Gender in Intimate Relationships

A MICROSTRUCTURAL APPROACH

TITLES OF RELATED INTEREST

Research Methods and Statistics

Earl Babbie, *The Practice of Social Research,* 5th ed.
William Sims Bainbridge, *Survey Research: A Computer-Assisted Approach*
Anthony Capon, *Elementary Statistics for the Social Sciences*
Joseph Healey, *Statistics: A Tool for the Social Sciences*
John Hedderson, *SPSS^X Made Simple*
John Lofland/Lyn Lofland, *Analyzing Social Settings: A Guide to Qualitative Observation and Analysis,* 2nd ed.
Allen Rubin/Earl Babbie, *Research Methods for Social Work*
June True, *Finding Out: Conducting and Evaluating Social Research,* 2nd ed.

Marriage and the Family

Mary Ann Lamanna/Agnes Riedmann, *Marriages and Families,* 3rd ed.
Marcia Lasswell/Thomas Lasswell, *Marriage and the Family,* 2nd ed.
Bud McClure/Robert Milardo, *The Marriage and Family Workbook*
Lloyd Saxton, *The Individual, Marriage, and the Family,* 6th ed.
Robert Staples, *The Black Family,* 3rd ed.

Specialized Texts

Susan Basow, *Gender Stereotypes,* 2nd ed.
Sally Bould/Beverly Sanborn/Laura Reif, *85+: The Oldest Old*
Daryl E. Chubin/Ellen W. Chu, *Science off the Pedestal: Social Perspectives on Science and Technology*
Donald Cowgill, *Aging Around the World*
Jack Levin/William Levin, *The Human Puzzle: An Introduction to Social Psychology*
Bernice Lott, *Women's Lives: Themes and Variations in Gender Learning*
Martin Marger, *Elites and Masses,* 2nd ed.
Martin Marger, *Race and Ethnic Relations: American and Global Perspectives*
Charlotte O'Kelly/Larry Carney, *Women and Men in Society,* 2nd ed.
Arnold Sherman/Aliza Kolker, *The Social Bases of Politics*
James Spates/John Macionis, *Sociology of Cities,* 2nd ed.
John Weeks, *Population,* 4th ed.
Fredric Wolinsky, *Sociology of Health: Principles, Practitioners, and Issues,* 2nd ed.

Computer Software for the Social Sciences

William Bainbridge, *Sociology Laboratory*
Rodney Stark/Cognitive Development, Inc., *Student ShowCase: Introducing Sociology through the Computer*

Gender in Intimate Relationships

A MICROSTRUCTURAL APPROACH

BARBARA J. RISMAN
North Carolina State University

PEPPER SCHWARTZ
University of Washington

WADSWORTH PUBLISHING COMPANY
Belmont, California
A Division of Wadsworth, Inc.

Sociology Editor: *Serina Beauparlant*
Production Editor: *Deborah Cogan*
Managing Designer: *Donna Davis*
Print Buyer: *Barbara Britton*
Designer: *Christy Butterfield*
Copy Editor: *Phyllis Cairns*
Compositor: *Omegatype*
Cover: *Donna Davis*

Printed in the United Stated of America 49

1 2 3 4 5 6 7 8 9 10———93 92 91 90 89

Library of Congress Cataloging-in-Publication Data

Gender in intimate relationships: a microstructural approach /
[edited by] Barbara J. Risman, Pepper Schwartz.
p. cm.
ISBN 0-534-09690-5
1. Interpersonal relations. 2. Sex role. I. Risman, Barbara J., 1956- . II. Schwartz, Pepper.
HM132.G43 1989 88-19723
305.3—dc19 CIP

Contents

Preface

This book has an idealistic and rather grand vision. We hope to change the terms of debate about gender and relationships. We want to convince the reader that gender, and even intimacy, are best understood using a sociological perspective.

Our ambition is to convince the reader that gender is never accomplished once and for all. Gender is an ongoing, ever-plastic process, and we can see its construction and evolution if we look closely at the circumstances of everyday life. In the language of sociology, we advocate a microstructural approach. The approach is simple but powerful: Men and women are not created all at once—at birth or during childhood socialization—but are continually changing throughout the life cycle. This perspective is well accepted in studies of class or ethnicity and in other areas, but it is oddly underutilized in gender studies—especially in studies of gender and intimacy.

One might think that all books on gender show how the norms and behaviors during courtship and marriage, within families, and at work mold gender roles and shape relationships. But unfortunately this is not the case. Most books on relationships, and certainly on gender, bypass sociology and concentrate rather narrowly on how the psychological differences between men and women, or the differences in their training, produce a gendered intimacy. Although this approach is useful, we find it incomplete. We decided to write a book that would remedy the situation by concentrating specifically on the forces that mold gender and, therefore, intimacy.

The first part of the book explains our theoretical stance. The majority of the book then presents articles on diverse social contexts that show, by example, how gender gets created and relationships get organized. We show how working-class gangs, same-sex couples, and dual-career marriages function as microenvironments that produce a gendered outcome. Finally, we examine how our perspective might influence strategies for achieving social change and equality. In a nutshell, we argue that equality will be achieved not by changing individuals but by changing social systems.

Examples of Gender and Intimacy in Everyday Life

We have made every effort to collect the best new research on intimate experiences in contemporary American society. Intimacy occurs in many settings; we have purposely expanded our concerns beyond the white, middle-class nuclear family. Thus we have included articles on male friendship, single parents, lesbians, working-class social gangs, elite dual-career couples, and black families. Intimacy exists within relationships based on friendship, romantic love, and parenthood, and even among coworkers. It concerns both men and women. We have worked hard to avoid the common mistake of confining the study of intimacy or the study of gender to the study of women. Men, too, are created by their intimate contacts and the institutional directives of their lives.

We have not, unfortunately, been able to cover as many aspects of people's lives as we would have liked, both because of space limitations and because of the type of research available. Most research on gender and intimacy focuses on the psychological differences between men and women and not on the kinds of structural variables we think are so critical. The articles we do present were selected because each one makes a clear point about how gender behavior in intimate relationships is embedded in social circumstances. Some of this research is exploratory and we hope the range of provocative topics will inspire student and professional alike to do more microstructural investigation—for example, a study of the effects of AIDS on homosexual and heterosexual intimacy, or an examination of the ways in which family relationships among recent immigrants to the United States change as new norms are encountered.

Sociological Visions and Social Change

Showing how social expectations and membership in social networks create gender should have direct implications for social change. Readers who find the articles in this book compelling will want to think about how social environments might be changed to promote gender equality and flexibility. The thoughtful reader and social activist may want to imagine how societal expectations and social opportunites could be reorganized so that men and women would have individual, rather than gendered, roles in their lives and in their relationships.

If one accepts the older but more common idea that socialization creates gender, it is rather hard to believe that all sex-role socialization can be reversed. But if the reader finds our approach convincing, then he or she can envision social change coming more rapidly by altering the conditions of interaction. One need not wait for major psychological breakthroughs. In this sense society can be remade—or at lease rethought—through collective as well as individual change. We believe this book will engage the reader on a personal and political level: If our perspective is correct, what about the world should be changed? And what will be the results? The data we look at concerns arenas that are near and dear to us: love, attachment, friendship, obligation, and community. And when we challenge and alter the ways our environment shapes these arenas, we change the world.

Acknowledgments

Any book is a collaborative venture; this one particularly so. The idea for an edited volume using a microstructural perspective on gender was first conceived during informal discussions in a gender studies group at the University of Washington. We would like to thank the following co-participants for sharing their ideas with us: Laura Bailey, Philip Blumstein, Mary Gillmore, Laurie Hatch, Charles Hill, Judith Howard, Anne Martin, and Mary Siedel. In addition, a number of people at North Carolina State University have been helpful. We particularly want to thank Maxine Atkinson, Michael Schwalbe, and Donald Tomaskovic-Devey. We thank Carol Gilbert and Evelyn Zobel for superb secretarial assistance. We are grateful to our Wadsworth editor, Sheryl Fullerton, for her enthusiasm and help. We would also like to acknowledge the reviewers of our manuscript: Pamela Hewitt, University of Northern Colorado; Ross A. Klein, Skidmore College; Susan E. Marshall, University of Texas at Austin; Charlotte G. O'Kelly, Providence College; and Carol A. Whitehurst, California State University, Fresno. And last, but certainly not least, we thank the national feminist sociological network, which has made a book on this subject possible. Many colleagues have worked very hard to create an intellectual climate and academic environment where gender studies can flourish.

Finally, we want to thank those people with whom we have our own most intimate relationships. Our parents, Gertrude and Isaac Risman and Gertrude and Julius Schwartz, have always given us their loving support for personal and intellectual endeavors. Our husbands, Richard Kane and Arthur Skolnik, have backed us up and given us the kinds of partnerships that are essential for work to occur and deadlines to be met. And we thank our children, Leah Nicole KaneRisman and Cooper and Ryder Schwartz-Skolnik, for providing us with so much joy and renewing our sense of commitment to the exploration of gender equality. We dedicate this book to all those we love—but especially to our mothers, for their never-ending nurturing, and to our children, with the hope that this book helps create a world in which they can be anything they want to be.

About the Contributors

Philip Blumstein is Professor of Sociology at the University of Washington. He is coauthor, with Pepper Schwartz, of *American Couples* (Pocket Paperback, 1985) and is working with Pepper Schwartz on a book on equality in marriage.

Francesca M. Cancian received her Ph.D. from Harvard in 1963, and is Professor of Sociology at the University of California at Irvine. Her publications include *Love in America* (Cambridge University Press, 1987), "The Feminization of Love" (*Signs,* 1986), and *The Family in Latin America* (special issue, *Journal of Family History,* 1978). She is currently editing a book on the social foundations of peace and war and is starting a new project that will apply participatory research methods and feminist analysis to investigating two-job and two-career families.

David Cheal was educated at the University of Birmingham (B. Soc. Sci., 1966; Ph.D., 1972), and is currently Professor of Sociology at the University of Winnipeg. His research interests include the sociology of the family and the sociology of the life course, as well as the study of interpersonal rituals. He is presently working on a paper on interaction ritual in mass society for the *Journal of the Theory of Social Behavior.* A series of his studies on ritualized gift giving has been integrated into a forthcoming book, *The Gift Economy* (Travistock/Routledge). His current research project, funded by the Social Sciences and Humanities Research Council of Canada, is on the moral economy of family life, concerning the allocation of resources within households.

Theodore F. Cohen is Assistant Professor of Sociology at Ohio Wesleyan University, where he teaches a variety of courses including The Family, Gender in Contemporary Society, and Masculinity and Men's Roles. He has authored papers on the impact of marriage and parenting on men and on men's attachment to work and family. His current research interests are men's experiences of marriage and fatherhood and the interconnections between gender, work, and family. He received his Ph.D. in sociology from Boston University in 1986.

Judith A. DiIorio is Assistant Professor of Sociology at Indiana University–Purdue University at Fort Wayne. She received her M.A. and Ph.D.

degrees from Ohio State University, where she became interested in the relationship between feminist theory, qualitative research methods, and the sociology of everyday life. Currently she is working on a book dealing with gender and sexuality in the vanning subculture.

Alice Echols teaches in the Women's Studies Program at the University of Michigan. Her book, *Daring to Be Bad: A History of the Radical Feminist Movement in America, 1967–75,* is being published by the University of Minnesota Press.

Lillian Faderman is Professor of English at California State University, Fresno. Her publications include *Surpassing the Love of Men* (William Morrow, 1981), *Scotch Verdict* (William Morrow, 1983), and numerous articles on women's relationships. She is presently at work on a book about the construction of lesbianisms in twentieth-century America.

Polly A. Fassinger, Assistant Professor of Sociology at Concordia College in Moorhead, Minnesota, received her doctorate from Michigan State University, where she specialized in the areas of gender, work, and families. For her recent Ph.D. dissertation, she studied men's and women's reactions to single parenting. In 1987, she was the recipient of the first annual Dissertation Paper Award of the American Sociological Association, Section on Sex and Gender. Dr. Fassinger's previous research focused on farm women's work.

Kathleen Gerson is Assistant Professor at New York University. She is the author of *Hard Choices: How Women Decide About Work, Career, and Motherhood* (University of California Press, 1985). She is currently a Visiting Scholar at the Russell Sage Foundation where she is wokring on a book examining men's changing commitments to family and work (Basic Books, forthcoming).

Rosanna Hertz is presently a research Fellow in the Department of Psychiatry at Harvard Medical School and Assistant Professor of Sociology at Wellesley College. She is working on a study of money and authority in the family at Harvard Medical School and she has just finished coauthoring an in-depth study of the effects of shiftwork on family life. *More Equal than Others: Women and Men in Dual-Career Marriages* was her first book.

Michael S. Kimmel is Assistant Professor of Sociology at the State University of New York at Stony Brook. His books include *Changing Men:*

New Directions in Research on Men and Masculinity (Sage, 1987), *Absolutism and Its Discontents: State and Society in 17th Century France and England* (Transaction, 1988), and *Men Confronting Pornography* (Crown, 1988). He is the editor of a book series with Beacon Press on men and masculinity, and he is currently working on a history of profeminist men in American history and a study of the relationship between sexual desire and gender.

Maureen Mulligan LaRossa is a registered nurse in the Department of Neonatal/Perinatal Medicine at Grade Memorial Hospital in Atlanta, and is a coauthor of *Transition to Parenthood: How Infants Change Families* as well as other works on premature infant care and foster grandmothers. She is currently involved in research on the effects of low birth weight on child development.

Ralph LaRossa is Associate Professor in the Department of Sociology at Georgia State University in Atlanta. His writings include *Conflict and Power in Marriage: Expecting the First Child; Transition to Parenthood: How Infants Change Families; Family Case Studies: A Sociological Perspective;* and *Becoming a Parent.* He is currently working on a book on the history of fatherhood in twentieth-century America.

Judith Lorber is Professor of Sociology at Brooklyn College and the Graduate Center, City University of New York. She is the author of *Women Physicians: Careers, Status, and Power* (Tavistock/Methuen, 1984) and numerous journal articles on gender and women and health care. Her current research is on the new reproductive technologies. She is editor of *Gender & Society,* the official publication of Sociologists for Women in Society.

Laurel Richardson is Professor of Sociology at Ohio State University. She has published extensively in the fields of gender and intimate relationships. Her books include *The New Other Woman: Contemporary Single Women in Affairs with Married Men* (Free Press, 1987); *The Dynamics of Sex and Gender: A Sociological Perspective,* Third Edition (Harper & Row, 1988); *Feminist Frontiers: Rethinking Sex, Gender, and Society,* Second Edition (Random House, 1989); and *Gender and University Teaching: A Synthesis of Interactionist and Feminist Theories* (forthcoming).

Barbara Risman is Assistant Professor of Sociology at North Carolina State University. Her work involves applying a microstructural perspective on gender to the fields of gender, sexuality, and sociology of the family. Recently she has published on the topics of homosexuality, single parents, and gender segregation in the labor force.

Pepper Schwartz is Professor of Sociology at the University of Washington. She is coauthor, with Philip Blumstein, of *American Couples* (Pocket Paperback, 1985) and is presently working with Philip Blumstein on a book on equality in marriage.

Joan Z. Spade is Assistant Professor at Lehigh University. Her research interests include the work/family nexus, gender stratification, and differentiation in education. She received her Ph.D. in sociology from the State University of New York at Buffalo.

Robert Staples was born in Roanoke, Virginia, and educated in the state of California. Presently he is Professor of Sociology at the University of California, San Francisco, and has held past faculty appointments at Howard University, Fisk University, California State University at Hayward, and Bethune-Bookman College. His publication record includes over 130 articles in popular and scholarly periodicals in the United States, Yugoslavia, Austria, Venezuela, and Australia. He has written or edited nine books on the black family. His latest books are *The World of Black Singles* (Greenwood Press, 1981), *Black Masculinity* (The Black Scholar Press, 1982), and *The Urban Plantation* (The Black Scholar Press, 1987).

Scott Swain completed his undergraduate work in Social Science at the University of California, Berkeley. He then counseled and taught high school students for three years on the Hoopa Indian Reservation in northern California. He returned to graduate work at the University of California, Irvine, in the field of Comparative Culture, and completed doctorate research on intimacy in men's same-sex friendships. He has also conducted research on the informant role in male-female friendships and on adolescent male contraceptive behavior. After a year of post-doctoral training at the Wellesley College Center for Research on Women, he is currently counseling at Acalanes High School in the San Francisco Bay Area.

Mary K. Zimmerman is Associate Professor of Health Services Administration and Sociology at the University of Kansas. Her research focuses on the social structuring of women's lives in relation to their health. She has used symbolic interactionist theory and methods as well as social epidemiology to examine a variety of women's health issues including abortion, contraception, hypertension, and stress. She is the author of *Passage Through Abortion: The Personal and Social Reality of Women's Experiences* and numerous articles including, most recently, "The Women's Health Movement: A Critique of Medical Enterprise and the Position of Women" for *Analyzing Gender: A Handbook of Social Science Research* (1987). Her newest research explores the social worlds and health of mothers caring for children with chronic disease.

Introduction

Being Gendered: A Microstructural View of Intimate Relationships

BARBARA J. RISMAN
PEPPER SCHWARTZ

A few years ago a group of sociology professors and graduate students at the University of Washington met informally to study gender. The reason for the group, besides intellectual camaraderie, was a shared view that we needed to discuss gender as a sociological rather than psychological phenomenon. We felt then, as we do today, that too much of the literature on men's and women's roles explained each sex's conduct on biological or psychological disposition. Although we found the literatures that advanced social learning and socialization hypotheses very useful, we felt they were inadequate and perhaps ultimately misleading about how male and female roles are truly constructed.

The more we read, the more convinced we became that an alternative explanation for gender in intimate relationships was necessary. What was needed was a *microstructural* theory of gender, a theory that took into account the impact of adult life experiences on men's and women's self-concept and actions. The theme of a microstructural theory is simple but powerful: men and women are not created all at once—at birth or during early socialization—but are continually re-created during the life cycle by the opportunities available to them and their interactions with others.

This strikes us as particularly true in male and female roles played in intimate relationships. We decided to gather together articles that would begin to explain intimacy by showing how microstructural forces help create men's and women's actions and beliefs. The articles that follow show, we hope, how the format of an institution (such as a bridal shower), the expectations of others (such as parents), the options available (social mobility through either marriage or work) operate to form stereotypically male and female behavior, what we shall call gendered behavior. But before presenting each example, we begin by explaining our theory in more detail.

The predominant model of gender in interpersonal relationships is called "individualist" because it rests on a theory of relatively inflexible personalities, which, once created, remain throughout life whatever other experiences or circumstances come about. This individualist paradigm posits that by adulthood men and women have developed sex-typed personalities that are quite different from one another. Females have become nurturant, person-oriented, and child-centered, and males have become competitive and work-oriented. Once formed, these core personality traits continue to influence behavior throughout life.

Researchers using such individualist perspectives are biased toward psychological explanations for sex differences and do not consider seriously enough how males and females are shaped by their immediate social settings. In an often-cited statement of the individualist perspective, Bem and Bem (1976) argue, for example, that a 21-year-old woman is not free to choose a nonstereotypical lifestyle because "society has controlled not only her alternatives, but her motivation to choose any but one of those alternatives."

The personality and socialization arguments are well stated, and many different kinds of individualist theories have been generated. Some of them have been extremely influential. For example, Chodorow's (1978) theory in the *Reproduction of Mothering* gave a great boost to feminist psychoanalytic explanations of how the earliest parent-child interaction (mothering) explains male and female personality differences. Individualist explanations are also expressed in differential reinforcement and socialization theory (for example, Bandura and Walters, 1963; Mischel, 1966; Weitzman, 1979; and others) and cognitive development theory (Kohlberg, 1966; Gilligan, 1982). Even sociobiological theories (for example, Wilson, 1978; Symons, 1979; Van den Berghe, 1979) and bio-social theories (Rossi, 1984) that integrate evolutionary, genetic, hormonal, and social variables, ultimately focus on individuals' preferences rather than on the social systems that influence them.

The defining characteristic of various individualist paradigms, from Chodorow's (1978) feminist psychoanalytic approach to a more traditional sex-role socialization theory, is the presumption that gendered behavior is the result of *internalized* traits. Although individualist theorists do not ignore the role of social structural influences on intimate behavior (see, especially, Chodorow), they focus on how culturally determined family patterns create gendered personalities, which then provide the motivations for individuals to fill their socially appropriate roles. All research within this tradition shares the central presumption that internalized psychological motivation is a more salient explanation for gendered behavior than immediate social relations.

We don't want to create a useless antagonism between an individualist and a microstructural explanation of gender and intimate conduct, but we do feel that sociological variables are given too little weight in individualist discussions of intimate relationships and that the more potent microstructural argument has been too often ignored. When individualist theorists assume relatively inflexible, internalized, gender-based personality traits, they are making incorrect assumptions that inevitably lead to wrong conclusions. An illustration may help explain our position. Individualist theories debate whether women desire to stay home with their children more than men because they have been mothered by same-sex parents and have therefore developed the desire for intense intimacy, or whether the social reinforcement girls receive for doll play and other nurturant behavior is a better explanation for exclusively female mothering. It is an interesting question—except that by assuming internalized predispositions exist we are directed only to inquire about the consequences of the female predisposition to mother. We have a more basic question: Do such sex-based predispositions really exist? Or would the social conditions that promote full-time mothering also promote full-time parenting in men equally well? If fathers were not only actually given the option of remaining at home with their babies, but also expected to do so, would more men choose the role of primary caretaker? And what if these same men earned considerably less than their wives? Different assumptions lead to different problems and therefore, potentially, to different answers. Most of the questions that are currently explored in the realm of intimate relationships assume sex-typed preferences and the overwhelming importance of sex-role socialization.

This presumption that gender is internalized as a stable personality trait is the thread that weaves through all the individualist theories, though they may conflict and disagree otherwise. Motivation becomes a central research question in this paradigm. Researchers look for answers about why someone would *want* to behave a certain way rather than why they may be merely behaving like other actors with the same constraints or rewards.[1]

We believe that individualist paradigms posit an oversocialized conception of masculine men and feminine women. The "oversocialized conception of *man*," first identified by Wrong (1961), would have us believe that once we know what people are trained to think and do, everything else about their lives is only secondarily important. Ongoing social relations are reduced to postscripts rather than to determinants of social forces. Individualist paradigms have led to an oversocialized conception of men and women, of gender.

How a Microstructural Perspective Helps Explain Interpersonal Relations

Taken to its logical extreme, our microstructural theory predicts that men and women would behave *exactly* the same way if they were given identical expectations and positions in society. More realistically, the theory has to take certain biological conditions into account, such as the impact of childbirth on interpersonal relations and placement in society. Our position is that biology and psychology are going to be relatively unimportant in contemporary Western societies and thus, most of what we continue to believe are gender differences in intimacy are continually constructed during interaction (see Risman, 1987). Social design has been mistaken for psychological reality. In other words, the overrepresentation of men at the top of Fortune 500 companies is less a consequence of greater male motivation and drive than the result of men's greater opportunities to join the right social networks and fulfill the expectations of the company. Our position, of course, is not to be taken on faith. This book is designed to support our thesis by comparing sex-based personality traits with the impact of social circumstances to see which best predicts male and female behavior.

Our microstructural theory assumes that the players in the game of life adapt to ongoing patterns of interaction that are themselves produced by a socially organized system. The factors at work are often called "structural," but sociologists have used this word in so many different ways that it is now too confused to be resuscitated with a nice, clear meaning. Classically, (Merton, 1975; Goode, 1960) structure has referred to the relationships between various economic historical forces and social institutions. The most restrictive definition (Mayhew, 1980) for structure is a macro-level one: relationships between societal forces. But others (Hewitt, 1979, and Stryker, 1980, 1981) have argued that structural forces also describe how social organization affects interactions between individuals. In this view, the "nature of situations" as people experience them helps shape behavior.

We will not debate here what is "true" structural theory—only to say that we are proceeding within the tradition of those who believe that situational interaction is necessarily a component of a structuralist approach. For clarity, when studying interpersonal relations we call this a microstructural theory. And it is this link, the world experienced by the individual, that we wish to define better for a more complete understanding of how and why gender evolves as it does. The guiding vision behind each article is the desire to go beyond the notion of socially created sex-typed personalities toward a theory that focuses on how the day-to-day social relations of men and women create gendered behavior.

There are three sociological traditions useful for the reader to think about when trying to understand gender: symbolic interaction theory, status expectations theory, and network theory. All three traditions help us focus on different aspects of the experiences we face every day.

Symbolic Interaction Theory

Symbolic interaction research has shown for decades that situational factors influence behavior over and above individual factors such as training or biological predisposition. Even today gender remains a "master status," an organizing principle of everyday life (Hughes, 1945). We all hold implicit and explicit expectations that differ by sex. Men are not expected to assume a subordinate identity to women in marriage (that is, Mr. Helen Smith). Nor are employed married women considered unsuccessful if they alone cannot earn enough money to support their families well. These expectations, known to the participants of an interaction and to everyone in our society, exert powerful constraints on how men and women are likely to behave.

Symbolic interactionists use the term *altercasting* to show one process by which such roles are formed by expectations (Weinstein and Deutschberger, 1963). When people are confronted with expectations that differ from their self image, they look for cues about how to proceed (Beckhouse et al., 1975). When the person they are dealing with shows them what he or she expects, they generally try to behave accordingly. No one likes the discomfort that can happen when we don't meet others' expectations. When we get mixed messages about who we are expected to be, we try to make sense of the conflicting transmissions so that interaction can continue smoothly. We all change our behavior in response to new or changing expectations. This inconsistency suggests that personality traits do not make us act only one way. Rather, behavior is often an attempt to meet expectations to do well at what we are *supposed* to do at any given moment.

We believe that understanding the process of social expectations and altercasting is important to the study of gender in two ways. First, even when men and women are in identical settings, they often face differential expectations. Second, men and women do not often even have access to identical settings or opportunities. For example, if ever there was a behavior supposed to be more biological and based more on feminine personality than sociological variables, it is mothering. From a symbolic interactionist perspective, however, it is the child's, the family's, and society's expectations of full-time mothering by females that may produce the behaviors we see in today's women. If expectations were changed (for example, if the child and society made it clear that "mothering" is expected from the father), the symbolic interactionist would predict that mothering behaviors would be produced by fathers.

We predict that males would respond to such changed expectations with mothering skills as they are altercast into the mothering role, if not right away then over time. At first they might find the child's expectations incongruent with their own self-images, but eventually fathers would become what the child expects and needs them to be (Risman, 1986). In fact, that does seem to happen when men become single fathers. Indeed, the same process of altercasting may be what turns many, though certainly not all, women into "good enough" mothers.

Many of the chapters illustrate how the expectations of others help create gendered behavior in intimate relationships. The research by LaRossa and LaRossa on infant care shows that mothers in our society are expected to lose more freedom to child care than are fathers. Interviews with new parents suggest that such expectations at least partly create the inequitable burden of childrearing that even employed mothers carry. Swain's study of male college students suggests that the societal constraints against men expressing their emotions shape the kind of intimacy possible within same-sex friendships. DiIorio's research on working-class youth suggests that even in a club with an expressed commitment to sexual equality, the norms and expectations attached to the status of boyfriend versus girlfriend vary so tremendously that girls remain subordinate.

Other chapters suggest not only that expectations differ for men and women, but also that the sexes rarely have access to similar experiences and opportunities. For example, Cancian suggests that when industrialization split the world of paid work from the hearth and home, women were for the first time expected to become specialists in love. Men had little option to devote themselves to the emotions of others; women had little option to do otherwise. Kimmel continues a historical analysis by suggesting that when the American frontier shrank, a definition of manhood based on physical prowess and bravery became unattainable. This created a crisis for the definition of masculinity. Such a crisis was irrelevant to femininity, which had never been defined in similar terms. Lorber suggests that social institutions—including family and sexual relationships—need not categorize persons by gender; institutions should be developed to provide similar experiences and opportunities to men and to women.

Status Expectations Theory

Status expectations theory can also help us understand gendered behavior in intimate relationships. A large literature shows that expectations of individuals differ based on the status ranking of the group to which they belong—even when that status is irrelevant to the task at hand (Berger et al., 1972; Ridgeway, 1982; Wagner et al., 1986). Lower-status groups have less influence. People who hold higher social status, white males in our society, tend to dominate groups even in small experimental settings (Meeker and Weitzel-O'Neill, 1977). Thus, men and women behave quite differently because responses to members of the higher-status male group are quite different than responses to lower-status females. For example, if you are a man, people tend to stop talking when you raise your voice just because you are a man. No matter what you say it is taken seriously, even if it is eventually repudiated. But if you are a woman you always have to fight to get the floor, and it is hard to be taken seriously even when you have a solution your colleagues may need. Experience has taught you that it is unlikely your proposal will be acted on. In this way sexual stratification organizes interaction even though the people may believe they are giving fair weight to the abilities of each person in the room.

Research has shown that if social status is experimentally manipulated, expectations based on sex can be subordinated to other status conditions. One study (Geis et al., 1984) showed how student reaction to television commercials changed when the high-status person was male and when the high-status person was female. The results were supportive of status expectations theory: high-status males and females were rated as independent, rational, dominant, ambitious, and good leaders while low-status men and women were rated as dependent, irrational, submissive, unambitious, and followers. Of course, in real life, males are more likely to be in the high-status position in commercials. But in this experiment, when sex was disassociated with social status, sexual stereotypes disappeared.

Network Theory

Symbolic interaction and status expectation theories independently suggest that actual social relations (expectations, opportunities, and altercasting during interaction) mold behavior that might otherwise be presumed motivated by gendered personality traits. Granovetter (1985) suggests we integrate the analysis of interaction and social status by studying how people are placed in or are embedded in social networks. They may be central actors, important and known to everyone else, or they may be peripheral to the social system, acquainted with only a few others and different from them in some fundamental way. We think that how people are embedded in social networks helps create gendered behavior, and such behavior is not merely the expression of personal gendered choices. Men and women have had different life options at least partly because of how they are differentially embedded in social networks. For example, mothers with young children are unlikely to find themselves in social networks that expect and demand achievement outside the home. Men of any age, married or single, however, can hardly escape such expectations.

Network embeddedness has been used as a particularly effective variable explaining women's performance in the labor force. In 1977, Kanter critiqued studies on female labor force participation for their individualist presumptions. The literature of the time was full of descriptions about why women workers were different from male workers. Kanter showed that when an individual had access to powerful mentors, interaction with people like themselves, and the possibility for upward mobility, they behaved like others with similar advantages—regardless of sex. These social network variables could explain work success far better than assumptions of masculine versus feminine work styles. Women were less often successful because they were more often blocked from network advantages. When they had such advantages, women behaved very much like their male colleagues. When men lacked such opportunities they did not advance, and they behaved with stereotypically female work styles. Other researchers (Thompson, 1981; Lorber, 1984; Geis et al., 1984) also report findings supportive of such a network approach.

This network perspective can be transferred to domestic settings. For example, studies have found structural explanations for what had seemed to be gender-linked language patterns. Kollock et al. (1985) compared conversations between homosexual partners and heterosexual partners and found that power dynamics accounted for some of the privileges (for example, who can interrupt, who talks more) in conversation that other researchers had attributed to sex-linked personality traits. Past research had shown that men interrupted and talked more. By comparing homosexual and heterosexual couples, the authors demonstrated that it was really power that conferred conversational privilege and that gender almost disappeared as a factor once it was known who was the more powerful person in the relationship. Since men are more often the more powerful person in heterosexual relationships, sex had been confounded with power. We have mistakenly thought that certain interactional styles were male and others were specifically female, but these styles are actually tied to power, not only to sex.

The chapter by Gerson also supports the importance of microstructural factors. Instead of attributing women's desire to mother to sex-role socialization, Gerson shows that whether employed women choose to remain childless or become mothers depends on their social context. Neither feminine personality traits nor biological instincts propelled women toward motherhood. What did predict childbearing was access to a stable heterosexual relationship, the kinds of jobs available in the labor force, and the relative interest of male partners in fatherhood.

Other chapters also focus on how social networks help shape gendered behavior. Richardson illustrates the importance of social networks for the very definition of relationships, even those secret and forbidden. She suggests that some of the subordination of single women to married men in extramarital liasons can be attributed to privileges based on marital status, rather than on gender per se. Being married seems to be an important determinant of interactional power. Marriage confers greater prestige and alternative avenues for social-psychological support upon the married partner in an extramarital liason. Hertz illustrates the strength of social networks with her focus on how the demands of corporate careers shape new types of interpersonal relationships. Cheal also looks at contemporary marriage, but his focus is on how a bride's new position in a network of married women helps define her role as wife.

Microstructural Theory and Social Change

Each chapter supports our basic argument: when the sociological traditions of symbolic interaction, status expectations, and social networks are integrated, we have a more powerful explanation for the continuing existence of gendered behavior in intimate relationships than if we continue to depend on individualist, oversocialized concepts of men and women. Until now, there really hasn't been much research that has avoided what we consider unjustified assumptions about the overwhelming influence sex-role socialization has on gender and intimacy. And so, we've collected what we consider to be the best new sociological work on gender and intimacy. The book is designed for use in classes on gender roles, sexual inequality, marriage and the family, and women's studies. It is organized into four sections. Part One, "Gender Relations and Historical Change: Past, Present, and Future," is designed to provide the reader with some understanding of the larger institutional forces that have created the conditions under which our current beliefs about gender have developed. The chapters in this first section illustrate how industrialization has helped to change the meaning and shape of our most intimate relationships. The rest of the book focuses more specifically on how the microstructural variables of social expectations and networks shape gendered behavior.

Part Two highlights the importance of social expectations, placement in social networks, and sexual inequality for relationships between friends and lovers. Part Three, "Becoming a Parent: Options and Realities," shows how microstructural variables help explain contemporary sex differences in parenting styles. The chapters in Part Four, "Interconnections Between Work and Family," illustrate that we can never study intimate relationships or gendered behavior isolated from the world of paid work. Economic needs and constraints set the context in which we experience our private desires.

Some of the chapters have been published before, others were written especially for this volume. We have not attempted to cover every kind of intimate relationship, nor every stage in the life cycle. Instead, each chapter was chosen to provide solid empirical evidence for our thesis, while helping the reader to better understand contemporary relationships in and outside the family.

We find the microstructural explanation convincing for ourselves and so we offer it to the reader. But we believe this book should do more than advance this perspective. We think this new approach to intimacy should have a profound impact on social policy about men and women in society today. If we adopt an individualist position, changing the relation of the sexes to one another in the labor force or in the family is a long and laborious process. The individualist approach assumes that in order to end sexual inequality we must re-socialize everyone—parents and children, husbands and wives, employers and employees. This laborious re-socialization process, plus the impediments of biology, will surely take a very long time to create an egalitarian society. Moreover, serious reluctance to re-socialization may surface because many will fear that by changing the "essential" nature of men and women, we may lose those personality capacities we find socially necessary (for example, competitiveness in men for career advancement or nurturance in women for family strength).

If our microstructural approach is correct, however, the assumptions of necessarily slow change and the loss of desirable traits are not accurate. Change need not be so slow if it comes by changing situational experiences and economic conditions rather than by re-socializing individuals or teaching them new directives from birth. Moreover, we will not lose valued personality traits if we keep the institutions that promote them. As long as we work in hierarchical institutions, we will maintain the competitive personalities and behaviors necessary to climb to the top. And if equal opportunities are truly available, competitiveness will be produced equally in both men and women. If we want to make sure that nurturance remains widely distributed (among women, or men for that matter), we will make sure that opportunities to "mother" and be involved in family systems are easy options to claim.

In other words, if the reader finds our theory of gender formation convincing, social change can be accomplished by restructuring the environment and designing new opportunities for men and women, not by re-training individuals. For example, social policy designed to reduce differences between men and women, based on our theory, would not only encourage but *expect* men to do substantial infant care, would provide parental leaves and flexi-time for both men and women, and would reduce the wage differential between male and female workers. Our vision is not therapeutic; it is architectural. Rather than focus on assertiveness training programs we feel that female assertiveness will grow when the jobs women hold demand it, when women are accorded high status, and when institutional forces support female aggressiveness. We believe male nurturance will develop when men are held responsible for caring for others. If we are right, that gender is created by everyday life and everyday institutions, then escaping gender constraints is a matter of redesigning the social structure.

We do not mean to imply that macro- and microstructural social forces together are deterministic, or that free will does not exist. Social structural forces do not develop magically, or spring full-formed from some mysterious celestial space. Human beings, in our creative attempt to solve everyday problems, have—over time—created the social forces that direct our lives. A full understanding of the social structure must include—not deny—the two-way relationship between individuals and society. We focus heavily on how microstructural forces create gendered behavior in intimate relationships, but we must all remain aware that when individuals collectively choose to defy current expectations and to organize new agendas, they eventually change the social structure itself. Indeed, this is what we recommend.

When social structural forces are in flux—when individuals face conflicting options, opportunities, and expectations—their choices shape, mold, and create the structural forces that future generations will take for granted. The choices we make today between conflicting work and family roles will shape tomorrow's social structure. These readings concentrate on showing how intimate relationships are currently constrained by socially created gender. We do not cover every aspect of life that helps construct gender, but this is one place, close to our hearts, to begin.

Note

1. We are not suggesting that stable personality traits do not exist, only that gendered behavior is not primarily a consequence of gendered personality traits.

References

Bandura, Albert, and Richard H. Walters. 1963. *Social Learning and Personality Development.* New York: Holt, Rinehart and Winston.

Beckhouse, Lawrence, Judith Tanur, John Weiler, and Eugene Weinstein. 1975. "And Some Men Have Leadership Thrust Upon Them," *Journal of Personality and Social Psychology* 31(3):557–566.

Bem, Sandra L., and Darby J. Bem. 1976. "Case Study of a Nonconscious Ideology: Training the Woman to Know Her Place," in Sue Cox (ed.), *Female Psychology: The Emerging Self.* Chicago: Science Research Associates, pp. 180–190.

Berger, Joseph, Bernard P. Cohen, and Morris Zelditch, Jr. 1972. "Status Characteristics and Social Interaction," *American Sociological Review* 37:241–255.

Chodorow, Nancy. 1978. *The Reproduction of Mothering.* Berkeley: University of California Press.

Geis, F. L., V. Brown, J. Jennings, and D. Corrado-Taylor. 1984. "Sex vs. Status in Sex-Associated Stereotypes," *Sex Roles* 11(9/10):771–785.

Gilligan, Carol. 1982. *In a Different Voice*. Cambridge, MA: Harvard University Press.

Goode, William J. 1960. "A Theory of Role Strain," *American Sociological Review* 24:38–47.

Granovetter, Mark. 1985. "Economic Action, Social Structure and Embeddedness," *American Journal of Sociology* 91(3):481–510.

Hewitt, John P. 1979. *Self and Society: A Symbolic Interactionist Social Psychology*. Boston: Allyn and Bacon.

Hughes, Everett C. 1945. "Dilemmas and Contradictions of Status," *American Journal of Sociology* 50:353–359.

Kanter, Rosabeth. 1977. *Men and Women of the Corporation*. New York: Harper and Row.

Kohlberg, Lawrence. 1966. "A Cognitive-Developmental Analysis of Children's Sex-Role Concepts and Attitudes," in Eleanor Maccoby (ed.), *The Development of Sex Differences*. Stanford: Stanford University Press, pp. 82–173.

Kollock, Peter, Philip Blumstein, and Pepper Schwartz. 1985. "Sex and Power in Interaction: Conversational Privileges and Duties," *American Sociological Review* 50(1):34–46.

Lorber, Judith. 1984. *Women Physicians: Careers, Status and Power*. New York: Tavistock.

Mayhew, Bruce H. 1980. "Structuralism Versus Individuals: Part I, Shadow Boxing in the Dark," *Social Forces* 59(2):335–375.

Meeker, B. F., and P. A. Weitzell-O'Neill. 1977. "Sex Roles and Interpersonal Behavior in Task-Oriented Groups," *American Sociological Review*, 42:91–105.

Merton, Robert K. 1975. "Structural Analysis in Sociology," in P. M. Blau (ed.), *Approaches to the Study of Social Structure*. New York: Free Press, pp. 21–52.

Mischel, Walter. 1966. "A Social Learning View of Sex Differences in Behavior," in Eleanor Maccoby (ed.), *The Development of Sex Differences*. Stanford: Stanford University Press.

Ridgeway, Cecilia L. 1982. "Status in Groups: The Importance of Motivation," *American Sociological Review* 47:76–88.

Risman, Barbara J. 1987. "Intimate Relationships from a Microstructural Perspective: Men Who Mother," *Gender and Society* 1(1):6–32.

———. 1986. "Can Men Mother: Life as a Single Father," *Family Relations* 35(1):95–102.

Risman, Barbara, and Kyung Park. 1988. "Just the Two of Us: Parent-Child Relationships in Single-Parent Homes," *Journal of Marriage and the Family*. Forthcoming.

Rossi, Alice S. 1984. "Gender and Parenthood," *American Sociological Review* 49:1–19.

Stryker, Sheldon. 1981. "Symbolic Interactionism: Themes and Variations," in Morris Rosenberg and Ralph H. Turner (eds.), *Social Psychology: Sociological Perspectives*. New York: Basic Books.

———. 1980. *Symbolic Interactionism: A Social Structural View*. Menlo Park, CA: Benjamin/Cummings.

Symons, Donald. 1979. *The Evolution of Human Sexuality*. New York: Oxford University Press.

Thompson, Martha E. 1981. "Sex Differences: Differential Access to Power or Sex-Role Socialization?" *Sex Roles* 7(4):413–424.

Van den Berghe, Pierre L. 1979. *Human Family Systems: An Evolutionary View*. New York: Elsevier.

Wagner, David G., Rebecca S. Ford, and Thomas W. Ford. 1986. "Can Gender Inequalities Be Reduced?" *American Sociological Review* 51(1):47–60.

Weinstein, Eugene, and Paul Deutschberger. 1963. "Some Divisions of Altercasting," *Sociometry* 26(4):454–466.

Weitzman, Lenore J. 1979. *Sex Role Socialization*. Palo Alto, CA: Mayfield.

Wilson, Edward O. 1978. *On Human Nature*. Cambridge, MA: Harvard University Press.

Wrong, Dennis H. 1961. "The Oversocialized Conception of Man in Modern Sociology," *American Sociological Review* 26(2):183–193.

Part One

Gender Relations and Historical Change: Past, Present, and Future

These chapters set the stage for the rest of the book and provide an understanding of how larger institutional forces create the conditions under which gender expectations develop. The beliefs we hold today, at this moment in history, are products of social changes that have occurred during the past two centuries. Cancian reviews the historical evidence and suggests that when income-producing labor was removed from the family setting during industrialization, the consequent split between the public and private spheres left emotional work—particularly love—in the private sphere, and thus assigned specifically to women. Cancian traces the consequences of love's feminization for marital relationships in the past and for today. Her discussion of love shows quite clearly how one of the most intimate of behaviors, marital love, is affected by social forces.

Faderman also illustrates how intimate relationships are affected by social forces, but focuses on how same-sex relationships are defined by culture and history. Love relationships between women were not only common but quite acceptable in pre-industrial America. Such relationships were sanctioned only if the women appeared to usurp male social or political privileges. Faderman suggests that as long as women were segregated in the private sphere, their emotional and sexual relationships were not strictly policed. But when female emancipation appeared possible, love between women was redefined as sick or evil.

Kimmel, Echols, and Lorber concentrate on how people act *collectively* to create new meanings and expectations about gender and intimate relationships. Kimmel, like Cancian, argues that industrialization—with the subsequent closing of the wilderness experience—led to a renegotiation of masculinity and femininity. Because structural changes made the old definitions of masculinity (for example, physical prowess, risk-taking, interpersonal dominance) unattainable, a "crisis of masculinity" developed. Kimmel identifies a variety of male reactions to the crisis and shows how important collective action is for social change and the redefinition of what it means to be male in twentieth-century America.

Echols tackles the issue of social movements more directly as she discusses how feminists today are attempting to influence the meaning of femininity. Echols criticizes a particular group of feminists because she believes that they have accepted contemporary definitions of masculinity and femininity, seeking primarily to increase the status and power of "feminine" behavior. But although the empowerment of a "female identity and culture" promises an immediate solution to women's powerlessness, Echols suggests that promise is illusory because it is based on a retreat from an understanding of the social and political creation of gender. Indeed, the data presented here by Cancian and Kimmel support Echol's argument that gendered behavior itself—including the feminine virtues extolled by cultural feminists—is historically specific and culturally variable.

Lorber provides ideas for the reorganization of society without gender. She suggests how nongendered families, sexuality, reproduction, and wage-work might be organized in post-industrial societies. Her analysis would surely be useful for feminist social movements that do not accept contemporary definitions of gender.

The five chapters in Part One support the importance of structural and institutional variables on gendered behavior and intimate relationships. Although the authors themselves do not focus on microstructural variables, they present an appropriate and useful introduction because they show that gender is constructed within a political and historical context. These readings help explain not only how the social forces of industrialization and modernization shaped the expectations we hold for gendered behavior, but also how men and women in the past shaped the world we now take for granted. They show how gender is changing—even as we speak—because of collective action.

1

Love and the Rise of Capitalism

FRANCESCA M. CANCIAN

Love is a personal experience, but it is socially constructed, shaped by economic institutions that structure our daily activities and by cultural understandings about the meaning of love, gender, and self. A historical analysis of conceptions of love in nineteenth-century America clarifies how our love relationships are socially structured. With the transformation from an agrarian to a capitalist economy, love also was transformed.

Two aspects of capitalist society have been most important in shaping marital love (which is the type of love relationship on which I am focusing). The first aspect, associated with early capitalism, is the separation of the home and the workplace. This structural change intensified the split between the feminine sphere of love and the family versus the masculine sphere of achievement and work. Men's and women's activities became separated, leading to a division of personality characteristics by gender, so that women were expected to be compliant, tender, and dependent, while men were expected to be assertive, rational, and independent. Love became feminized, controlled by women and identified with feminine qualities like tenderness and weakness. Although this split has softened in recent decades, it continues to structure marital love.[1]

The second aspect that has transformed personal relationships, associated with late capitalism, is the cultural emphasis on individualism and emotional self-expression for both women and men. With wives increasingly joining the labor force, the growth of leisure and consumerism, the improving standard of living, and the rise of wives' employment, men and women came to value self-development and internal experience. Ideals of marital love became more intimate and androgynous. But these trends did not emerge strongly until the third or fourth decade of the

---

This is a revised version of Chapter 2 in Francesca Cancian's *Love in America: Gender and Self-Development.*

twentieth century. In this paper I will focus on the first transformation—the feminization of love that accompanied the separation of the home and the workplace during the nineteenth century.[2]

Love in Agrarian New England

Before the nineteenth century, the dominant image of family life was that women and men were both responsible for love, and family members were dependent on each other both materially and emotionally. The ideal of the independent individual was still weak; gender roles were not polarized, and the private sphere of family life was closely integrated with the public community.[3]

In the colonial communities of New England, the household was the arena for affection, economic production, education, and social welfare. The typical family was, in the words of the historian John Demos, "a little commonwealth," a miniature community governed by the same rules as the wider community.[4]

The integration of activities in the family produced a certain integration of instrumental and expressive traits in the personalities of men and women.[5] Husbands and wives were involved in similar economic activities, and shared the task of caring for household members. The patriarch was expected to guide and nurture all the dependents in his household, which often included apprentices and servants, and both sexes were instructed by their ministers to be loving and affectionate within the family. Benjamin Wadsworth's book, *The Well-Ordered Family,* published in 1712, advised that "the duty of love is mutual, it should be performed by each to each of them." Husbands were instructed to temper their authority with love: "Though he governs her, he must not treat her as a servant but as his own flesh, he must love her as himself." And love included sexuality. Men were told, in the words of the Bible, to "rejoice with the wife of thy youth. Let her breasts satisfy thee at all times. And be always ravished with her love."[6]

Men did monopolize almost all the property and positions of power in the community, while women were responsible for the care of infants and of the sick and disabled, but the activities and personality traits associated with love were not highly differentiated by gender. As the historian Mary Ryan summarizes the evidence:

> When early Americans spoke of love they were not withdrawing into a female byway of human experience. Domestic affection, like sex and economics, was not segregated into male and female spheres. . . . The reciprocal ideal of conjugal love . . . grew out of the day-to-day cooperation, sharing, and closeness of the diversified home economy.[7]

The Separation of Men's and Women's Activities in a Cash Economy

By the end of the eighteenth century, a great transformation was occurring. The family and personal relationships were being separated from economic production, and there was a parallel separation of human personality traits by gender. Love and family attachments were being defined as women's sphere while economic production and individual achievement were in men's sphere. The feminization of love and the masculinization of work intensified the divergence between men's and women's activities and personalities, and produced ways of loving that were more congenial to women than to men. Mary Ryan describes how this transformation took place in upstate New York. A similar transformation has occurred in much of the world during the past two centuries.[8]

At the beginning of the nineteenth century, Oneida County was a sparsely populated frontier, where most families lived on subsistence farms. Households were headed by the patriarch and produced their own food and clothing, bartering some of their produce for spices, liquor, and other luxury goods in one of the few local stores. The household also conducted family worship, educated its children, and took care of the sick and the indigent. The church and town watched over the household and tried to ensure that it carried out these duties.[9]

Personal relationships within the household were relatively formal and hierarchical. Obedience of the wife and apprentices to the household head and of children to their parents was a primary virtue, and all adults were expected to be hardworking and religious. Children were viewed as miniature adults, and stern discipline was used to break a child's will and turn the child from individual desire to obedience to parents and church. The emotional bonds beween husband and wife were not emphasized, and there was little physical privacy in the house for the couple. Marital intimacy, in the modern sense of emotional expression and verbal disclosure of personal experience, was probably rare. Instead, husband and wife were likely to share a more formal and wordless kind of love, based on duty, working together, mutual help, and sex.

The activities of both men and women focused on productive work near the home and on caring for household members. Women had a major role in economic production, usually taking charge of planting the family vegetable garden, caring for poultry and cattle, and making thread, cloth and clothing, and other products. Men as well as women were responsible for the well-being of household members, and for their religious education, although men were doubtless expected to be more severe and demanding. Men worked near their homes, often assisted by family members, and were home during the day for meals and other family activities. Moreover, there was no sharp distinction between "private" and "public." The household was a hierarchical work group supervised by church and town, and intimate attachments or individual self-expression were not cultivated; thus people behaved much the same at home and in the community.

The patriarchal household began to disintegrate between 1815 and 1840. As land became scarce, shops and crafts began to replace agriculture as the major economic activity. Cash replaced barter as a mode of exchange, and merchants in the 1830s lured farmers with advertisements such as "cash for wool."[10] The new economic opportunities to work as artisans, shopkeepers, or commercial farmers were mostly open to men, but the cotton mills offered employment to young unmarried women. At first, the factories were small; families worked together under the father's leadership and were often paid in kind rather than cash. Thus an advertisement in the Utica *Patriot* in 1813 announced, "A few sober and industrious families of at least five children each, over the age of eight years, are wanted at the Cotton Factory."[11] But by 1840, the factories were larger; workers were all recruited individually, not as families, and they were paid in cash. Husbands in the towns typically worked as craftsmen or shopkeepers in establishments that were attached to the homes, but the most prosperous merchants worked away from home. Wives stayed at home and did not work for money.

As the workplace became more separate from home and family, relationships at work became impersonal. The distinction between the warm, personal private sphere and the cold, public sphere was emerging. Paul Johnson describes the changes in the shoe factories and building crews of Rochester, New York, a community that became the fastest growing city in the nation in the 1820s as agriculture became commercialized and the Erie Canal was completed. In 1820, merchants and master craftsmen "lived above, behind, or very near their places of business, and employees boarded in their homes." The master was responsible for the moral behavior of his workmen; they were defined as dependents in his household. "Work, leisure and domestic life were acted out in the same place and by the same people. . . ."[12]

In the following decade, the size of workshops grew larger, and workmen increasingly lived apart from their employer. For example, while in 1827 one in four shoemakers lived with his employer, only one in twenty was doing so by 1834.[13] Masters were becoming businessmen, spending most of their time away from the workshops buying labor and raw materials and selling finished goods. At the same time, they were demanding new standards of discipline at work. "Masters increased pace, scale, and regularity of production, and they hired young strangers with whom they shared no more than contractual obligations."[14]

By the 1840s, the split between men's sphere at work and women's sphere at home was well under way. The male world of business and public life had become an unpredictable arena of competition among individuals. People moved from farm to town and from one town to another in search of work, competing with the growing number of foreign workers and fearful of recurrent business slumps. Men's daily work increasingly became divorced from personal relationships and cooperation, and men also became separated from religion, as they stopped attending church and leading family prayers. Historians detect a mood of expansiveness and unlimited opportunity in American public life in the early nineteenth century. At the same time, there was an undercurrent of fear, a sense of slipping away into a chaos of "individual men devouring each other in the struggle for success."[15]

As public life became more impersonal, immoral, and uncertain, the female world of the family was becoming more intensely personal, pure, and circumscribed. Households became smaller as the birth rate declined and fewer households had apprentices and boarders. The ties between household, church, and town diminished, as husbands withdrew from the family and from the church, and town governments became more impersonal. The family less often acted as an efficient work team, and economic production, education, and health care moved out of the home into factories, offices, schools, and hospitals. Women continued to work hard at home, producing clothing, preparing food, and caring for family members, but the focus of their lives was to care for their children and their husbands.

Women's task of child rearing expanded as children were defined as vulnerable innocents in great need of care. Moreover, the proper raising of children became increasingly important to the middle class as the class position of sons and daughters came to depend more on character and education than on inheritance of land. Child rearing, according to Paul Johnson, "fell more and more to mothers. They were warned not to beat their children . . . , but to mix discipline with love, and to develop moral sensibilities that would make them useful citizens of a Christian republic."[16] The relationship between mother and child became emotionally intense and oriented to the individual development of the child (but not the mother). In Ryan's words, the center of the household shifted "from patriarchal authority to maternal affection."[17]

Between the worlds of work and home, a new arena of lodges, clubs, and missionary societies was developing. Young men joined lodges to have a place to stay when they left home and went to clubs for fellowship. Women joined religious and moral reform societies as a way to have an impact on the wider society and find a context for carrying on close friendships with women. These sex-segregated voluntary organizations bridged the growing gap between the public and private spheres.

The Ideology of Separate Spheres

As the daily activities of men and women grew farther apart, a new world view emerged. It exaggerated the differences between "the home" and "the world" and polarized the ideal personalities of women and men. It was an ideology that was adopted by affluent Americans as well as the working class and is still influential today.[18]

The ideology of separate spheres is clearly evident in the magazines, church newsletters, and sermons of the nineteenth century, and has been well described by several historians.[19] In brief, this ideology portrayed the home as an "oasis in the desert," a spiritual "sanctuary." A New England minister proclaimed in 1827 that

> it is at home, where man . . . seeks a refuge from the vexations and embarrassments of business, an enchanting repose from exertion, a relaxation from care by the interchange of affection: where some of his finest sympathies,

> tastes, and moral and religious feelings are formed and nourished;—where is the treasury of pure disinterested love, such as is seldom found in the busy walks of a selfish and calculating world.[20]

Home is good and pure in this image and also somewhat immaterial and unreal—home centers on feelings and ideals, not productive physical activities like preparing meals or caring for infants.

In contrast, in the tough, material outside world "we see the general good, sacrificed to the advancement of personal interest," according to the *Ladies' Magazine* in 1830. "We behold every principle of justice and honor, and even the dictates of common honesty disregarded, and the delicacy of our moral sense is wounded."[21]

These two different worlds were dominated by two different personalities—the feminine and the masculine. The ideal woman was pious, pure, domestic, and submissive, in the words of historian Barbara Welter; a pious, emotional giver of care who depended on her husband to provide money and to deal with the threatening outside world. The ideal was described in a sermon on women:

> How interesting and important are the duties devolved on females as WIVES . . . the counsellor and friend of the husband; who makes it her daily study to lighten his cares, to soothe his sorrows, and to augment his joys; who like a guardian angel, watches over his interests [and] . . . constantly endeavors to render him more virtuous. . . .[22]

A letter from General William Pender to his wife during the Civil War illustrates how husbands expected their wives to be moral arbiters:

> Honey, whever I try to reflect upon the future and to resolve to do better, I think of you first and your image rises up . . . so that I have almost come to feel that you are a part of my religion. Whenever I find my mind wandering upon bad and sinful thoughts I try to think of my good and pure wife and they leave me at once. My dear wife you have no idea of the excellent opinion I have of your goodness and sweetness. You are truly my good Angel.[23]

Motherhood was the key to being a real woman. The virtues of motherhood were extolled in *The Ladies' Companion* in 1838. Fathers could not inculcate morality in children because the father,

> weary with the heat and burden of life's summer day or trampling with unwilling foot the decaying leaves of life's autumn, has forgotten the sympathies of life's joyous springtime. . . . The acquisition of wealth, the advancement of his children in wordly honor—these are his self-imposed tasks.

It was his wife's duty to develop the child's character, to form "the infant mind as yet untainted by contact with evil . . . like wax beneath the plastic hand of the mother."[24] An ideal woman centered her life on love of husband and children, a love expressed mostly through emotions and piety, not practical action.

The ideal woman could also be powerful, both as the ruler of her domestic domain and as a moral reformer working with other women to help the weak and punish the wicked. Thus popular magazines between the mid-eighteenth and mid-nineteenth century portrayed women as increasingly powerful, especially in child rearing, morality, and courtship.[25] But if she were to avoid censure, her power had to be based on her special feminine qualities—her superior ability to love, to be good, and to serve others—and not on masculine qualities such as self-interest, anger, or a desire for control.[26] According to an 1839 article on matrimony, "The man bears rule over his wife's person and conduct. She bears rule over his inclinations: he governs by law; she by persuasion. . . . The empire of the woman is an empire of softness . . . her commands are caresses, her menaces are tears."[27]

The masculine ideal, tailored to fit the emerging capitalist economy, was to be an independent, self-made man. Key male virtues included self-control, economic success, courage, and upright character. *A Voice to the Married,* published in 1841, advised young men that "a good character must be formed, it must be made—it must be built by our individual exertions." Nineteenth-century writers called on men to be disciplined and courageous and to concentrate their energies, in order to prosper in the world outside the home, which was "a vast wilderness" where they were "naked and alone surrounded by savages" in "a rage of competitive battle."[28] Thus Demos identifies the central masculine virtues as strength, cunning, and endurance.

Men's strength depended on controlling and restraining their emotions and their sexuality. A medical text counseled men that "reserve is the grand secret of power everywhere. Be noble, generous, just, self-sacrificing, continent, manly in all things—and no woman worthy of you can help loving you in the best sense of the word."[29] An abundant medical literature described the dire consequences of masturbation and excessive sexual intercourse. One text warns that with masturbation "all the intellectual faculties are weakened. The man becomes a coward; sighs and weeps like a hysterical woman. He loses all decision and dignity of character."[30] With the polarization of gender roles, male vices are female virtues, as Charles Rosenberg has commented.

The masculine conception of self-development that is still influential today is rooted in this nineteenth-century male ideal. Independence, self-control, and achievement are the major values of this ideal self while intimacy, emotional expression, and other feminine qualities are devalued.

An ideal man was not perfectly suited for family life. Trained for competitive battles and self-reliance, he might well suffocate in a cozy Victorian home. This conflict was reflected in the existence of two contradictory male ideals: the family man and the independent adventurer. From the point of view of most mothers, ministers, and prospective brides, the ideal man was probably a dependable family man who was a good provider and a devout Christian. Nineteenth-century marriage manuals defined the ideal husband as a home-loving Christian and a man of good character who avoided "idleness, intemperate use of intoxicating drinks . . . licentiousness in every form, gambling, swearing and the keeping [of] late hours at night."[31]

But many of the nineteenth-century heroes—the mountainmen, ships' captains, and cowboys—were undomesticated adventurers. They had abandoned the civilized world of women and the family for a life of danger and comradeship among men. According to Leslie Fiedler's analysis of novels, the central myth of American culture is the tale of a boy or man who escapes from society to an island or wilderness where mother can't come and where he can enjoy innocent, violent adventures with a special male companion.[32] In this myth, marriage represents captivity and emasculation by sexless, virtuous women. The ideal is heroic action with men, not passionate love with women, as it usually is in European novels. Heroes from Tom Sawyer and Captain Ahab to the contemporary private eye all fit this pattern, which is an extreme version of the myth of male independence from women and families.

In sum, the ideology of separate spheres reinforced the new division of labor, and portrayed a world of independent, self-made men and dependent, loving women. The ideal family was portrayed as a harmonious, stable, nuclear household with an economically successful father and an angelic mother.

The reality of family life in the nineteenth century was of course much more diverse and turbulent than this ideal, even among the white middle class. Death disrupted many families. Marriages were just as likely to be broken in 1850 as 1950, if we combine the effects of death and divorce, because in 1850 so many people died young. Not until the 1960s was there a substantial rise in broken marriages, because of a sharp increase in divorce. Many households included other people besides the nuclear family. Affluent families usually had servants, while poorer families took in boarders[33] Husbands sometimes rebelled against the provider role and deserted their wives, and wives were often less docile and more interested in sex than the Victorian image of "the angel in the house." Many women retreated into illness or rebelled against their confinement at home by joining religious or reform organizations or by remaining single.[34]

For the working class, immigrant groups, and black slaves, reality was probably farther from the ideal, although the evidence for these groups is scanty. Working-class men and their families often moved from city to city in search of work. For example, only 40 percent of the unskilled laborers who had lived in Newburyport, Massachusetts, in 1850 were still there in 1860.[35] When work was available, the husband's wages often could not support his family, and his children and wife had to work. Less than 36 percent of the men working in Massachusetts factories in 1897 earned enough to support their families.[36] Immigrant groups often maintained the family patterns of their homelands, and slave families also had special traditions as well as a unique burden of oppression. Despite this diversity, however, these families too were strongly influenced by Victorian ideals. According to historian Carl Degler:

> The majority of Afro-American children in the 19th and 20th centuries lived in a nuclear family with both parents present, in which the father was not only the recognized head of the household but the primary breadwinner as well. . . . Among the immigrants, as among the Black and native families, the wife and mother was the heart of the home; it was she who managed the home and reared the children. Upon her fell the responsibility for seeing that the home was a proper place for the children and an attractive place for the husband.[37]

The Feminization of Love

With the split between home and work and the polarization of gender roles, love became a feminine quality. A Unitarian minister described the female as "accustomed to feel, oftener than to reason." An Episcopalian praised women for possessing "all the milder virtues of humanity," and "a more exquisite sensibility than men. . . . The God of heaven has more exquisitivily [sic] attuned their souls to love, to sympathy and compassion."[38] Women's superior ability to love was seen as enabling them to comfort and care for their children and husbands.

As women gained control of love, the cultural images of love shifted toward emphasizing tenderness, expression of emotion, and weakness. When mothers replaced fathers as the parent with day-to-day authority, the methods of child rearing shifted from the stern will-breaking methods of agrarian times to socialization through giving and withholding love. Conceptions of God's love also shifted toward sweetness and tenderness. God was seen as an "indulgent parent," a "submissive, meek and forgiving" Christ.[39] In religious revivals, and in women's friendships, there was a new emphasis on recognizing private feelings and communicating them in an intimate relatinship in which one could unfold one's whole heart.[40] Conceptions of marital love also shifted toward greater emphasis on affectionate feelings.

In *The Feminization of American Culture,* Ann Douglas argues that religion and popular literature were dominated by middle-class women and Protestant ministers in the nineteenth century. Women's status was declining as the household lost many of its functions, and ministers were becoming less powerful as the church lost its control over daily life and society became secularized. Excluded from effective public action, they took over activities devalued in industrializing America, and created an ineffectual, sentimental mass culture reflecting their own powerlessness. The literature and the religion they produced emphasized subjective feelings and suffering, and opposed virile action, rebellion, and objective analysis. As this simplified outline of her argument may show, Douglas is more admiring than I am of "masculine" assertion and independence, more critical of "feminine" emotion, and less interested in integrating the two spheres. But her analysis suggests how love was changed and distorted by being identified with women.

Feminized love was defined as what women did in the home; it had nothing to do with how men related to each other at work. Love became a private feeling, disassociated from public life, economic production, and practical action to help others. Many middle-class women challenged this private conception of love in the latter part of the nineteenth century. They expanded domestic love to include being "social housekeepers" and "mothers of the world." In the name of feminine love, hundreds of thousands of women organized to stamp out the vice of liquor, and smaller numbers worked to help the poor or abolish child labor.[41] But by the 1920s women's love was private once again.

Equating woman's activities with love and men's activities with work produced a distorted perception of the activities of both sexes. Men's attachments and dependency were obscured, and women's productive labor was labeled love. A great deal of work remained to be done at home, especially for the majority of women who lacked servants. But women's domestic labor was less visible and less respected than it had been in the agrarian economy.[42] Women were not paid for housework, while outside the home people usually worked for wages. The labor involved in women's expanding new task of shopping—spending money for goods—was especially obscured by identifying work with getting money. There was also an increasing divergence in the quality of work experience. Women's work at home "retained the irregularity, the responsiveness to immediate and natural demands, and the intermixture with social occasion common to preindustrial occupations."[43] Outside the home, work was regulated by clock time and the demands of machines. Gradually the concept of work excluded women's labor in the home and emphasized the masculine ideals of individualism, achievement, discipline, and competition.

Another effect of the feminization of love was the encouragement of a florescence of intimate friendships between women in the late eighteenth and the nineteenth century. The historian Nancy Cott points out that "the identification of women with the heart . . . implied that they would find truly reciprocal interpersonal relationships only with other women."[44] Moreover, the equality between women compared favorably to women's subordination to men. Friendship among women was also encouraged by the sociability among women in all-female schools and charitable and religious societies.

Frontier women bitterly complained about the absence of female friends, and the correspondence of educated women often reveals a passionate, enduring commitment to a life-long woman friend. Luella Case, a married woman from Massachusetts, wrote to her old friend Sarah in the 1830s after discovering a poem that Sarah had written to her: "Words seem inadequate to express the sense I feel of your—what shall I say, *friendship?* No, I will rather call it affection, for you know I confessed as one of my weaknesses, an inordinate desire *to be loved.*" And as a visit from Sarah ended, she felt "most lonely" having "no gentle voice to talk with, or read to me, no sweet beaming countenance to echo the feelings expressed, none of that gentlest of all sympathies, that of a pure, and truehearted female. . . ."[45] Intense love between women friends, more accepted in the nineteenth century than now, was expressed in fondling, endearments, and love letters, concludes historian Lillian Faderman, but rarely included genital sex.[46] Victorian women thus turned to other women and to their children for love, more than to men.

Love, Dependency, and Power

Power relations in the family and the economy were also affected by the new beliefs in feminine love and masculine independence. These beliefs strengthened men's power advantage at home. They also covered up the material dependency and exploitation that were the major causes of power differences in the family and the workplace.

Women in the nineteenth century became extremely economically dependent on their husbands, probably more so than before or after the Victorian era. In the colonial period, women were actively involved in the domestic economy; after the Victorian era, increasing numbers of women entered the workforce. But in the nineteenth century it was shameful for a wife to work, even if she was a widow. An advice book for married women pointed out that "the average woman recognizes the value of money," but her desire to make money "battles perpetually with her desire to do nothing which is strong-minded and unladylike."[47] Married women who had worked as teachers usually would not be rehired after they married, and offices and stores often would not employ older married women.[48] Three-fourths of the female industrial workers in large cities in the 1880s were younger than twenty-five and 96 percent of them were single.[49]

Other family relationships became less dependent with the transition to capitalism. Economic survival was no longer based on working in the family farm or shop; individual wage labor was an alternative. Sons and daughters no longer depended on inheriting land from their father, and family members increasingly turned to outside government and private organizations rather than each other for education and health care. But wives became more dependent on husbands.

For example, Emma Goldman reports matter-of-factly that despite the poverty of her family, she quit her factory job in 1887 when she married the young man who worked next to her in the shop. After describing her reactions to her husband's impotence, she continues:

> My own passion had subsided. The material anxiety of making ends meet excluded everything else. I had stopped work: it was considered disgraceful for a married woman to go to the shop. Jacob was earning fifteen dollars a week. . . . Life became insupportable.[50]

Increasing economic dependency was the basis for what many social historians see as a decline in the power of wives during the Victorian era,[51] but the connection was obscured by the ideology of innate differences between the sexes. In this world view, women were powerless because they were naturally affectionate and docile, as an article by the antislavery writer Lydia Maria Child illustrates:

> The comparison between women and the colored race is striking. Both are characterized by affection more than by intellect; both have a strong development of the religious sentiment; both are exceedingly adhesive in their attachments; both, comparatively speaking, have a tendency to submission, and hence, both have been kept in subjection by physical force, and considered rather in the light of property, than as individuals.[52]

This perspective denies the material basis of women's dependency, and emphasizes women's need for affection and their natural morality and submissiveness. Part of the feminization of love was the belief that women had an enormous need for love and tenderness while men were naturally independent and had much less need for enduring, nonsexual love. This imbalance in emotional dependency bolstered the power of men over women.

In the workplace, too, relations of material dependency were obscured by polarized gender roles. Men were defined as naturally independent, amoral, and isolated, the other side of defining women as naturally dependent, moral, and affectionate. This ideology of the isolated (male) individual accompanied and justified the rise of capitalism, as Marxist scholars have pointed out.[53] Workers were encouraged to see themselves as independent, competitive, and self-made. If they were rich or poor, it was the result of their own individual merit, not relations of dependency with other people. And if they were real men, they would thrive on the impersonal, competitive relationships that prevailed at work. Personal, caring relationships were restricted to women and the home; they should not be expected in the public sphere.

The ideology of independent individuals and "free" workers replaced the old patriarchal model of dependent workers who were subordinate members of their master's household. Johnson describes how new ideals of independence and self-control emerged in Rochester in the 1820s and 1830s, fueled by a religious revival that emphasized the "moral free agency" of each individual to reject evil and choose Christ.[54] This ideology implied that employers had no responsibility to their workers beyond paying them a minimal wage:

> the belief that every man was spiritually free and self-governing enabled masters to present a relationship that denied human interdependence as the realization of Christian ideals . . . workmen who continued to drink and carouse and stay away from church were no longer considered errant children; they were free moral agents who had chosen to oppose the Coming Kingdom. They could be hired when they were needed, fired without a qualm when they were not.[55]

Thus the new division of labor in the family and the workplace intensified the material dependency of wives and of workmen, but these relations of unequal resources and power were covered over by an ideology that focused on the characteristics of individuals. The economic dependency of women was masked by the belief that women were inherently loving. The economic dependency of workers was masked by the belief that men were independent and self-made and free to determine their own social position.

The ideals of love and self-development that emerged in the nineteenth century justified inequality, especially at the workplace, by denying the material dependency among people. Twentieth-century ideals of love and self continue to ignore material interdependence, perhaps because recognizing this interdependence would threaten the legitimacy of our economic system.

Androgyny and Intimacy

As we have seen, the transition from an agrarian to a capitalist society polarized gender roles, feminized love, and led to a masculinized ideal self. But in the long term, the transition led to more androgynous conceptions of gender, love, and self, and more intimacy between husband and wife. The new androgynous ideal combined masculine autonomy and feminine affection. Emotional expression became more valued for both sexes and intimate relationships in the private sphere became the main arena for developing one's unique self. In contrast, the masculine ideal self that accompanied the rise of capitalism emphasized independence, emotional control, and success in the public sphere. Conceptions of love also became more androgynous, as feminized love was superseded by new ideals of husband-wife companionship and open communication. Ideals of intimacy and androgyny did not become powerful in American culture until the twentieth century, in my view, although these ideals were visible much earlier, during the transition to capitalism.

Lawrence Stone, a historian of the English family, argues that the rise of capitalism was accompanied by new values of "affective individualism" that emphasized self-development and intimate bonds with others. Stone describes how "human relationships were increasingly seen in economic terms, governed by the rules of the free market" because of the growth of a market economy and wage labor, together with other trends such as urbanization and geographical mobility. In the old-world view, "the purpose in life was to assure the continuity of the family, the clan, the village or the state, not to maximize the well-being of the individual."[56] The new-world view emphasized

> firstly, a growing introspection and interest in the individual personality; and secondly, a demand for personal autonomy and a corresponding respect for the individual's right to privacy, to self-expression, and to the free exercise of his will within limits set by the need for social cohesion. . . .

Combining individualism with a focus on personal experience and feelings, the new-world view was manifest in warmer, more affectionate family relationships and in "a wholly new scale and intensity of interest in the self."[57]

However, affective individualism probably did not predominate until much later than Stone asserts. The evidence that he cites primarily shows that love became feminized, not androgynous, with the rise of capitalism. For example, he notes the enormous popularity of romantic novels (read mostly by women) and the greater intimacy of the mother-child relationship.

Other scholars have noted signs of affective individualism during the rise of capitalism in nineteenth-century America. William Goode argues that with industrialization the American family became more affectionate and equalitarian, increasingly emphasizing the need for all its members to develop their unique selves. Eli Zaretsky discusses the emergence of a new sphere of personal life in nineteenth-century America as work became less satisfying and people turned to personal relationships and internal experiences for gratification.[58] And Robert Bellah and his colleagues describe the "expressive individualism" that began to develop in the mid-nineteenth century. In this new perspective, "the expansive and deeply feeling self" was the mark of a successful life, along with rich experience and the freedom to express oneself. In contrast, the older "utilitarian individualism" advocated "a life devoted to the calculating pursuit of one's own material interest."[59]

Some historians argue that this trend to affection produced more intimate and equal marriages in the nineteenth century, and they cite letters and diaries exhibiting a high degree of mutual love and dependency in marriages.[60] However, my reading of the evidence is that intimacy between wife and husband remained rare as long as their activities were so different and their power was so unequal. Thus Nancy Cott points out that "exaggerated sex-role distinctions may have succeeded in making women uncomfortable with men (and vice versa) as often as rendering the two sexes complementary."[61] She also argues that marital love was weakened by the subservience of women to men in a period in which traditional dependency relations were dissolving and peer relationships were increasingly valued.

Evidence of the lack of intimacy between husband and wife comes from nineteenth-century marriage manuals, which rarely mention affection or companionship. According to these manuals, a sound marriage is based on being religious, industrious, and healthy, and sex is for the purpose of procreation only. Women are advised to seek a husband who values home life and has good morals and then to obey him and be hardworking and good tempered. The quality of the relationship between husband and wife is relatively unimportant.[62] Other signs of marital estrangement include the complaints of married people in their letters and diaries, the disapproval of sexuality, the enormous rise in prostitution, and the decrease in the marriage rate toward the end of the nineteenth century.[63] In sum, the primary effect of the rise of capitalism in the nineteenth century was to create inequality and estrangement between the sexes, and a split between feminine love and masculine self-development.

In the twentieth century, these marital patterns reversed. As wives joined the labor force and women's education increased, husband and wife became more equal; they also probably developed more similar personalities and became more capable of intimacy, as their daily activities converged. Emotional experience and self development in the private sphere became more important, fueled by the growth of advertising and consumerism, which encouraged people to develop new personal needs and try to fulfill them.

By the 1920s, the new ideal of "companionship" marriage emerged, emphasizing marital intimacy and the personal development of both partners. By the 1970s, intimate, open communication of feelings had become the most important part of marital love. Self-development was a major goal in life, and love had become the joint responsibility of both partners, who were now expected to diligently "work on" their relationship.

We are now in the midst of this change toward intimacy and androgyny, caught between new cultural ideals of androgyny and intimacy, and the reality of persisting differences in men's and women's job opportunities and family responsibilities. These cultural understandings and structural arrangements will continue to shape our experience of love, as they have in the past.

Notes

1. For an analysis of feminized love in contemporary marriage, see Cancian, 1985.

2. The change to androgyny and intimacy in the twentieth century is examined in my book *Love in America.*

3. This historical description, which focuses on the white middle class in New England and in other Eastern states, is based primarily on the work of Ryan, 1979; Cott, 1977; Welter, 1966; and Degler, 1980.

4. Demos, 1979.

5. This description of family and gender roles in the Colonies draws heavily on Ryan, 1979.

6. Ibid., pp. 23–24.

7. Ibid., pp. 24–25.

8. Ryan, 1981. See Stone, 1979, on the transformation in England; and also Goode, 1963, and Shorter, 1975.

9. Thus the Oneida Baptists pledged to "extend a faithful watch over all its members, also in every private relation," and to "promote true piety and family religion." In a typical court case, the Oneida County Court ordered a man to support his aging father in order to avoid expense for the town. Ryan, 1981, pp. 39 and 24.

10. Ibid., p. 9.

11. Ibid., p. 44.

12. Johnson, 1978, p. 43.

13. Ibid., p. 46.

14. Ibid., p. 57.

15. Demos, 1974, p. 433. Also see Johnson, 1978.

16. Johnson, 1978, p. 7. Degler, 1980, and Ryan, 1981, describe childbearing in the nineteenth century. For an incisive analysis of mother-child intimacy and its relation to Freudian theory, see Poster, 1978.

17. Ryan, 1981, p. 102.

18. Both Degler, 1980, and Cott, 1977, conclude that this ideology was widely accepted in different social classes.

19. See especially Welter, 1966; Cott, 1977; Degler, 1980; and Ryan, 1979. See also Rosenberg, 1975, and Demos, 1979. An interesting analysis of how the ideology was created in female religious groups in the early nineteenth century is presented by Ryan, 1981.

20. Quoted in Cott, 1977, p. 64

21. Ibid., pp. 64–65.

22. Welter, 1966, p. 325.

23. Degler, 1980, p. 31.

24. Quoted in Welter, 1966, p. 326.

25. Lantz et al., 1975.

26. Some historians argue that the separation of spheres increased women's status; see, for example, Cott, 1977, and Degler, 1980.

27. Welter, 1966, p. 325.

28. The quotes are from Ryan, 1981, p. 147; and G. J. Barker-Benfield, in Gordon, 1978, p. 374.

29. Demos, 1974. The quote is from Rosenberg, 1980, p. 229. Historians tell us less about the masculine ideals in the nineteenth century because there is as yet no male equivalent to the feminist-inspired research on women's roles.

30. Rosenberg, 1980, p. 237.

31. Gordon and Bernstein, 1970.

32. Fiedler, 1966. Also see Swidler's (1980) discussion of male aversion to domestic love in our culture. Wahlstrom, 1979, shows how this image persists in contemporary mass media portrayals of men. The psychoanalyst Erik Erikson has also noted that American myths and folk songs glorify the womanless, unattached man without roots.

33. See Bane, 1976, on marital dissolution, and Degler, 1980, p. 155, on household composition. Around 1870, 1 out of every 6.6 white families had servants. Taking in boarders was a popular way for a woman to bring in income, and about 20 percent of urban households had lodgers.

34. This discussion relies on Ryan, 1979; Degler, 1980; and Flexner, 1974.

35. Thernstrom, 1964.

36. Calhoun, 1917, p. 74.

37. Degler, 1980, pp. 131 and 136.

38. Quoted in Cott, 1977, p. 160.

39. Douglas, 1977, p. 149.

40. Cott, 1977, p. 186.

41. Women's reform activities are well described by Ryan, 1979, and Rothman, 1978.

42. See Ryan, 1981, for a description of the domestic work of women in the nineteenth century and men's devaluation of this work. Douglas, 1977, also describes the increasing invisibility of women's domestic work in the nineteenth century.

43. Cott, 1977, p. 60. See Braverman, 1975, for a description of increasing discipline and alienation at work.

44. Cott, 1977, p. 168. Smith-Rosenberg, 1975, and Faderman, 1981, describe women's friendships.

45. Cott, 1977, p. 185.

46. Faderman, 1981.

47. Quoted in Rothman, 1978, p. 86.

48. See Rothman, 1978, p. 85.

49. From Ryan, 1979, p. 124.

50. Goldman, 1931, p. 23.

51. Historians who take this position include Ryan, 1979; Demos, 1974; and Douglas, 1977. A related change in the nineteenth century was that children became more dependent on their parents as schooling increased and apprenticeships declined; see Kett, 1977.

52. Quoted in Rose, 1982.

53. For example, see Jacoby, 1975, and Marcuse, 1964.

54. Johnson, 1978, p. 7.

55. Ibid., pp. 138 and 141.

56. Stone, 1979, pp. 172–173.

57. Ibid., pp. 151 and 155. Stone avoids clear causal arguments and does not assert a necessary connection between individualism and affect (see Chapter 6 of his book). For other evidence on the rise of individualism and a concern with the self and psychological perspective, see Lyons, 1978, and Zweig, 1968.

58. Goode, 1963. Goode labels this the "conjugal" family system. Another sign of affective individualism is romantic novels, which were extraordinarily popular in America in the mid-nineteenth century, while in England they became very popular at the end of the eighteenth century; see Zaretsky, 1976, and Ryan, 1979. The religious revivals that swept over the northern states in the 1820s and 1830s might also be considered as a sign of affective individualism.

59. Bellah et al., 1985, pp. 33–34.

60. It is possible that intimacy increased as patriarchal authority based on the family farm declined, as the family no longer functioned as a productive, formally organized work group, and as the values of freedom and individualism spread. Degler sees the family of this period as characterized by affection and respect between spouses along with an increasing separation of men's and women's spheres, a growing focus of women on child rearing, and a decrease in family size. See, for example, Parsons, 1954; Goode, 1963; Degler, 1980; and Shorter, 1975.

61. Cott, 1977, p. 190.

62. Gordon and Bernstein, 1970.

63. On the decrease in the marriage rate, see Degler, 1980, p. 152; Stone, 1978; and Goode, 1963. On the decline in husband-wife affection, see Ryan, 1979; Barker-Benfield, 1976; and Demos, 1974. The increase in intimate friendships among women also suggests that women may have been missing something in their relations with their husbands; such friendships were rare for wives who had very affectionate marriages, according to Degler, 1980, Chapter 7.

References

Bane, Mary Jo (1976). *Here to Stay: American Families in the Twentieth Century.* New York: Basic Books.

Barker-Benfield, G. J. (1976). *The Horrors of the Half-known Life: Male Attitudes Toward Women and Sexuality in 19th Century America.* New York: Harper and Row.

Bellah, Robert, Richard Madsen, William Sullivan, Ann Swidler, and Steven Tipton (1985). *Habits of the Heart.* Berkeley: University of California Press.

Braverman, Harry (1975). *Labor and Monopoly Capital: The Degradation of Work in the 20th Century.* New York: Monthly Review Press.

Calhoun, Arthur W. (1917). *A Social History of the American Family.* Cleveland: Arthur Clark.

Cancian, Francesca (1985). *Marital Conflict over Intimacy.* Pp. 277–292 in G. Handel (ed.), *The Psychosocial Interior of the Family,* Third Edition. New York: Aldine.

Cancian, Francesca (1987). *Love in America: Gender and Self-Development.* New York: Cambridge University Press.

Cott, Nancy F. (1977). *The Bonds of Womanhood.* New Haven: Yale University Press.

Degler, Carl N. (1980). *At Odds: Women and the Family in America from the Revolution to the Present.* New York: Oxford University Press.

Demos, John (1974). "The American Family in Past Time." *American Scholar* 43:422–446.

Demos, John (1979). "Images of the American Family, Then and Now." Pp. 43–60 in V. Tufte and B. Myerhoff (eds.), *Changing Images of the Family.* New Haven: Yale University Press.

Douglas, Ann (1977). *The Feminization of American Culture.* New York: Knopf.

Faderman, Lillian (1981). *Surpassing the Love of Men.* New York: William Morrow.

Fiedler, Leslie A. (1966). *Love and Death in the American Novel,* Revised Edition. New York: Stein and Day.

Flexner, Eleanor (1974). *Century of Struggle.* New York: Atheneum.

Goldman, Emma (1931). *Living My Life.* New York: Knopf.

Goode, William (1963). *World Revolution and Family Patterns.* New York: Free Press.

Gordon, Michael (1978). "From Unfortunate Necessity to a Cult of Mutual Orgasm: Sex in American Marital Education Literature, 1830–1940." Pp. 59–84 in J. Henslin and E. Sagarin (eds.), *The Sociology of Sex,* Revised Edition. New York: Schocken.

Gordon, Michael, and M. Charles Bernstein (1970). "Mate Choice and Domestic Life in the Nineteenth-Century Marriage Manual." *Journal of Marriage and the Family* 32:665–674.

Jacoby, Russell (1975). *Social Amnesia.* Boston: Beacon Press.

Johnson, Paul E. (1978). *A Shopkeeper's Millennium.* New York: Hill and Wang.

Kett, Joseph (1977). *Rites of Passage.* New York: Basic Books.

Lantz, Herman R., Jane Keyes, and Martin Schults (1975). "The American Family in the Preindustrial Period: From Base Lines in History to Change." *American Sociological Review* 40:21–36.

Lyons, John O. (1978). *The Invention of the Self.* Carbondale, Ill.: Southern Illinois University Press.

Marcuse, Herbert (1964). *One-Dimensional Man.* Boston: Beacon Press.

Parsons, Talcott (1954). "The Kinship System of the Contemporary United States." Pp. 177–197 in *Essays in Sociological Theory,* Revised Edition. Glencoe, Ill.: Free Press.

Poster, Mark (1978). *Critical Theory of the Family.* New York: Seabury Press.

Rose, Willie Lee (1982). "Reforming Women," *New York Review of Books,* October 7.

Rosenberg, Charles E. (ed.) (1975). *The Family in History.* Philadelphia: University of Pennsylvania Press.

Rosenberg, Charles E. (1980). "Sexuality, Class and Role in 19th Century America." In Elizabeth Pleck and Joseph Pleck (eds.), *The American Man.* Englewoods Cliffs, N.J.: Prentice-Hall.

Rothman, Sheila M. (1978). *Woman's Proper Place: A History of Changing Ideals and Practices 1870 to the Present.* New York: Basic Books.

Ryan, Mary P. (1979). *Womanhood in America (From Colonial Times to the Present),* Second Edition. New York: New Viewpoints.

Ryan, Mary P. (1981). *The Cradle of the Middle Class: The Family in Oneida County, N.Y., 1790–1865.* New York: Cambridge University Press.

Shorter, Edward (1975). *The Making of the Modern Family.* New York: Basic Books.

Smith-Rosenberg, Carroll (1975). "The Female World of Love and Ritual." *Signs* 1:1–29.

Stone, Lawrence (1979). *The Family, Sex and Marriage in England, 1500–1800.* New York: Harper Colophon.

Swidler, Ann (1980). "Love and Adulthood in American Culture." Pp. 120–147 in N. Smelser and E. Erikson (eds.), *Themes of Work and Love in Adulthood.* Cambridge, Mass.: Harvard University Press.

Thernstrom, Stephan (1964). *Poverty and Progress: Social Mobility in a Nineteenth Century City.* Cambridge, Mass.: Harvard University Press.

Wahlstrom, Billie Joyce (1979). "Images of the Family in the Mass Media." Pp. 193–229 in Virginia Tufte and Barbara Myerhoff (eds.), *Changing Images of the Family.* New Haven: Yale University Press.

Welter, Barbara (1966). "The Cult of True Womanhood: 1820–1860." *American Quarterly,* Summer: 151–174.

Zaretsky, Eli (1976). *Capitalism, the Family and Personal Life.* New York: Harper Colophon.

Zweig, Paul (1968). *The Heresy of Self-Love.* Princeton, N.J.: Princeton University Press.

2

A History of Romantic Friendship and Lesbian Love

LILLIAN FADERMAN

The correspondence of women in America, England, France, and Germany during the sixteenth through the nineteenth centuries illustrates innumerable examples of passionate commitment by one woman to another. There are also many fictional examples of such female love relationships, all of them without any hint that the women involved had the slightest sense of wrongdoing, or any suggestion that such affection could be considered abnormal. Common terms used to describe love relationships between women, such as "the love of kindred spirits," "Boston marriage," and "sentimental friends," are found in the writings of the nineteenth century.

These romantic friendships were love relationships in every sense except perhaps the genital, since women in other centuries often internalized the view of females as having little sexual passion. Thus they might kiss, fondle each other, sleep together, utter expressions of overwhelming love and promises of eternal faithfulness, and yet see their passions as nothing more than effusions of the spirit. If they were sexually aroused, bearing no burden of visible proof as men do, they might deny it even to themselves if they wished. But whether or not these relationships had a genital component, the novels and diaries and correspondence of these periods consistently showed romantic friends opening their souls to each other and speaking a language that was in no way different from the language of heterosexual love: They pledged to remain "faithful" forever, to be in "each other's thoughts constantly," to live together, and even to die together.

Society appeared to condone these romantic friendships rather than to view them as disruptive of the social structure. What was it that made such relationships, which have certainly been seen as threatening in our day, seem nonthreatening in other eras? Not all female same-sex relationships were condoned. Transvestite

---

This article has been revised from the Introduction and Chapter IIIB in Lillian Faderman's 1981 book, *Surpassing the Love of Men.* Copyright © 1981 by Lillian Faderman. Used by permission of William Morrow & Co.

women (that is, those who dressed and frequently attempted to pass as men) who engaged in same-sex love were often persecuted and sometimes even executed. Why was a woman's choice of dress such a weighty factor in determining whether men would praise her love for another woman as being noble and beautiful or flog her for it?

An obvious answer was that if a woman dressed like a man, it was assumed that she behaved sexually as a man. If she dressed in clothes suitable to her sex, it might be assumed that she was not sexually aggressive, and two unaggressive females together would do nothing to violate men's presumptive property rights to women's bodies. The answer was in fact more complex: There were many instances of women who were known to engage in lesbian sex, and they did so with impunity. As long as they appeared feminine, their sexual behavior would be viewed as an activity in which women indulged when men were unavailable or as an apprenticeship or appetite-whetter to heterosexual sex. But if one or both of the pair demanded masculine privileges, the illusion of lesbianism as *faute de mieux* behavior was destroyed. Ultimately it was not the sexual aspect of lesbianism as much as the attempted usurpation of the male prerogative by women who behaved like men that many societies appeared to find most disturbing.

Most female romantic friends in the nineteenth century probably did not have sexual relationships. Was that then the primary difference between romantic friendship and lesbian love? The definition of lesbianism is somewhat confused because many of the lesbian cases cited by the early sexologists such as Havelock Ellis and Sigmund Freud (who were among the first to offer modern definitions of the term) were of Victorian and post-Victorian women whose love relationships were nongenital. If lesbianism was not a specifically sexual phenomenon to them, what was it? It appeared in many respects no different from the romantic friendships of earlier eras. Even the sexologists' evidence seemed to suggest that homo*sexuality* was generally no more appropriate a term to describe lesbianism than it was to describe romantic friendship. It would seem that women's love relationships have seldom been limited to that one area of expression, that love between women has been primarily a sexual phenomenon only in male fantasy literature. "Lesbian" describes a relationship in which two women's strongest emotions and affections are directed toward each other. Sexual contact may be a part of the relationship to a greater or lesser degree, or it may be entirely absent. By preference the two women spend most of their time together and share most aspects of their lives with each other.

In our post-sexual-revolution day, we may have difficulty accepting that most female love relationships before the twentieth century were probably not genital, or we might believe that those relationships were not genital, but cannot accept the idea that they were nevertheless serious, that the women's professions of commitment to each other were real and not simply another example of sentimental excessiveness. This attitude has to do with our assumption that what is true of behavior and attitudes today has been true at all times.

But sexual patterns in general have altered tremendously over the centuries, and it can be demonstrated that people in Europe and the United States have probably become more sexual than they were in former times.[1] Even in the twentieth century it is apparent that great changes have occurred, particularly with regard to female sexual expression. For example, we can infer that in the nineteenth century, middle-class urban women seldom had sexual intercourse outside of wedlock from the information that among 339 "illegitimate" mothers whose occupations were known in several London parishes during the 1850s only three were "gentlewomen." Most were domestic servants. It was not until the beginning of this century that premarital sex became a significant reality in the lives of middle-class women who, with their increasing independence, began to see themselves as "like" (that is, equal to) men, and therefore capable of sexual enjoyment, and having the right to that pleasure. Attitudes and experiences continued to change in more recent times. In the 1950s, when Alfred Kinsey was studying sexual behavior among unmarried women, only 20 percent of those he interviewed had had intercourse by the age of nineteen. In 1971 the number in a comparable sample had risen to almost 50 percent.[2] In 1969, 68 percent of Americans believed "it is wrong for people to have sexual relations before marriage." Four years later, the number fell to 48 percent.[3] It is more difficult to trace sexual patterns of love between women, since lesbian sex leaves no evidence in "illegitimate" offspring, and there have been few surveys which deal with women's views of lesbian sexuality. But we can assume that female homosexual relationships followed a pattern similar to that of heterosexual relationships. Therefore, although there is abundant evidence of love between women in the diaries, correspondence, and fiction of earlier centuries, there are not many hints of sexual expression of that love.

My studies have led me to conclude that it is in the twentieth century that love has come to be perceived as a refinement of the sexual impulse, but in many other centuries romantic love and sexual impulse were often considered unrelated.[4] Certainly the degree of sexual expression among romantic friends must have varied, just as it does among women who are avowedly lesbian today. However, it is likely that most love relationships between women during previous eras, when females were encouraged to force any sexual drive they might have to remain latent, were less physical than they are in our times. But the lack of overt sexual expression in these romantic friendships could not discount the seriousness or the intensity of the women's passions toward each other—or that if by "lesbian" we mean an all-consuming emotional relationship in which two women are devoted to each other above anyone else, these ubiquitous sixteenth-, seventeenth-, eighteenth-, and nineteenth-century romantic friendships were "lesbian."

Passionate romantic friendship between women was a widely recognized, tolerated social institution before our century. Women were, in fact, expected to seek out kindred spirits and form strong bonds. It was socially acknowledged that while a woman could not trust men outside her family, she could look to another female for emotional sustenance and not fear betrayal. But her relationship to another female went beyond such affectionate exchanges. It was not unusual for a woman to seek in her romantic friendship the center of her life, quite apart from the demands of marriage and family if not in lieu of them. When women's role in society began to change, however—when what women did needed to be taken more seriously because they were achieving some of the powers that would make them adult persons—society's view of romantic friendship changed.

Love between women—relationships which were *emotionally* in no way different from the romantic friendships of earlier eras—became evil or morbid. It was not simply that men now saw the female sexual drive more realistically. Many of the relationships that they condemned had little to do with sexual expression. It was rather that love between women, coupled with their emerging freedom, might conceivably bring about the overthrow of heterosexuality—which has meant not only sex between men and women but patriarchal culture, male dominance, and female subservience. Learning their society's view of love between women, females were compelled to suppress natural emotion; they were taught to see women only as rivals and men as their only possible love objects, or they were compelled to view themselves as "lesbian," which meant "twisted" either morally or emotionally. What was lovely and nurturing in love between women, what women of other centuries clearly understood, became one of the best-guarded secrets of the patriarchy.

In the sophisticated twentieth century women who chose to love women could no longer see themselves as romantic friends, unless they enveloped themselves in a phenomenal amount of naïveté and were oblivious to modern psychology, literature, and dirty jokes. If they persisted in same-sex love past adolescence, they would at least have to take into account what society thought of lesbians, and they would have to decide to what extent they would internalize those social views. If they were unusually strong or had a strong support group, they might escape regarding themselves as sick sinners. For many of them, without models to show that love between women was not intrinsically wrong or unhealthy, the experts' pronouncements about lesbianism worked as a self-fulfilling prophecy. They became as confused and tormented as they were supposed to be. But it was only during this brief era in history that tragedy and sickness were so strongly attributed to (and probably for that reason so frequently found in) love between women.

This changed with the rise of the second wave of feminism. Having made a general challenge to patriarchal culture, many feminists have recently begun to challenge its taboos on love between women too. They saw it as their job to divest themselves of all the prejudices that had been inculcated in them by their male-dominated society, to reexamine everything regarding women, and finally to reclaim the meaning of love between women. Having learned to question both the social order which made women the second sex and the meaning behind the taboos on love between women, they determined to live their lives through new definitions they would create. They called themselves women-identified-women, or they consciously attempted to lift the stigma from the term "lesbian" and called themselves lesbian-feminists, by which they meant that they would put women first in their lives because men had proven, if not on a personal scale then on a cultural scale, that they were not to be trusted. Lesbian-feminists see men and women as being at odds in their whole approach to the world: Men, as a rule, are authoritarian, violent, cold; and women are the opposite. Like romantic friends before them, lesbian-feminists choose women, kindred spirits, for their love objects. Unlike most romantic friends, however, they understand through feminist doctrine the sociopolitical meaning of their choice.

Lesbian-feminists differ from romantic friends in a number of ways. Most significantly, the earlier women generally had no hope of actually spending their lives together despite often reiterated fantasies that they might; but also romantic friends did not have an articulate doctrine which would help them explain why they could feel closer to women than to men. And the primary difference which affected their relationship to the world is that romantic friends, unlike lesbian-feminists, seldom had reason to believe that society saw them as outlaws—even when they eloped together like the Ladies of Llangollen did. Lesbian-feminists understand, even when they are comfortable within a large support group, that the world outside views them as criminal and reduces their love to a pejorative term. Whatever anger they began with as feminists is multiplied innumerable times as lesbian-feminists as soon as they experience, either in reality or by observation, society's hostility to what is both logical and beautiful to them. Even if they do not suffer personally—if they do not lose their children in court or if they are not fired from their jobs or turned out by their families because of their political-sexual commitments—lesbian-feminists are furious, knowing that such possibilities exist and that many women do suffer for choosing to love other women. Romantic friends never learned to be angry through their love.

There is a good deal on which lesbian-feminists disagree, such as issues concerning class, whether or not to form monogamous relationships, the virtues of communal living, whether separatism is necessary in order to live as a lesbian-feminist, the nature of social action that is efficacious, etc. But they all agree that men have waged constant battle against women, committed atrocities or at best injustices against them, reduced them to grown-up children, and that a feminist ought not to sleep in the enemy camp. They all agree that being a lesbian is, whether consciously or unconsciously perceived, a political act, a refusal to fulfill the male image of womanhood or to bow to male supremacy. Perhaps for romantic friends of other eras their relationship was also a political act, although much more covert: With each other they could escape from many of the externally imposed demands of femininity that were especially stringent throughout much of the eighteenth and nineteenth centuries. They could view themselves as human beings and prime rather than as the second sex. But they did not hope that through their relationship they might change the social structure. Lesbian-feminists do.

They see their lesbian-feminism not just as a personal choice regarding life-style, even though it is certainly a most personal choice. But it is also a political choice which challenges sexism and heterosexism. It is a choice which has been made often in the context of the feminist movement and with an awareness of the ideology behind it. It has seemed the only possible choice for many women who believe that the personal is political, that to reject male supremacy in the abstract but to enter into a heterosexual relationship in which the female is usually subservient makes no sense. Contemporary lesbianism, on the other hand, makes a great deal of sense. It is a combination of the natural love between women, so encouraged in the days of romantic friendships, with the twentieth-century women's freedom that feminism has made possible.

While romantic friends had considerable latitude in their show of physical affection toward each other, it is probably that, in an era when women were not supposed to be sexual, the sexual possibilities of their relationship were seldom entertained. Contemporary women can have no such innocence. But the sexual aspect of their lesbian-feminist relationships generally have less significance than the emotional sustenance and the freedom they have to define themselves. While many lesbian-feminist relationships can and do continue long after the sexual component has worn off, they cannot continue without emotional sustenance and freedom of self-definition. Romantic friends of other eras would probably have felt entirely comfortable in many lesbian-feminist relationships had the contemporary label and stigma been removed.

But many women today continue to be frightened by love between women because the pejorative connotation of the contemporary label and the stigma are still very real for them. Such fear is bound to vanish in the future as people continue to reject strict orthodoxy in sexual relationships: Women will be less and less scared off by the idea of same-sex love without examining what it entails beyond "sexual abnormality." The notion of lesbianism will be neutralized. As females are raised to be more independent, they will not assume that heterosexual marriage is necessary for survival or fulfillment; nor will they accept male definitions of womanhood or non-womanhood. They will have no need to repress natural feelings of affection toward other women. Love between women will become as common as romantic friendship was in other eras. The twentieth-century combination of romantic friendship and female independence will continue to yield lesbian-feminism.

In an ideal world lesbian-feminism, which militantly excludes relationships with men, would not exist. And, of course, the romantic friendships such as women were permitted to conduct in other centuries—in which they might be almost everything to each other but in which a male protector was generally needed in order for them to survive—would not exist either. Instead, in a utopia men would not claim supremacy either in social or personal relationships, and women would not feel that they must give up a part of themselves in order to relate to men. Women with ambition and strength and a sense of themselves would have no reason to see men as the enemy out to conquer and subdue them. Nor would there be any attempt to indoctrinate the female with the notion that to be normal she must transfer the early love she felt for her mother first to her father and then to a father substitute—a man who is more than she is in all ways: older, taller, better educated, smarter, stronger. Women as well as men would not select their love objects on the basis of sexual politics, in surrender or in reaction to an arbitrary heterosexual ideology. They would choose to love another only in reference to the individual needs of their own personalities, which ideally had been allowed to develop untrammelled and free of sex-role stereotyping. Potential or actual bisexuality, which is today looked on by lesbian-feminists as a political betrayal and by heterosexuals as an instability, would be normal, both emotionally and statistically. But until men stop giving women cause to see them as the enemy and until there ceases to be coercion to step into prescribed roles without reference to individual needs and desires, lesbian-feminists will continue to view their choice as the only logical one possible for a woman who desires to be her own adult person.

Notes

1. See, e.g., Edward Shorter, *The Making of the Modern Family* (New York: Basic Books, 1975), especially chapter III.

2. John Kantner and Melvin Zelnik, "Sexual Experience of Young Unmarried Women in the United States," *Family Planning Perspectives,* IV, 4, (Oct. 1972), 9–19.

3. Shorter, *The Making of the Modern Family,* p. 114.

4. See, e.g., Emil Lucka, *The Evolution of Love,* trans. Ellie Schleussner (London: George Allen and Unwin, 1922); Gordon Rattray Taylor, *Sex in History* (New York: Harper and Row, 1954); A. J. Denomy, "Fin' Amors: The Pure Love of the Troubadors, Its Amorality, and Possible Sources," *Mediaeval Studies,* vol. III (1945), 139–207.

3

From Separate Spheres to Sexual Equality: Men's Responses to Feminism at the Turn of the Century

MICHAEL S. KIMMEL

Doubt is in the air. There is an upheaval of traditions and conventionalities. . . . With no firm ground to stand upon, the self-confidence of the past has vanished. Disbelief in everything involves disbelief in one's self.
—A. W. Warner, 1909

The emergence of the modern feminist in the late nineteenth and early twentieth century is a well-documented and much celebrated phenomenon. Less well understood and far less well documented are the variety of reactions to her emergence by American men. Such a lacuna can be explained by the convergence of several problems in the historical study of gender in the United States. For one thing, students of gender have most frequently adopted a "sex-role" model to study masculinity and femininity, a model that is designed to specify the ways in which biological males and biological females become socialized as men and women in any particular culture. This model can be labeled "individualist" (Risman, 1987) because it focuses on learned personal behaviors. This paradigm implies an ahistorical inevitability, which is contradicted by its emphasis on cultural relativity; in each culture, the researcher can identify a kind of static sex-role container into which all biological males and females are forced to fit. As such, the paradigm ignores the extent to which our conceptions of masculinity and femininity—the content of either the male or female sex role—is relational, that is, the product of gender relations that are historically and socially conditioned. Masculinity and femininity are relational constructs; the definition of either depends upon the definition of the other. "Male" and "female" may have some universal characteristics (though even here, the research on biological dimorphism suggests a certain fluidity), but one cannot understand the social constructions of either masculinity or femininity without reference to the other. The sex-role so-

---

An earlier version of this essay appeared as a part of "The Crisis of Masculinity in Historical Perspective" in Harry Brod, ed., *The Making of Masculinities* (Boston: Allen and Unwin, 1987) and a substantially revised version appeared in *Gender and Society* 3, Fall 1987. I have benefited from valuable comments, criticism, and support from Rhoda Blumberg, Harry Brod, Martin Duberman, Anne Foner, John Gagnon, Judy Gerson, Frances Goldin, Janet Goldstein, Cathy Greenblat, Meredith Gould, Barbara Laslett, Judith Lorber, Joseph Pleck, Barbara Risman, and Pepper Schwartz.

cialization paradigm has been critically discussed and evaluated in detail (see, for example, Gerson and Peiss, 1985; Gould and Kern-Daniels, 1977; Lopata and Thorne, 1978; Shapiro, 1982; Stacey and Thorne, 1985; and Tresemer, 1975). These writers, though, tend to stress the problems with the model as it applies to the study of gender in general, or more often to women in particular. Little, if any, attention has been paid specifically to men and masculinity as a social scientific problematic, which is my intention here.

The sex-role socialization model is ahistorical in another sense. Almost all sex-role research focuses on attributes, indicating behavioral or attitudinal traits that are associated with the particular sex role. Thus, changes in sex roles appear as changes in the list of traits or attitudes associated with masculinity or femininity. But masculinity and femininity are more the products of role *enactments*; instead of specifying traits, research might detail the ways in which people negotiate their "roles," the historically fluid and variable enactments of specific role prescriptions. Such a focus on gender relations allows articulation of traits at separate times, but also the processes by which the changes occur.

The sex-role paradigm also minimizes the extent to which gender relations are based on power. Not only do men as a group exert power over women as a group, but the historically derived definitions of masculinity and femininity reproduce those power relations. Masculinity becomes associated with those traits that imply authority and mastery, femininity with those traits that suggest passivity and subordination. By undervaluing the historical and social bases for gender relations, then, the sex-role paradigm can reproduce the very problems it seeks to understand.

An emphasis on gender relations as historically and socially constructed also sheds different light on another problem. (The gender relations model is similar to the "microstructural" model proposed by the editors.) The sex-role model had assumed fixed, static, and mutually exclusive role containers with no interpenetration. Further, bipolar mutual exclusivity of sex roles reinforces oppositional assumptions about masculinity and femininity; though defined in reference to abstract ideals, sex roles reinforce the popular notions of the "otherness" of the "opposite" sex.

I believe therefore that the sex-role socialization model is theoretically inadequate on conceptual grounds. But it's explanatory weakness is best revealed when one looks at those historical moments in which gender issues assume a prominent position in the public consciousness, moments of gender confusion and the vigorous reassertion of traditional gender roles against serious challenges to inherited configurations—moments, we might say, of "crisis" in gender relations, historical moments not unlike our own.

The late nineteenth and early twentieth centuries were also such an historical moment of crisis in gender relations, when the meanings of both femininity and masculinity were challenged and various groups attempted to reconstitute gender along different relational lines. The rise of feminism and the emergence of the New Woman and the articulation of distinctly different identities for the heterosexual and the homosexual—prior to the late nineteenth century, identity did not inhere in sexual behaviors, and especially in the gender of one's sexual partner—explicitly challenged inherited constructions. And responses to these challenges ranged from frightened retreat to traditional configurations to demarcating institutional spheres for the vigorous assertion of a renewed masculinity, to the rise of sex-role theory itself, an historical popularization of the Freudian notion that appropriate gender organization and sexual orientation were products of cultural interventions in the child's life, that the development of personality was, as he put it, "a work of culture—not unlike the draining of the Zuider Zee" (Freud, 1965:80).

When, in the late nineteenth and early twentieth centuries, gender relations were challenged, men were suddenly confused; no one knew what it meant to be a "real man." (Fortunately for the scholar, such periods of confusion yield a rich set of texts that give popular readers advice on how to recapture or reconstruct their gender identity.) Men's responses can be organized into three separate categories, which suggest three alternate strategies for the reconstitution of gender. Some men, whom I call the "anti-feminists," demanded the return of women to the private sphere of hearth and home, yearning nostalgically for a mythic separation of spheres that helped to keep women from explicit challenges to men in the public realm. Other men, though not entirely indifferent to women's invasion of the public sphere, sought solutions in developing separate public institutions for men. This "pro-male" response could combat the perceived "feminization" of American culture (Douglas, 1977) through institutions to train young men in a virile hardiness appropriate to their gender. Finally, a small but visible group of men believed that the solution to the gender crisis at the turn of the century rested on embracing the feminist model of social reconstruction. These "pro-feminist" men actively supported campaigns for women's public participation, especially suffrage, as well as more personal demands for sexual autonomy.

The explication of these three distinct trajectories of men's responses to feminism at the turn of the century provides an historical counterpoint to sex-role socialization models, revealing that model's conceptual inadequacy to fully encompass shifting gender relations. For example, though historically linked, the anti-feminist and the pro-male responses articulate different strategies for restoring the traditional balance between women and men, which rest on the shifting relations between public and private spheres. The sex-role socialization model, resting on acquisition of individual psychological traits, is particularly ill-suited to account for these two trajectories. Nor is it well equipped to account for the historical emergence of pro-feminist men at specific historical junctures and not at others. One could resort to a sex-role deviant model that questions the appropriateness of fit between these men and the male sex-role, which is precisely what many antagonists of pro-feminist men actually did. But the historical question of the emergence of pro-feminist men at some times and not at others would remain.

To the historical sociologist, crises in gender relations occur at specific historical junctures, when structural changes transform the institutions of personal life, such as marriage and the family, and hence the possibility for gender identity. In this paper, after specifying these structural shifts, I shall turn to the rise of the New Woman, who became the target for the three male responses to feminism. Understanding these responses requires discussion of several ideological currents of the period, especially the rise of scientific discourse as a counter to anti-modernist sentiments. In its nineteenth-century incarnation, feminism represented a paragon of modernist thought, and male responses to feminism were inextricably bound to responses to modernity.

One sociological implication of a gender relations model is that it allows the observer to specify not only the reconstitution of gender over time, but also the *directionality* of changes in gender relations. The historical evidence suggests that though both masculinity and femininity are socially constructed within an historical context of gender relations, definitions of masculinity are historically *reactive* to changing definitions of femininity. Such a claim runs counter to traditional formulations of gender—such as David Riesman's comment that "characterological change in the West seems to occur first with men" (1950:18). Instead, my argument suggests that since men benefit from inherited definitions of masculinity and femininity, they would be unlikely to initiate change. In fact, it would appear that men as a group have benefited from the sex-role socialization *model* that has governed behavioral science's treatment of gender, since it uses masculinity as a normative standard of reference and maximizes the distance between the two genders while it minimizes the extent to which these definitions reproduce existing power relations, are historically variable, and are therefore open to challenge.

The New Woman challenged traditional gender relations, which called into question the definition of masculinity, which, in turn, prompted a set of male responses at the turn of the century. Let us begin the explication of those responses by examining the circumstances under which the New Woman emerged.

Structural Changes and the Erosion of Traditional Gender Arrangements in the Late Nineteenth Century

The early nineteenth century provided a fertile environment for an expansive American manhood. Geographic expansion—the taming of the West and the "pacification" of its native population—combined with rapid industrial and urban growth to fuel a "virile" optimism about social possibilities. The Jacksonian assault on "effete" European bankers, and the frighteningly "primitive" Native American population, grounded identity in a "securely achieved manhood" (Rogin, 1975:162).

By mid-century, though, "the walls of the male establishment began to crack," as social and economic changes also transformed the social institutions in which gender relations were negotiated (marriage, family, sexuality). Westward expansion came to an abrupt end as the frontier closed; the unspoiled virgin land that "gave America its identity" (Rogin, 1975:79) was gone. "For nearly three centuries," wrote Frederick Jackson Turner in 1896, "the dominant fact in American life has been expansion. And now the frontier is gone, and with its going has closed the first period of American history."

Rapid industrialization in the late nineteenth century radically transformed men's relationship to their work. The independent artisan, the autonomous small farmer, the small shopkeeper, were everywhere disappearing. Before the Civil War, almost nine of every ten American men were farmers or self-employed businessmen; by 1870 that figure had dropped to two-thirds, and by 1910, less than one-third of all American men were so employed. Increased mechanization and the routinization of labor accompanied rapid industrialization; individual workers were increasingly divorced from control over the labor process as well as dispossessed of ownership. Thus Henry George wrote in *Social Problems* (1883) that labor-saving devices were "absolutely injurious" and result in "positive evils" for the working man, "degrading men into the position of mere feeders of machines":

> rendering the working man more dependent; depriving him of skill and the opportunities to acquire it; lessening his control over his own condition and his hope of improving it; cramping his mind, and in many cases distorting and enervating his body. (Trachtenberg, 1982:43)

In such an atmosphere, the dramatic international economic collapse of 1873 was especially powerful. A series of bankruptcies, bank failures, and foreclosures sharpened political conflict. (In 1874 alone, over 6,000 businesses closed, and 900 closed every month during one quarter in 1878.) In the South, Southwest, and Midwest, dispossessed farmers fought back against big capital through the Farmers Alliance and the Populist movement, perhaps the United States' only genuine mass leftist political movement. In the burgeoning cities, a widening class rift and waves of immigrants fueled hostilities, which erupted in a wave of strikes and revolts in 1877 that brought the nation to the brink of armed insurrection. "Sudden as a thunderburst from a clear sky the crisis came upon the country," wrote journalist J. Dacus in 1877. "It seemed as if the whole social and political structure was on the very brink of ruin" (Trachtenberg, 1982:70–71).

And indeed it was. During the last decade of the century, American men were increasingly restless, besieged by a seemingly endless string of structural problems: "the failures and corruption of reconstruction, the longest depression in American history, insatiable trusts, swarms of what were held to be sexually potent and racially inferior immigrants, and a government discredited at all levels" (Barker-Benfield, 1976:84).

One set of responses to this cultural crisis was the anti-modernist critique of American culture. A convulsively anti-modernist sentiment captured the imaginations of many groups, although it was often expressed in contradictory ways. For some, anti-modernism glorified individual achievement; for others, it revealed a desperate longing for community. Resurgent medievalism, a fascination with oriental culture, and religious revivalism all celebrated the annihilation of the ego and its immersion into a transcendent community. The anti-modernist vision thoroughly rejected the city, with its "dark satanic mills," as the breeding ground for both "idleness" and "vicious classes" according to Wendell Phillips (Leach, 1980:334). Frank Lloyd Wright's tirade against New York captures part of the anti-urban sentiment. He described it in *The Future of Architecture* as

> a place fit for banking and prostitution and not much else . . . a crime of crimes . . . a vast prison . . . triumph of the herd instinct . . . outgrown and overgrown . . . the greatest mouth in the world . . . humanity preying upon humanity . . . carcass . . . parasite . . . fibrous tumor . . . pig-pile . . . incongruous mantrap of monstrous dimensions . . . enormity devouring manhood, confusing personality by frustration of individuality. Is this not anti-Christ? The Moloch that knows no God but *more*? (cited in Muschamp, 1983:15)

To others, the city was less a sinkhole of vice and violence than an enervating seductress, skillfully sapping men of their virility. In contrast to the frontier, "the city represents civilization, confinement, and female efforts to domesticate the world" (Pugh, 1983:150). Its effect, as Ernest Thompson Seton put it, was to make us "degenerate. We know money grubbing machine politics, degrading sports, cigarettes . . . false ideals, moral laxity, and lessening church power, in a word 'city rot' has worked evil in the nation" (Macleod, 1983:32). The city was cast as cultural villain, either because of its effete feminizing refinement, or because of the ominous danger lurking in the rows of working-class tenements that housed the unwashed immigrant hordes. Each strain of thought saw a threat to masculinity.

Responses to Structural Change by Women and Men

Feminism and the New Woman

Against this background of dramatic structural change and ideological developments, the family and the relations between women and men were undergoing upheaval and conflict in the late nineteenth century (Rosenberg, 1980:235). Rapid capitalist industrialization "increasingly subverted the older sexual division of labor . . . [and] created conditions favorable to the emergence of women into the public realm with men" (Leach, 1980:123). Women were involved in arenas that directly touched the lives of men

> in temperance, social science, and moral education; in the reforms . . . of the marriage laws . . . that legally permitted women to transact their own business, keep their own separate earnings, and retain ownership of their separate estates; in the reform of many state laws . . . that sanctioned the rights of women, whether married or single, to employment in the professions; and in the growing employment of large numbers of women in the industrial sector of the economy and . . . in the professions, especially medicine, journalism, and education. (Leach, 1980:123)

Women's increased public presence was buttressed by changes in the family, such as shrinking family size, increasing nuclearization of family structure, and a clear demarcation between workplace and household as separate units of production and consumption, respectively (Chafetz and Dworkin, 1986:4). The median age for marriage for men was higher in 1890 than in any subsequent year until 1986, and a statistical imbalance between the sexes, with women outnumbering men, was observed (*New York Times,* December 10, 1986, and Todd, 1867:20). Motherhood was increasingly professionalized, cast as a "calling," which coincided with a decline in the number of household servants and greater absence of busy fathers from the home, which "made the mother-son relationship appear threatening to proper masculine socialization" (Hantover, 1980:290). Everywhere, "motherhood was advancing, fatherhood was in retreat" (Rotundo, 1983:30).

Such changes placed contradictory demands on a woman; she was to be both the True Woman, "emotional, dependent, and gentle—a born follower," and the Ideal Mother, "strong, self-reliant, protective, an efficient caretaker in relation to children and home" (Smith-Rosenberg, 1985:199). By "combining piety and domesticity with submissiveness and passivity," the notion of the True Woman "controlled women and narrowed their options" (Degler, 1980:26–27). But both the Ideal Mother and the True Woman were confined to the home and other arenas of social reproduction, so that culture became "increasingly the sphere of women, of ladies of charity as well as schoolteachers and librarians" (Trachtenberg, 1982:145). That American culture was increasingly "feminized" became a dominant theme in the discourse between women and men. The separation of work and home, the privatization of family life, and other changes meant that childhood socialization—by parents, teachers, and religious leaders—was increasingly the work of women, as mothers, schoolteachers, and Sunday school teachers (Douglas, 1977). By the late nineteenth century, "women were teaching boys to be men" (Rotundo, 1983:32).

Several social changes—the rise of women's colleges, increased literacy, delayed age of marriage, an ideology of upward mobility, and capitalist development—gave rise to the New Woman, a single, highly educated, economically autonomous woman who "challenged existing gender relations and the distribution of power" (Smith-Rosenberg, 1985:245). Since, as Sarah Norton observed in 1870, the "inequality of women finds its origins in marriage," and to make political equality possible, "social equality of the sexes must precede it" (Leach, 1980:190), the New Woman eschewed marriage and "fought for professional visibility, espoused innovative, often radical economic and social reforms, and wielded real political power" (Smith-Rosenberg, 1985: 245). The New Woman was an avowed feminist, who campaigned for suffrage and asserted her autonomy in the world of men. "My aim," said one, "is to make myself a true woman, one worthy of the name, and not to be one of the delicate little dolls or the silly fools who make up the bulk of American women, slaves to society and fashion" (Lasch, 965:67). Such expressions of autonomy carried serious costs for women; many, believing that the price of independence was femininity, took on men's names, dressed as men, and behaved as men. "The determination to be a 'true woman' forced one in effect to lead a man's life" (Lasch, 1965:68). The rise of the women's movement is a direct outcome of those structural changes, arising "during times of, and in response to, general socioeconomic and cultural change, changes that include, but are not restricted to alterations in the family and the roles of women" (Chafetz and Dworkin, 1986:38).

The Crisis of Masculinity

Thus the stage was set for a new "crisis of masculinity," in late nineteeth- and early twentieth-century United States. Structural changes had transformed the structure of gender relations; both men and women struggled to redefine the meanings of masculinity and femininity.

> What did it mean to be masculine or feminine? What did the adjectives signify? The intensity of the speculation about these questions discloses anxieties which lie much deeper than anything associated with the greater leisure of the modern woman or the flight of housework from the home. (Lasch, 1965:57)

One historian argues that, in fact, the "real gender drama in this period involve[d] the changes in men's lives and their reactions to them" (Hartman, 1984:13). Writers acknowledged that "their readership was hungry to be told of what true manhood and true womanhood consisted," and though they often "flew to the simplest, most extreme kind of definitions" (Barker-Benfield, 1976:210) a serious reexamination was also under way. Men felt themselves besieged by social breakdown and crisis, as "the familiar routes to manhood [became] either washed out or roadblocked" (Hartman, 1984:13), and as male anxieties intensified by democracy and industrialization.

> Men . . . were jolted by changes in the economic and social order which made them perceive that their superior position in the gender order and their supposedly "natural" male roles and prerogatives were not somehow rooted in the human condition, that they were instead the result of a complex set of relationships subject to change and decay. (Hartman, 1984:13)

At both the textual and the institutional levels—in works of fiction, sermons, and scientific tracts as well as in public policy and voluntary associations—the late nineteenth-century crisis of masculinity revealed three important reactions to the perceived feminization of American popular culture. First, there was a considerable anti-feminist backlash, which, casting women as the source of men's troubles, sought to reestablish the male dominance that was perceived to have eroded. Second, we can observe a pro-male backlash, which sought to vigorously reassert traditional masculinity, especially as a cultural and political ethos, against social and political trends of which feminism was but a symptom, not a cause. Finally, a small but important group of men openly embraced feminist ideas and ideals as the signposts pointing toward a radically different future.

The Anti-Feminist Backlash

For some men, the need to redefine masculinity was caused by women's ill-advised challenge to their traditional role; if masculinity was in crisis, it was women's fault, and the solution to the crisis was the revival of a hypermasculine subordination of women. A strongly misogynist current runs through a number of religious tracts, medical treatises, and political pamphlets of this period, as the assault against women's gains came largely from the religious and medical spheres and from the opposition to women's suffrage. All three discourses resorted to a revivified emphasis on the "natural" differences between men and women as the basis for social differentiation; opponents of increasing economic, political, and social equality between men and women almost always resort to arguments about the "natural order of things" as counters to progressive social trends.

For example, pamphlets about women and sexuality written by women and clergy "played with stereotypic sex distinctions," providing "a testament of sexual tension, of covertly stated hatred of women by men and the reverse" (Douglas, 1977:228). A new "muscular Christianity" hailed a remasculinized Jesus: He was "no dough-faced, lick-spittle proposition," proclaimed Billy Sunday, but "the greatest scrapper who ever lived" (Douglas, 1977:327). Texts such as Thomas Hughes's *The Manliness of Christ* (1880) and Carl Case's *The Masculine in Religion* (1906) echoed this remasculinization of Jesus. And the Right Reverend John L. Spalding, Catholic bishop of Peoria, fused political repression and sexual repression of women when he wrote:

> Sensuality and love, though mysteriously related, are contrary as religion and superstition. The baser passion grows upon the grave of the finer virtue. Woman, like religion, appeals to what is highest in man. Her power over him is that of sentiment, and to seek to place her in rivalry with him in the rude business of life is an aim worthy of an atheistic and material age. (Gardella, 1984:116)

Men's anti-suffrage organizations sprang up around the nation to rally men behind the masculine cause. Suffrage was seen as the "ultimate invasion of the male domain by women in their drive to save the Republic" (Dubbert, 1979:86). Some organizations, like the Man Suffrage Association, were composed of men representing the industries that had been active in the anti-suffrage cause (Flexner, 1975:311; see also Chafetz and Dworkin, 1986:31). Horace Bushnell, a mid-nineteenth-century reformer, went so far (1867) as to claim that women would be physiologically damaged if they got the vote, growing larger, developing heavier brains, and losing their unique feminine mannerisms and features. It wasn't so much, he argued, that they should be deprived of the vote as *exempted* from it, because of their lofty position and female role (see Frothingham, 1890:177). Opposition to women's suffrage reasserted a natural division between women and men and often rested on a distinction between natural right and civil right. "It would seem best," wrote John Todd (1867:25), "for those who, at any hazard or labor, earn the property, to select the rulers, and have this responsibility." Opposition to suffrage was hailed as a patriotic act. "The American Republic stands before the world as the supreme expression of masculine force," claimed the Illinois Association Opposed to Women's Suffrage in 1910. Those who supported women's advance, or progressive reformism generally, were considered less than American and hence less than real men.

> Reformers and genteel intellectuals who stood above party battles invited the scorn of the regulars, a scorn couched frequently in images fusing anger at feminizing culture with sexual innuendo, and manly braggadocio of the stalwarts: "political hermaphrodite," "miss-Nancys," "man-milliners." Nonpartisans were a "third sex," "the neuter gender not popular in nature or society." (Trachtenberg, 1982:163)

Men used the "natural" division between the sexes as the justification for opposition to women's education. "I think the great danger of our day is forcing the intellect of woman beyond what her physical organization will possibly bear," wrote John Todd (1867:23). He counseled (1867:25) giving women "all the advantages and all the education which her organization so tender and delicate, will bear; but don't try to make the anemone into an oak, nor to turn the dove out to wrestle with storms and winds, under the idea that she may just as well be an eagle as a dove."

Medical texts revealed the twin terrors of sexuality and women's advances, and many manuals conflated their effects, casting women as both lustful temptresses and pious guardians of home and hearth. The male response to the New Woman underscores how scientific discourse came to dominate the arguments over women's equality. Men first attacked the New Woman for her rejection of motherhood. Edward Bok, editor of *Ladies Home Journal,* linked this to structural changes when he wrote that "[t]wenty years ago, a change in economic conditions, caused chiefly by the invention of labor saving devices, found thousands of women suddenly thrown with leisure on their hands." As a result, women were drawn away from the "great and fundamental problems directly touching the marriage relation and the home" (Bok, 1910:5–6). Soon, armed with new medical evidence, the New Woman was attacked for her rejection of femininity in general. Thus Dr. Alfred Stille observed in his presidential address to the American Medical Association in 1871:

> Certain women seek to rival men in manly sports . . . and the strongminded ape them in all things, even in dress. In doing so, they may command a sort of admiration such as all monstrous productions inspire, especially when they tend towards a higher type than their own. (Ehrenreich and English, 1979:65)

Rejecting motherhood and femininity, the New Woman was also cast as rejecting men. She was a third sex, an intermediate sex, a "mannish lesbian." By linking social protest to biological differences, male anti-feminists could claim that this war against the socially constructed gender was really a war against nature.

> Men's growing sense of vulnerability after the Civil War—their notion of social crisis and the concomitant gynecological crescendo—cannot

> be disassociated from the increasing vociferousness of women at the same time, most noticeably on the suffrage front. Doctors like other men also displayed persistent anxiety over the growing numbers of the new, conspicuously consuming, fashionable life style of city women, their style dangerously attractive to all women. (Barker-Benfield, 1976:123)

From this growing fear came an episode of reactionary mythmaking; commentators "clothed gender distinctions specific to late 19th century industrial countries in the unchangeability of human biology," making the social appear natural and immutable (Smith-Rosenberg, 1985:289).

On the other side, physicians warned against feminized boys, and spent tremendous energy in advising parents on proper socialization to manhood. In the same presidential address cited above, Dr. Stille, warned that "a man with feminine traits of character or with the frame and carriage of a female is despised by both the sex he ostensibly belongs to and that of which he is at once a caricature and a libel" (Barker-Benfield, 1976:86). One physician wrote that "a woman admires in a man true manliness, and is repelled by weakness and effeminacy. A womanish man awakens either the pity or the contempt of the fair sex" (Rosenberg, 1980:231). And Dr. Augustus Kinsley Gardner stressed the imperative of different childrearing techniques for boys and girls. His extensive consideration of male masturbation in *Our Children* (1872) led him to argue against feather beds for boys, because "the very softness is not desirable, while the very excess of heat conduces to a frame of mind not desirable, engenders and ferments lascivious thoughts in the adolescent, and is otherwise very objectionable" (Barker-Benfield, 1976:232). Parents had an enormous responsibility, and manuals proliferated to help them guide their children through the perilous journey to maturity. Several cautioned against dancing, book-learning, and even fraternities, since they would corrupt the young, (see McKeever, 1913:passim). Barely concealed were views of children, especially young boys, as increasingly impressionable and vulnerable to feminine wiles, and of women as dangerous and tempting threats to masculinity. Male anti-feminists were wary of the feminizing clutches of mothers and teachers, whose refined civility would be the undoing of American masculinity, and they sought to push women out of the public domain and return them to the home as passive, idealized figurines, so that their influence could no longer sap the vitality of the nation.

Nowhere is the male anti-feminist backlash better expressed than in Henry James's novel *The Bostonians* (1886), whose hero, the dashing Basil Ransom, is afraid that the natural masculinity of political leaders would be rendered impotent by meddling, aggressive women; he "projects his anxiety onto women and provides . . . an explicit literary example of the castration complex" (Pugh, 1983:109).

> The whole generation is womanized; the masculine tone is passing out of the world; it's a feminine, nervous, hysterical, chattering canting age, an age of hollow phrases and false delicacy and exaggerated solicitudes and coddled sensibilities, which, if we don't soon look out, will usher in the reign of mediocrity, of the feeblest and flattest and most pretentious that has ever been. The masculine character, the ability to dare and endure, to know and yet not fear reality, to look the world in the face and take it for what it is . . . that is what I want to preserve, or rather . . . recover; and I must tell you that I don't in the least care what becomes of you ladies while I make the attempt! (James, 1965:343)

The assertion of masculinity required the resubordination of women.

The Pro-Male Response

Other men were equally anxious and distressed about masculinity, but saw solutions to gender crisis in a vigorous reassertion of traditional masculinity in other, more public domains. Women, themselves, were not the enemy; women's increased power was but symptomatic of cultural changes that had reduced the importance and visibility of masculinity. Masculinist sentiments countered feminization as a cultural process, rather than women, either as a group or as individuals. Several well-known authors jumped on the masculinist bandwagon. Melville argued that masculinity was a "resistance to sentimentalism," and "effort at a genuinely political and philosophical life" (Douglas, 1977:294), and Harvard senior John Dos Passos complained to a friend in 1917:

> I think we are all of us a pretty milky lot, don't you? With our tea table convictions and our radicalism that keeps up so consistently within the bounds of decorum. . . . And what are we to fit when they turn us out of Harvard? We're too intelligent to be successful businessmen and we haven't the sand or the energy to be anything else. (Filene, 1984:10)

William James wrote that there was "no more contemptible type of human character than that of the nervous sentimentalist and dreamer, who spends his life in a weltering sea of sensibility and emotion, but who never does a concrete manly deed" (Bellah et al., 1985:120).

Several antidotes to this perceived feminization were offered, antidotes that would increase male fellowship and instill those masculine virtues that could rescue an enfeebled nation. Whereas anti-feminist men wanted to press women back into the private sphere, pro-male men were concerned about women's dominance of the private sphere, and sought to dislodge her in the home by creating distinctly male agencies of socialization. There was something "mentally enervating in feminine companionship" (Dubbert, 1979:97). The separation of boys and girls became a "kind of mania"; Hartman (1984:11) notes that in some libraries it was normative to segregate the volumes authored by men from those authored by women. William James prescribed a stiffening of American ideals with the tonic of the common laborer's "sterner stuff of manly virtue." Such an infusion of masculinity into the predominantly feminine precincts of refinement would allow the entire society to "pass toward some newer and better equilibrium" (Trachtenberg, 1982:141–142). Senator Albert Beveridge of Indiana counseled, in his *Young Man and the World* (1906), one of the many manuals that advised parents and children on the proper behavior for boys and girls, that boys should "avoid books, in fact avoid all artificial learning for the forefathers put America on the right path by learning from completely natural experience" (Dubbert, 1980:310).

Curiously, pro-male men believed that separation of the sexes would also serve as an antidote to increasing homosexuality. If the sexes mingled, these authors claimed, then men would become feminized, and hence homosexual. Separation of the sexes—or homosociality—was a necessary precondition of heterosexuality. As G. Stanley Hall, the eminent psychologist, argued in his textbook *Adolescence,* familiarity and camaraderie produced a disenchantment and diluted the "mystic attraction of the other sex" (1904:641).

This compulsive reassertion of traditional masculinity resonated with the anti-urbanism and the reactivated martial ideal that characterized a strain of anti-modernist sensibility at the turn of the century. "Get your children into the country," one real estate advertisement for Wilmington, Delaware, urged potential buyers in 1905. "The cities murder children. The hot pavements, the dust, the noise, are fatal in many cases, and harmful always. The history of successful men is nearly always the history of country boys" (Jackson, 1985:138).

Revived martial idealism also pushed the nation even closer to war. If, as Maurice Thompson wrote in 1898, "the greatest danger that a long period of profound peace offers to a nation is that of [creating] effeminate tendencies in young men" (610), then war could be a sensible policy for the nation and a remedy for feminized men. The building of empire through military domination was fueled by an emotional fervor to prove masculinity. The *Washington Post* editorialized in 1898:

> A new consciousness seems to have come upon us—the consciousness of strength, and

> with it a new appetite, a yearning to show our strength. . . . Ambition, interest, land-hunger, pride, the mere joy of fighting, whatever it may be, we are animated by a new sensation. . . . The taste of empire is in the mouth of the people, even as the taste of blood in the jungle. (Booth, 1982:27)

General Homer Lea linked the two explicitly, when he noted that "[as] manhood marks the height of physical vigor among mankind, so the militant successes of a nation mark the zenith of its physical greatness" (Roszak and Roszak, 1975:92). At least some writers believed that it worked. "The slouching, dissipated, impudent lout who seemed to typify young America has disappeared," editorialized the *Washington Post* in 1918 at the end of the First World War (Filene, 1980:325).

Perhaps no one better captures this militarist strategy and the view of the soldier as moral exemplar than Theodore Roosevelt, who elevated compulsive masculinity and military adventurism to the level of national myth. Roosevelt's triumph over his own youthful frailty and his transformation into a robust vigorous man served as a template for a revitalized American social character; he "symbolized a restoration of masculine identity at a time . . . when it appeared to be jeopardized," and "typified the male oriented conquest of the wilderness that seemed to be the new 'safety valve' or 'frontier,' " (Dubbert, 1980:313; Green, 1986:237). William Allen White, a Kansas newspaper editor, praised Roosevelt's "hard muscled frame" and his "crackling voice"; here was a "masculine sort of person with extremely masculine virtues and palpably masculine faults" (Dubbert, 1980:131). Roosevelt's foreign policy was military expansion; his style was hypermasculine, proven in imperial adventures in the Caribbean and the Philippines. "The nation that has trained itself to a cancer of unwarlike and isolated ease is bound, in the end, to go down before other nations which have not lost *the manly and adventurous virtues,*" he thundered. "There is no place in the world for nations who have become enervated by the soft and easy life, or who have lost their fibre of vigorous hardiness and masculinity" (Roszak and Roszak, 1975:92).

The masculinist response to the crisis of masculinity also manifested less bellicose institutional responses, such as the founding of the Boy Scouts of America in 1910. The Boy Scouts celebrated a masculinity tested and proven against nature and other men, removed from the cultural restraints of home, hearth, school, and church. Scouting could "counter the forces of feminization and maintain traditional manhood," Hantover (1980:293) writes. Here was "a boy's liberation movement, to free young males from women, especially from mothers" (Dubbert, 1979:152). "Manliness can only be taught by men," observed Lord Baden-Powell, the founder of the organization in England, "and not by those who are half men, half old women" (Rosenthal, 1986:226). If "spectatoritis" had "turned robust, manly, self-reliant boyhood into a lot of flat-chested cigarette smokers with shaky nerves and doubtful vitality," according to Chief Scout Ernest Thompson Seton in his *The Boy Scouts of America* (1910), then the BSA could counter the forces of feminization and maintain traditional manhood (Macleod, 1983:49). Americans found in the BSA "an institutional sphere for the validation of masculinity previously generated by the flow of daily social life and affirmed in one's work" (Hantover, 1980:299). Here was the place to re-create an ideal boyhood and its natural small-town setting, masculine preserves against the urban world of enfeeblement, refinement, civility, and women. To the BSA fell the "noble ideal of restoring the primitive past" (Dubbert, 1979:156), resolving a cultural Oedipal angst by removing boys from mothers and reinserting them back into nature with the band of the brothers, the primal horde, re-created in the American small town. As Walter Lippman put it, the Boy Scouts made boys' gangs "valuable to civilization" as a "really constructive reform" (1962:41–43).

Such organized "primitiveness" requires quotation, because the goal of the BSA was hardly to encourage political rebellion against an enervating culture, but it was a "quest for disciplined vitality," to redirect male anxieties, to channel and sublimate adolescent sexual yearning—"the curse and bane of boyhood" as health reformer Horace Fletcher put it (Green, 1986:261)—and to reassert a traditional masculinity, but all within the bounds of an extended complacency and obedience to the emerging industrial order (Green, 1986:262). Lord Baden-Powell understood this campaign for moral redemption well. England was "shamed by the Boer War, concerned about the vulnerability of its vast empire and the specter of social unrest among its own laboring classes," when Baden-Powell wrote that the brotherhood of scouts consisted of

> real *men* in every sense of the word . . . they understand living out in the jungles, and they can find their way anywhere . . . they know how to look after their health when far away from any doctors, are strong and plucky, and ready to face any danger, and always keen to help each other. (Rosenthal, 1984:46)

Neither anarchistic nor individualistic, Scouting's cult of masculinity requires that they "give up everything, their personal comforts and desires, in order to get their work done. They do not do all this for their own amusement, but because it is their duty to their king, fellow country-men, or employers" (Rosenthal, 1984:45–46). In the United States as well, the goal of all this "stodgy fun" was therapeutic, to turn boys into docile middle-class workers, tuned to middle-level occupations, with some responsibility, but subordinate and able to take commands from superiors (Macleod, 1983; see also Rosenthal, 1984:30). If boys were provided a place away from the city, from women, and from culture—where they "could be boys"—then they would surely become the "real men" required by early twentieth-century industrial capitalism.

The Pro-Feminist Response

Although fewer in number and less influential institutionally, a significant group of American men openly embraced feminist principles as a potential solution to the crisis of masculinity. Inspired by women's increasingly visible public presence (in reformist movements such as abolition, populism, and labor, and socially redemptive groups such as the WCTU and the Social Purity movement), many men believed that women's political participation, symbolized by the extension of suffrage to women, would be a significant gain for all Americans, male and female. Other men supported feminist women's goals to revolutionize the relations between men and women in the family and in sexuality. Still others maintained a firm belief in the division of the sexes, but argued that increased feminization might prove a palliative to the dangers of compulsive masculinity.

Male support for women's public participation came first from the founders and early leaders of the newly opened women's colleges. Matthew Vassar, William Allan Neilson and Joseph Taylor (both of Smith), and Henry Durant (Wellesley) were articulate champions of women's citizenship. Durant wrote that "the real meaning of the Higher Education for Women" was "revolt."

> We revolt against the slavery in which women are held by the customs of society—the broken health, the aimless lives, the subordinate position, the helpless dependence, the dishonesties and shams of so-called education. The Higher Education of Women . . . is the cry of the oppressed slave. It is the assertion of absolute equality . . . it is the war of Christ . . . against spiritual wickedness in high places. (Horowitz, 1984:44)

Vassar President Henry Noble MacCracken chartered trains at his own expense to transport Vassar students to suffrage demonstrations in New York, where he proudly led the college's contingent, holding one end of the Vassar College Suffrage Association banner before a jeering crowd.

The movement for coeducation was also supported by pro-feminist men, whose political views were often based upon scientific advances. John Vleck, for example, who presided over Wesleyan's experiment with coeducation, believed that "egalitarian coeducation represented the true index of the scientific advancement of the race" (Leach, 1980:73). Floyd Dell argued that the patriarchal system had "labored under a . . . disadvantage of having to assert that its artifices were laws of nature" (Dell, 1930:131) while pro-feminist men had science on their side. And Burt Green Wilder, a scientist at Cornell, condemned the "barbaric cruelty" and "repression" that had "crushed" women's spirit and transmuted sexual "equivalence" into sexual disequilibrium. "The real creed of the future," he wrote in *Atlantic Monthly,* "is equal but not identical; diverse yet complementary; the man for the woman, and the woman for the man" (Leach, 1980:49).

Men also directly supported women's suffrage, believing with Dr. Charles Taylor that the repression of women was "the greatest evil of modern society" (Degler, 1980:256), and that political equality might relieve the world of oppressively masculine politics. The Men's League for Women's Suffrage had both English and American branches; in the United States, Greenwich Village radical Max Eastman was its guiding light. His pamphlet, *Is Woman Suffrage Important,* linked a socialist economic critique of the leisured class with an analysis of the social construction of gender differences; these combine to turn women's "enforced feebleness into a holy thing," he wrote (Strauss, 1983:229).

Men participated regularly in suffrage demonstrations as well. An editorial from *La Follette's* (May 1911) praises the 85 "courageous and convinced men" who marched in a demonstration, among them John Dewey, Hamilton Holt, Oswald Garrison Villard (editor of the *New York Evening Post*), and Edward Markham. Although "hooted and jeered," and "guyed in the streets," one counted being "booed and hissed down the Avenue . . . a very thrilling and inspiring experience. I am determined," he continued, "that if I can help to that end, there shall be a thousand men in line next year." He wasn't very far off target. An editorial in the *New York Times* the next year predicted 800 men would march in a suffrage demonstration the next day, and suggested, somewhat smugly, that these "courageous" men would face an "unsympathetic multitude" as they stood publicly for what they believed.

But suffrage was but a public expression of a deeply social challenge that feminists had issued to the social order that bound them to unattainable ideals and repressive social conditions. "Woman's suffrage is not primarily a political but a social question," wrote Jesse Jones, a Boston Unitarian minister, in the *Woman's Journal,* "and means a profounder revolution in the whole structure of society that many advocates seem ever to have dreamed of" (Leach, 1980:15). Within the personal sphere, men sought to resolve the crisis of masculinity by supporting women's claims for autonomy, both within the family and the marriage relationship, and in their demands for sexual freedom.

Many men supported feminists' repudiation of the traditional hierarchical principles of patriarchal authoritarianism. "For them personal love was the determinant factor in marrying. The problem for them was how to transform sexual love into an egalitarian relation while at the same time preserving social order and community" (Leach, 1980:126). In fact, Floyd Dell argued that since modernity eliminates necessity, it could reestablish "family life on the basis of romantic love" (Dell, 1930:7). Reverend Jesse Jones championed the notion of divorce "so far as women take the initiative in it [as] one phase of the revolt of women against the harem idea." Although it seemed "corrupting," he wrote in the *Woman's Journal,* it was "a movement for good, for it is a movement to escape out of tyranny into freedom" (Leach, 1980:145). Many men followed Henry Blackwell's earlier admonitions that women's maintaining careers after marriage was essential to the survival of their equal union (Leach, 1980:196). In the language of late nineteenth-century magazines, the pro-feminist man married neither "drudge nor ornament." He would not try to transform his wife into a woman chained to "sexual servitude or bodily toil" or to conditions in which "her mind rises no further than the roof that shelters it" (Leach, 1980:30). Dell linked work and marriage explicitly:

> The recognition of women's work outside the home, and of educational preparation for such

> work as *being a part of the marriage system, and not something alien and hostile to it,* would modernize our social and economic system at this point. (1930:357; italics in original)

Birth control reformer Margaret Sanger's husband William actively supported her participation in the public sphere. "You go ahead and finish your writing," she quotes him as saying, "and I'll get the dinner and wash the dishes" (Forster, 1985:252).

The sex radicals who clustered around Greenwich Village in the first two decades of the twentieth century supported women's sexual equality while they challenged traditional notions of masculinity and wrestled with these issues of equality and autonomy in their own lives. They believed that sexual repression was an essential underpinning of capitalism, and based their critiques on socialist politics and scientific advances, both of which posited an equality of sexual desire between women and men. Sex radicals tried to transform the entire sexual relation between men and women. Denlow Lewis wrote in 1900 that "the sexual act must be performed with satisfaction to both participants in the conjugal embrace" (Degler, 1980:274). Ben Reitman, a Greenwich Village Bohemian and longtime lover of Emma Goldman, supported her work in birth control reform, and was well identified with the feminist cause himself. When Reitman was on trial, one prosecutor denounced him as "an Anarchist, who comes to our fair city to defy our laws. . . . If you will let him break the law on birth control, our property and our wives and daughters will not be safe . . . [from their] dirty, filthy, stinking birth control literature" (Falk, 1985:254).

Floyd Dell, who believed that feminism was the only antidote to ruling-class pretense and materialistic value culture, also claimed that men were "tired of the subservient woman—the pretty slave with all the slave's subtlety and cleverness" (Strauss, 1983:249). The liberation of women from the oppressive bonds of traditional femininity—women were "world builders" to Dell—implied the liberation of men from the restrictive moorings of traditional masculinity. Such a pro-feminist sensibility required women's access to birth control. "Modern contraceptive methods are not yet all that might ideally be desired," he wrote, "but *they do enable people to live sexual lives which they need not be ashamed to think about*" (Dell, 1930:196; italics in original). And in a 1914 essay entitled "Feminism for Men," Dell made this connection explicit.

> The home is a little dull. When you have got a woman in a box, and you pay rent on the box, her relationship to you insensibly changes character. . . . It is in the great world that a man finds his sweetheart, and in that narrow little box outside of the world that he loses her. When she has left that box and gone back into the great world, a citizen and a worker, then with surprise and delight he will discover her again and never let her go. (Trimberger, 1984:136)

Conclusion

These three responses to late nineteenth- and early twentieth-century feminist claims for reconstruction of gender relations—anti-feminist, pro-male, and pro-feminist—presented different strategies for the reconstitution of masculinity, but all agreed that masculinity was in crisis because of profound structural transformations. Does it surprise us today, in the wake of transformations of work, the closing of the imperial frontier, and new gains for women, that masculinity is seen as an "endless trial" (Emerson, 1985:188) and although books, films, and even presidential addresses counsel us on appropriate behavior for "real men," we again find these three responses to the crisis of masculinity. Some men suggest a return to traditional gender differences (through a distortion of "scientific" evidence of "natural" differences); others proclaim a reinvigorated masculinity and support for wounded men (as well as anti-feminist challenges to divorce, alimony, child custody, and abortion rights); and an increasing number of men who, recognizing the ways in which their ability to transform masculinity is inspired by and made possible by the women's movement, have joined their sisters in the difficult and painful process of dismantling masculinity in order to create a vision of sexual equality and gender justice.

References

Barker-Benfield, G. J. (1976). *The Horrors of the Half Known Life: Male Attitudes Toward Women and Sexuality in 19th Century America.* New York: Harper and Row.

Bellah, Robert, Richard Madsen, William Sullivan, Ann Swidler, and Steven Tipton. *Habits of the Heart.* Berkeley: University of California Press.

Bok, Edward (1910). "My Quarrel with Women's Clubs," *Ladies Home Journal* 27.

Booth, John (1982). *The End and the Beginning: The Nicaraguan Revolution.* Boulder, CO: Westview Press.

Bushnell, Horace (1867). *Woman's Suffrage: A Reform Against Nature.* Boston: Picknor.

Chafetz, Janet Saltzman, and Anthony Gary Dworkin (1986). "In the Face of Threat: Organized Antifeminism in Comparative Perspective." Paper presented at the annual meetings of the Southern Sociological Society, April.

Degler, Carl (1980). *At Odds: Women and the Family in America from the Revolution to the Present.* New York: Oxford University Press.

Dell, Floyd (1930). *Love in the Machine Age: A Psychological Study of the Transition from Patriarchal Society.* New York: Farrar and Rinehart.

Douglas, Ann (1977). *The Feminization of American Culture.* New York: Knopf.

Dubbert, Joe (1979). *A Man's Place: Masculinity in Transition.* Englewood Cliffs, NJ: Prentice-Hall.

———. (1980). "Progressivism and the Masculinity Crisis," in Elizabeth Pleck and Joseph Pleck, eds., *The American Man.* Englewood Cliffs, NJ: Prentice-Hall.

Ehrenreich, B., and D. English (1979). *For Her Own Good.* New York: Doubleday.

Emerson, G. (1985). *Some American Men.* New York: Simon and Schuster.

Falk, Candace (1985). *Love, Anarchy and Emma Goldman.* New York: Holt, Rinehart and Winston.

Filene, Peter (1980). "In Time of War," in Elizabeth Pleck and Joseph Pleck, eds., *The American Man.* Englewood Cliffs, NJ: Prentice-Hall.

———. (1984). "Between a Rock and a Soft Place: A Century of American Manhood." Chapel Hill, NC: unpublished manuscript.

Flexner, E. (1975). *Century of Struggle.* Cambridge: Harvard University Press.

Forster, Margaret (1985). *Significant Sisters: The Grassroots of Active Feminism.* New York: Knopf.

Freud, Sigmund (1965). *New Introductory Lectures in Psychoanalysis.* New York: W. W. Norton.

Frothingham, O. B. (1890). "The Real Case of the Remonstrance Against Woman Suffrage," *The Arena* II, July.

Gardella, Peter (1985). *Innocent Ecstasy.* New York: Oxford University Press.

Gerson, Judith, and Kathy Peiss (1985). "Boundaries, Negotiation, Consciousness: Reconceptualizing Gender Relations," *Social Problems* 32(4).

Gould, Meredith, and Rochelle Kern-Daniels (1977). "Toward a Sociological Theory of Gender and Sex," *The American Sociologist* 12.

Green, Harvey (1986). *Fit for America.* New York: Pantheon.

Hall, G. Stanley (1904). *Adolescence,* Vol. II. New York: Appleton.

Hantover, Jeffrey P. (1980). "The Boy Scouts and the Validation of Masculinity," in Elizabeth Pleck and Joseph Pleck, eds., *The American Man.* Englewood Cliffs, NJ: Prentice-Hall.

Hartman, Mary (1984). "Sexual Crack-up: The Role of Gender in Western History." New Brunswick, NJ: unpublished paper, Rutgers University.

Horowitz, Helen Lefkowitz (1984). *Alma Mater: Design and Experience in the Women's Colleges from Their 19th Century Beginnings to the 1930's.* New York: Knopf.

Jackson, K. (1985). *Crabgrass Frontier.* New York: Oxford.

James, Henry (1965). *The Bostonians.* New York: Modern Library.

Lasch, Christopher (1965). *The New Radicalism in America, 1889–1963.* New York: Knopf.

Leach, William (1980). *True Love and Perfect Union: The Feminist Reform of Sex and Society.* New York: Basic Books.

Lippman, Walter (1962). *A Preface to Morals.* New York: Harper and Row.

Lopata, Helena Z., and Barrie Thorne (1978). "On the Term 'Sex Roles,' " *Signs* 3.

"Marrying Later in Life" (1986). *New York Times*, December 10 (chart).

Macleod, David (1983). *Building Character in the American Boy: The Boy Scouts, YMCA, and Their Forerunners, 1870–1920*. Madison: University of Wisconsin Press.

McKeever, William (1913). *Training the Boy*. New York: Macmillan.

Muschamp, Herbert (1983). *Frank Lloyd Wright and the City*. Cambridge: Massachusetts Institute of Technology Press.

Pugh, David (1983). *Sons of Liberty: The Masculine Mind in Nineteenth Century America*. Westport, CT: Greenwood Press.

Riesman, David (1950). *The Lonely Crowd*. New Haven, CT: Yale University Press.

Risman, Barbara J. (1987). "Intimate Relationships from Microstructural Perspective," *Gender and Society* 1(1).

Rogin, Michael (1975). *Fathers and Children*. New York: Pantheon.

Rosenberg, Charles (1980). "Sexuality, Class and Role in 19th Century America," in Elizabeth Pleck and Joseph Pleck, eds., *The American Man*. Englewood Cliffs, NJ: Prentice-Hall.

Rosenthal, Michael (1984). "Recruiting for Empire: Baden-Powell's Boy Scout Law," *Raritan* 4(1), Summer.

———. (1986). *The Character Factory: Baden-Powell's Boy Scouts and the Imperatives of Empire*. New York: Pantheon.

Roszak, Theodore, and Betty Roszak (1975). *Masculine/Feminine*. New York: Harper and Row.

Rotundo, E. Anthony (1983). "Body and Soul: Changing Ideals of American Middle Class Manhood, 1770–1920," *Journal of Social History* 16(4).

Shapiro, Judith (1982). " 'Women's Studies': A Note on the Perils of Markedness," *Signs* 7.

Smith-Rosenberg, Carroll (1985). *Disorderly Conduct: Visions of Gender in Victorian America*. New York: Knopf.

Stacey, Judith, and Barrie Thorne (1985). "The Missing Feminist Revolution in Sociology," *Social Problems* 32(4).

Strauss, Sylvia (1983). *Traitors to the Masculine Cause: The Men's Campaign for Women's Rights*. Westport, CT: Greenwood Press.

Thompson, Maurice (1898). "Vigorous Men, A Vigorous Nation," *Independent*, September 1.

Todd, John (1867). *Woman's Rights*. Boston: Lee and Shepard.

Trachtenberg, Alan (1982). *The Incorporation of America: Culture and Society in the Guilded Age*. New York: Hill and Wang.

Tresemer, David (1975). "Assumptions Made About Gender Roles," in Marcia Millman and Rosebeth M. Kanter, eds., *Another Voice: Feminist Perspectives on Social Life and Social Science*. Garden City, NY: Anchor.

Trimberger, Ellen Kay (1984). "Feminism, Men and Modern Love: Greenwich Village, 1900–1925," in Ann Snitow, Christine Stansell, and Sharon Thompson, eds., *Powers of Desire: The Politics of Sexuality*. New York: Monthly Review Press.

Wright, Frank Lloyd (1970). *The Future of Architecture*. New York: Dover.

4

The New Feminism of Yin and Yang

ALICE ECHOLS

Introduction

For any oppressed group it is tempting to seek solace in the reclamation and rehabilitation of that identity which the larger culture has systematically denigrated. This approach becomes especially compelling when the possibilities for radical structural change seem remote, and the only alternative seems to be the liberal solution of token representation and assimilation into an oppressive and inegalitarian system. Unfortunately, as recent feminism has become synonymous with the reclamation and establishment of a so-called female principle, it has come to reflect and reproduce dominant cultural assumptions about women.

This is particularly ironic since early radical feminists, rather than accept such assumptions about women, had sought the abolition of gender as a meaningful category: "We believe that the male world as it now exists is based on the corrupt notion of 'maleness vs. femaleness,' that the oppression of women is based on this very notion and its attendant institutions."[1] "Masculinity" and "femininity" were thus defined as socially constructed rather than biologically determined. Today's radical feminists, however, are more likely to discuss gender differences as though they reflect deep truths about the intractability of maleness and femaleness. Some have argued, for example, that women are more concerned with ecology and peace and less with sexuality than men.[2] Women's traditional orientation away from what one feminist terms the "purely sexual" is interpreted as a virtue or an advantage rather than an emblem of oppression.[3] This preoccupation with defining the female sensibility not only leads these feminists to indulge in dangerously erroneous generalizations about women, but to imply that this identity is innate rather than socially

---

This is a revised version of an article in *The Powers of Desire: The Politics of Sexuality,* edited by Ann Snitow, Christine Stansell, and Sharon Thompson (Monthly Review Press).

constructed. At best, there has been a curiously cavalier disregard for whether these differences are biological or cultural in origin. Thus Janice Raymond argues: "Yet there are differences, and some feminists have come to realize that those differences are important whether they spring from socialization, from biology, or from the total history of existing as a woman in a patriarchal society." For Raymond the source of these differences is irrelevant because as women "we know who *we* are."[4]

To be sure, since the beginning of the women's movement there have been radical feminists for whom gender is an absolute rather than a relative category. Valerie Solanas's 1967 *S.C.U.M. Manifesto* is the earliest articulation of this view.[5] However, it has only been in the past few years that this perspective has gained legitimacy and achieved hegemony within the radical feminist movement. This view represents such a fundamental departure from the early radical feminist vision that it is important to differentiate the two. I will therefore refer to this more recent strain of radical feminist as *cultural feminism* because it equates women's liberation with the development and preservation of a female counter-culture. The phrase *radical feminism* will be used to describe the earlier antecedent of this movement.[6] Of course, to maintain that there exists a theoretical coherence to cultural feminism is not to suggest that it is monolithic.

This essay is intended as a critical examination of cultural feminism. This movement's belief in a male and a female sexual essence has disturbing implications for future feminist practice and has already had deleterious political consequences. After defining the basic characteristics of cultural feminism, I will examine one especially troubling consequence of this movement, the feminist anti-pornography crusade.

Defining Cultural Feminism

How does cultural feminism both derive and depart from radical feminism? Compared with today's cultural feminists, radical feminists of the late 1960s and early 1970s seem like raging materialists. Some radical feminists, especially the original Redstockings, stressed the material basis of patriarchy. For instance, they suggested that a woman's decision to marry should be interpreted as a rational strategy rather than confirmation of false consciousness. At the same time, most radical feminists understood sexism as a primarily psychological dynamic that was manifested in material conditions. Cultural feminism exaggerates this tendency and subordinates material reality to a supporting role. Andrea Dworkin, for instance, argues that "freedom for women must begin in the repudiation of our masochism."[7] Thus the goal of feminism becomes the development of an alternative consciousness, or what Mary Daly terms the "spring into free space."[8] Unlike most radical feminists, cultural feminists assume that individual liberation can be achieved within a patriarchal context. This analysis has the disadvantage of denying agency to those who are "unliberated" or "male-identified" by cultural feminist standards. It can also encourage a dangerously elitist attitude among those who consider themselves "woman-identified." Daly's argument illustrates this problem:

> It is obvious to Hags that few gynecologists recommend to their heterosexual patients the most foolproof of solutions, namely Mister-ectomy. It is women who choose to be agents of be-ing who have pointed out that tried and true, and therefore, taboo, "method." The Spinsters who propose this way by our be-ing, liv-ing, speak-ing can do so with power precisely because we are not preoccupied with ways to get off the hook of the heterosexually defined contraceptive dilemma.[9]

In Daly's view heterosexual women are preconscious lesbians who simply need to "choose to be agents of be-ing."

By promoting an overdetermined psychological analysis of gender asymmetry, cultural feminists focus attention away from the structure of male supremacy onto male behavior. Thus Robin Morgan contends that "the Man's competitiveness and greed" are responsible for "sexism, racism . . .

hunger, war and ecological disaster."[10] If the source of the world's many problems can be traced to the dominance of the male principle, its solution can be found in the reassertion of the female principle. To make this explanation work, cultural feminists reduce women and men to mere caricatures of themselves. Nowhere is this clearer than in their characterization of male sexuality as compulsive and violent and female sexuality as muted and ethereal. For instance, Kathleen Barry maintains that her mother correctly advised her to beware of the infamous "male sex drive":

> If I allowed a boy to kiss me and one thing led to another, then I would be getting him all excited and he wouldn't be able to control himself. His "thing" would get hard and then he couldn't be expected to stop. I would no longer be a nice girl.[11]

For Barry, as for her mother, it is women's responsibility to tame and restrain the irresponsible and irrepressible beast that is male sexuality.

Even more troubling than this attachment to traditional stereotypes of masculinity and femininity is the growing tendency among some cultural feminists to invoke biological explanations of gender differences. It is ironic to find cultural feminists advancing biological explanations of gender given the energy that radical feminists devoted to refuting biological justifications of gender hierarchy. Such arguments generally attribute patriarchy to the rapaciousness or barrenness of male biology. Thus Susan Brownmiller argues in *Against Our Will* that rape is a function of male biology. According to Brownmiller, male biology is destiny: "By anatomical fiat—the inescapable construction of their genital organs—the human male was a predator and the human female served as his natural prey."[12] For Daly, the "emptiness" of male biology explains male dominance. And, as though this proved her point, Daly cites arch-conservative George Gilder's view that " 'while the female body is full of internal potentiality, the male is internally barren.' "[13]

While radical feminists viewed female biology as a liability and thus mirrored the culture's devaluation of the female body, cultural feminists have overreacted to this earlier position by arguing that female biology is in fact a powerful resource.[14] Cultural feminists distinguish between patriarchally conditioned femininity, which they characterize as passive and submissive, and female nature, which they define as nurturant, loving, open, and egalitarian. According to their logic, female passivity is but a conditioned response whereas male violence is a reflection of maleness.

Not all cultural feminists are enthusiastic supporters of biologically based explanations of gender. Both Florence Rush and Andrea Dworkin have expressed their skepticism about this approach. However, for others, like Morgan, the danger lies less in the concept itself than in the control of its application. Morgan warns us against embracing "biological-determination theories . . . until we have enough feminist scientists to right the current imbalance and bias and to create a genuinely value-free science."[15]

Radical feminism departed from both liberal and early socialist feminism by maintaining that individual men do oppress individual women. They argued that although men would benefit ultimately from the dismantling of male supremacy, they would resist changes that would diminish their power and privilege. However, most radical feminists were careful to identify the male role rather than maleness as the problem; men were the enemy only insofar as they identified with their role. As Anne Koedt contended, "Thus the biological male is the oppressor not by virtue of his male biology, but by virtue of his *rationalizing* his *supremacy* on the basis of that biological difference."[16] This distinction, so significant in its implications, has become buried with the rise of cultural feminism. By interpreting masculinity as immutable, the cultural feminist analysis assumes that men are the enemy by virtue of their maleness rather than the power a patriarchal system lends them.

problem with the left is not the inadequacy of its analysis in explaining gender hierarchy, or its continued resistance to feminism, as radical feminists had maintained, but rather that its perspective is irrelevant to women.[17] For cultural feminists, the left, like pornography, is an intrusive and contaminating force that prevents us from fully "dispossessing ourselves" of our patriarchal past.[18] In fact, cultural feminism began to emerge as philosophically distinct from radical feminism in early 1975 with the establishment of the Circle of Support for Jane Alpert. Rather than deny the charge that Alpert had supplied the FBI with information about fellow members of the underground, the Circle rejoiced in her defection from the left and her conversion to feminism.[19]

But it was in the mid-1970s phenomenon of feminist capitalism that cultural feminism really took shape. These early cultural feminists treated capitalism as a relatively benign system that could be enlisted in the struggle to defeat patriarchy.[20] Some even embraced capitalism while repudiating democratic process and rationalized this position by invoking women's superiority and commonality of interests.[21] Those feminists who criticized their attempt to wed capitalism with feminism were characterized as "aping" the "correct-line politics" and "trashing" style of the male left.[22]

Cultural feminists vilify the left because its analysis so completely contravenes their belief system, especially their faith that truly radical change will be achieved only when the culture "returns" to female values and that race and class are merely ancillary to the gender hierarchy. In fact, cultural feminists treat race and class oppression like patriarchal fallout that will be swept away by a women's revolution.

Cultural feminists believe that the degree of dissidence within the women's movement demonstrates, not the diversity of the movement, but the extent to which patriarchy has defiled the mother-daughter bond and, by extension, all relationships between women.[23] They further make feminism synonymous with female bonding and contend that the rehabilitation of the mother-daughter relationship is central to feminism.[24] Their idealization of the mother-daughter relationship may explain why the cultural feminist analysis of incest blames the father while exonerating the mother:[25] if incest is explained as the confluence of male lust and female powerlessness, the cultural feminist fantasy of the idyllic mother-daughter bond can remain intact. For cultural feminists it is perhaps too threatening to acknowledge the extent to which women feel betrayed by one another.

Finally, cultural feminists are committed to preserving rather than annihilating gender distinctions. In *The Transsexual Empire,* Raymond argues that those women who support the integration of male-to-female lesbian transsexuals into lesbian communities "would have us believe that all boundaries are oppressive. Yet if feminists cannot agree on the boundaries of what constitutes femaleness, then what can we hope to agree on?"[26] In contrast with radical feminists, for whom women's oppression derived from the very construction of gender, cultural feminists argue that women's oppression stems from the repression of the female principle.

This difference is, of course, reflected in their respective visions. Radical feminists envisioned an androgynous society as their long-term goal. In the "Bitch Manifesto," Joreen described the rebellious woman, or the "Bitch":

> What is disturbing about a Bitch is that she is androgynous. She incorporates within herself qualities traditionally defined as "masculine" as well as "feminine." A Bitch is blunt, direct, arrogant, at times egoistic. She has no liking for the indirect, subtle, mysterious ways of the "eternal feminine." She disdains the vicarious life deemed natural to women because she wants to live a life of her own.[27]

This rather skewed idea of androgyny seems characteristic of those radical feminists who found "femininity" even less attractive than "masculinity." By contrast, cultural feminists explicitly reject androgyny as a masculinist concept and propose the reclamation of a female principle. Sally Gearhart suggests that

> in the spirituality arena of the women's movement there is the world's most radical political potential, for in its redemption of female values and female epistemology, woman-spirit re-

> turns to and begins again with the fundamental female nature of the race.[28]

Of course, many of the values commonly associated with the female or private sphere should be redefined as vital human values. However, cultural feminists encourage us to "maximize female identity" without questioning the extent to which that identity has been conditioned.[29] They correctly assume that mother-daughter conflict has implications for female bonding, but, by attributing this conflict to patriarchy, they encourage us to repress the ambivalence present in any relationship.

Given strong countervailing theoretical tendencies, how did radical feminism devolve into cultural feminism? The debate around lesbianism and feminism was to a large extent responsible for promoting the assumptions that underlie cultural feminism. The struggle for lesbian visibility and recognition in the early 1970s was extremely important because it forced feminists to acknowledge that sexuality is socially constructed. But the homophobia, and to a lesser extent the anti-sex attitudes within certain elements of the movement, precluded lesbian feminists from promoting lesbianism as a sexual rather than a political choice. Many heterosexual feminists, reflecting larger cultural assumptions, defined and dismissed lesbianism as a solely sexual experience. For instance, Ti-Grace Atkinson cautioned:

> A case could be made that lesbianism, in fact *all* sex, is reactionary, and that feminism is revolutionary. . . . Because lesbianism involves role-playing and more important, because it is based on the primary assumption of male oppression, that is, sex, lesbianism reinforces the sex class system.[30]

Given the context, it is understandable that many lesbian feminists found it easier to justify their sexuality on exclusively political grounds.

Lesbian recognition was achieved by locating the discussion within the already established framework of separatism.[31] Lesbian separatists such as the Washington D.C. Furies collective argued that heterosexual women were impeding the movement's progress. Rita Mae Brown opined:

> Straight women are confused by men, don't put women first. They betray lesbians and in its deepest form, they betray their own selves. You can't build a strong movement if your sisters are out there fucking with the oppressor.[32]

By defining lesbianism as a political choice, implying the immutability of gender differences, and promoting a sentimental view of female sexuality, lesbian feminists deprived heterosexual feminists of one of their favorite charges against lesbianism—that it was male-identified.[33] However, the assumption that relationships with men are inevitably debilitating while those with women are automatically liberating has had, as we shall see, serious consequences for lesbian sexuality. Furthermore, in establishing lesbianism as a true measure of commitment to feminism, lesbian separatists distorted the meaning of "the personal is political," giving it a prescriptive rather than a descriptive meaning. Of course, the tendency to judge a woman on the basis of her sexual preference, marital status, or hair length did not originate with lesbian separatism, but it was further legitimated by it.

Lesbian separatism's open hostility to heterosexual feminists guaranteed that it would remain a minority view. However, in its reincarnation as cultural feminism, lesbian separatism has been modified and refined in such a way as to make it more acceptable to a wider audience. Whereas lesbian separatists advocated separation from men, cultural feminists advocate separation from male values. And rather than promote lesbianism, cultural feminists encourage woman-bonding and thus avoid estranging heterosexual feminists.

With the rise of cultural feminism, relations between gay and heterosexual feminists have become more cordial. However, the very terms of this reconciliation have ensured that suspicion and acrimony would be preserved, though often below the surface. First, lesbian recognition has been achieved by further abstracting it from the realm of sexuality and cloaking it as female bonding. Lesbian acceptance is contingent upon the extent to which our relationships conform to feminist standards of egalitarianism. Second, heterosexual feminists are still made to feel as though they are the movement's backsliders by virtue of their proximity to contaminating maleness. Occasionally hostility surfaces as it did at the 1979 Women Against Pornography (WAP) conference when a lesbian separatist called Susan Brownmiller a "cocksucker." Brownmiller retaliated by pointing out that her critic "even dresses like a man."[34]

With the anti-pornography movement, cultural feminism has succeeded in mobilizing feminists regardless of sexual preference—not an inconsiderable task. Unfortunately, anti-pornography activists have united feminists by manipulating women's traditional sexual conservatism and appealing to widely held assumptions about male and female sexuality. In advocating a return to a female sexual standard, cultural feminists ignore the extent to which femaleness functions as the complement to maleness and therefore reflects dominant cultural assumptions—assumptions that encourage political expediency. By further treating femaleness as an unalloyed force for good, cultural feminists have tried to accommodate feminism with capitalism and sexual repression. As its brief history demonstrates, cultural feminism degenerates into the view, so eloquently articulated by cultural feminist entrepreneur Laura Brown, that "feminism is anything we say it is."[35]

Sexual Repression: The Case of Women Against Pornography

Take Back the Night, a recent cultural feminist anthology on pornography, opens with this excerpt of an 1853 letter from Elizabeth Cady Stanton to Susan B. Anthony:

> Man in his lust has regulated long enough this whole question of sexual intercourse. Now let the *mother of mankind, whose prerogative it is to set bounds to his indulgence,* rouse up and give this whole matter a thorough, fearless investigation.[36]

One fears this citation is more appropriate than its anthologizer intended. For despite the fact that the historical conditions confronting today's feminists differ significantly from those faced by nineteenth-century women, the current cultural feminist view of sexuality bears a striking similarity to that articulated by activists a century earlier. For the most part, nineteenth-century feminists, many of whom were active in the temperance movement, held conservative views on marriage, the family, and sexuality.

Radical feminists sometimes spoke of sexuality as incompatible with women's freedom, but they were far more likely to identify women's subjugation with the repression of female sexuality.[37] They understood that women's sexual inhibition was related to the lack of accessible and effective contraception, which rendered women sexually vulnerable. They believed that women's attachment to traditional morality stemmed less from the immutability of female sexuality than from their economic dependence on men. This consciousness was reflected in the radical feminist struggle for abortion and safe, effective contraception. Radical feminists understood, as does the New Right, that the fight for reproductive rights is the struggle for women's sexual freedom and self-determination. As we shall see, cultural feminists, by contrast, argue that sexual freedom and feminism stand in mutual opposition.

The cultural feminist perspective on sexuality has emerged and crystallized only recently with the development of the feminist anti-pornography movement. Women Against Pornography maintains that pornography not only reflects our culture's misogyny, but causes violence against women as well.[38] The avowed purpose of the anti-pornography movement is to enlighten the public about the dangers of pornography. Many women involved in this struggle, including Susan Brownmiller, Andrea Dworkin, Diana Russell, and Kathleen Barry, further recommend some form of censorship to eliminate pornography. While the elimination of violence is crucial, there is reason to be dismayed by the movement's assumption, despite the dearth of solid, confirming evidence, that pornography is a causative factor. And there is reason to be alarmed by its casual attitude toward establishing causality. For instance, Kathleen Barry has cautioned us against getting "bogged down in academic research" and urged us to "rely more on our common sense, our own convictions, and 'what we see in front of us.' "[39]

Fantasy

What are the assumptions that underlie the cultural feminist understanding of sexuality and inform the anti-pornography movement? The argument that "pornography is the theory, rape the practice" represents cultural feminism's contribution to the domino theory of sexuality.[40] It identifies pornography as the scourge that leads inexorably to violence against women.

More recently, anti-pornography activists have extended their critique to encompass fantasy, which they suggest is dangerous because it entails the substitution of an illusion for the "social-sexual reality" of another person. If internalized, pornography compels women to accept dehumanization over personhood. In rejecting as so much "male-identified mind-body dualism" the notion that fantasy is the repository of our ambivalent and conflictual feelings, cultural feminists have developed a highly mechanistic and behavioristic analysis that conflates fantasy with reality and pornography with violence.[41] Such a view assumed that we can and should be held accountable for our fantasies and bedroom exploits. And if we fail to banish those dreaded fantasies, we can console ourselves with Julia Penelope's suggestion that fantasy may be another "phallocentric 'need' from which we are not yet free."[42]

However, cultural feminists' enthusiasm for correlating fantasy with reality wanes considerably when female fantasies are under discussion. Although some seem to attribute women's masochistic fantasies to their masochism, most argue either that they are a patriarchal invention or that they reveal women's powerlessness and socialization rather than their masochism.[43] Of course, men's sadistic fantasies are still seen as confirmation of their fundamentally murderous nature.

Male and Female Sexuality

Cultural feminists define male and female sexuality as though they were polar opposites. Male sexuality is driven, irresponsible, genitally oriented, and potentially lethal. Female sexuality is muted, diffuse, and interpersonally oriented. Men crave power and orgasm, while women seek reciprocity and intimacy. Robin Morgan claims:

> Every woman here knows in her gut the vast differences between her sexuality and that of any patriarchally trained male's—gay or straight . . . that the emphasis on genital sexuality, objectification, promiscuity, emotional noninvolvement, and coarse invulnerability was the *male style,* and that we, as women, placed greater trust in love, sensuality, humor, tenderness, commitment.[44]

Morgan assumes that somehow women's sexuality is not "patriarchally trained."

For cultural feminists, male sexuality is not only compulsive, but, as Dworkin has described it, "the stuff of murder, not love."[45] Thus, for men, sexuality and violence are inextricably linked and find their cultural expression in pornography. Cultural feminists are so convinced that male sexuality is, at its core, lethal that they reduce it to its most alienated and violent expressions. The actions of the Marquis de Sade or Son of Sam come to symbolize the murderousness of male sexuality, and sexual intercourse becomes a mere euphemism for rape.[46] Liberal and leftist men who oppose censorship are characterized as having a prurient interest in pornography, and men's growing interest in their partner's sexual satisfaction is said simply to demonstrate men's obsession with sexual performance. Everything, no matter how contradictory, confirms the premise that male sexuality is selfish, violent, and woman-hating.

By contrast, women's sexuality is assumed to be more spiritual than sexual, and considerably less central to their lives than is sexuality to men's. For instance, Adrienne Rich describes female sexuality as an "energy which is unconfined to any single part of the body or solely to the body itself."[47] And Ethel Person maintains that "many women have the capacity to abstain from sex without negative psychological consequences." For Person, women's more highly developed "capacity for abstinence, repression, or suppression [has] adaptive advantages" over male hypersexuality.[48] Person fails to understand that women's apparent mental health in the face of anorgasmia or abstention testifies to women's conditioning to subordinate and repress sexual drive.[49] Cultural feminism in fact feeds what one feminist has described as "our society's treasured illusion that male sexuality is like a bludgeon or a speeding train" and its equally cherished corollary that women seek affection rather than orgasm in their sexual encounters.[50]

Conclusion: The Retreat from Theory into Fantasy

By equating feminism with the so-called reassertion of a female identity and culture, cultural feminism seems to promise an immediate solution to women's powerlessness in the culture at large. Its growth is attributable to the frustrating fragmentation of the women's movement and the erosion of feminist gains in the recent past. Cultural feminism represents a retreat from the difficulties of political struggle into the self-validation that community-building offers. It further substitutes the fantasy of a united sisterhood for political theory.

Unfortunately, it seems that many feminists and leftists have abandoned transformative politics for the familiarity of sexual repression and the nuclear family respectively. For instance, Tom Hayden claims that liberalism failed because it "lost God, the flag, national defense, tax relief, personal safety and traditional family values to conservatives."[51] And Michael Lerner suggests that Americans could be sold on socialism were they to understand its salutory impact on family life.[52]

The years ahead promise to be turbulent. It would be most unfortunate if feminists respond to the inhospitality of the 1980s by further retreating into this fantasy of a morally pure sisterhood. Ultimately, cultural feminism offers us little more than the illusion of power and will fail us very badly in the difficult period ahead.

Notes

I want to thank the following individuals for reading and commenting on an earlier draft of this paper: Susan Contratto, Constance Samaras, Kathleen Steward, Ellen Willis, Marilyn Young, and Patricia Yeghessian. Editing efforts by Sandra Silberstein, Ann Snitow, and Sharon Thompson have improved this essay appreciably.

1. Bonnie Kreps, "Radical Feminism 1," in *Radical Feminism,* ed. Anne Koedt, Ellen Levine, and Anita Rapone (New York: The New York Times Book Co., 1973), p. 239.

2. Adrienne Rich, Mary Daly, and Susan Griffin are the best known proponents of these views. However, the notion that women's more extensive experience with nurturance makes them natural pacifists is fairly widespread among feminists.

3. Julia Penelope, "And Now for the Hard Questions," *Sinister Wisdom* (Fall 1980):103.

4. Janice Raymond, *The Transsexual Empire* (Boston: Beacon Press, 1979), p. 114.

5. Valerie Solanas, *S.C.U.M. Manifesto* (New York: Olympia Press, 1970).

6. The *reconstituted* Redstockings, a New York radical feminist group, termed this theoretical tendency "cultural feminism" in their 1975 publication *Feminist Rev-*

olution. Although their critique identified some of the problems with cultural feminism, it was seriously marred by its paranoia and homophobia. More recently, Ellen Willis has critiqued cultural feminism especially as it informs the anti-pornography movement and eco-feminism. See her fine collection of essays, *Beginning to See the Light* (New York: Knopf, 1981) and her *Village Voice* articles. Major cultural feminist texts include: Adrienne Rich, *Of Woman Born* (New York: W. W. Norton, 1976); Mary Daly, *Gyn/Ecology* (Boston: Beacon Press, 1978); Janice Raymond, *The Transsexual Empire* (Boston: Beacon Press, 1979); Kathleen Barry, *Female Sexual Slavery* (Englewood Cliffs, N.J.: Prentice-Hall, 1979). The now defunct Los Angeles–based magazine *Chrysalis* has also served as a major outlet for cultural feminist work since its founding by Susan Rennie and Kirsten Grimstad in 1977. The best single radical feminist anthology is Koedt, Levine, and Rapone, *Radical Feminism.* Also see Shulamith Firestone, *The Dialectic of Sex* (New York: Morrow, 1970).

7. Andrea Dworkin, *Our Blood* (New York: Harper and Row, 1976), p. 111.

8. Daly, *Gyn/Ecology,* p. 12.

9. Ibid., p. 239.

10. Robin Morgan, *Going Too Far* (New York: Random House, 1978), p. 93.

11. Barry, *Female Sexual Slavery,* p. 218.

12. Susan Brownmiller, *Against Our Will* (New York: Simon and Schuster, 1975), p. 16.

13. Daly, *Gyn/Ecology,* p. 360. For an especially astute analysis of Gilder see Michael Walzer, "Gilderism," *The New York Review of Books,* 2 April 1981, p. 3.

14. Firestone's *The Dialectic of Sex* exemplifies the problem with the radical feminist view of female biology. For the cultural feminist view see Rich, *Of Woman Born,* p. 39.

15. Morgan, *Going Too Far,* p. 164.

16. Anne Koedt, "Lesbianism and Feminism," in Koedt, Levine, and Rapone, *Radical Feminism,* p. 249.

17. See Kathleen Barry, "Did I Ever Really Have a Chance? Patriarchal Judgment of Patricia Hearst," *Chrysalis* I (1977); Morgan, *Going Too Far;* Rich, *Of Woman Born,* p. 285; Jane Alpert's germinal "Mother-Right," *Ms.* (August 1973).

18. Barbara Deming, "To Fear Jane Alpert Is to Fear Ourselves," *Off Our Backs (OOB)* (May/June 1975).

19. Rennie and Grimstad of *Chrysalis* were instrumental in establishing the Circle of Support. It is worth noting that upon Alpert's surrender, her lawyer stressed her "renunciation of radical activities and her conversion to the feminist movement." This prompted *OOB* reporter Madeleine Janover to ask with great prescience, "What does this mean for radical feminism?" See *OOB* (December 1974):5.

20. See Jennifer Woodul, "What's This About Feminist Businesses?" *OOB* (June 1976).

21. It was this view that informed the ill-fated and short-lived Feminist Economic Network (FEN) founded in Detroit in 1975 and dissolved less than one year later. FEN was the brainchild of the Oakland Feminist Women's Health Center, the Detroit Feminist Federal Credit Union, and Diana Press. For detailed accounts see Belita Crown and Cheryl Peck, "The Controversy at FEN," *Her-Self* (May 1976); Jackie St. Joan, in *Big Mama Rag (BMR)* 4, no. 1; Martha Shelley, "What Is FEN?" circulated by author; Janis Kelly et al. in *OOB* (March 1976). For an exoneration of FEN see Kathleen Barry et al., *OOB* (January 1977).

22. Barry et al., ibid.

23. See Rich, *Of Woman Born;* Pauline Bart, review of *The Reproduction of Mothering, OOB* (January 1981): 19.

24. See Daly, *Gyn/Ecology,* p. 39.

25. For the cultural feminist view, see Florence Rush, *The Best Kept Secret* (Englewood Cliffs, N.J.: Prentice-Hall, 1980); for a trenchant feminist counter-analysis, see Judith Herman and Lisa Hirschmann, "Father-Daughter Incest," in *Signs* 2, no. 4 (Summer 1977).

26. Raymond, *Transsexual Empire,* pp. 109–110.

27. In Koedt, Levine, and Rapone, *Radical Feminism,* p. 52.

28. Sally Gearhart, "The Spiritual Dimension: Death and Resurrection of a Hallelujah Dyke," in *Our Right To Love,* ed. Ginny Vida (Englewood Cliffs, N.J.: Prentice-Hall, 1978), p. 192. See also Daly, *Gyn/Ecology,* pp. xi, 387; Rich, *Of Woman Born,* pp. 76–77; Raymond, *Transsexual Empire,* pp. 154–164. Raymond argues, "Androgyny becomes a synonym for an easily accessible human liberation that turns out to be sexual liberation" (p. 162).

29. Ann Snitow, "The Front-Line: Notes on Sex in Novels by Women, 1969–1979," in *Women: Sex and Sexuality,* ed. Catharine Stimpson and Ethel Person (Chicago: University of Chicago Press, 1980), p. 174.

30. Ti-Grace Atkinson, "Lesbianism and Feminism," *Amazon Odyssey* (New York: Links Books, 1974), p. 86.

31. The conviction that feminism is conditional on separation from men predated lesbian separatism. For instance, the radical feminist group The Feminists established a quota system to limit the number of members living with men.

32. Rita Mae Brown, "The Shape of Things to Come," in *Plain Brown Rapper* (Baltimore: Diana Press, 1976), p. 114.

33. See ibid.; Charlotte Bunch and Nancy Myron, eds. *Lesbianism and the Women's Movement* (Baltimore: Diana Press, 1975); Martha Shelley, "Notes of a Radical Lesbian," in *Sisterhood Is Powerful,* ed. Robin Morgan (New York: Random House, 1970), p. 309.

34. Susan Chute, "Backroom with the Feminist Heroes: Conference for Women Against Pornography," *Sinister Wisdom* (Fall 1980):2.

35. Quoted in Cowan and Peck, "The Controversy at FEN," *Her-Self* (May 1976).

36. Laura Lederer, ed. *Take Back the Night* (New York: William Morrow, 1980), p. 21; emphasis added.

37. For the minority view, see Dana Densmore, "On Celibacy," in *Voices from Women's Liberation,* ed. Leslie Tanner (New York: New American Library, 1970), p. 264. For the majority view, see Anne Koedt, "The Myth of the Vaginal Orgasm," in Koedt, Levine, and Rapone, *Radical Feminism,* p. 199.

38. There are two major feminist anti-pornography organizations, Women Against Violence in Pornography and Media (WAVPM), established in the Bay Area in 1976, and Women Against Pornography (WAP), established in New York City in 1979. Though I refer only to WAP in this paper, the two groups share the same analysis.

39. Quoted in Deb Friedman, "Feminist Perspectives on Pornography," *OOB* (January 1979).

40. This slogan originated with Robin Morgan's 1974 article "Theory and Practice: Pornography and Rape," reprinted in Morgan, *Going Too Far.*

41. See Rich's critique of "male-identified" dualism in *Of Woman Born,* pp. 56–83; Susan Griffin, *Pornography and Silence* (New York: Harper and Row, 1981). For an insightful analysis of Griffin's indictment of dualism see Robert Christgau in *Village Voice,* 15–21 July 1981.

42. Penelope, *Sinister Wisdom,* "And Now for the Hard Questions," p. 103.

43. See Diana Russell, "Pornography and Violence: What Does the New Research Say?" in Lederer, *Take Back the Night,* p. 231. In *Homosexuality in Perspective* (Boston: Little, Brown & Co., 1979), Masters and Johnson report that in their sample, heterosexual men's second most frequent fantasy was about forced sex and they fantasized being forced slightly more frequently than they did forcing another.

44. Morgan, *Going Too Far,* p. 181.

45. Andrea Dworkin, "Why So-Called Radical Men Love and Need Pornography," in Lederer, *Take Back the Night,* p. 152.

46. In "Compulsory Heterosexuality and Lesbian Existence," in *The Politics of Desire,* ed. Ann Snitow, Christine Stansell, and Sharon Thompson (New York: Monthly Review Press, 1983), Rich praises Catharine MacKinnon, author of *Sexual Harassment of Working Women: A Case of Sex Discrimination* (New Haven, Conn.: Yale University Press, 1979), for criticizing Brownmiller's unexamined premise that " 'rape is violence, intercourse is sexuality.' "

47. Ibid.

48. Ethel Person, "Sexuality as the Mainstay of Identity: Psychoanalytic Perspectives," in *Women: Sex and Sexuality,* pp. 50, 57.

49. See Larry Bush and Richard Goldstein, "The Anti-Gay Backlash," *Village Voice,* 8–14 April 1981; Deirdre English, "The War Against Choice," *Mother Jones* (February/March 1981).

50. Snitow, "The Front-Line," in *Women: Sex and Sexuality,* p. 165.

51. Tom Hayden, "The Future Politics of Liberalism," *The Nation,* 21 February 1981.

52. Michael Lerner, "Recapturing the Family Issue," *The Nation,* 2 February 1982. For a pithy response to Lerner, see Barbara Ehrenreich, "Family Feud on the Left," *The Nation,* 13 March 1982.

5

Dismantling Noah's Ark

JUDITH LORBER

[T]hou shalt come into the ark, thou and thy sons, and thy wife, and thy sons' wives with thee. And of every living thing of all flesh, two of every sort shalt thou bring into the ark, to keep them alive with thee; they shall be male and female.[1]

"Did she have a boy or a girl?" I asked. "Why do you want to know?" said my 13-year-old.[2]

It is a paradox of feminist politics that women must act politically as a group in order to defuse gender as a discriminative status. In the current climate, and no doubt for a long time to come, if women are to gain anything like equal representation in existing institutions, they must push for their rights *as* women. Another necessary political stance has been the valorization of women's characteristics and special perspectives to counter their devaluation in male-dominated cultures. However, both strategies have limits that caution us to keep in mind that equal rights for women as a group and the celebration of the female are effective only as short-term politics. The permeation of existing institutions with gender inequality makes the long-term goal of equal opportunity within them a sham (Eisenstein, 1981). Glorifying womanliness consolidates female unity and power, but when pushed to extremes it comes dangerously close to reviving the cult of true womanhood and the ideology of separate spheres (Jagger, 1983; Stacey, 1983a). The long-term goal of feminism must be no less than the eradication of gender as an organizing principle of postindustrial society.

Feminist theory and research have shown us that gender is a linchpin of social order, but they have not seriously envisaged a social order without gender. Examination of the social bases of gender demonstrates that gender is essentially a social construction, and the relations between women and men are essentially social relations. What is socially constructed can be reconstructed, and social relations can be rearranged. A modern social order is possible without gender, and I would like to sketch what it might look like. So that it is clear what I mean when I speak of *gender* as a set of oppositional relationships that sustain and are sustained by institutionalized

Written with research support from PSC-CUNY Grant #14010. An earlier version was presented at the Eastern Sociological meetings, Boston, Massachusetts, March 1984. I am indebted to Nona Glazer for her comments. This is slightly revised from an article of the same name that appeared in *Sex Roles,* Vol. 14, Nos. 11/12, 1986.

patterns of behavior, I begin by analyzing the concept of gender as a social construct.

The Social Bases of Gender

Gender supposedly rests on an obvious physiological and biological dichotomy, but it can be argued that the concept of physiological and biological dimorphism emerges from our firmly held belief in two and only two genders. In everyday life and in scientific research, Kessler and McKenna (1978) argue, we first attribute sexual dimorphism, and then look for evidence of it in order to have "good reasons" for the original sorting of people into the categories "female" and "male." From the perspective of dialectical materialism, Alison Jagger (1983, pp. 109–112, 125–132) points out, physiological sex differences are socially produced by differences in diet, exercise, work, and selective breeding, and reproduction and sexuality are as socially constructed as they are biologically based (see also Longino & Doell, 1983; Naftolin & Butz, 1981). Most human beings produce both androgens and estrogens, and these are chemically converted into each other, so that "the endocrine nature of the human species is hermaphroditic" (Briscoe, 1978, p. 31). Physiological sex differences may be quantitative, but the boundaries between "female" and "male" are socially located and differentiated by what Gayle Rubin calls a "sameness taboo . . . dividing the sexes into two mutually exclusive categories, a taboo which exacerbates biological differences between the sexes and thereby *creates* gender" (1975, p. 178, her emphasis).

But what about menstruation, lactation, and pregnancy? Do they not demarcate females from males? They do not. Some females are pregnant some of the time; some do not have a uterus or ovaries. Some females breastfeed some of the time; some men lactate (Jagger, 1983, p. 165fn).

Extensive studies on early socialization have demonstrated beyond quarrel the social creation of gender identity and genderized behavior in children (Safilios-Rothschild, 1979). Through the example, teaching, rewards, and admonishments of parents, siblings, teachers, and other significant adults, the child learns, first, that there are two genders, second, which gender she or he belongs to (and how to refer to them), and finally, how to be (and not be) a proper member of their gender (Bem, 1981). The gender division of parenting deepens the development of female and male personality and character (Chodorow, 1978).

As children develop pubescent physical characteristics, their behavior is further dichotomized and organized around gender-appropriate sexual scripts, which vary from society to society, and within societies, by class, race, religion, and ethnic group (Gagnon & Simon, 1973). Anatomical secondary sex characteristics are of less importance as gender markings than the extensive display signals Birdwhistell (1970, pp. 39–46) calls "tertiary sexual characteristics." These create an elaborate communication code of masculinity as contrasted with femininity, that, Birdwhistell says, is made necessary by the relative unimorphism of human beings.

Gender and Social Structure

Although physiological distinctions have seemed to be a natural starting place for the social construction of gender, anthropological studies suggest that the division of duties pertaining to reproduction and child rearing is more central to gender as a socially organizing principle than dichotomous reproductive biology.

Gender probably emerged as part of a more efficient division of labor for food production and distribution, for child care, and for teaching of survival skills. Gender assumed importance only with the invention of projectile human hunting and the use of fire for food production, Lila Leibowitz (1983) argues. The necessity of teaching these more elaborate skills encouraged a division of labor that increased food supply (Leibowitz, 1983; Marwell, 1975). Because of the need for women to be both food producers and nurturers, women's work developed certain characteristics

(Brown, 1970). It is likely to be relatively repetitious and interruptible so that small children can be watched as women work; it is likely to be done where children can be carried along; and it must be relatively safe, so as not to jeopardize the precious societal resources of mothers and surviving children. Men (and adolescents of both sexes) do the work that is dangerous, that requires distant travel and that needs close attention (Freidl, 1975).

The division of labor by the requirements of subsistence technology, and the need for the group to reproduce itself, fits the work women and men do in gathering and hunting societies, in societies based on hoe cultivation (women's work) and plow agriculture (men's work). It also affects the relative status of women and men. When the subsistence technology is compatible with child minding, women contribute significantly to the economic resources of the societal group and their status tends to be equal with that of men, as in gathering and hunting and horticultural societies (Blumberg, 1978; Leacock, 1978). When the subsistence technology is not compatible with the care of small children, women tend to be less valued as producers and their consequent social status is low, as in patriarchal agricultural societies based on plow farming and herding. In these societies, women are valued as secondary producers, but the primary production is controlled by land-owning men.

Interwoven with the gendered division of labor are kinship systems that allocate responsibilities for the socialization and social placement of older children, for the care of the elderly, and for the bonding ties between families through out-marriage on the basis of gender. In primitive societies, the resources embedded in food distribution, mate choice, and rights to the services and marriage portions of children were ascribed by gender, and were proliferated into gender-based systems of property ownership and political dominance (Cucchiari, 1981; Rubin, 1975). The ideological justifications and supports for these arrangements are found in oral and written histories, myths, and religious symbols and rituals (Sanday, 1981). In short, in preindustrial society, gender organizes the social order through kinship and the sexual division of labor.

The shift to industrial capitalism weakened kinship as an organizing principle of society but ironically built gender into the new economic institutions (Blaxall & Reagan, 1976; Matthaei, 1982; Pinchbeck, [1930] 1969). Working-class women were hired, along with their children, as part of a family unit of wage workers headed by the husband (Hartmann, 1976). Married women who remained in the work force continued to be considered secondary workers, and this designation carried over to all women workers, who were systematically paid less than men, and to occupations dominated by women, which consistently have wage structures below that of comparable male-dominated occupations (Milkman, 1980; Treiman & Roos, 1983).

In today's capitalist economies, women who alternate between work in the home and work in the marketplace provide the necessary reserve army of labor that can be called on during economic expansion and dismissed during recessions. Married women who do not work in the marketplace are also vital to capitalism, for, without pay, they organize consumption and philanthropy, socialize the next generation of male workers and managers, and prepare their daughters to be housewives, mothers, part-time workers, and occupants of the perpetually gender-segregated work force (Glazer, 1984; Ostrander, 1984; Safilios-Rothschild, 1976; Sokoloff, 1980; Zaretsky, 1976). Socialist economies, despite an ideological commitment to equality for women and high rates of life-long female labor-force participation, also have dual labor markets divided on gender lines, male-female income differentials, and a concentration of women workers at the lower ends of work hierarchies (Dalsimer & Nisonoff, 1984; Lapidus, 1976, 1978; Loi, 1981; Nazzari, 1983; Swafford, 1978).

The persistence of gender segregation and stratification in the economies of all industrialized countries has ensured that most women would also be barred from significant political participation because of their limited power-base resources (Bengelsdorf & Hageman, 1979; Eisenstein, 1981; Hartsock 1983; Lapidus, 1978; Nelson, 1984; Stacey 1983b). As Virginia Woolf succinctly put it in *Three Guineas* (1938, p. 22), "What real influence can we bring to bear upon law or business, religion or politics—we to whom many doors are still locked, or at best ajar, we who have neither capital nor force behind us?" But even those women to whom doors have opened—professional women, and women with financial and political capital—have, except for a few well-known male-oriented prime ministers, been kept from the inner circles of power by covert denigration of their competence and legitimacy as leaders (Amundsen, 1977; Epstein, 1970; Fennel et al., 1978; Lipman-Blumen, 1976; Lorber, 1984; Martin & Osmond, 1982; Reskin, 1978; Wolf & Fligstein, 1979).

Given the embeddedness of gender in all social structures that make up modern society, would not the erosion of gender boundaries result in social chaos and individual normlessness? In actuality, the solidity of gender as an organizing principle of society has already been eroded by feminist challenges of its petty absurdities and exploitative functions. But no feminist perspective has kept clearly in focus the revolutionary aim of restructuring social institutions without a division of human beings into the social groups called men and women. Liberal feminists have concentrated on espousing equality between the two groups, but not eliminating them as significant social categories. Radical feminists have emphasized the positive aspects of women's traditional qualities, and so have polarized women and men. Marxist feminists have suggested industrializing women's work, but have not suggested how to get men to share in it. Socialist feminism has come closest to envisaging "a society in which maleness and femaleness are socially irrelevant, in which men and women, as we know them, will no longer exist" (Jagger, 1983, p. 330), but their program has tended to concentrate on promulgating democratically run, communally organized workplaces without specifying how to build in genderlessness. They also have tended to pay less attention to restructuring sexuality, friendship, and parenting so as to eliminate gender as an organizing principle of intimate relationships.

What follows is not an attempt to provide a complete prescription for revolution, or a utopian description of a society without gender, which Gilman (1979), Piercy (1976), and LeGuin (1969) have done so well. Rather, I want to take forward tendencies and policies already familiar to us to show how, if carried through, they could go a long way to a genderless restructuring of postindustrial society.

Social Structures Without Gender

In many societies there have been people who moved from one gender to another temporarily or permanently—transvestites, berdaches, manly-hearted women, hijras, actors and impersonators, and in our time, transsexuals. While they challenge the fixedness of gender boundaries and the sex-gender overlap, they do not challenge gender itself. Indeed, cross-dressing, impersonation, transsexuality, male wives and female husbands, and butch-femme homosexuality in many ways strengthen gender, since without a notion of gender differences there is no rationale for crossing over (Altman, 1982; Billings & Urban, 1982; Blackwood, 1984; Raymond, 1979).

No more challenging to gender are unisex styles, which may be as simple as a neutrally colored jump suit, as ubiquitous as the polo shirts, jeans, and sneakers seen across the Western world, or as the stylish androgyny recently described in the *New York Times* as follows:

> Seen from the back, a young person, radiating a certain sense of style, may be wearing an oversize man's jacket, tight pegged pants, crushed down boots. Slung over the shoulder is a big, soft, pouchy bag. The hair will be worn short with some fluff on top. If there is a bit of

> pierced earring visible, it is probably a woman. Then again, it could also be a young man. (Donovan, 1983, p. 108)

To be more than a passing fashion, nongendered dressing would have to start early, be consistent, and include dress-up as well as play clothes. The unisex style described above is not consistent—males wear earrings in one ear, women in both. Dress makes personal and social statements. As long as gender categories are socially significant, dress will reflect difference and signal gender identification. We cannot erode gender from the skin out.

Similar problems arise with attempts to teach children about biological dimorphism without a cultural overlay (Bem, 1983; Money & Ehrhardt, 1972; Morgan & Ayim, 1984). The significance of genitalia, reproductive capacities, and sexuality arise from the social construction of gender, and its evaluations and power relations. There is no way to discuss sex and reproduction neutrally, that is, free of social and cultural meanings. If we could, the evidence of diverse sexual persuasions throughout history would long ago have made clear that sexuality is not neatly dichotomous. An increasingly sophisticated reproductive technology of artificial insemination, *in vitro* fertilization, egg and sperm donations, and embryo transplants will boggle the mind with combinations and permutations of biological parentage, but the likelihood is that the innovations will be contained in the conventional strictures of heterosexual, two-parent families (Rothman, 1982, 1984).

However, the separation of sexuality and reproduction, and biological and social parenting, if carried through into new family and kinship structures, might help to dislodge gender from its central place in recreational sex, child rearing, and intimate emotional relationships. The components of dimorphic sex would then clearly belong to the biological needs of procreation. As Chodorow says:

> We cannot know what children would make of their bodies in a nongender or nonsexually organized social world, what kind of sexual structuration or gender identities would develop. But it is not obvious that there would be major significance to biological sex differences, to gender difference, or to different sexualities. There might be a multiplicity of sexual organizations, identities, practices, perhaps even of genders themselves. Particular bodily attributes would not necessarily be so determining of who we are, what we do, how we are perceived, who are our sexual partners. (1979, p. 66fn)

Nongendered Families

In postindustrial society, kinship is no longer socially necessary to allocate reciprocal rights and responsibilities for economic cooperation, child rearing, and care of dependents. Without interlocked networks of blood relations and affines, women do not have to be exchanged so that men can gain brothers-in-law, and mothers do not have to be socially suppressed so that men can lay claim to children (Paige & Paige, 1981; Rubin, 1975). Therefore we can envisage responsible intimate relations and economic cooperation among adults, and between adults and children, that do not depend on gender.

For adults, each must be treated as a single unit for purposes of income, taxation, and all legal rights and responsibilities. Whatever permanent linkages or household arrangements or personal economic exchanges are made in a person's lifetime will then be a matter of formal or informal contracts among consenting adults. Competent adults must take responsibility for children, the frail elderly, the sick, and the mentally incompetent either through state-financed and publicly administered organizations, or personally, through a kind of kinship system, or through a mixture. In an earlier attempt to think through nongendered parenting arrangements, I suggested that every adult might take legal responsibility for at least one child, and for the parent-child line to become the kinship line for purposes of legal responsibility and emotional sustenance (Lorber, 1975). A basic dependent support allowance from the state, and well-financed public caretaking, nursing, medical, and educational services would help significantly in smoothing out the differentials in adult resources in these vertical families. If single parenting is felt to be too hermetically intense, several adults could commit themselves to legal responsibility for several dependents as an identifiable family, as Hooks (1984, pp. 133–146) recommends for single mothers.

Nongendered Sexuality

Incest taboos, which have always been designations of whom one can and cannot marry, could apply to sexual relationships within the kin groups to protect the dependent from sexual demands from those responsible for them. Other limits to sexual behavior are likely to emerge from community norms, ethics, values, and social priorities. Like other social relations, nongendered sexual relationships are likely to involve interpersonal manipulation, if not power and exploitation. But if interpersonal and institutional power is not gendered, then the norms and laws governing intimate personal relationships, including the sexual, cannot be oppressive to women or to men, for these will not be significant social categories.

Nongendered Reproduction

The common presumption has been that without reinforced heterosexuality and displays of masculinity and femininity, no children would be born. While it is highly unlikely that in a random, polymorphous sorting, no heterosexual coupling would take place, no conceptions would occur, no pregnancies would be sustained, and no children born, societies that value reproduction are likely to encourage it. As in the present society, pronatalist and antinatalist policies in a nongendered society can be expected to be political decisions. But these reproductive decisions would not be made by the men in power for all women, nor would all women be categorized as potential child bearers and child rearers, nor would mothers alone be expected to bear all the burdens of creating and raising the next generation.

There would be social categories of parenting other than "mother" and "father"—child bearers and child rearers, professional caretakers and educators, sperm and egg donors and gestators, legal kin and emotional supporters. These would not be based on dichotomous differentiations, attached to central social statuses, or designations of ownership. In short, the social roles of mother and father in a nongendered society would not be indicative of the connection between "parent" and "child." What would be needed are terms of reference more specific to the variety of relationships between responsible adults and dependent children.

Nongendered Wage Work

Ideally, all work should be equally valued and all wage workers should receive equal compensation for their labor. This would be a radical socialist solution to wage inequities. The liberal solution has been to concentrate on the historical discriminatory practices built into the present wage structure and, using the theory of comparable worth, attempt to create a wage structure based on the characteristics of the work itself and the worth of that work to the employer (Feldberg, 1984; Treiman & Hartmann, 1981). As applied to gender inequities in wages, comparable worth would place women workers on an equal footing with men workers, and thus eliminate much of the basis for women's economic dependence. Ideologically, it would remove the justification of low wages for women as secondary wage earners, eliminate the concept of a higher male family wage, and thus support the erosion of the family sexual division of labor (Feldberg, 1984). Indeed, without a restructuring of the compensation for women's work to bring it up to the level of compensation for comparable men's work, treating everyone as an individual unit would exacerbate women's subordinate status and disadvantage those who are legally dependent on them.

If the trend toward single-parent families is to be encouraged so as to break down the gendered pattern of kinship, then a corollary tactic must be to support the fight for a gender-neutral wage structure. In turn, a gender-neutral wage structure would help dismantle the gendered division of labor within the family since it would make women economically self-sufficient. Without superior wages, men would not be able to claim women's domestic services in exchange for primary economic support. Since the two cornerstones of the sexual division of labor—in the family and in the marketplace—are intertwined in industrial societies, they must be dismantled at the same time.

If all competent adults are to have roughly equal responsibility for those who are dependent, they must be compensated equally in one or more ways: a basic public support allowance, payment for their services, payment for wage work other than caretaking. So that care of dependents does not continue to devolve on one group—women (with the cultural justification that they alone have the appropriate skills and temperament)—all adults should get a support allowance for themselves and their dependents. Professional caretaking must be compensated according to its real skill level (Phillips & Taylor, 1980), and wages should be based on the content of the work, not the social status of the workers.

Gender-Neutral Authority and Political Power

Whether authority and political power are seen to derive from membership in strategically placed inner circles of elites, or from ownership and control of the means of production, women have been an excluded class, except through their connection with powerful men. Without at this point arguing for a nonhierarchical state or for more democratic ownership of the means of production, both of which are goals feminists might wish to achieve as feminists and/or as socialists, I would like to consider the strategies for, and possible effects of, gender-neutral access to positions of authority and political power.

I feel that nongendered access to capital resources and to positions of significant policy making and authority are dependent on the erosion of gendered kinship and work. Such a structural and ideological shift would drastically alter social relations. Without gendered kinship, gendered inheritance of capital and businesses should disappear. Without a gendered wage structure, the male monopoly of leadership positions in work hierarchies should also diminish, since the underpinnings in a sex-segregated and sex-stratified occupational structure would be gone.

The converse view, that significant numbers of women in positions of leadership and in control of economic resources can make a difference in social values and in allocations of those resources, is dependent on the maximalization of gender differences and the assumption that women in power will act in the interests of other women (Lorber, 1981). But the same purported gender differences and woman-oriented outlook are, in my view, what blocks women from access to those positions and resources. To the extent that women and men are seen as different, dominant men will not trust even women of their own class, religion, race, and training as colleagues, will not sponsor them for entry into elite inner circles of power, nor allow them control of important areas of the economy. The carefully chosen women who do make it to the top do so because they have demonstrated their loyalty to male values, and so, lest they jeopardize their positions, they cannot act in the interests of women (Laws, 1975). Men will no longer see women as essentially different when gender loses its salience as a social category. For this to happen, significant areas of the social order must first be restructured on a nongendered basis.

Gender Equality and the Erosion of Gender

For categories of people to be equal, a social order must be structured for equality of outcome. Equality is a political goal that can encompass equality of gender, but the history of liberal political philosophy demonstrates that women are usually excluded when ascribed statuses are no longer the basis for full-fledged citizenship (Okin, 1979). If gender is removed as a qualification for equal treatment under the law, as the Equal Rights Amendment would have done, women and men would have legal equality, but not necessarily social equality. To achieve social equality, we would need scrupulous equality of women and men in care of dependents, allocation of work, wage structure, and control of resources and societal decision making (Chafetz, 1984).

In my mind, gender equality is too limited a goal. Unless women and men are seen as socially interchangeable, gender equality does not challenge the concept of sex differences that leads to separate spheres in the family and marketplace division of labor, which in turn results in women's lesser access to control of valued resources and positions of power. Scrupulous equality of categories of people considered essentially different needs constant monitoring. I would question the very concept of gender itself, and ask why, if women and men are social equals in all ways, there needs to be two encompassing social statuses at all.

Notes

1. King James Version, Book of Genesis.
2. Conversation between author and child, 1982.

References

Altman, D. *The homosexualization of America.* Boston: Beacon Press, 1982.

Amundsen, K. *A new look at the silenced majority.* Englewood Cliffs, N.J.: Prentice-Hall, 1977.

Bem, S. L. Gender schema theory: A cognitive account of sex typing. *Psychological Review,* 1981, *88,* 354–364.

Bem, S. L. Gender schema theory and its implications for child development: Raising gender-aschematic children in a gender-schematic society. *Signs,* 1983, *8,* 598–616.

Bengelsdorf, C., & Hageman, A. Emerging from underdevelopment: Women and work in Cuba. In Z. R. Eisenstein (Ed.), *Capitalist patriarchy and the case for socialist feminism.* New York: Monthly Review Press, 1979.

Billings, D. B., & Urban, T. The socio-medical construction of transsexualism: An interpretation and critique. *Social Problems,* 1982, *29,* 266–282.

Birdwhistell, R. L. *Kinesics and context.* Philadelphia: University of Pennsylvania Press, 1970.

Blackwood, E. Sexuality and gender in certain native American tribes: The case of cross-gender females. *Signs,* 1984, *10,* 27–42.

Blaxall, M., & Reagan, B. B. (Eds.) *Women and the workplace: The implications of occupational segregation.* Chicago: University of Chicago Press, 1976.

Blumberg, R. L. *Stratification: Socioeconomic and sexual inequality.* Dubuque, Iowa: William C. Brown, 1978.

Briscoe, A. M. Hormones and gender. In E. Tobach & B. Rosoff (Eds.), *Genes and gender: Hereditarianism and women.* New York: Gordian Press, 1978.

Brown, J. K. A note on the division of labor by sex. *American Anthropologist,* 1970, *72,* 1073–1078.

Chafetz, J. S. *Sex and advantage.* Totowa, N.J.: Rowman & Allanheld, 1984.

Chodorow, N. *The reproduction of mothering.* Berkeley, Calif.: University of California Press, 1978.

Chodorow, N. Feminism and difference: Gender, relation, and difference in psychoanalytic perspective. *Socialist Review,* 1979, *9,* 51–69.

Cucchiari, C. The gender revolution and transition from bisexual horde to patrilocal band: The origins of gender hierarchy. In S. B. Ortner & H. Whitehead (Eds.), *Sexual meanings: The cultural construction of gender and sexuality.* Cambridge: Cambridge University Press, 1981.

Dalsimer, M., & Nisonoff, L. The new economic readjustment policies: Implications for Chinese urban working women. *Review of Radical Political Economics,* 1984, *16,* 17–43.

Donovan, C. A question of self-expression. *The New York Times Magazine,* December 18, 1983, 108.

Eisenstein, Z. R. *The radical future of liberal feminism.* New York: Longman, 1981.

Epstein, C. F. Encountering the male establishment: Sex status limitations on women's careers in the professions. *American Journal of Sociology,* 1970, *75,* 965–982.

Feldberg, R. L. Comparable worth: Toward theory and practice in the United States. *Signs,* 1984, *10,* 311–328.

Fennell, M. L., Barchas, P. R., Cohen, E. G., McMahon, A. M., & Hildebrand, P. An alternative perspective on sex differences in organizational settings: The process of legitimation. *Sex Roles,* 1978, *4,* 589–604.

Friedl, E. *Women and men.* New York: Holt, Rinehart & Winston, 1975.

Gagnon, J. H., & Simon, J. W. *Sexual conduct: The social sources of human sexuality.* Chicago: Aldine, 1973.

Gilman, C. P. *Herland.* New York: Pantheon, 1979.

Glazer, N. Y. Servants to capital: Unpaid domestic labor and paid work. *Review of Radical Political Economics,* 1984, *16,* 61–87.

Hartmann, H. Capitalism, patriarchy, and job segregation by sex. In M. Blaxall & B. B. Reagan (Eds.), *Women and the workplace: The implications of occupational segregation.* Chicago: University of Chicago Press, 1976.

Hartsock, N. C. M. *Money, sex, and power.* New York: Longman, 1983.

Hooks, B. *Feminist theory: From margin to center.* Boston: South End Press, 1984.

Jagger, A. M. *Feminist politics and human nature.* Totowa, N.J.: Rowman & Allanheld, 1983.

Kessler, S. J., & McKenna, W. *Gender: An ethnomethodological approach.* New York: Wiley, 1978.

Lapidus, G. W. Occupational segregation and public policy: A comparative analysis of American and Soviet patterns. In M. Blaxall & B. B. Reagan (Eds.), *Women and the workplace: The implications of occupational segregation.* Chicago: University of Chicago Press, 1976.

Lapidus, G. W. *Women in Soviet society.* Berkeley: University of California Press, 1978.

Laws, J. L. The psychology of tokenism: An analysis. *Sex Roles,* 1975, *1,* 51–67.

Leacock, E. Women's status in egalitarian society: Implications for social evolution. *Current Anthropology,* 1978, *19,* 247–255.

LeGuin, U. K. *The left hand of darkness.* New York: Ace Books, 1969.

Leibowitz, L. Origins of the sexual division of labor. In M. Lowe & R. Hubbard (Eds.), *Women's nature: Rationalizations of inequality.* New York: Pergamon Press, 1983.

Lipman-Blumen, J. Toward a homosocial theory of sex roles: An explanation of the sex segregation of social institutions. In M. Blaxall & B. B. Reagan (Eds.), *Women and the workplace: The implications of occupational segregation.* Chicago: University of Chicago Press, 1976.

Loi, M. Chinese women and the "fourth rope." *Feminist Issues,* 1981, *1,* 51–85.

Longino, H., & Doell, R. Body, bias, and behavior: A comparative analysis of reasoning in two areas of biological science. *Signs,* 1983, *9,* 206–227.

Lorber, J. Beyond equality of the sexes: The question of the children. *Family Coordinator,* 1975, *24,* 465–472.

Lorber, J. Minimalist and maximalist feminist ideologies and strategies for change. *Quarterly Journal of Ideology,* 1981, *5,* 61–66.

Lorber, J. *Women physicians: Careers, status and power.* New York & London: Tavistock, 1984.

Martin, P. Y., & Osmond, M. Gender and exploitation: Resources, structure, and rewards in cross-sex social exchange. *Sociological Focus,* 1982, *15,* 403–415.

Marwell, G. Why ascription? Parts of a more or less formal theory of the functions and dysfunctions of sex roles. *American Sociological Review,* 1975, *40,* 445–455.

Matthaei, J. *An economic history of women in America: Women's work, the sexual division of labor and the development of capitalism.* New York: Schocken, 1982.

Milkman, R. Organizing the sexual division of labor: Historical perspectives on "women's work" and the American labor movement. *Socialist Review,* 1980, *49,* 95–150.

Money, J., & Ehrhardt, A. A. *Man & woman, boy & girl.* Baltimore, Md.: Johns Hopkins University Press, 1972.

Morgan, K. P., & Ayim, M. Comment on Bem's "Gender schema theory and its implications for child development: Raising gender-aschematic children in a gender-schematic society." *Signs,* 1984, *10,* 209–231.

Naftolin, F., & Butz, E. (Eds.) Sexual dimorphism. *Science,* 1981, *211,* 1263–1324.

Nazzari, M. The "woman question" in Cuba: An analysis of material constraints on its solution. *Signs,* 1983, *10,* 246–263.

Nelson, B. J. Women's poverty and women's citizenship: Some political consequences of economic marginality. *Signs,* 1984, *10,* 209–231.

Okin, S. M. *Women in western political thought.* Princeton, N.J.: Princeton University Press, 1979.

Ostrander, S. A. *Women of the upper class.* Philadelphia: Temple University Press, 1984.

Paige, K. E., & Paige, J. M. *The politics of reproductive ritual.* Berkeley, Calif.: University of California Press, 1981.

Phillips, A., & Taylor, B. Sex and skill: Notes towards a feminist economics. *Feminist Review,* 1980, *6,* 79–88.

Piercy, M. *Woman on the edge of time.* New York: Fawcett Crest, 1976.

Pinchbeck, I. *Women workers and the industrial revolution, 1750–1850.* London: Virago Press, [1930] 1969.

Raymond, J. G. *The transsexual empire.* Boston: Beacon Press, 1979.

Reskin, B. F. Sex differentiation and the social organization of science. *Sociological Inquiry,* 1978, *48,* 3–37.

Rothman, B. K. How science is redefining parenthood. *Ms. Magazine,* July/August, 1982, *11,* 154–158.

Rothman, B. K. The meanings of choice in reproductive technology. In R. Arditti, R. D. Klein, & S. Minden (Eds.), *Test-tube women.* London: Pandora Press, 1984.

Rubin, G. The traffic in women: Notes on the "political economy" of sex. In R. Reiter (Ed.), *Toward an anthology of women.* New York: Monthly Review Press, 1975.

Safilios-Rothschild, C. Dual linkage between the occupational and family systems: A macrosociological analysis. In M. Blaxall & B. B. Reagan (Eds.), *Women and the workplace: The implications of occupational segregation.* Chicago: University of Chicago Press, 1976.

Safilios-Rothschild, C. *Sex role socialization and sex discrimination: A synthesis and critique of the literature.* Washington, D.C.: National Institute of Education, 1979.

Sanday, P. R. *Female power and male dominance.* Cambridge: Cambridge University Press, 1981.

Sokoloff, N. J. *Between money and love.* New York: Praeger, 1980.

Stacey, J. The new conservative feminism. *Feminist Studies,* 1983, *9,* 559–583. (a)

Stacey, J. *Patriarchy and socialist revolution in China.* Berkeley: University of California Press, 1983. (b)

Swafford, M. Sex differences in Soviet earnings. *American Sociological Review,* 1978, *43,* 657–673.

Treiman, D. J., & Hartmann, H. (Eds.), *Women, work and wages: Equal pay for jobs of equal value.* Washington, D.C.: National Academy Press, 1981.

Treiman, D. J., & Roos, P. Sex and earnings in industrial society: A nine-nation comparison. *American Journal of Sociology,* 1983, *89,* 616–650.

Wolf, W. C., & Fligstein, N. D. Sex and authority in the workplace. *American Sociological Review,* 1979, *44,* 235–252.

Woolf, V. *Three guineas.* New York: Harcourt, Brace & World, 1938.

Zaretsky, E. *Capitalism, the family, & personal life.* New York: Harper & Row, 1976.

Part Two

Bonds That Tie: Friends and Lovers

The chapters in Part Two highlight the importance of societal expectations, placement in social networks, and sexual inequality in personal relationships. The first three are exploratory studies based on small, specialized samples; all use their data to illustrate the impact of microstructural variables on relationships. Swain and Cheal study how social expectations affect same-sex relationships (for example, friendship and kin relations), while DiIorio and Richardson look at the emergence of female subordination in heterosexual couples. Blumstein and Schwartz present a critique of the theory of invariate sexual preferences. They argue instead that both gender roles and the social organization of sexual possibilities actually create the form of sexual desire we experience.

Swain uses in-depth interviews with college students to critique the sex-role socialization hypothesis that males are inexpressive because of a trained incapacity to share. He argues instead that male/male friendships are indeed intimate, but such intimacy must be covert because men are aware of the negative evaluations of those who express emotions. It is not that men are trained to be inexpressive and thus do not desire intimate friendships; rather, they both desire and achieve intimate friendships but use covert strategies to avoid social sanction.

Cheal analyzes how one particular interaction ritual performed by women alone, the bridal shower, supports and reinforces female subordination and sexual segregation. Bridal showers are one of several rites of passage that mark the transition to the status of wife. Cheal suggests that the organization of bridal showers symbolizes female collusion in the construction of family-role specialization and female domestication. Although the particular bridal showers that Cheal uses for illustration will be exotic to many readers (Polish and Ukrainian affairs), their basic form and content will be quite familiar: all-female occasions where gifts are given to the bride. These gifts (for example, dishes, pots and pans, towels, and so forth) make explicit the expectation that the bride is soon to become a domestic wife. Male exclusion from this gift-giving ritual symbolizes the expectation that domesticity is a female specialization. The new bride enters not only a marriage but also a sexually segregated occupation, housewifery, with its own social organization.

DiIorio uses expectations about future female economic dependence to help explain why sexual inequality develops in working-class heterosexual couples. In her participant observation of a van club that explicitly recognizes the equality of male and female members, DiIorio found that males dominated group talk and activities. Their subcultural devotion to "having a good time" was often focused on what they considered the "best time"—having sex. The rules of heterosexual relationships, however, included a sexual double standard, and this led to the exclusion of "lady vanners" from much of the informal camaraderie and socializing. In addition, the men controlled their girlfriends' behavior and benefited from their emotional labor. DiIorio suggests that the women accepted these rules for conduct because heterosexual relationships, particularly future marriage, were so vital to them. As working-class women, these "lady vanners" knew that sometime in the future they would be dependent upon husbands for economic survival. This led them to accept whatever rules for heterosexual relationships appeared to result in stable and satisfactory marriages.

Richardson discusses the social construction of secret and forbidden relationships, focusing on affairs between married men and single women. Basing her conclusions on interviews with single women involved in such relationships, Richardson identified two stages of intimacy: (1) becoming confidants and (2) becoming a "we." This research suggests that the unequal distribution of power in these forbidden relationships is better explained by the advantages of being married (such as access to alternative support networks) than by male personality traits (such as dominance or aggression).

Blumstein and Schwartz concentrate on one key aspect of marriage and relationships—sexuality. They suggest that the study of human sexuality has been dominated by the presumption that men and women are biologically programmed to be different and that each individual has a true sexual core self that does not change. Their essay suggests, instead, that sexual desire is created by its cultural context, a product of socialization, opportunity, and interpretation. They use examples from a large study of couples to help explain their thesis that even the most intimate of experiences—sexual desire—is itself shaped by social context.

In each of these chapters, the authors show how the gender-typed expectations of others and contemporary sexual inequality help shape behavior that might otherwise appear to be the product of internalized masculinity and femininity. Swain suggests that male sex-role socialization has not created a generation of inexpressive males; rather men express intimacy covertly to avoid social sanctions. Similarly, Cheal suggests that bridal showers are rituals that help create and transmit the expectations for female domestic behavior. DiIorio suggests that male dominance within heterosexual couples may have less to do with internalized female submissiveness and male aggressiveness than an anticipated future economic dependence of girls on their boyfriends. Richardson suggests that the dominance of married men over single women with whom they are involved may be attributed to marital status as well as male privilege. And finally, Blumstein and Schwartz suggest that even the very desire of most people in our society to enter sexually monogamous heterosexual unions may itself be a function of the lack of socially acceptable alternatives. In each chapter, microstructural forces help explain what might easily be attributed to masculine or feminine personality traits.

6

Covert Intimacy: Closeness in Men's Friendships

SCOTT SWAIN

This study is an analysis of college men's intimate behavior in same-sex friendships and their standards for assessing intimacy. It documents the development, causes, and manifestation of a covert style of intimate behavior in men's friendships. Covert intimacy is a private, often nonverbal, context-specific form of communication. The concept of covert intimacy is rooted in the behaviors that men reported as indicative of closeness and intimacy in their friendships with other men.

First, I trace differences in the development of men's and women's adolescent friendships that shape and promote differing styles of intimacy. Next, such contexts are linked to the emergence of the separate worlds of men and women and how such separate worlds and microstructural contexts continue into adulthood. I analyze these separate worlds for the specific behaviors and values that shape intimacy among same-sex friends, and then clarify the distinctive cues and nuances of men's intimate behavior by comparing them to behaviors in male-female platonic friendships and friendships among women. I conclude the study with an assessment of the strengths and limitations of men's covert style of intimacy with men friends and its relationship to the inexpressive male.

The Inexpressive Male, or Sex-Specific Styles of Intimacy

Sex-role theorists have characterized men as instrumental (Parsons and Bales, 1955), agentive (Bakan, 1966), and task-oriented (Komarovsky, 1964). Women have been characterized as expressive (Parsons and Bales, 1955), communal (Bakan, 1966), and empathic (Hoffman, 1977; Bem, 1976). Consistent with these theoretical formulations, researchers on the male role have

I would like to thank Francesca Cancian, Joseph Pleck, and Marjorie Robertson for helpful comments on this paper. Portions of the analysis and writing of this paper were supported by NIMH training grant MH 17058.

interpreted men's interpersonal behavior as nonintimate and have stressed the restraints and limitations that cultural conceptions of masculinity impose on intimate expression. Examples of this *deficit approach* to men's intimate capabilities are Jack Balswick's "The Inexpressive Male" (1976) and Mirra Komarovsky's concept of men's "trained incapacity to share" (1964).

In recent years many of these generalizations, which were based on slight yet significant sex differences, have been reexamined. The majority of studies that measure interpersonal skills and relationship characteristics report nonsignificant sex differences (Maccoby and Jacklin, 1974; Pleck, 1981; Tavris and Wade, 1984). When studies report significant sex differences, the results have been mixed and sometimes conflicting. In support of the male deficit model, men are reported to be less likely than women to disclose sadness and fears (Rubin, 1983; Allen and Haccoun, 1976; Davidson and Duberman, 1982), less affective and spontaneous with friends than women (Booth, 1972), and less adept than women at nonverbal decoding skills (Henley, 1977). Men are also reported to be more homophobic than women, which may inhibit the use of certain interpersonal skills in men's friendships (Lehne, 1976; Morin and Garfinkle, 1978).

However, the majority of self-disclosure studies reveal nonsignificant sex differences (Cozby, 1973); and related analyses report that men score higher than women on nonverbal decoding skills (Hall and Halberstadt, 1981), rate their friendships as more trusting and spontaneous than do women (Davidson and Duberman, 1982), and value intimacy in friendship as much as do women (Caldwell and Peplau, 1982). In view of such findings and the conflicting results of other related studies, sex differences in interpersonal behavior appear to be minor or not adequately measured. However, notions of the "inexpressive male" continue to persist and guide research on men's interpersonal behavior.

Perhaps the most consistently reported difference in men's and women's friendships is men's preference for joint activities and women's preference for talking (Caldwell and Peplau, 1982; Cancian, 1985). Men's emphasis on instrumental action has been interpreted by past researchers as a less personal and less intimate form of interaction than verbal self-disclosure (Komarovsky, 1964; Rubin, 1983; Davidson and Duberman, 1982). This interpretation may be influenced by researchers' reliance on measuring feminine-typed styles of behavior to assess topics involving love and interpersonal behavior. This bias has been critiqued by Cancian as the "feminization of love" (1986). Researchers concerned with intimacy have assumed that verbal self-disclosure is the definitive referent for intimacy, and have thus interpreted alternative styles that involve instrumental action as a less intimate, or nonintimate, behavior. [Previous definitions of intimacy relied primarily on verbal self-disclosure as an indicator of intimacy. But, the relationship between intimacy and self-disclosure is usually only implied and not specifically defined.]

Caldwell and Peplau (1982) suggest that men and women may place the same value on intimacy in friendships, yet have different ways of assessing intimacy. Men are reported to express a wider range of intimate behaviors, including self-disclosure, while participating in gender-validating activities (Swain, 1984). Men may develop sex-specific contexts, cues, and meanings, which connote feelings and appraisals of intimacy similar to those connoted by self-disclosure for women.

Intimacy is defined in the present study as *behavior in the context of a friendship that connotes a positive and mutual sense of meaning and importance to the participants*. This definition allows respondents to determine what behaviors are meaningful and intimate, and assumes that there may be several avenues that may result in the experience of intimacy.

The results presented here are based on in-depth interviews with fifteen men and five women. The college sample was young and white with a mean age of 22.5 years. This small sample was used to further explore sex-specific friendship behaviors, which have been significantly documented using larger samples of similar populations (Swain, 1984; Caldwell and Peplau, 1982).

The interview protocol was based on two empirical studies; the first was a pilot study (N = 232) that measured the relative value of activities in men's and women's same-sex friendships, and the second (N = 140) measured the relative importance and meaning that men and women attributed to those activities (Swain, 1984).

Interviews lasted an average of an hour and a half, with a female interviewer working with female subjects and a male interviewer (myself) working with the male subjects. For analysis, we then transcribed and organized the interviews by question and content. A disadvantage of such a focused sample is that the results may not generalize across age groups, or even represent this particular subgroup. However, we selected a private and personal interview setting to collect more detailed data about sensitive information concerning intimacy in friendships than would otherwise be possible when using larger samples and less personal data-collection techniques. Because of the college setting, we expected the sample to have more friends and contact with same-sex friends than men and women from the general population. The advantages of this sample of young adults are their temporal closeness to the development of adolescent friendships and their frequent interaction with friends because of the college environment. This should promote clarity in their recollections of the development of adolescent friendship behaviors and give them a sharpened and more sensitive vantage point from which to describe their current friendships with men and women.

The Development of Sex-Specific Styles of Intimacy: The Separate Worlds of Boys and Girls

Men and women grow up in overlapping, yet distinctively different worlds. Sex segregation begins at an early age when boys and girls are differentially rewarded for various play activities. Boys are encouraged to actively participate in the outside environment by parental acceptance of the risks of physical injury and parents' flexible attitude toward personal hygiene and appearance. Torn clothes, skinned knees, and dirty hands are signs of the normal growth of healthy boys. If girls choose these same activities, they may be tolerated; however, they may be sanctioned differently. For example, the term "tomboy" is used to distinguish a girl with "boyish" behaviors, and to designate a stage of development that deviates from normative expectations of the female child. Several men attributed the distinctive friendship behaviors of men to this early segregation while growing up. Jim said:

> Well, you do different things. Little boys, they'll play in the dirt and things, whereas a guy and a girl they might play in the house or something. The guys like . . . they don't mind getting dirty. I don't want to stereotype or anything, but it's just the way I see it. The guys are more rugged and things.

Pete responded to the question, "How do you act just around the guys?"

> You'd talk about anything, do anything. You aren't as polite. You don't care as much how you look, how you dress, what you wear, things of that nature. Even if we're just platonic friends, for some reason when you're around girls you're different. In the United States men and women don't share bathrooms together in the public restrooms. That's a good example, right there—obviously men and women are segregated then. That segregation exists in friendships, too.

Separate restrooms are a concrete manifestation of the different realms experienced by boys and girls as they grow up and of the restrictions on crossing over into the other sex's domain. The curiosity that boys and girls experience about what the bathrooms are actually like for the other sex is evidence of this separateness. A boy who is teased and pushed into the girl's bathroom is called a "girl" as he hastily exits. Thus, children internalize sex-segregated boundaries and enforce these restrictions. Evidence of the long-term influence of this segregation is the humiliation and embarrassment an adult feels when accidentally entering the "wrong" bathroom. The association between gender and specific contexts is also suggested by men referring to a woman who is included in a men's poker game as being "just like one of the guys." The separate contexts of men and women continue throughout the life cycle to shape the ways they express intimacy.

The male world is the outside environment of physical activity. Boys share and learn activities with male friends that involve an engagement with this outside world. Social encouragement is evident in such organizations as the Boy Scouts (Hantover, 1978), sports and recreation programs (Coleman, 1976; Stein and Hoffman, 1978), and a division of labor that often has boys doing home chores that are outdoors, such as mowing lawns. These outside activities have a shaping influence on their interests and values. Jack recalled his adolescence:

> I can remember only one friend that I had from years past. My friend Jim. Just kind of all the fun we had, boyhood fun. We built a fort, lit firecrackers, and all that stuff.

He refers to "boyhood" rather than "childhood" fun, implying that these experiences tended to be shared with other males. Another man recalled:

> The activities shared were a lot of outdoor-type things—fishing, hunting, Tom Sawyer type things. It's a commonality that we both shared that helped bring us together.

Men mentioned activities that ranged from dissecting lizards, riding bikes, and childhood sports to four-wheeling, lifting weights, playing practical jokes on friends, problem solving, and talking about relationships as they reached adulthood. By the time high school graduation arrives, most males have had more experiences and time with men friends than with women friends. Several men commented on this early division in their friendships. For instance, Rick replied:

> Up to the sixth or seventh grade girls are "stay away from the girls!" So during that whole time you only associate with the guys, and you have all these guy friends. And after that you kind of, you know, the first time you go out, you're kind of shy with the girls, and you don't get to know them too well. . . . I really didn't get over being shy with girls until my senior year.

His first contact with girls is in the dating context of "going out," which implies a heterosexual coupling dimension to the relationship in addition to friendship. The segregated contexts of men and women continue into adulthood, and shape the opportunities for expressing intimacy and the expectations of how that intimacy is to be expressed. As a result, men are more familiar with their men friends, and women are more familiar with their women friends.

Consequences of the Separate Worlds of Men and Women

Self-Disclosure: Profanity, Sameness, and Group Lingo

As boys move through adolescence surrounded and immersed in friendships with other boys, behavioral differences emerge that distinguish men's and women's friendships. Men develop language patterns that often rely on blunt, crude, and explicitly sexual terms. Bluntness, crudity, and profanity legitimize masculinity by tending to roughen the tone of any statement that a man may make. Swearing serves as a developmental credential in an adolescent boy's maturation process, much as do smoking, drinking, and getting one's drivers license. The "rugged" and "dirty" environment that boys share is translated into a coarser language during adolescence, which is also labeled as "dirty." Men felt that this language was more appropriate around other men, and they often related this sex-specific language to all-male contexts such as military service and sports. Greg responded:

> Well (laugh), not that I cuss a lot, but when I, you know, get around the baseball field and stuff like that. . . . They [women] don't like that. I try to stay away from the crude or harsh humor as much as I can (laugh).

Greg's laughing suggested a tense recognition that men's use of language in "harsh humor" does not easily translate in the company of women.

Men's harsh language and sexual explicitness in joking behavior are censored and muted when interacting with women friends. The censoring of humor to avoid offending women friends testifies to the different meaning and value men and women attribute to the same behaviors. Mike related:

> Around girls you act more of a gentleman. You don't cuss. You watch what you say. Because you don't want to say anything that will offend them.

Men felt more at ease with close men friends, partially from a perception of "sameness." Men assume that male friends will be more empathetic concerning sexual matters since they have similar bodies. Jack related:

> I find it much easier to talk about sexual things with guys, which makes sense.

A majority of the men said it was easier to talk to men about sexual matters than to women. Another man responded to the question, "What are some of the things that would be easier to talk over with a guy?"

> Anything from financial problems to problems with relationships. That's a big thing I really don't like talking to girls about. For some reason I just . . . I don't know . . . I get . . . usually because what I'm saying is from a male's point of view. And I know this is all sounding really sexist. But you know, there are certain things that I view that girls don't necessarily view the same way. And it's just easier talking to guys about that. Well, lately sex is one of those. I mean you can talk about certain sexual things; there are certain things. I had a conversation the other day, and he was talking to me about a sexual act that his girlfriend, his new girlfriend, wanted to do. And he really doesn't care to do it. There's no way I could talk to a girl about what he's talking about.

The men appeared to generalize a common world view to other men that fostered a feeling of comfort. Frank commented:

> I'm more relaxed around guys. You don't have to watch what you say. Around friends like that [men] I wouldn't . . . what could you say? I wouldn't be careful I shouldn't say something like this, or I shouldn't do this. That's because with the guys, they're just like you.

Men friends used the degree of comfort and relaxation experienced with men friends as an indicator of closeness. Matt described this feeling when asked about the meaningful times he has shared with men friends.

> Last week some really good friends of mine in my suite . . . one guy plays the guitar. And so he was just sitting around playing the guitar and we were making up tunes. We were making up songs to this, and that was really a lot of fun. The fun things come to mind. We rented a VCR and some movies and watched those, and just all the laughing together comes to mind as most memorable. As to the most meaningful, those also come pretty close to being the most meaningful, because there was just total relaxation, there. That I felt no need to worry. There's no need to worry about anyone making conversation. The conversation will come. And we can laugh at each other, and you can laugh at yourself, which is handy.

Men were asked to compare their friendships with men to their platonic friendships with women. Generally, men felt more at ease and relaxed when with close men friends than with women friends. John answered the question, "Are there any differences between your friendships with men and your friendships with women?"

> You don't have to worry about the situation you're in. If you have to go to the bathroom, you just run up and go. You don't have to worry about "please excuse me" or anything. And it's a lot more relaxed. A lot more. Like in Jack's house we just go into the kitchen and make ourselves something to eat, you know, part of the family.

The "situation" is comfortable because the men's shared assumptions, cues, and meanings of behavior allow them "not to have to worry" whether they are acting appropriately. The formality associated with women friends is suggestive of Irving Goffman's concept of "frontstage" behavior, which is more rule-bound and distanced, while the "backstage" behavior with men friends is more intimate because of the lack of censoring and the feeling of informality associated with being "part of the family." The shared history, activities, and perception that other men are "just like you" gave a predictable familiarity to men's interactions. Women also felt that their similarity to each other produced an empathy unique between women friends. A woman responded to a question about the differences between her men and women friends:

> There are some things about a woman's feelings that I don't think a man, having never been in a woman's mind, could ever really understand. Because I think most women are a little more sensitive than men.

Men also developed unique terms with their close friends that expressed their history and connectedness. These terms acknowledged the particular experiences shared between friends and underlined their special relationship. When asked about his most meaningful experiences with his men friends, Tim related:

> The best thing, well the thing is, Rick, Mike, and me kind of have our own lingo. I haven't seen other people use them, like "Bonzo" is one of them. Like "go for Bonzo," and anybody else would just go "Well, whatever."

The "lingo" was derived from activities experienced by the group. The private meaning of the language served as a boundary separating friends from people outside the group.

Doing Versus Talking: The Intimacy of Shared Action

The men were asked, "What was the most meaningful occasion spent with a same-sex friend, and why was it meaningful?" The men mentioned a total of 26 meaningful occasions with men friends, and several men mentioned more than one meaningful experience. We analyzed the responses to clarify the link between sharing an activity and feeling close to a friend. Of those occasions, 20 meaningful times were spent in an activity other than talking. Men related a wide variety of meaningful experiences from "flirting with disaster" in an out-of-control car and winning a court case to being with a close friend the night that the friend found out his sister had committed suicide. Activities such as fishing, playing guitars, diving, backpacking, drinking, and weightlifting were central to men's meaningful experiences.

Nine meaningful experiences directly referenced the sharing of skills and accomplishments. These meaningful times involved the shared enjoyment of learning and mastering skills and accomplishing goals ranging from a sexual experience with a woman to staying up all night on a weeknight. The essential ingredients in these experiences seemed to be comfort with a competitive challenge and a sense of shared accomplishment. A man responded to the question of what was the most meaningful experience he had shared with a male friend, and later a group of male friends:

> I've always been extremely shy with women, and one of my friends in between, after high school . . . women were always chasing after him like crazy—and I'm defensive and stuff with women when one time we went to the

> river. And a couple of girls picked us up and we got laid and everything. And it was kind of, this is going to sound like the standard male thing, but we all kind of went, after, we went and had a few beers and compared notes. You know, and I felt totally accepted because I had just as many good things to say as they did, and I could relate. I knew what they were talking about, because most of my life I've never known what these guys were talking about sexually.

Although this quote might imply sexual exploitation, several aspects should be considered. First, this man admits he is shy with women, and furthermore he indicates that the women initiated the interaction. He was able to discuss with his men friends a new experience that had been alien to him until this occasion. The argument here is not that the sexual experience was exploitive or intimate; it appears to have been a purely physical encounter between strangers. However, the commonality gained from a shared life experience did provide meaningful interaction among the men.

We further examined the influence of men's active emphasis and women's verbal emphasis on intimate friendship behavior by asking men to compare their friendships with men to their friendships with women. Tim responded to the questions, "What part of you do you share with your men friends and what part of you do you share with your women friends? How would you characterize those two different parts of you?"

> I think that the men characteristics would be the whole thing, would be just the whole thing about being a man. You know, you go out and play sports with your brothers, and have a good time with them. You just . . . you're doing that. And there are some things that you can experience, as far as emotional, [with] your best friends that are men . . . you experience both. And that's what makes it so good is that. With most of the girls you're not going to go out and drink beer and have fun with them. Well, you can, but it's different. I mean it's like a different kind of emotion. It's like with the guys you can have all of it. . . .

Tim says that you can have "the whole thing" with men, suggesting that he can do things and talk about things with his close men friends. With women friends doing things is "different." Tim refers to a "different kind of emotion" and speaks of a "good time" when he is with his men friends. This good feeling may result from the ease and comfort of interacting with close friends who have developed a familiar style of communication from sharing activities.

The value of doing things is apparent in Matt's response, which described his most meaningful times with men friends:

> It was like we were doing a lot of things together. It just seemed like we just grew on each other. Can't think of just one thing that stood out in my mind. It was more like a push-pull type thing. Like I'd pull him through things and he'd pull me through things. It wasn't like there was just one thing I can just think of right now, just a lot of things he did, whatever. Just the things we like to do, we just did them together, and just had a good time.

The closeness is in the "doing"—the sharing of interests and activities. When Matt was asked about his meaningful times with his women friends, he responded:

> It's like the things that you'd talk—it's really just like "talk" with them. It's not so much like you'd go out and do something with them, or go out and maybe be with them.

Several men said that with women friends it's "just talking" and referred to interaction with women as "the lighter side of things." For men, it appears that actions speak louder than words and carry greater interpersonal value.

Women were also aware of a difference in men's style of expressing caring. A women commented on the differences in how her men and women friends let her know that they like her:

> Women talk more about feelings than men do. A man might let me know that he likes me because when he was in New York, he saw a book I'd been looking for and he brought it to me. And so I know that he likes me because he did that. Where a woman might say, twelve days in a row, "I've been looking all over for that book, but I can't find it."

Her male friend expressed his caring through a direct action, while her female friend expressed her caring verbally.

The emphasis on activities in men's friendship shapes their communication of closeness and caring. The significance of the doing/talking emphases in men's and women's styles of intimacy is apparent in the following response of a man to the question, "Why do you think they'd [women friends] be more verbal than your guy friends [in showing that they like you]?"

> I don't know why. I think there's just more ways to . . . I think there's more ways for the males to show me their appreciation that's nonverbal. I don't know why. I just think that if, in the way that they respond to things we do together and stuff like that. There's more ways to show it. Like if we're, I make a good shot in a game or something, just give me a high-five or something like that. You don't have to say anything with the guys. That's just an example, it doesn't have to be just sports. But the same type of things, off the field or whatever, just a thumbs-up type thing from a guy or whatever. There's just more ways to show being around [each other]. Where with the girls, you know, what can they do? You know, run up and just give you a kiss or something, I know girls who would do that in high school. So it—I think their options are just less—so they opt for the verbal type of thing.

He views talking as one option or style of expressing caring. From his activity-oriented perspective, he actually views women as restricted by a lack of alternatives to verbal expressiveness. These expressive alternatives are available to men through cues developed by sharing and understanding common activities. Nonverbal cues, expressed in active settings, contribute to private, covert, and in general, sex-specific styles of intimacy. This suggests that each sex tends to overlook, devalue, and not fully comprehend the other sex's style of expressing care.

Men and women have different styles of intimacy that reflect the often-separate realms in which they express it. The activities and contexts that men share provide a common general experience from which emerge certain values, gestures, and ways of talking about things that show intimacy. Both men and women are restricted in crossing over into each other's realm by early sex segregation, which results in a lack of experience with the meanings and contexts of the other sex. Researchers often underestimate this segregation because of an emphasis on the loosening of sex-related boundaries in the past several decades. Despite such changes, sex segregation still influences men and women, especially during the development of friendships in adolescence.

Covert Intimacy in Sports and Competition

Sports are the primary format for rewarding the attainment and demonstration of physical and emotional skills among adolescent boys. A man stated:

> I would have rather taken my basketball out than I would a girl . . . you know how young men are in the seventh, eighth, and ninth grade . . . if I had the choice I'd play basketball with the guys instead of going out that night.

Researchers have documented detrimental interpersonal consequences that may result from sports participation (Stein and Hoffman, 1978; Coleman, 1976). However, the productive aspects of the sports context have received less attention from researchers. For men, the giving and receiving of help and assistance in a challenge context demonstrates trust and caring in a friendship. Engaging in the risk and drama of performing in a competitive activity provides the glue that secures the men in an intimate process of accomplishing shared goals. Jim responded to the question, "What situations or activities would you choose or would you feel most comfortable in with your close men friends?"

> I'm very comfortable, like playing racquetball. A lot of one-on-one things where you're actually doing something. Playing backgammon. Now being competitive makes it a little easier, because it's like a small battle going on. Not that you're out to show who's best, but it gives you something more that you two have in common in the situation.

The competition provides a structured context where friends can use their skills to create "something more" than they previously had in common. Each friend brings his own experiences and talents to join the other friend in the common arena of a competitive activity. The competition provides an overt and practical meaning; the covert goal, however, is not to "show who's best" but to give "something more that you two have in common."

The sports context provides a common experience whereby men can implicitly demonstrate closeness without directly verbalizing the relationship. Nonverbal communication skills, which are essential for achieving goals in the fast-moving sports context, also provide avenues for communicating intimacy. Greg responded to the question, "What were the most meaningful times that you spent with your men friends?"

> In athletics, the majority of these friends that are close to me were on teams of mine. We played together. We were on the same team, me playing first and him catcher, or at times he played third. You know, first and third looking across the infield at each other. Knowing that we were close friends, and winning the CIF championship. I could just see that it meant a lot to me in terms of friendship too. As soon as that last pitch was made, we just clinched the title, to see the first person that he looked for to give, you know, to hug or congratulate, or whatever, was me. And the same for me to him. That was a big, another emotional thing for the two of us. Because I could just . . . it's just . . . you could just see how close your friends really are, or something like that. When there's twenty-five guys on the team and they're all going crazy, you're just trying to rejoice together, or whatever, for the victory. And the first, the main thing you wanted to do was run across the diamond and get to each other, and just congratulate each other first. And that meant a lot to me emotionally as well as far as friendship is concerned. It was only a split second, because after it was just a mob.

The two friends had grown up playing baseball together. Sharing the accomplishment of winning the championship provided a context where a close friendship could be affirmed and acknowledged nonverbally in "only a split second." Other members of the team, and perhaps even family members, may not have been aware of the intimacy that took place. The nonverbal nature of the glance and the context of excitement in the team's rejoicing after the victory allowed the intimacy to be expressed privately in a covert fashion. Both the intimate style and the context in which the intimacy was expressed contributed to an environment that was relatively safe from ridicule.

How Do I Know You Like Me: Intimacy and Affection in Men's Friendships

When asked, "How do you know that your men friends like you?" only one man responded that his friend tells him directly that he likes him. If men do not tend to self-disclose to each other the closeness of their friendship, how do they evaluate closeness and intimacy with a man friend? In men's friendships with other men, doing something together and choosing a friend and asking him if he wants to participate in an activity demonstrate that they like one another and enjoy being together. These acts have a meaning similar to a boy who asks a girl to a dance; it's assumed that he likes her by the nature of the action. Mike responded to the question, "How do you know or get the idea that they [men friends] like you?"

> When I suggest that we do something I can tell in their voice or the way their actions are that they want to do it. Like hey! they really want to do it. Like, "Anyone want to go to the baseball game?" "Yeah, great! That's exactly what I want to do." That's a good feeling to know that you can make some sort of a suggestion that fits. Laughter, the joking, the noise. Knowing that they like to do the things that I like to do and that I like to do the things that they like to do. And it's the same in reverse, and basically I want to do it as well, me agreeing with them. As far as that goes, you'd say, I like it when they show me by asking me, if they want to do it with me.

Men mentioned physical gestures, laughing at jokes, doing one another favors, keeping in touch, "doing stuff," teasing, and just being around friends as ways they know that men friends like each other. The most common responses to the question of how their men friends let them know that they liked them were "doing things together" and "initiating contact." John responded:

> I think it's just something you can sense, that you feel by . . . obviously if you continue to go out and do things with them.

Mike responded:

> Well, they'll call me up and ask me to do stuff, if they have nothing to do, or if they do have something to do and they want me to be a part of it.

Men feel liked by other men as a result of being asked to spend time in activities of common interest. Within such active contexts, reciprocated assistance, physical gestures, language patterns, and joking behaviors all had distinctive meanings that indicated intimacy between male friends.

Reciprocity of Assistance. Men mentioned doing favors, which included mailing a letter, fixing a car, loaning money, and talking about problems relating to heterosexual relationships. The men emphasized a reciprocity of assistance and a goal-orientation to both problem solving and situations that involved self-disclosure. This reciprocity demonstrated mutual interest and also was a means to achieve a balanced dependency. Pete responded to the question, "How do your friends let you know that they like you?"

> We help each other out, just like doing favors for someone. Like right now, me and my roommate were going to class, and he was asking me questions because he slept in and didn't study. So I go "what's this—ok, here, just have my notes." Even though I'm going to need them for my thing at three. You know, just little stuff like that.

Matt referred to the assistance given between his closest male friend and himself as a "barter" arrangement.

> Jack and I had a good relationship about this. He's a very good mechanic, and I would ask him. And I would develop something that I do that was rewarding for him. Like I could pull strings and get free boat trips and stuff like that when I was an [diving] instructor. And he would work on my car and I would turn him on to the Islands and dives and stuff. It was sort of a barter situation.

The sharing of their skills and access to opportunities fostered interdependency, yet also maintained their independence through a mutual give-and-take.

Physical Gestures. Men also reported physically demonstrating affection to each other. However, the physical gestures had a distinctively masculine style that protected them from the fear of an interpretation of a homosexual preference. Men mentioned handshakes, bear hugs, slaps on the back, and an arm on the shoulder as ways that friends demonstrated affection.

Handshakes were the most frequently mentioned. Handshakes offer controlled physical contact between men and are often considered an indicator of strength and manliness. A strong, crisp, and forthright grip is a sign of "respectable" masculinity while a limp and less robust handshake may be associated with femininity and a homosexual orientation. A bear hug also offers a demonstration of strength, often with one friend lifting another off the ground. Gary described an occasion in his response to the question, "How do your men friends let you know that they like you?"

> I came back from a swim meet in Arkansas last week, and I hadn't seen Mike for two weeks. When I came back he came right at me and gave me a big old bear hug, you know, stuff like that. And my mom and dad were in the room, and they're going, "Hey, put my son down!" and we were all laughing.

Men give the affectionate hug a "rugged," nonfeminine veneer by feigning playful aggression through the demonstration of physical strength. The garb and trappings of roughness allow a man to express affection while reducing the risks of making his friend uncomfortable or having his sexual identity ridiculed. A slap on the back is much less risky for a man than a caress on the cheek, although they may have a similar message in the communication of closeness.

Joking Behavior. Men developed joking behaviors that communicate closeness and similar ways of viewing the world. Ken responded to the question, "How do you get the idea that they [men friends] are close friends?"

> Laughter is one of them. I'll admit, when I'm around anybody really, not just them, I try to be the world's best comic. Like I said, humor is just important and I love it. I'd rather . . . I just like to laugh. And when they laugh, and they get along with me, and we joke with each other, and not get personal, they don't take it too harshly.

Although Ken says he attempts to be a comic "when I'm around anybody," he goes on to elaborate about the differences in joking when around men or around women:

> For the girls, not so much the laughter because you can't, with the comedian atmosphere, or whatever, you can't tell with the women. . . . Because, you know, if you get together with some girl or someone that likes you a little bit, or whatever—you can tell them that your dog just died, and they'll laugh. You know what I mean, you know how it goes. It's just, they'll laugh at anything, just to . . . I don't know why it is. But you get together with certain girls and they'll just laugh no matter what you say. So it's kind of hard to base it on that. Because the guys, you know, you can judge that with the guys. Because they'll say it's a crappy joke or something like that, or say that was a terrible thing.

Women friends did not respond to his humor in as straightforward and rigorous a manner as did his men friends. This appears to be a result of a covert sexual agenda between the cross-sex friends and a misunderstanding of the cues and nuances of male joking behavior by his women friends. Joking behaviors often are rooted in the contexts of men's shared experience, an experience that women may have little access to. Joking relationships are used by men to show caring and to establish trust in the midst of competitive activities. The following response to the question, "What are the most meaningful occasions that you spent with a male friend?" demonstrated a context where joking behavior expressed intimacy in the midst of competitive action. First, Greg describes the context in which the joking took place.

> The first time I'd been waterskiing was last summer. And among these guys I was really athletic, maybe more so than them even. And he knew how to waterski and I didn't. And we got there, and I tried maybe six or eight times, and couldn't do it, just couldn't do it. I don't

> know what the deal was because I'm really an athletic person and I figure it wouldn't be that tough, and it was tough. As far as the friendship goes, for Mark, for him to sit there and have the patience to teach me what to do, what was going on, it must have taken an hour or so or more of just intense teaching. Like he was the coach and I was the player, and we got done with that and I did it. And the next time we went I was on one ski, thanks to him. It was that much of an improvement. And to know that we could communicate that well around something that I love, sports, and to know that we could communicate that well in something that we both like a lot, athletics, that meant a lot to our friendship.

Mark provided assistance that altered a potential traumatic experience into a positive success. Specifically, Mark used a joking relationship to reduce the pressure on Greg and allowed him to perform while in a vulnerable position. Mark did not exploit his superior capabilities, but shared them and empowered his friends. Greg explains:

> We were just able to make jokes about it, and we laughed at each other all day. And it finally worked out. I mean it was great for me to be that frustrated and that up-tight about it and know the only thing he was going to do was laugh at me. That may seem bad to some people. They'd have gotten more upset. But for me that was good. . . . It really put things in perspective.

The joking cues expressed acceptance and communicated to Greg that it was okay to fail, and that failing would not jeopardize continuing the lesson. Mark's acceptance of a friend's failures reduced the performance pressure on Greg, and thus released him to concentrate on learning to water-ski.

Joking behavior is important to men because it offers a style of communication that consists of implicit meanings not readily accessible to people outside the group. "In" jokes between friends demand attentiveness to an individual's thinking, emotional states and reactions, and nuances of behavior. They provide a format where a man can be meticulously attentive to the feelings and tastes of another man. An elaborate reciprocation of jokes can be a proxy for more overt forms of caring. Yet, because joking behavior is often used as a distancing gesture and hostile act, joking behavior is not interpreted as an expression of attachment. This adds to the covert nature of the act and further protects men from possible ridicule. The tenuous line between aggression and affection is demonstrated by Tim's response to the question, "Can you think of any other qualities that would be important to a close friendship?"

> Basically that they'll understand you. Like if you do something wrong and they go, "Oh, what a jerk." I mean they can say it, but they'll say it in a different way than some guy who shoots his mouth off, "What a jerk, you fell off your bicycle."

Tim was questioned further, "How would it be different—I know what you mean—but can you describe it?"

> You know, they'll poke fun at you but they'll say it in a friendly way. Where someone else will just laugh, "What an idiot," and they'll mean it. Where your friend will say . . . you know, just make fun of you and stuff. I don't know if I explained it too well.

The same words used by two different men are interpreted and reacted to in very different ways. The tone of voice and social distance between the two men are essential factors in the determination of an understanding friend as opposed to an aggressive enemy. Tim's reactions to both cues reveal the different meanings. The question was asked, "Okay, maybe if I ask another question to get at it, say you fell off your bike, how would you feel when your friend joked about you as opposed to . . . ?"

> I would just start laughing, you know. I mean he'd start laughing at me and I'd just look and

> he'd go, "You jerk," and I'll start laughing. We know each other and stuff. Some guy off the street—I'll just cuss at him and flip him off, you know. So it's a little different.

Such discriminations are difficult for men to explain and describe. This would suggest that the discriminating task may be even more difficult for women, who have not had the experience in the contexts from which men's friendships have developed. Matt explained how he lets his closest male friend know that he likes him.

> I'll have a tendency to say, "Well, why don't you write?" in a teasing way, and "Okay, when are we going to get together? . . . and this bullshit of you being up there in Stockton."

Coarse language is injected into the teasing to legitimize the implicit meaning that he misses his friend and wishes that they were together. Joking relationships provide men with an implicit form of expressing affection, which is an alternative to explicit forms such as hugging and telling people that they care about them. Joking also may be more personal, since it often relies on a knowledge and sensitivity to a friend's attitudes and tastes, thus recognizing and affirming a unique part of him. The following portion of an interview demonstrates this masculine style. Jim responds to the question, "Why do you think [women are more likely than men to come out and tell you that they like you] that is?"

> Oh, it's just the way you were raised. It's society. You might hug a girl and say, "See you later and good luck on your test tomorrow." Whereas you'll joke around with a guy about it.

"Why would you joke around with a guy?"

> It's just a . . . it's just a different relationship, you know. I think society would accept two girls hugging each other and a guy hugging a girl, but it's a little different when you're two guys. I don't know if you saw the movie *Grease* where there, like Danny and that other guy who's driving the car, they do it, well like they hug each other right? After they pull the car out of the shop, it's kind of like that, they stop, they realize what they did. You might even want to, you might wanna say, "Hey, thanks a lot." You do stuff like that. But you don't act silly. You might shake their hand.

Jim was asked if he hugged his closest male friend, to which he responded, "No, I don't do that." He was then asked, "How would it feel if you went up to hug Fred [closest male friend]? How do you think he would react?"

> Well, I can remember a couple of times that we had . . . after a football game when you're real excited and things. It all depends on the situation. If I just did it, you know, out of the clear blue sky, he'd probably look at me and, you know. I could do it jokingly. It might even be pretty funny. I might try that. But I don't think he'd like it. He'd probably think it was a little strange.

Jim was able to hug his friend after a football game, when emotions ran high, and the men's masculinity had just been validated by participating in, and presumably winning, the game. The football context insulated the hugging from being interpreted as unmanly or gay. Jim says, "It depends on the situation." At one point when Jim was asked what it would be like to hug his friend, he interpreted it as a challenge or a dare. "I could do that." However, he translates the act into a joking behavior, "I could do it jokingly," in an effort to stylize the hug as masculine. Men's styles of intimacy attempt to minimize the risks taken when overtly expressing affection. These risks are summed up best by Jim when asked why he would feel strange if he hugged his best male friend. Jim said:

> The guys are more rugged and things, and it wouldn't be rugged to hug another man. That's not a masculine act, where it could be, you know, there's nothing unmasculine about it. But somebody might not see it as masculine and you don't want somebody else to think that you're not, you know—masculine or . . . but

> you still don't want to be outcast. Nobody I think wants to be outcast.

Thus Jim could not hug his friend "out of the clear blue sky," overtly and without a gender-validating context. The styles of male intimacy attempt to limit these risks. Joking behavior camouflages the hidden agenda of closeness by combining elements of a private awareness of a friend's history and personal nuances with a public tone of aggression and humiliation. A man describes his most meaningful times with men friends.

> The conversation will come and we can kind of laugh at each other. And you can laugh at yourself, which is really handy.

Much as the slap on the back covers an affectionate greeting with an aggressive movement, joking behavior provides a covert avenue in which to express caring and intimacy.

Conclusions

These findings suggest that microstructural variables, particularly interactional expectations, are powerful explanations for male intimacy styles. Intimacy between men is influenced by their awareness of the restrictive sanctions that are often imposed on men who express certain emotions, such as sadness or fear. Men's intimate verbal style is partially shaped by the fear of sanctions that may be imposed on emotional behaviors deemed culturally unacceptable. Homophobia and the difficulty men have disclosing weaknesses testify to the limitations they experience when attempting to explore certain aspects of their selves. These limitations of male intimacy may distance men from all but their closest men friends, and may also create a premium on privacy and trust in close friendships. Such limitations may be more detrimental later in life where structural settings are less conducive and supportive to maintaining active friendships. A college environment fosters casual access to friendships, and friendships may also be integral and functional for the successful completion of a degree. Thus, the sample in the present study may be experiencing an intimacy that is more difficult for men to maintain in job and career settings.

The interview data show that although constraints in the masculine role limit men in certain situations and in verbal intimacy, men do develop intimate friendship behavior that is based on shared action. Men's intimacy often depends on nonverbal cues that are developed in contexts of active engagement. Men expressed intimacy with close friends by exchanging favors, engaging in competitive action, joking, touching, sharing accomplishments, and including one another in activities. The strengths of men's active style of intimacy involve sharing and empowering each other with the skills necessary for problem solving, and gaining a sense of engagement and control of their lives by sharing resources and accomplishments. Nonverbal cues offered an intimacy based on a private affirmation and exchange of the special history that two men share. This unique form of intimacy cannot be replicated solely by self-disclosure.

In addition to the men's active style of intimacy, they also reported self-disclosure to friends. Contrary to previous research, most men reported that they were more comfortable expresssing themselves to a close male friend than to female friends. These men assumed that close male friends would be more understanding because of their shared experiences. Men said that self-disclosure and hugging "depended on the situation," and were more likely to self-disclose in a gender-validating context. Thus, men overcome cultural prohibitions against intimacy with this gender-validating strategy.

There are advantages and disadvantages to both feminine and masculine styles of intimacy. Feminine intimacy is productive for acknowledging fears and weaknesses that comprise a person's vulnerability. Admitting and expressing an emotional problem are enhanced by verbal self-disclosure skills. Masculine styles of intimacy are productive for confronting a fear or weakness with alternative strategies that empower them to creatively deal with a difficulty. Both styles appear necessary for a balanced approach to self-realization and the challenge of integrating that realization into a healthy and productive life.

Although this study focused on generalized sex differences to document a previously unrecognized active style of intimacy, women also demonstrated active styles of intimacy, and men demonstrated verbal styles of intimacy. Thus, although the results are based on generalized tendencies, the data also support the flexibility of gender-based behavior and the ability of men and women to cross over and use both active and verbal styles of intimacy.

The documentation of active styles of intimacy sharpens the understanding of intimate male behavior, and it provides a more accurate and useful interpretation of the "inexpressive male." The deficit model of male expressiveness does not recognize men's active style of intimacy, and stresses men's need to be taught feminine-typed skills to foster intimacy in their relationships. This negation or denial of men's active style of intimacy may alienate and threaten men who then assume that intimacy is a challenge they will fail. An awareness of the strengths in men's covert style of intimacy provides a substantive basis from which to address and augment changes in restrictive and debilitating aspects of masculinity. The finding that gender-validating activities foster male self-disclosure suggests that strategies for developing more intimate capabilities in men would be most successful when accompanied by a gender-validating setting that acknowledges, enhances, and expands the use of the intimate skills that men have previously acquired.

The data suggest the influence that sex-segregated worlds exert on the ways women and men choose, and are most comfortable in expressing, intimacy. The separate adult social worlds that women and men often experience shape the opportunities and forms of intimacy shared between friends. These structural opportunities and the styles of intimacy that become integral to specific opportunities become familiar, expected, and assumed between friends of the same sex, and often are bewildering, inaccessible, and misinterpreted by cross-sex friends or partners.

The implications are clear: men and women will have to be integrated in similar microstructural realms in the private and public spheres if we are to expect men and women to develop fluency in what are now termed "male" and "female" styles of intimacy. If such integration does indeed take place, the reduction of misunderstanding, frustration, and abuse in cross-sex relationships could be profound.

References

Allen, J., and Haccoun, D. "Sex Differences in Emotionality: A Multidimensional Approach." *Human Relations* 29 (1976):711–722.

Bakan, D. *The Duality of Human Existence.* Chicago: Rand McNally, 1966.

Balswick, J. "The Inexpressive Male: A Tragedy of American Society." In D. David and R. Brannon (eds.), *The Forty-Nine Percent Majority.* Reading, MA: Addison-Wesley, 1976:55–67.

Bem, S.; Martyna, W.; and Watson, C. "Sex Typing and Androgyny: Further Explorations of the Expressive Domain." *Journal of Personality and Social Psychology* 34 (1976):1016–1023.

Booth, A. "Sex and Social Participation." *American Sociological Review* 37 (1972):183–192.

Caldwell, R., and Peplau, L. "Sex Differences in Same-Sex Friendship." *Sex Roles* 8 (1982):721–732.

Cancian, F. M. "Marital Conflict Over Intimacy." In A. Rossi (ed.), *Gender and the Life Course.* Hawthorne, NY: Aldine, 1985.

———. "The Feminization of Love." *Signs* 11 (1986):692–709.

Coleman, J. "Athletics in High School." In D. David and R. Brannon (eds.), *The Forty-Nine Percent Majority.* Reading, MA: Addison-Wesley, 1976:264–269.

Cozby, P. "Self-Disclosure: A Literature Review." *Psychological Bulletin* 79 (1973):73–91.

Davidson, J., and Duberman, L. "Same-Sex Friendships: A Gender Comparison of Dyads." *Sex Roles* 8 (1982):809–822.

Goffman, Irving. *Presentation of Self.* Garden City, NY: Doubleday, 1959.

Hall, J., and Halberstadt, A. "Sex Roles and Nonverbal Communication Skills." *Sex Roles* 7 (1981):273–287.

Hantover, J. "Boy Scouts and the Validation of Masculinity." *Journal of Social Issues* 34 (1978):184–195.

Henley, N. *Body Politic, Power, Sex and Nonverbal Communication.* Englewood Cliffs, NJ: Prentice-Hall, 1977.

Hoffman, M. "Sex Differences in Empathy and Related Behaviors." *Psychological Bulletin* 84 (1977):712–722.

Komarovsky, M. *Blue-Collar Marriage.* New York: Vintage, 1964.

———. *Dilemmas of Masculinity: A Study of College Youth.* New York: Norton, 1976.

Lehne, G. "Homophobia Among Men." In D. David and R. Brannon (eds.), *The Forty-Nine Percent Majority.* Reading, MA: Addison-Wesley, 1976:66–88.

Maccoby, E., and Jacklin, C. *The Psychology of Sex Differences.* Stanford: Stanford University Press, 1974.

Morin, S., and Garfinkle, E. "Male Homophobia." *Journal of Social Issues* 34 (1978):29–47.

Parsons, T., and Bales, R. *Family, Socialization, and Interaction Process.* New York: Free Press, 1955.

Pleck, J. *The Myth of Masculinity.* Cambridge, MA: MIT Press, 1981.

Rubin, L. *Intimate Strangers.* San Francisco: Harper and Row, 1983.

Stein, P., and Hoffman, S. "Sports and Male Role Strain." *Journal of Social Issues* 34 (1978):136–150.

Swain, S. "Male Intimacy in Same-Sex Friendships: The Influence of Gender-Validating Activities." Conference paper presented at the American Sociological Association Annual Meetings, San Antonio, 1984.

Tavris, C., and Wade, C. *The Longest War: Sex Differences in Perspective* (Second Edition). San Diego: Harcourt Brace Jovanovich, 1984.

7

Women Together: Bridal Showers and Gender Membership

DAVID J. CHEAL

The principal justification for a microstructural approach to gender must be that it reorients the terms in which the social organization of gender is presented in sociology. The sociology of gender, like sociology in general, has traditionally been concerned with the relationship between the individual and society. At the individual level, the sociology of gender has been concerned with *gender identities,* that is with individuals' images of themselves in relation to the cultural ideals of how men and women are believed to act. Thus, gendered behavior is held to be produced by individuals' efforts to conform to their learned identities. At the collective level, sociologists have focused upon *gender roles* (or sex roles), which are positions in social systems. Here, gendered behavior is thought to be due to the constraining effects of role norms.

In opposition to those approaches that focus upon the individual or upon society, microstructuralism is proposed as a third term for sociology of the interaction order (Goffman, 1983). The object of investigation here is situated interaction (Knorr-Cetina, 1981, p. 19), understood as the joint action of individuals within a particular context. From this perspective, gendered behavior is held to be the result of the ways in which meanings are constructed within social relationships (Gerson and Peiss, 1985). Gender stereotypes are mapped onto the sexes from the typical activities in which men and women engage as a result of their roles in the sexual division of labor. Thus, the stereotypical characteristics of women may be the result of their work as secretaries in organizations (Kanter, 1977), and as nurturers in a variety of public and private contexts (Graham, 1983; Risman, 1987).

Parts of this chapter are reprinted with the kind permission of Norman K. Denzin, for whom the ethnography of ceremonial activity at hall showers was originally prepared (Cheal, 1988a). The research materials are drawn from the author's project on Winnipeg Gift Behaviour, supported by the Social Sciences and Humanities Research Council of Canada, grant no. 410-82-0041 and grant no. 410-85-0082.

Typically, service occupations and caring for others have been regarded as proper work for women. Being a secretary or being a nurse has therefore come to mean being feminine, and the organization of work within these gendered occupations is constituted by the conventional characteristics of femininity (Gamarnikow, 1978). Men who are in fact employed in such occupations may find that their masculinity is called into question (Segal, 1962). In other words, they are likely to have problems with *gender membership*. It is gender membership and its social organization that we will be concerned with here.

Gender Membership

Gender membership consists of being recognized by others as belonging to a particular gender. This social process of status attainment has the following important features:

1. Acknowledgement of gender occurs during encounters, and it is therefore expressed in interaction rituals.
2. Gender rituals involve constructs of sameness and difference.
3. Attaining gender membership must not be confused with successful socialization, although the former may follow the latter.

Gender membership is neither an inherent trait of individuals, nor is it a property of social systems. It is, rather, accomplished during interaction. It occurs whenever an individual's claims (explicit or implicit) to belong to a gender category are accepted by others (Garfinkel, 1967). As Erving Goffman showed (1967), it is principally through the deference rituals of interpersonal relationships that social statuses are confirmed in everyday life. At a minimum, interaction rituals are used to convey an image of the individual as belonging to one socially defined category rather than another. The social construction of gender in interaction rituals therefore involves identifying the individual as the same type of person as others who are also members, and as different from those who are not members. A common example of this occurs in the ritual display of difference between women and men in gender etiquette (Goffman, 1977). It is also important to understand the social construction of gender sameness in rituals that are unique to the members of a gender. These shared experiences are consequences of the social separation of men's and women's lives in segregated roles (Smith-Rosenberg, 1975).

Interaction rituals among women and among men are endemic in everyday life, and are therefore found at all stages of the life cycle. Unlike theories of sex-role socialization, the concept of gender membership directs our attention to the adult stages of the life cycle, and in particular to the transition into adulthood (Hudson, 1984). Gender membership is not attained learning sex-typed behavior, but through being accepted by others as a competent member. Thus, membership is the result of an unending chain of interaction rituals (Collins, 1981), which are independent of socialization. The implications of this perspective have been spelled out by Erving Goffman (1979, p. 8).

> What the human nature of males and females really consists of, then, is a capacity to learn to provide and to read depictions of masculinity and femininity and a willingness to adhere to a schedule for presenting these pictures, and this capacity they have by virtue of being persons, not females or males. One might just as well say there is no gender identity. There is only a schedule for the portrayal of gender.

If Goffman is correct, the central topic for the microanalysis of gender should be the schedules for gender display that structure the *gender careers* of men and women. In other words, we should be concerned with the process of becoming, remaining, and perhaps ceasing to be, a member of a particular gender. That process is most evident in rites of passage, although we have little information about them for Western industrial societies (Bush and Simmons, 1981).

According to van Gennep (1960), rites of passage facilitate the movement of individuals from one well-defined social position to another. The transition stage is sometimes spread out over a considerable length of time, and a number of subsidiary rituals may be performed during that period. In the period between betrothal and marriage, for example, it is not uncommon to find rituals that have as much to do with adjusting the individual's changing relationships to stratified sex groups as they do with the acquisition of the role of husband or wife. Marriage, van Gennep claimed, does not only involve the incorporation of the individual into the new family group; it also involves incorporation of adult married men or women into a same-sex category (van Gennep, 1960, pp. 129–130, 144). For both women and men, marriage entails new patterns of interaction, within the married couple and within networks of kin and friends. However, these changing relationships have particularly important effects upon women, due to their lesser economic opportunities in the labor market and to their providing most of the unpaid domestic labor within the family economy.

Women are generally more dependent financially upon men than men are upon women. As a result of this inequality in dependence, a woman's social status is changed more by marriage than is a man's (Eichler, 1973). The attainment of adulthood via marriage is therefore more important to women than it is to men (Leonard, 1980, p. 259). Social recognition of this fact is ritualized in wedding ceremonies that focus on the bride rather than the groom (Barker, 1978, p. 74), and in the elaboration of pre-marriage ceremonies such as engagement rings (Westwood, 1984, pp. 106–111) and bridal showers in which brides-to-be receive tokens of their new status. Traditional rituals associated with marriage therefore typically reenact the dependence of women upon men. But they also often emphasize the interdependence of women who rely upon each other for support in serving the needs of their husbands and children. Ritual occasions such as "hen parties" thus make statements about the solidarity and affection between women and about the durability of the bonds that unite them in their ambiguous relations with men (Westwood, 1984, p. 119). In North America that is conspicuously evident at bridal showers.

Symbols of Solidarity: An Ethnography of Bridal Showers

In interaction rituals, material and ceremonial transactions are often fused into complex occasions (Goffman, 1967, pp. 53–56). This is the case with bridal showers, whose importance as a separate sphere of female activity deserves recognition. Bridal showers are something more than excuses for the redistribution of property. They are also occasions for ceremony. Some women, at least, take considerable pride in them, because "this is something that we women do together."

Bridal showers are planned occasions for female relatives, friends, and neighbors to give a bride-to-be things that will be useful in her new status as a married woman. They are normally organized and attended exclusively by women. The most widespread type of bridal shower is the *house shower* held at the home of a friend, or a friend of the family, or an older relative. Several showers may be held on a bride's behalf, attended by different (though sometimes overlapping) groups of women. By the time the wedding day arrives the bride has usually already received an array of goods that will be useful in her new home and in her new role as wife. In some parts of Canada these ritual transfers of domestic goods have been amplified into large occasions that are held in church or community halls.

Hall showers, or *community showers,* are large events, with the number of women in attendance ranging from 50 to 300 or more. In spring 1984 the author attended two such showers in Winnipeg. In one case the bride's family was of Polish origin, and in the other case the family was of Ukrainian origin. For the sake of convenience the two showers will be referred to as the "Polish" shower (70–75 guests) and the "Ukrainian" shower (110–120 guests). The author attended the Polish shower as a peripheral observer, joining two male photographers (who were the only other men present). At the Ukrainian shower (which would otherwise have been a purely female occasion), the author was a passive participant, seated with the other guests. The advantage of direct observation of hall showers is that it provides access to information about situated behavior that cannot easily be obtained in any other way. Details about hall showers can thus be used to illustrate general themes that are likely to be true for all female bridal showers. Despite their unique forms, hall showers unequivocally demonstrate the importance of marriage for women's gender membership, and the collusion of women in reproducing the domestic system that has traditionally defined female gender identity.

Students of female networks (Stack, 1974; Ross, 1983) have observed that the redistribution of resources among women can be of vital importance in helping them achieve a certain standard of living. This is true not only for the poor and those whose family arrangements are unstable, but also for those who are trying to make it in an affluent society in which social status is based on the abundance of consumer goods.

Large quantities of domestic utensils and household furnishings are conveyed at hall showers. In addition, major appliances, pieces of furniture, and money may also be given. At the Ukrainian shower the largest of the gifts—a 7-cubic-foot freezer from the bride's mother (who was present) and a chesterfield from her father (who was not present)—were not brought into the hall. For these gifts, an announcement was made, and a photograph of the freezer was held up for the guests to see. Whether or not they bring a gift, most people attending a hall shower in Winnipeg contribute money, which may be done at the door as they come in. At the Polish shower the expected value of the contribution ($10.00) was stated in advance on the invitation. The Ukrainian shower had been announced as a monetary or miscellaneous shower, with no stated value for a monetary donation. After the gifts presented at each shower had been opened, the total value of the money that had been raised was announced. At the Ukrainian shower it was reported that $350.00 had been collected "at the door." At the Polish shower it was announced that $470.00 had been collected, and that an additional $565.00 had been received from people who were unable to attend (most of whom lived outside of the city). Clearly, the material dimensions of a hall shower are considerable, and the participants certainly find them impressive. The ceremonial features of this economic ritual are also noteworthy, at least to the uninitiated.

Both hall showers were held on a Sunday afternoon, since this was a time when most women could expect to be free from other responsibilities for a few hours. In the morning, relatives and friends of the family had prepared food (which they donated), decorated the hall, and set the food out on tables ready for the arrival of the guests. Tables for the guests had been arranged in the body of the hall, and three additional tables had been set up at the end farthest from the main door. The latter consisted of a long head table with chairs facing into the body of the hall, and one empty table on each side. As the guests arrived, their gifts (all gift wrapped) were stacked on one of these tables. Gaily colored streamers and balloons were used to decorate the hall, the head table, and the chair of the bride-to-be. At the Polish shower balloons were placed on her chair beneath concealing pillows. After the bride was seated and the welcoming ceremonies had been completed, the concealed balloons were burst by the bride's companions. The bride's shock, and her embarrassment at displaying alarm in front of so many people, caused general laughter.

The main business at a hall shower is undoubtedly the opening of the gifts, which takes from one to two hours. Assistants carried the gifts one by one from the storage table (on the right of the head table party) to the bride, who opened them. The gifts were then removed to the table on the left. Throughout this stage in the proceedings the guests kept up an active conversation, mainly about their personal and family affairs.

The penultimate activity at both showers was the adornment of the bride-to-be. This was anticipated with some relish by most of the guests and with visible reluctance by the brides who were being "honored." Most of the gifts had been decorated with brightly colored ribbons, which were collected by the attendants as the gifts were being unwrapped. These ribbons were worked into a large garish habiliment during the opening of the presents. At the Polish shower this took the form of a chain that was hung around the bride's neck, and at the Ukrainian shower it took the form of a hat that was placed on her head. The announcer at the Polish shower (a recently married woman) stated with obvious irony that here was one last gift that she knew the bride would cherish "for many, many years to come."

Ritual in Female Communities: The Social Construction of Female Consciousness

Bridal showers, such as those described above, reveal the existence of a female community in which women are the agents of their own culture. Men appear in relation to these occasions as minor figures who are excluded from full participation. If they are present at all, it is in supporting roles such as driver or photographer, whose minor status is marked by the peripheral spaces that they occupy. The socially situated inferiority of men at hall showers is also expressed in their deference toward women. Within the environs of the hall men speak in subdued voices (which may contrast sharply with the boisterous conversations of some of the women), and in other ways they subordinate themselves to the requirements of an occasion that they know is not theirs. Men are, in fact, sometimes providers of gifts, but they are truly without standing. Their gifts must be turned over to female intermediaries, since it is women who control the ritual process of gift giving.

The special ritual powers of women with respect to gift giving are consequences of the unequal sexual distribution of caring for others, and especially nurturing the young (Cheal, 1987). Nurturing involves attention to the needs of others and a preparedness to sacrifice oneself for them. These dispositions are facilitated by sentiments of caring for others and denial of self. In the sexual division of labor, this complex of meanings is unequally distributed, so that it is incorporated into the roles of women but not of men (Hartsock, 1983; 1985).

The nurturing complex can be ritualized in a number of ways. One of them is gift giving. In a gift transaction the existence of a social tie is affirmed, and a willingness to give up something of value for the other is demonstrated (Cheal, 1988b). As we should expect from the sexual distribution of nurturing, women in Winnipeg are more active gift givers than men (Cheal, 1987). Although some gift giving is performed by women on behalf of male family members, much of it is conducted on their own account. Through these and other expressions of caring, women maintain and strengthen their bonds with other women within a specifically female community (Smith-Rosenberg, 1975).

Female solidarity within social support networks has been described as one consequence of the fact that the major responsibility for child rearing is assigned to women (Wearing, 1984). At bridal showers, gifts circulate among women in ways that dramatize the solidarity and power of women acting together within networks of interpersonal ties (Cheal, 1988a). However, the solidarity that women achieve within these networks produces a female consciousness, rather than a feminist consciousness (Kaplan, 1982). That is to say, women acquire a heightened consciousness of their obligations to preserve and nurture life through their domestic labor. Those obligations are made visible in the most direct fashion at bridal showers. Bridal shower gifts consist of items that are "for the home," and especially for the kitchen (toasters, soup bowls, and so forth) and the bedroom (sheets, pillow cases, and so forth). At the two showers described here, the majority of the household equipment given was for the preparation and serving of food. The domestic characteristics of the gifts document the stereotypical contents of the female world within the family, and thereby confirm its legitimacy. They are, in other words, part of the symbolic order of domesticity by which female adulthood has traditionally been defined (Leonard, 1980; Csikszentmihalyi and Rochberg-Halton, 1981).

Conclusion

The social origins of female solidarity rituals have been shown to lie in the regular cooperation of women as they fulfill their customary domestic obligations (Young, 1965). This fact has important consequences since rituals reinforce women's roles as care-givers. In the absence of external forces for change (such as pressures for female participation in desegregated occupations), women's networks reproduce the domestic ideology that assigns them to the private sphere of service to husband and children (Wearing, 1984; Westwood, 1984).

We have seen that the ritualization of giving to others, which is so characteristic of women in their intimate family relations, can become the basis for female communities that link large numbers of women from many different families. We have also seen that the resulting collective rituals equip young women to establish independent families, and display the subjects' femininity by committing themselves to women's responsibilities within marriage. In short, the consequence of female solidarity is to constitute women in their private, domestic roles.

What has been described here is how women's rituals reproduce the gendered experience of domestic intimacy. Communal rituals such as hall showers enable and encourage women to serve others in the intimate environments of their homes. It is through this unending cycle of intimacy-community-intimacy that women's gender careers have been managed, and their gender membership constructed.

References

Barker, Diana Leonard. 1978. "A Proper Wedding." Pp. 56–77 in *The Couple,* edited by Marie Corbin. Harmondsworth, Middlesex: Penguin.

Bush, Diane Mitsch, and Roberta G. Simmons. 1981. "Socialization Processes over the Life Course." Pp. 133–164 in *Social Psychology,* edited by Morris Rosenberg and Ralph H. Turner. New York: Basic.

Cheal, David. 1987. "Showing Them You Love Them." *Sociological Review* 35:150–169.

———. 1988a. "Relationships in Time." In *Studies in Symbolic Interaction,* Vol. 9, edited by Norman K. Denzin. Greenwich: JAI Press.

———. 1988b. *The Gift Economy.* London: Routledge.

Collins, Randall. 1981. "On the Microfoundations of Macrosociology." *American Journal of Sociology* 86:984–1014.

Csikszentmihalyi, Mihaly, and Eugene Rochberg-Halton. 1981. *The Meaning of Things.* Cambridge: Cambridge University Press.

Eichler, Margrit. 1973. "Women as Personal Dependents." Pp. 36–55 in *Women in Canada,* edited by Marylee Stephenson. Toronto: New Press.

Gamarnikow, Eva. 1978. "Sexual Division of Labour." Pp. 96–123 in *Feminism and Materialism,* edited by Annette Kuhn and AnnMarie Wolpe. London: Routledge.

Garfinkel, Harold. 1967. *Studies in Ethnomethodology.* Englewood Cliffs, NJ: Prentice-Hall.

Gerson, Judith, and Kathy Peiss. 1985. "Boundaries, Negotiation, Consciousness." *Social Problems* 32:317–331.

Goffman, Erving. 1967. *Interaction Ritual.* New York: Doubleday.

———. 1977. "The Arrangement Between the Sexes." *Theory and Society* 4:301–331.

———. 1979. *Gender Advertisements.* New York: Harper and Row.

———. 1983. "The Interaction Order." *American Sociological Review* 48:1–17.

Graham, Hilary. 1983. "Caring." Pp. 13–30 in *A Labour of Love,* edited by Janet Finch and Dulcie Groves. London: Routledge.

Hartsock, Nancy. 1983. "The Feminist Standpoint." Pp. 283–310 in *Discovering Reality,* edited by Sandra Harding and Merrill Hintikka. Dordrecht: Reidel.

———. 1985. "Exchange Theory." Pp. 57–70 in *Cur-*

rent Perspectives in Social Theory, Vol. 6, edited by Scott G. McNall. Greenwich: JAI Press.

Hudson, Barbara. 1984. "Femininity and Adolescence." Pp. 31–53 in *Gender and Generation,* edited by Angela McRobbie and Mica Nava. London: Macmillan.

Kanter, Rosabeth Moss. 1977. *Men and Women of the Corporation.* New York: Basic.

Kaplan, Temma. 1982. "Female Consciousness and Collective Action." *Signs* 7:545–566.

Knorr-Cetina, Karin. 1981. "The Micro-Sociological Challenge of Macro-Sociology." Pp. 1–47 in *Advances in Social Theory and Methodology,* edited by Karin Knorr-Cetina and Aaron V. Cicourel. Boston: Routledge.

Leonard, Diana. 1980. *Sex and Generation.* London: Tavistock.

Risman, Barbara. 1987. "Intimate Relationships from a Microstructural Perspective: Mothering Men." *Gender and Society* 1(1):6–32.

Ross, Ellen. 1983. "Survival Networks." *History Workshop* 15:4–27.

Segal, Bernard. 1962. "Male Nurses." *Social Forces* 41:31–38.

Smith-Rosenberg, Carroll. 1975. "The Female World of Love and Ritual." *Signs* 1:1–29.

Stack, Carol. 1974. *All Our Kin.* New York: Harper and Row.

van Gennep, Arnold. 1960 [1908]. *The Rites of Passage.* Chicago: University of Chicago Press.

Wearing, Betsy. 1984. *The Ideology of Motherhood.* Sydney: Allen and Unwin.

Westwood, Sallie. 1984. *All Day Every Day.* London: Pluto Press.

Young, Frank. 1965. *Initiation Ceremonies.* Indianapolis: Bobbs-Merrill.

8

Being and Becoming Coupled: The Emergence of Female Subordination in Heterosexual Relationships

JUDITH A. DIIORIO

Since the writings of Kate Millet (1970) and Shulamith Firestone (1970), the politics of sexuality has been the central focus of radical feminist thought. The revolutionary analysis developed by these and other feminist theoreticians following in their tradition has been based upon the critique of that area of social life that appears most natural, most personal, most apolitical: the emotional and sexual relationships between women and men. In demystifying these relationships and distinguishing between appearance and reality, feminists have attempted to show how the cultural ideals, social rules, and social psychological processes by which gender and sexuality are created are controlled by men, in their own interests. These cultural and interactional relations are one aspect of the web of forces that creates patriarchal social relations. As stated by Catharine MacKinnon (1982: 516):

> The organized expropriation of the sexuality of some for the use of others defines the sex, woman. Heterosexuality is its structure, gender and family its congealed forms, sex roles its qualities generalized to social persona, reproduction a consequence and control its issue.

Men and women may be coerced into exclusive heterosexual relationships by an institutional apparatus that few escape, and then with much to fear. It is at least partly through the institution of compulsory heterosexuality that women come to be subordinated to men and denied to each other (Rich, 1980).

These insights are indeed powerful and important. If correct, they suggest that efforts to equalize women's status through legal reforms guaranteeing women equal rights and formal equality may be insufficient for creating true sex equality since in the private and intimate spheres of life—those spheres unaffected by legal guarantees of equal rights—women will still find themselves subordinate to their boyfriends, lovers, or husbands.

Unfortunately, despite the important political implications of this perspective, its development has been hindered by two major weaknesses, one empirical and one theoretical. Empirically, there has been little research looking at the concrete, everyday processes by which heterosexual relations are created and conducted. We know little about how women and men actually accomplish "being-in-love" and how these microdynamic processes engender patriarchal relations. Theoretically, although the institution of sexuality is a major basis of women's social subordination, it is neither the sole basis nor an autonomous basis. Women also suffer from an inferior economic status that not only reflects the patriarchal dimensions of production systems, but which engenders their dependence on marriage for survival—a material dependency that contributes to the exploitative dynamics of heterosexual relations (Bernard, 1971; Hartmann, 1976; Eisenstein, 1979). As I have argued elsewhere (DiIorio, 1980), the development of feminist social theory must be based upon an analysis of gender and sexuality grounded in the microrealities created by women and men in their everyday lives and must probe the dynamic relationship between these realities and the macroforces (ideological, economic, and political) impinging upon them.

The research I present here is an admittedly small beginning for such a project. It involves a qualitative analysis of gender relations in a small, primary group of youths. In it I seek to examine the cultural beliefs and social rules through which heterosexual relations were shaped, the effects of these relationships on women's overall status in the group, and how these relations were affected by the economic conditions the women faced. For several reasons, the group I studied presented a particularly good opportunity for investigating these questions. The members were the same age and social class, enabling me to control for the possible interactive effects of these variables on personal relations. In addition, as a small, play group existing outside the institutionalized settings of family and work, I could witness the formation of heterosexual relations in a context where they were both a legitimate and explicit part of the members' activities and where they were fairly open to observation. Finally, this club explicitly acknowledged the formal equality of female members thereby allowing me to see whether, at least in this particular group setting, institutional equality was a sufficient basis for establishing egalitarian gender relations or whether the informal dynamics of heterosexual relations precluded real sex equality. Let me begin by describing the group and the method I used to study it in slightly greater detail.

A Description of the Group

The small group I studied was a van club that I call Nomad Vans. Nomad Vans was a mixed-sex group of young people committed to being friends, owning vans, and pursuing a good time. At its largest, there were fifteen dues-paying members, eleven males and four females, ranging in age from eighteen to thirty with a modal age of nineteen. They were primarily working-class youths who had neither the will nor the resources to go to college and who, with a few exceptions, were still living with their parents while working at minimum-wage jobs that payed them enough to own and operate a van, but little more.

Besides the fifteen actual members, there were many other friends and acquaintances who participated regularly in club activities but who were referred to as "outsiders." In keeping with the linguistic practices of the group members, I will refer to its male members as "guys" or "vanners," "guys" being their generic term for males and people in general. I will refer to its female members as "lady vanners" or "girls," "girls" being their generic term for females. When referring to individual members of the club I will use the unusual but colorful pseudonyms each chose for his or her "CB handle," the name used when speaking over citizens band radios. Star Baby, Wild Fire, and Spacy were the names of the three lady vanners besides myself. All other names refer to guys unless otherwise indicated.

Altogether, I was with the club from its inception to its dissolution, approximately eleven months. I was with the club as a member and a friend, as well as a researcher. What I came to know about the organization of this group stemmed from observing the talk and actions of other members and from reflecting upon the relationships and experiences I had as a female (and feminist) member of this club.

Early in my study of this club, I became aware of an apparent paradox with regard to the nature of its gender relations. Contrary to other youth subcultures that have been studied (Willis, 1978; Brake, 1980; Frith, 1978), Nomad Vans admitted girls as autonomous and equal members. Lady vanners had the same membership rights as male vanners. They could and did raise issues, speak out and be heard on matters that concerned them and, of course, vote on issues as specified within the club bylaws. Explicitly as well, the vanners—guys and girls—were committed to forming relationships based on friendship. They believed that the members of this club should get to know each other well, treat each other with mutual respect, and support each other in the face of any external adversity. Their shared status as vanners and club members were supposed to supersede any other social statuses in the relationships they formed and the patterns of interaction they engaged in. But despite this rhetorical and formal equality, the vanners and lady vanners did not participate equally in group activities. Gender was an important social and political division. Although assertive and outspoken at business meetings, the lady vanners were more passive and invisible at precisely those events that were culturally the most important: parties, van-ins, and social gatherings by which the vanners sought to have a good time. At these events, gender did supersede club membership in determining the nature of people's participation. The guys, both members and outsiders, remained in control of public discourse, engaged in the antics and rituals that symbolized having fun, and got drunk. The girls, both members and outsiders, participated on the fringes, observing the guys or at times engaging in quiet dyadic conversations with each other. Control over the club and its activities and, as a result, control over the resources for creating the subcultural realities remained with the guys.

The Heterosexual and Pro-Masculine Biases: The Vanners' Ideology of Sexuality and Gender

By analyzing talk, jokes, and rituals I became aware rather forcefully of the heterosexual bias and the pro-masculine bias of this subculture. The guys glorified sexual intercourse. In a group devoted to pursuing a good time, "having sex" was seen not just as a good time but as the best time. Wanting to have sex, planning on having sex, and seeking to have sex were constant themes of their conversations and jokes; and the planning of events typically involved considerations of where there might be girls available for the guys to meet and "get it on with." Although sex was considered a highly pleasurable and important activity, sexual encounters were only right, natural, and pleasurable if they occurred between a male and female. This heterosexual bias was reflected not only in the condemnation of "fags" and of any physical intimacy between two guys, but also in their perceptions of all heterosocial interactions as well. The vanners eroticized most interactions between guys and girls. If having sex was wonderful and if a guy could only have sex with a girl, then they also assumed that that was the overt or hidden agenda in all heterosocial interaction. Whenever a guy was seen talking privately to a girl, he was invariably teased about it by other guys.

The pro-masculine bias of the club's culture was rooted in a double standard of sexual conduct that afforded guys far greater freedom of sexual expression than girls while simultaneously defining and denigrating girls as sexual objects of men's desires. The vanners believed that males had a strong sex drive and that sexual intercourse was a basic and, at times, consuming need of all normal males; and they continually celebrated its achievement in their bantering with each other. Being male meant wanting sex, needing sex, and seeking to satisfy this need as frequently as possible.

In fulfilling this need, moreover, the guys could choose between two alternative modes of heterosexual activity. They either could engage in sex-as-consumption, where they pursued sex for its own sake with girls who represented nothing more than objects-that-give-pleasure; or they could engage in sex-with-commitment, where they would restrict their sexual activity to a specific girl with whom they were in love. For most of the vanners, the latter mode was the preferred form because it was perceived to satisfy emotional needs as well as sexual ones and because it offered greater security with less cost. Nonetheless, both modes of sexual activity were seen as legitimate, a matter of personal choice rather than morality. The following incident illustrates these perceptions.

One evening Quickdraw, Travelin' Man, Wizard, Free Bird, Vandura, Zookeeper, and myself had gathered at a pizza parlor to have a few beers and talk. At one point Wizard asks if everyone would like to go camping at a lake the following weekend. Travelin' Man responds that he can't go because he works on Saturday and has a date with his girlfriend on Saturday evening. Free Bird, who was dating Star Baby but who was also known to see other women occasionally, responds by saying that Travelin' Man should not be in love.

FREE BIRD: Love is no good really. It ties you down and I can't afford it 'cause someone always gets hurt. Star Baby and I have a nice understanding since we both know we can see other people. You know, even though we spend most of our free time together, we still know we can see others and that's great.

WIZARD: I don't agree. Man, there's something really special about being in love. I'm serious. You find yourself a good woman and you've got it made. Sometimes I get so tired of playin' all the little games.

ZOOKEEPER: Yeah, you just want someone who's right there when you need 'em.

WIZARD: And you don't have to worry about what to do and everything. You know what I'm sayin'?

FREE BIRD: I know what you're sayin' but I don't agree. As soon as you say you're in love it's like you're not supposed to do anything else or even look at anybody else. It drives me crazy.

WIZARD: Well, yeah, there's that part of it, too, 'course you can always try to get a little piece on the side. (Laughter.)

In essence, for the male vanners (as well as for the females) the heterosexual relationship based on love prescribed sexual monogamy. However, a guy was not morally constrained from being sexually active outside of this type of relationship. If he was willing and able to have sex with any number of women who were also willing and if he refrained from becoming committed to any of them, he suffered no loss of esteem or respect in the eyes of other guys. Indeed, he gained respect and esteem.

Girls were afforded no such choice. In the abstract, females were reduced to and denigrated as the objects of male sexual desires. Whether at meetings, gatherings, or parties, allusions to women-as-sex and men-as-consumers-of-women permeated male talk about planning or having fun, as the following conversations occurring at two separate club meetings reveal.

FREE BIRD: I think we should all go down to the Pumpkin Festival in Watersville next weekend. It's really a good time. They got anything you can think of made out of pumpkin and it's a great time.

VANDURA: Hey, Free Bird, they got pumpkin pie?

FREE BIRD: They got pumpkin hamburgers, pumpkin cake. They even got pumpkin (he puts his hands together in a gesture symbolizing a vagina meaning "eat it").

ZOOKEEPER: You can guarantee that, Free Bird? If you can guarantee that, I'll go.

Another time Earthquake suggested that the club attend a van and auto show called the Van-O-Rama being held at a local fairgrounds.

GORILLA: Is that the one with the Dallas Cheerleaders?
EARTHQUAKE: Yeah, the Dallas Cheerleaders are gonna be there.
GORILLA: That's worth three-fifty (the $3.50 admission price).
ZOOKEEPER: If all you get to do is look at it, it ain't!
GORILLA: What do you want for three-fifty?
ZOOKEEPER: As much as I can get.

On a more individualized basis, girls were constantly being evaluated by guys along two dimensions of their perceived worth: their desirability as erotic objects and their respectability as "nice girls" who limited their sexual encounters to monogamous, love relationships. Whether driving by one or more females during convoys, watching girls enter a bar where they were sitting, or walking around looking at girls during van-ins, the male vanners routinely discussed the sexual attractiveness or desirability of the girls they saw. Although they did not always agree on the relative desirability of a girl, they did agree upon the distinctions to be made in ranking girls as sexual commodities. At one end of their erotic continuum was the "fox," the girl any man would like to have; at the other end was the "dog," the girl too ugly to be of any value as a sexual object. The following conversation, which occurred over CB radios while the club was on a convoy traveling down a busy thoroughfare, shows these distinctions in use.

BEER BARREL: Just point to the brown car two back from you and tell 'em they can ride in this one but they'd better not be blimps.
JACKRABBIT: If I see 'em in a yellow '78 Camaro, I'll send 'em back.
WIZARD: You guys referring to the Gruesome Twosome?
BEER BARREL: Uh, that's right. One ain't bad. The other one, the skinny one, she's a dog. We can throw her right out the window.
FREE BIRD: Yeah, one of 'em . . . wow, that fox can ride in my van any time she wants.
BEER BARREL: You know how it be there, uh, Jackrabbit? We can take the skinny one, you know, that blond, we can throw her out the window. Only problem is she's liable to stick right through somebody's chest and then we'd be up on murder charges.

A female either too fat (blimp) or too skinny was an object of no value—an object that might be thrown out of a moving van the way one discarded an empty beer can.

Not only did the male vanners define and rank females in terms of their perceived value as sexual objects, they also evaluated them according to their perceived sexual conduct with and demeanor toward males. A girl deemed worthy of respect by guys was the "nice girl," "lady," or "good woman" who was sexually attractive but also sexually monogamous, limiting her sexual activity to a relationship with one guy to whom she was emotionally committed. Contrary to male sexual codes in other social contexts (Whyte, 1943), the vanners did not expect girls to be virginal until marriage. They acknowledged that girls, like guys, have sexual needs and enjoy sexual intercourse but only as an outgrowth of an emotional involvement and not as a mere physical act. They believed that girls should be sexually active if they were in love but only if in love and only with the guy with whom they were in love. No matter how attractive she might be, no matter how many other males she might be capable of "getting," she should want only one man. Like a vanner's van, a nice girl should be loyal, dependable, and fulfill the needs of the guy she cared about. A conversation that several of the vanners had concerning Quickdraw's girlfriend, Susan, illustrates the qualities they associated with nice girls. Quickdraw and Susan had just broken up for the third time in two months. Although they had been involved with each other at the time the club formed, Quickdraw had seldom brought her with him to club functions, and she had never become a member of the club. The vanners had assumed that this was Susan's choice, that she did not want to participate in club activities because she did not like them or the club members. As a result, the vanners had labeled her a "bitch." After a brief but pleasant conversation with Susan, Wizard attempted to reinterpret the reasons for her absence at club events and in so doing to redefine her as a nice girl.

WIZARD: Susan is really a nice girl. I mean it. At first, I wasn't really sure about her but I ran into her the other night in the department store and we had a good talk. I guess she puts up with a lot of shit which surprised me.

ZOOKEEPER: Whatdya mean, "she puts up with a lot of shit"?

WIZARD: Well, like, I don't know, I guess he [Quickdraw] doesn't call her and well, like, for example, she said that she really would like to be around the club more but that it's him. That he doesn't want her to be around us or something.

ME: How come he doesn't want her to be around us?

WIZARD: I don't know. Jealous, I guess. She's really goodlookin' and, I don't know. Anyway, she really loves him and I guess she really wants to get back together with him. She said she just wants to make him happy so I think they'll probably get back together.

ZOOKEEPER: Well, if they don't he's a fool!

EARTHQUAKE: I'll say he is. She sounds pretty damn nice to me.

As distinct from and opposed to the nice girl, the vanners referred to three other types of females: bitches, teases, and sluts. Although they made important distinctions between these three types, what set all of them apart from the nice girl or lady was their deviation from standards of appropriate female heterosexual demeanor.

The label having the broadest, most variable, and most frequent usage was that of "bitch." Judging from the numerous occasions upon which it was used, a bitch was a female who insulted or hurt a guy and thereby failed to act like a good woman should—putting the needs or interests of a guy before her own. A girl could be called a bitch for refusing to act friendly toward a guy (even though if she did act friendly she could be seen as romantically or sexually interested in him). She could be labeled a bitch for being friendly with too many males, for refusing to become sexually and emotionally involved with one, or for expressing anger at a guy who in some way insulted or hurt her. In essence, a female could be called a bitch for failing in any way to respond to a guy the way he wanted, to submit to his wishes, or to accept his overtures.

If a girl could be called a bitch for failing to reciprocate a guy's interest in her, she could be called a "tease" for appearing to like a guy and then failing to "put-out," that is, have sexual intercourse with him. Teases were seen as male manipulators—females who would use their sexual powers to attract a guy's attention and extract his time, concern, and money without giving him what he wanted the most in return—sex.

Although Zookeeper claimed to believe there was no woman worse than a tease, most of the vanners disagreed. For them, the worst type of female was the "slut" or "whore," the immoral or "dirty" female unworthy of respect. The slut was the female who appropriated a masculine sexuality. She was the hypersexual girl who whether single or involved in a heterosexual relationship would have sexual intercourse with several guys, solely for fun, without becoming emotionally committed to any.

The vanners made the slut the subject of jokes and obscene songs but only rarely used this epithet when talking about girls they actually knew. An exception were two girls, Becky and Marie, who were disparagingly referred to as "the gruesome twosome" by the male vanners. Although they had boyfriends, they were also known or believed to have had sex with other guys when the opportunity arose. Nonetheless, although the vanners would speak disparagingly of Becky and Marie when the two girls were not present, whenever they would appear at a van party or gathering, the single vanners would compete with each other for their attention. The implication was that while their reputations served as a basis for degrading them when they were not present, they were a basis for pursuing them when they were. Such behavior on the part of the vanners also signified that although these women were soiled or "dirty," having sex with them did not soil or dirty the character of a guy. The males who had sex with a slut were not themselves immoral; they were simply taking advantage of a free but useful commodity.

Hence, by the masculine double standards they employed, a girl had to be physically attractive yet confine her sexual activity to a monogamous relationship with a guy whom she loved to achieve status in the eyes of the guys. Girls were normatively and symbolically denied control over their own sexuality, the right to enjoy casual sex with multiple partners or sexual intimacy with each other. The vanners did not expect a female to remain virginal until marriage or to remain committed to one man for life. Nonetheless, they did expect her to have sex only as an expression of love and to be in love with only one guy at a time. They expected her to want and need to become part of a couple.

These ideologies of gender and sexuality influenced the consciousness, identities, and perceived interests of the lady vanners. As vanners they saw themselves as different from other typical or stereotypical girls, as more assertive, independent, and self-reliant. As club members, they expected to be treated with respect by the guys. However, they also accepted the fact that as ladies, their primary needs, interests, and value came from achieving love and respect in a coupled relationship with a guy. Becoming some guy's girlfriend and making that relationship last was what we talked about and why we supported each other. What we seldom recognized and never challenged were the double standards of sexuality or the political consequences of being in coupled relationships. Understanding these consequences and the ways in which male defined and controlled sexuality perpetuated male dominance requires a discussion of the social rules and sex-based division of labor through which heterosexual coupling was achieved and maintained.

Being Boyfriend and Girlfriend

Club members recognized several types of heterosocial relationships. They acknowledged that a guy and girl could be "just friends," a type of relationship characterized by emotional but not sexual intimacy. Such friendships were rare and were perceived as tenuous and suspect because of the natural and inevitable growth of erotic interest whenever an unrelated male and female were physically or emotionally close. In addition, they recognized a form of heterosocial relationship referred to as "just dating," a relationship intentionally formed by a guy and girl to see whether a romantic interest might become something deeper and more permanent. These relationships were seen as temporary and short-lived since they would either develop into a more enduring commitment or would be ended by the choice of one or both parties.

As the modifier "just" in the names of these heterosocial relationships indicates, both forms were being compared to and described in terms of a third more common and ideal form of relationship: the heterosexual couple who were boyfriend and girlfriend. For the vanners, it was this latter type of relationship based on bonds of love and exclusive sex that was the preferred form, the one that both guys and girls were ultimately seeking to achieve with each other. Explicit acknowledgment of the importance of these relationships was formally made in the club bylaws, which permitted any vanner to bring his girlfriend (or her boyfriend) into the club as a member with all the rights and responsibilities membership afforded. Such a right was not formally given to a vanner's same-sex friends.

Although the guys and girls in the club perceived the heterosexual relationship as a special and preferred relationship, there was a sex-based division of labor regarding the creation and maintenance of these relationships that reflected the club's sexual double standard and that ultimately prevented women from participating autonomously in club activities. Essentially, it was the guy's right and responsibility to initiate the contact and elicit a commitment; but once a mutual commitment had been made, it was the female's responsibility to do most of the work necessary for maintaining it. The net effects of this division were to enhance male control over these relationships and, ironically, to elicit from females active collusion in their own subordination. To elucidate these effects, I will first discuss the process by which couplings were established and then look at the rules guiding their maintenance.

Becoming Coupled

Beginning a relationship involved dating and initiating a dating relationship—a process viewed as something guys and not girls should assume responsibility for. If a guy was interested in a girl, he could ask her out, but a girl interested in a guy should wait to be asked out. Nonetheless, given that achieving masculinity was dependent in part on being able to "get" girls, the guys perceived this work as risky. To ask and be refused, or to decide that they wanted to have a more involved relationship than did the girl they were dating, was experienced by the guys as hurtful and damaging to their self-esteem; so the ability to refuse a date or end a dating relationship represented a potential form of female power.

As a strategy for minimizing this risk and countering female power, the guys typically engaged in "flirting." Flirting was virtually synonymous with being friendly to a girl, talking to and joking with her. Hence, there was enough ambivalence in the definitions that could be given to a specific encounter that a guy who approached a girl at a bar or during a party could seek to control the definitions others gave to his action so as to lessen the potential negative repercussion ensuing from a failed attempt. If a girl he approached acted cooly toward him, he could say he was just trying to be friendly and she was a bitch. If, on the other hand, she "flirted back," then he could interpret her behavior as a sign of interest and ask her for a date. Then, should he ask a girl for a date and be refused, or want more of a commitment from a girl than she was willing to give, he could save face either by denying any real interest or by claiming that the girl was not really "nice" and hence unworthy of any serious commitment.

The guys recognized that the work of initiating heterosexual involvements was theirs and considered this a burdensome and unfair responsibility that girls could also assume but refused to do so. Nonetheless, they also implied that a girl who would "go after" a guy by initiating interactions or asking for a date lessened her value by such actions. A nice girl would not be willing to pursue a guy because to do so would be to risk being "used" by him and therefore to cheapen herself. Hence, both the guys and the lady vanners saw any girl's attempt to initiate a heterosexual relationship with a guy as indicative of a female who is either "hard-up" (so unattractive that she had to pursue a guy or remain forever dateless) or an immoral woman lacking sexual control. An incident illustrates each of these attributions.

Kim was a friend of Spacy who had for several months accompanied Spacy to almost every club party, get-together, or meeting. She was also very interested in Travelin' Man and repeatedly told Spacy, Wizard, and me how much she wanted to go out with him. When Travelin' Man failed to show any interest in her, Kim took the initiative and began to call him and ask him out. Travelin' Man always refused, telling her that he was still emotionally involved with another girl with whom he had recently broken up. He told the rest of us that the real reason he did not want to go out with Kim was because he simply did not find her physically attractive. ("She's too fat.") Kim persisted, however. One evening, while the rest of the club was sitting in a bar, Travelin' Man came in in a huff and said that Kim was driving him crazy and he did not know what he was going to do about her. He then left and the rest of us began to talk about the situation.

EARTHQUAKE: I don't know why he doesn't just say, "Hey, bitch, leave me alone." I'll bet that would solve his problem.

JAY BIRD: Naw, he can't say that exactly. That wouldn't be right. But he should lay it on the line with her. Just tell her right up front that he doesn't want to date her.

STAR BABY: Yeah, I agree. There ain't no sense in being mean to her. Poor kid is pretty hard-up. I think Spacy should take her aside, though, and tell her, "Listen, you're not helpin' anything by goin' after Travelin' Man that way. No guy really likes a girl who chases him."

Kim was seen as a rather pathetic female whose heterosexual aggressiveness resulted from her unattractiveness as a sexual object. Aggressiveness on the part of females who were sexually attractive was not tolerated.

Being Coupled

Once a heterosexual relationship had been established and a guy and girl were known to be "going together," another set of social rules came into play. One was the rule of co-sociality, which meant that the couple should exist and act as a single unit for purposes of social activity. Interactional restraint was the second rule and meant that, for purposes of expressing monogamous commitment, both partners should limit the nature and amount of their interaction with members of the other sex. The third and final rule was that of emotional primacy, which meant that persons in love should see that relationship as the primary relationship in their lives and experience their emotional well being as contingent upon the state of this relationship.

These rules represented a set of expectations regarding heterosexual monogamy (being boyfriend and girlfriend) that were overtly supposed to restrain the activities of the guy and the girl. However, the effects of these rules upon the behavior of boyfriends and girlfriends were differentially mediated by the vanners' masculine ideology. As a result, girls involved in coupled relationships actually did most of the work of maintaining the relationship and conforming to these rules and, in the process, were socially segregated from single girls and all other guys in a way that was not true for their boyfriends. In order to explicate these rules and their effects more fully, I will discuss and illustrate each.

Co-sociality. The most direct and immediate way in which two people displayed their "coupledness" was through co-association. A boyfriend and girlfriend were expected to act as a social unit, to want to be together, to go places together, and to stay close to each other when at these places. The vanners always knew when one of the guys was in love because we would either see him with his girlfriend or we would not see him at all, and this was considered appropriate behavior. If a vanner was known to be involved in a heterosexual relationship and came to some club function without his girlfriend, he would generally be asked to account for her absence. Furthermore, not only were a boyfriend and girlfriend expected to come to events together, they were also expected to sit, stand, and interact together while at these events.

Nonetheless, in observing and experiencing the demands of co-sociality during club parties and outings, I came to realize that the effects of this rule were not the same for guys-as-boyfriends as they were for girls-as-girlfriends. Differential effects resulted because the activities the couple participated in and their movements at these activities were controlled primarily by the male. The guys tended to control when and with whom the couple would talk. Girlfriends moved about as their boyfriends' appendages, a social status conveyed visually by the tendency for a guy, while standing and talking to the others, to throw a possessive arm around the shoulders of his girlfriend. If a girl did not accompany her boyfriend, it was generally because he wanted to be considerate of her when she was already busy talking to someone and he wanted to go see someone else; but she was supposed to stay where he left her. Although she might not know exactly where he was and with whom he was talking, chances were good that he knew exactly where she was and with whom she was talking. If he cared about her, then he was not supposed to leave her alone for very long, but neither should he have to follow her around. Being-in-love meant that he should want her by his side wherever he went and she should want to be there. As a result, she simply had far less control of autonomy over the social interactions she could have and the social relationships she could develop.

One incident, involving Travelin' Man and a girl named Chris with whom he had been going for several weeks, illustrates this rule and the effects of its violation. Earthquake was giving a party for the club and Travelin' Man brought Chris to it. During the evening, however, Chris repeatedly left Travelin' Man to talk to some people she knew. On one occasion she went to talk to a girl; on several other occasions, she went to talk to guys. That Chris's behavior was considered unusual for a girl involved in a heterosexual relationship was first brought to my attention by Wild Fire who at one point during the evening leaned over and whispered in my ear, "You'd never know she came with him (Travelin' Man), would you?"

Travelin' Man evidently also thought Chris's activities were inappropriate for he became increasingly upset as the evening progressed—an anger perceived as legitimate by the other vanners. Zookeeper and Earthquake finally decided that Travelin' Man should "show Chris a thing-or-two" and persuaded Travelin' Man to go with Zookeeper to pick up a couple of other girls who wanted to come to the party. Travelin' Man and Zookeeper left the party without telling Chris, and by the time they returned she was upset. As far as the vanners were concerned, she had gotten what she deserved and the following afternoon, Zookeeper, Earthquake, Travelin' Man, and Wizard talked about the event and laughed at Chris's reaction.

Interactional Restraint. Being a member of a heterosexual couple meant that the guy and girl were to be sexually monogamous. But being sexually monogamous entailed different normative requirements for the girlfriend than it did for the boyfriend, primarily because she was expected to refrain not just from having sexual intercourse with another guy but from any actions that might signify she was interested in having sexual encounters with any other guy. Given the tendency for the vanners to eroticize all but the most superficial interactions between a guy and girl, a violation of the commitment to sexual monogamy could be attributed to almost any interaction between a male and female when one or both were involved in a coupled relationship with someone else. When this happened, it was typically the girl, whether single or coupled, who was held responsible for the breach by other girls and other guys. In order to remain free of any accusation of being unfaithful to her boyfriend—an accusation that would jeopardize not only her love relationship but also her reputation as a nice girl—a girl could legitimately interact with other guys only if her boyfriend was present. Similarly, single girls could interact with coupled guys only when their girlfriends were present, or they risked being accused of "going after" another woman's man and being labeled a "tramp" or "slut." As a result, patterns of social interaction in the club were organized around the dyadic relationships of boyfriends and girlfriends. All guys, whether single or coupled, could legitimately interact with each other; but coupled girls tended to have relationships only with other coupled girls, and single girls could interact easily only with other single girls and single guys. A girl who crossed these interactional barriers risked incurring the wrath either of her boyfriend, if she was coupled, or of other girls, if she approached a coupled guy. In only the rarest of circumstances did I observe an instance where a guy was held accountable for attempting to challenge the sanctity of the monogamous bond, and that involved a single guy who was believed to be seeking to get a coupled guy to interact with some other girls. There were, however, a number of incidents involving violations of the rule of interactional restraint that illustrate that almost any interaction between a male and female could be interpreted as sexual and that it was almost always the girl who was held responsible.

One example occurred during the early weeks of the club's existence when the members were attending their first camping trip together. I had not been able to go with them, but I did talk to the other lady vanners about their experiences. In one conversation with Wild Fire, she told me that she was really angry with Spacy and that she did not think Spacy could be trusted.

ME: Why can't she be trusted?

WILD FIRE: Because I know she went after Crazy Horse (Wild Fire's guy) at the van-in and I'm not the only one who knew it.

ME: Why? What did she do?

WILD FIRE: Nuthin' really except she would stand and just stare at Crazy Horse. She would just stare at him with this weird look. You couldn't help but notice and several other people told me she was after him.

From that point on, Wild Fire made frequent reference to the incident and to her dislike of Spacy and, although both were members of the club, the two women seldom interacted during the first few months of the club's existence. This incident also illustrates the precariousness of a single girl's status in this world since, as Wild Fire herself admitted, Spacy had done little more than look at Crazy Horse. Nonetheless, this minimal interaction was sufficient for her to earn Wild Fire's wrath as a "little whore."

Displaying sexual commitment essentially imposed upon coupled women the necessity of restraining their interactions with all other males and imposed upon single women the necessity of restraining their interactions with already "taken" or coupled guys. The results of this rule were not only to segregate all coupled women from the guys but to pit coupled women against single women.

Emotional Primacy. The final expectation associated with boyfriend-girlfriend relationships concerned the personal and interpersonal experiences that the vanners' perceived to be a natural result of being-in-love. Being-in-love was the social bond upon which heterosexual relationships were based, and it was a bond perceived as stronger in its personal saliency than any other bonds a person might experience, including those of friendship and bonds with parents, siblings, or others.

The emotional primacy attributed to this affective state was expressed in two major ways. First, a person's emotional well being was considered to be intricately dependent upon how well her or his heterosexual relationship was going. Coupled males and females had their emotional highs and lows attributed to the state of their heterosexual relationships. Hence, when a guy would show up at a party "actin' down" or depressed, it was generally assumed that he had had a fight with his girlfriend. Second, because the love attachment was perceived to be of greater importance than any other interpersonal bond, when a conflict between it and other relationships would arise, an individual was expected to resolve the conflict by remaining with his or her lover. For example, when Spacy incurred the wrath of Star Baby and Wild Fire both women expected the guys with whom they were in love to refrain from any future interaction with Spacy, despite the fact that she had previously been their friend. And when toward the end of the club's days, Star Baby and Wizard came into conflict, Star Baby stopped interacting with me—her best friend in the club—because I was going with Wizard and as she later told me, "I just knew you would naturally have to side with him."

Despite the power that love was believed to hold over both the guys and girls, the emotional work of maintaining the love commitment in the face of internal or external threats was experienced by the girls involved in heterosexual couples as disproportionately their burden. They spoke often about the greater potential labor and higher personal costs that being-in-love extracted from them, as the following conversation between Star Baby and myself indicates. Star Baby and Free Bird had had a fight following which they had not seen each other for several days. She then calls me up to tell me that they are back together, feeling better, and all is well.

STAR BABY: Free Bird and I are doing great again.
ME: Great! What happened?
STAR BABY: Well, I drove up to the park yesterday afternoon and I saw his van there and he was just sittin' in it listening to music. I could tell he was actin' sort of depressed. So, anyway, I just went over and said, "Hey" and asked him how he was doin'. And we started to talk and we just talked everything out.
ME: So the two of you are doing well again?
STAR BABY: Yeah, I guess so. At least for the time being. I don't know. You know, how come . . . I don't know I've just never been able to figure out why it always has to be the woman who makes the first move. I know he wanted to get back together but he wasn't going to do anything until I did first. Seems like that's always the way it is, though. They get mad and then we have to apologize whether it's our fault or not. I guess it's worth it if you really love somebody but sometimes I get tired of it. . . . I don't think anything I've done has been wrong. Yet somehow we end up in a fight and then I have to say I'm sorry. It just don't make sense (laugh). I guess they really are all a bunch of little boys.

Conclusion

If one defines as political those social processes involving the exercise of power and power as the ability of some to control the behavior of others, then the rules and ideologies informing heterosexual relations in this group had important political consequences. In particular, they gave men power over women and served men's interests at the expense of women's.

Some of these political consequences are fairly evident. The rules of heterosexual relationships enabled the male vanners to benefit from the emotional labor of their girlfriends while controlling their girlfriends' activities. For the lady vanners, being coupled meant they could earn respectability but at the expense of their autonomy and their ability to participate fully in club activities. Instead, in the name of love and respectability, the lady vanners assumed the burden of maintaining these relationships under a system of rules that reflected masculine privilege and interest. To show commitment and to preserve sexual monogamy, they stayed physically close to their boyfriends allowing his patterns of interaction to determine theirs; they took his side against all others and smoothed over any emotional difficulties; they refrained from any actions that would make them appear either sexually promiscuous or sexually interested in some other guy; and they tried to prevent any other girl from attracting the sexual interest of their guys. As a result, coupled women were distanced from all other guys; a sense of distrust and competition characterized the relations between coupled girls and single girls; and the lady vanners became the sexual and emotional servicers of their boyfriends.

Despite a rhetorical emphasis on friendship and equality in members' relationships, so long as the lady vanners' actions and perceived interests were determined by masculine and heterosexual beliefs, they remained the social and cultural subordinates of the guys. To the extent that masculine and feminine sexuality are defined by a double standard and to the extent that monogamous heterosexual relations turn women into property and limit their ability to act and interact freely, those formal rights of membership represent little more than an ideological distortion of women's real subordination. Ostensibly afforded a high degree of independent participation and formal equality as vanners, the lady vanners were simultaneously denied this status by the rules of heterosexism.

But the question remains as to why these rules existed and why women conformed to them. Why was there a double standard of sexual conduct? Why was the division of labor in heterosexual relations organized as it was? And why did the lady vanners accept and strive to meet these discriminatory expectations? One possible answer could be derived from what Risman (1987) refers to as an "individualistic perspective." According to this perspective, the heterosexual relations I observed could be seen as an expression of gender differences in personality traits and motivations that the guys and girls of this club acquired during early socialization. The lady vanners had been socialized as "feminine" beings to be nurturant, emotionally expressive, and submissive, and these traits carried over into their heterosexual relations as did the male vanners "masculine" tendencies toward aggression, emotional inexpressiveness, and egocentrism and gave rise to the patterns of interaction I observed. Although plausible, this explanation is belied by the situational variability of the lady vanners' behavior, including their behavior toward the guys. There were situations, such as business meetings, where their behavior was far from submissive and indeed, where they would take charge and the guys would submit.

A better answer, therefore, can be found in what Risman (1987; Chapter 13, this volume) calls a microstructural perspective, which examines the relationship between the heterosexual relations of these individuals, the material conditions of their lives, and traditional beliefs about the institution of marriage that affected, in gender-differentiated ways, their responses to material conditions and to their heterosexual interests. To state it as succinctly as possible, I believe that the disadvantaged economic position of these persons, given a shared acceptance of a quasi-traditional view of gender roles in marriage, created competing interests between the guys and girls in heterosexual relations, which engendered the girls' greater dependency on marriage and enabled the guys to exercise greater power in premarital relations. As working-class "kids," neither the vanners nor lady vanners faced bright economic futures. Both were trapped in low-paying, dead-end service jobs earning less than they needed to fully support themselves, much less a family. Both also believed that it was a husband's responsibility to shoulder the primary financial burden for wives and children. Wives might work to supplement the income provided by their husbands, but not as an equal or greater provider and not when children were small. Because of these traditional beliefs, the vanners and lady vanners had different needs for the future and different interests in the present.

As working-class females, the lady vanners' economic survival was dependent upon marriage. Exploited as females in certain sex-typed occupations within the existing production system, they looked toward marriage to improve their material existence. They did not see marriage as an institution based on the exploitation of women as domestic laborers, reproducers, sexual servicers, and financial providers. They were conscious only of their problems at work and, perhaps, falsely conscious of marriage as meaning security, happiness, and love. Nonetheless, the material conditions of their life make their desire for marriage and their willingness to accept traditional beliefs about marriage understandable. Unfortunately, under these conditions, their future dependency on marriage put them in a position where dominance by their boyfriends became possible. The lady vanners clung to their heterosexual relations not merely for the emotional and sexual rewards these relations offered but as a possible means of economic survival that they did not wish to jeopardize.

The male vanners also had traditional beliefs about gender roles in marriage. They believed that as adult men they should be able to provide economically for their wives and children. Unfortunately, as young, working-class males, they realized that they were presently incapable of doing so and knew that it might take some time, some luck, and some special training before a good-paying job came along. As a result, they were in no hurry to get married, but they wanted the sexual and emotional pleasures associated with marriage. The heterosexual and masculine ideologies of their subculture permitted them to achieve the benefits of heterosexual monogamy without its costs. They could couple with a woman, and once coupled could expect her to provide emotional support and to be sexually available only to them, while avoiding the economic responsibility of marriage.

I do not wish to give the impression that the male vanners had lives of ease and pleasure while the lady vanners assumed all the social costs. Heterosexual relations were organized around male dominance and gave males greater benefits, but many guys had great problems establishing these relations. Fortunately, they also understood that it was sometimes just as well that they did not get too involved too soon; and they could legitimately still have sex—casual encounters for physical pleasure—outside of their relationship. Their masculine consciousness also created the means for their ideological control by the capitalist system. Rather than challenging the economic structure that provided them with so few opportunities and kept them in such low-paying jobs, they sought to establish their masculinity in the world of play and through sexual relationships. Their private lives provided them with the meaning and happiness denied them in work—a sense of authority and control otherwise absent from their young lives. With bleak futures and little power, they sought only to create a pleasurable present. Unfortunately, both they and the lady vanners needed much more.

References

Bernard, Jessie. 1971. "The paradox of the happy marriage." Pp. 145–63 in V. Gornick and B. K. Moran (eds.), *Woman in Sexist Society: Studies in Power and Powerlessness.* New York: New American Library.

Brake, Michael. 1980. *The Sociology of Youth Culture and Youth Subcultures.* London: Routledge and Kegan Paul.

DiIorio, Judith. 1980. "Toward a phenomenological feminism: A critique of gender role research." Paper presented at the National Women's Studies Association meetings. Bloomington, Indiana.

Eisenstein, Zillah. 1979. *Capitalist Patriarchy and the Case for Socialist Feminism.* New York: Monthly Review Press.

Firestone, Shulamith. 1970. *The Dialectic of Sex.* New York: Bantam Books.

Frith, S. 1978. *The Sociology of Rock.* London: Constable.

Hartmann, Heidi. 1976. "Capitalism, patriarchy and job segregation by sex." *Signs* 1:137–69.

MacKinnon, Catharine. 1982. "Feminism, Marxism, method and the state: An agenda for theory." *Signs* 7:515–44.

Millett, Kate. 1970. *Sexual Politics.* New York: Avon Books.

Rich, Adrienne. 1980. "Compulsory heterosexuality and lesbian existence." *Signs* 5:62–91.

Risman, Barbara. 1987. "Intimate relationships from a microstructural perspective: Men who mother." *Gender and Society* 1, 1:6–32.

Smith, Dorothy. 1977. "Some implications of a sociology for women." Pp. 15–29 in N. Glazer and H. Waeher (eds.), *Woman in a Man-Made World.* Chicago: Rand McNally.

Willis, Paul E. 1978. *Profane Culture.* Boston: Routledge and Kegan Paul.

Whyte, William Foote. 1943. "Slum sex code." *American Journal of Sociology* 49:24–31.

9

Secrecy and Status: The Social Construction of Forbidden Relationships

LAUREL RICHARDSON

Introduction

Eighty years ago, Georg Simmel proposed that all social relationships "can be characterized by the amount and kind of secrecy within them and around them" (1950:331). Yet, how status and secrecy affect the construction of social relationships has been little studied. The purpose of this paper is to theorize how status and secrecy affect the construction of a particular category of relationships: secret, forbidden, sexual relationships.

The secret, to paraphrase Simmel (1950: 330), was one of the major achievements of humankind because it permitted an immense enlargement of the world, the possibility of hiding reality and creating a second world alongside the manifest one. The secret, he argued, is a general sociological form of major significance, regardless of its content. Because some measure of secrecy exists in all relationships, ignoring it limits our understanding of how social relationships are constructed and maintained.

Analytically, Simmel distinguished two kinds of secrets. There are secrets about the self that are privately constructed and held and secrets about a social unit that are socially constructed and held, such as the private language of twins, the plots of co-conspirators, or the very existence of the co-conspirators. Secrets are possessions whose value is enhanced by denying knowledge of them to others. If secrets are shared, there is the risk of betrayal; if they are not shared, relationships are circumscribed. Following Simmel, understanding how secrecy is managed can tell us a great deal about how relationships are constructed. However, Simmel did not focus on the issue that concerns us here, namely, how status imbalances affect the continuing social construction of secret relationships.

A major proposition of the social constructionist school is that the meanings attached to rela-

This article is reprinted from *American Sociological Review* 53(April 1988):209–219. Reprinted by permission of The American Sociological Association and the author.

tionships vary according to status and that status differentials have consequences for the relationship's construction. Interactionally, status differentials are *power* differentials, and face-to-face interactions reflect the constraints or freedoms of relative social positions (cf. Karp and Yoels, 1979:124–81). Constructionists note that we simultaneously inhabit a micro world of face-to-face relationships and a macro world of abstract and remote institutional arrangements. The micro world makes full sense only in the context of the macro one that enfolds it (cf. Berger and Berger, 1975:8). Analyses of face-to-face relationships must take account of broader institutional arrangements, including those of status differentials (cf. Reynolds, 1987).

Secret *intimate* relationships are particularly salient for an analysis of secrecy and status in relationship construction. In secret relationships, ample opportunity exists both to reveal secrets about the self and to conceal one's biography, identity, and purposes. Second, ample opportunity exists to create mutual secrets, including the very existence of the relationship. Moreover, because intimate relationships are privatized, secret ones are doubly removed from the routine world. In such situations, restraints are minimized, so the impact of status is in greater relief.

One category of secret relationships, forbidden sexual relationships, is arguably the largest and most significant class of secret relationships. More individuals are likely to be so involved and more individuals are likely to be deeply affected by their own or significant others' involvements than any other kind of secret relationship. For example, somewhere between 18 percent and 32 percent of single women become involved with married men (Richardson, 1986); approximately 50 percent of husbands and 35 percent of wives have extramarital relationships (Atwater, 1982; Reiss, Anderson, and Sponaugle, 1980); approximately 25 percent of adult women were sexually molested by adult men when they were girls (under 16) (cf. Russell, 1986). Untold numbers of professors become involved with students, doctors with patients, ministers with parishioners, employers with employees. The emotional significance of these relationships can be intense and long-lasting. Women sexually harassed at work experience extreme stress (MacKinnon, 1979). Single women involved with married men often find themselves more emotionally committed than they had expected to be (Richardson, 1985). And childhood sexual experiences, including incest, have major, long-lasting emotional consequences (Koch, 1980).

A feature of cross-sex secret, forbidden sexual relationships is that they are typically constructed between *status unequals*. One status imbalance usually exists: age, class, or marital status. Consequently, the construction of cross-sex secret liaisons should reflect the major consequences of status differences, *power* differences. Secret sexual liaisons are likely to be *power-imbalanced* relationships.

Liaisons between single women and married men should provide the paradigmatic case for these secret, forbidden, power-imbalanced relationships, not only because of their numerical abundance, but for cultural-historical, interactional, and structural reasons. Adulterous relationships provide a world in which self-disclosures and mutually created secrets can proliferate. De Rougemont (1956), in his review of love in the Western world, argued that there is an inescapable conflict between passion and marriage in the West, with adultery nearly synonymous with passion. He speculated that Westerners are drawn to adultery, an act that destroys marital happiness, as much as they are to acts that ensure marital happiness, because marriage and ardor are in opposition.

Because of social-structural and social-psychological reasons, men have greater power than women. Men are more highly valued, have better jobs, and earn more than women (cf. Reskin and Hartmann, 1986). The male and the masculine are viewed as superior to the female and the feminine, and a double standard exists such that differential rewards and sanctions are given to men and women for the same behavior (cf. Eichler,

1980). Further, gender differences exist regarding the meaning of love and the importance of intimate relationships (cf. Gilligan, 1982; Hochschild, 1983; Diamond, 1983). Because women tend to value relationships more highly than men, work more to sustain them, and feel more responsible for their outcomes, women are likely to care more about having and preserving a relationship than men are. The "principle of least interest" holds (Waller, 1938; Blau, 1964). Whoever has the lesser interest in maintaining a relationship has the greater power within it.

In single woman/married man liaisons, the male has greater structural and social-psychological resources because of his marital status, as well. Being married confers greater prestige than being single, gives a veneer of stability and access to a network of couples (Stein, 1981), as well as an immediate alternative sexual partner. The effect of marital status difference on the construction of the relationship can be set in relief. Since the men in these liaisons are usually of a higher socioeconomic class than the women, there are also socioeconomic status differences. But, in addition, because socioeconomic peers are getting involved (Richardson, 1979; 1985), how socioeconomic inequalities interact with differences in gender and marital status can be explored.

Based on intensive interviews with single women involved with married men, I generate theories about the links between secrecy and status in the social construction of forbidden sexual liaisons. Two sequential stages of intimacy construction emerge and demand analysis: (1) exchanging secrets about the self, or *Becoming Confidantes;* and (2) creating mutual secrets, or *Becoming a We.* My analysis focuses on how the clandestine nature of these liaisons transforms, heightens, and/or intensifies normative social expectations and structures, including the impact of status differences. I find that the man's marital status, reinforced by his gender status and superior socioeconomic status, has major and significant consequences for the construction of the liaison.

Procedures

The data come from intensive interviews with 65 single women who had or were having long-term (over a year) intimate relationships with married men. The interviewees came from three sources. First, whenever I attended a public or social occasion, I mentioned the project, and women I met in these settings volunteered to be interviewed. Second, a respondent would occasionally suggest other potential interviewees. Third, women, hearing of the project, requested to be interviewed.

The frequently reinstituted "snowball" sampling procedure generated an extensive list of potential interviewees from a wide variety of social networks. After 48 interviews with a diverse set of women over a period of five years, saturation (cf. Glaser and Strauss, 1967) was experienced. Since I was fairly accurately predicting the women's accounts, I discontinued interviewing. During the analysis and writing stages, though, I followed 17 women who contacted me during the early stages of their liaisons. I interviewed them at approximately three-month intervals over a minimum period of 12 months. Because these women's accounts were substantially in agreement with those of other women I interviewed, the usual issues regarding the reliability and validity of retrospective biography are somewhat muted.

The women resided in rural and urban areas in all regions of the country. When their relationships began, they ranged in age from eighteen to fifty-six with a median age of twenty-eight. Sixteen women were high school graduates, thirty-six were college graduates, and fourteen had advanced degrees. Nine were students at some point during their liaisons. Occupationally, they held a variety of blue-collar, pink-collar, clerical, administrative, and professional positions. Twenty-seven of them had never been married, thirty-eight were divorced. Fifteen were raising children. Fifty-three were younger and less established than the men; eighteen had been supervised or mentored by their lovers at some point during their relationships; seven of them were occupational peers; and five were socioeconomically superior to their lovers. When the relationships began, all of the husbands were living with their wives, and fifty-two of them had minor or college-aged children. None of the husbands claimed to be in "open marriages," although five explicitly said their wives overlooked their infidelity. The relationships studied lasted from one to twenty-five years, and more than half were over at the time of, or shortly after, the interview.

The interviews were conducted in private settings such as the respondent's home or mine, a private office, or a hotel room. An open-ended format elicited detailed information on the woman's feelings, attitudes, and behaviors during different phases of the liaison. Interviews were tape recorded and transcribed.

Because the sample of women was not randomly drawn, precise representativeness is unknown.[1] The sample, however, is heavily weighted toward women with high education and white-collar occupations. The analysis searches for patterns and themes in the women's accounts, and presents these as processes and types. Because the women's accounts make sense within the growing substantive and theoretical understanding of women's experiences, considerable face validity can be claimed for the study. Because the relations are long-term ones, however, the analysis is not generalized to one-night stands or abbreviated affairs.

I looked at how features of these liaisons resemble features of normatively approved relationships and how the forbiddenness and secrecy of the liaisons transform or intensify those features. My conceptualizations are grounded in the data, and theoretical ideas are inductively generated (Glaser and Strauss, 1967). All generalizations are based on the dominant pattern or the clear majority of the respondents. When I quote from a particular interview, it represents a common interview theme. Since the interviews were fluid and open ended, not all respondents volunteered all themes. However, I do not discuss themes of processes that are not general.

Stage One: Becoming Confidantes

Building an intimate relationship is an accomplishment that is affected by the context in which the intimacy is being built. Yet little attention has been paid to the structural contexts that impede or enhance self-disclosures and intimacy (but, notably, see Davis, 1973). I find that the man's marital status creates a context of privacy, time constraints, and expectations of temporariness that encourage revealing secrets about the self. Revealing them increases the woman's trust in and idealization of her lover and their relationship, which, in turn, intensifies the woman's commitment. The intimacy process is a dynamic one greatly affected by the fact that the involved man is a *married* man.

Single women see the beginning and middle phases of their relationships with married men as "total," "emotionally pure," and "uniquely intimate." All the women I interviewed described their lovers as special people. They were seen as "compassionate and exciting," "like no man ever known before," and "every woman's dream." Even women who did not expect to adulate their lovers, women who were "career driven" or usually "emotionally reserved" commented on the "truly special qualities" of their lovers, their "generosity," "openness," "strength of character," and "spontaneity."

The pattern of idealization suggests that sociological factors of the relationships are operative, rather than the psychological characteristics of the women. The relationships have in common that they begin as a secret and that the man is married, the woman is not. Because the man is married, the relationship's existence is kept secret from particular significant others, such as her children, her employer, and his wife (Richardson, 1985). Because of his marital status, moreover, three structural conditions arise: privacy, time constraints, and expectations of nonpermanence. It is precisely these conditions that are structurally conducive to the woman's idealization of her lover and the relationship.

First, because the man is married, activities that sustain the relationship are carried on predominantly in *privacy.* The world-out-there, the normative social structure with its roles and rules, expectations and obligations, can be laid aside as the couple constructs a world-in-here, a world freer of normative social constraint and cultural definitions. Alone-together, the pair can construct the relationship, its boundaries, and its focus. Between them, they have the resources, such as their incomes and her home, to create and sustain the requisite privacy. Privacy leads subsequently to greater relational autonomy. As one woman summarized it, "We didn't have expectations of each other, and we didn't have to exploit each other. The relationship didn't have to have a goal. We could just be."

Second, because he is married, the relationship's *time constraints* are affected by his marital obligations. When time constraints exist and when energy is invested to achieve a rendezvous, positive expectations rise. Time spent together is labeled "special," "important," "encapsulated," "never mundane." Although these time constraints often become problematical later in the relationship, in the beginning they are viewed favorably (for example, "Because our time was special, neither of us wanted to mess it up"; "There was a purity" because we "never wasted time fighting or worrying about the relationship."). "Purity" is sustained because the clandestineness of the relationship separates it from the commonplace world. The liaison does not "deteriorate" into "a day-to-day domestic situation where demands are made that are unpleasant or mundane." The couple can "stop the clock, freeze the relationship" when it is "particularly romantic . . . encapsulated."

Third, because the man is married, the single woman anticipates that the liaison will be *temporary.* In the beginning stage, not one woman expected a long-term or permanent relationship with her married lover. One, who met her lover (of four years) at a conference, stated, "I knew when the conference ended, I would never see him again and I had no intention of keeping up the relationship." Another, whose relationship lasted five years, stated, "Since I knew it was temporary—I really thought that!—I felt it was a very safe thing to do." Entering these relationships believing they will be short-lived liaisons, women can be vulnerable to their lovers because they have no designs on his (their) future. Because the relationship is defined as temporary, it is safe. One emotionally reserved woman commented, "I'm willing to take a risk. I don't have to keep myself under control, because it's not so dangerous because it can't go anywhere."

Space and time, then, are both controlled by the man's marital status. Privacy leads to semi-autonomous definitions of the meaning of the relationship, time constraints to quality time together, and temporariness to feelings of freedom and safety. This context induces feelings of great emotional intimacy.

Typically, the feeling of emotional closeness grows as the man talks about his life, disclosing his fears, hopes, and secrets. One woman said her lover told her "family secrets" that he had shared with no one else, including his wife. Another said, "I know everything about him . . . *Everything.*" The woman feels *trusted.* The married man's apparent emotional openness and his willingness to be vulnerable is what draws her closer to him. In turn, the woman feels freer to talk about herself, a process much "like an add-a-pearl necklace," where both are "putting pearls [secrets] on the string." A context is established where a woman can let her "guard down" and "let a man know" more about her than "other men ever have." Through these self-disclosures, a feeling of intimacy based on "knowing about another" and "telling about oneself," as distinct from the creation of mutual secrets, is experienced.

Simmel (1950:334) noted that the secret is the primary basis for individualization and that, in modern societies, people identify more with the characteristics they hide than with the ones they publicly tout. He proposed that people tend to hide those characteristics that conflict with their public image and that they wittingly disclose secrets only to those who are indifferent to the discrepancies or who are otherwise harmless (1950: 334–35). Simmel's proposal is further explicated by Davis (1973: 103–4). What individuals try to hide are their *weaknesses*. People identify their uniqueness with their secret weaknesses. When people allow someone to see their vulnerabilities, they feel as though they are seen as they truly are. From Aristotle's view that "we feel friendly . . . toward those . . . who will tell us of their own weak points" (quoted in Davis, 1973: 114), through Simmel's and Davis's perceptive analyses, to Lorenz's ethological research (1966), being vulnerable is arguably a way of establishing bonds. "As animals bare their throats, so humans bare their secrets" (Davis, 1973: 115).

Once secrets about the self have been shared, Davis contends, the discloser becomes a "psychological hostage" of the listener. Knowledge confers power. If both parties exchange secrets, they reach a state of "mutual deterrence, for neither can now harm the other without having unacceptable damage inflicted upon himself in return" (1973: 112). Davis further proposes that "the potentially damaging secret knowledge of each other's weaknesses that both acquire" is a major force in the transformation of isolated individuals into intimates (1973: 130).

If this analysis is correct, the tension between concealing and revealing secrets about the self is intensified in modern societies. Sharing secrets about the self makes one a psychological hostage, but only through such sharing do people feel they are truly known as unique individuals. But does this analysis hold true for single woman/married man relationships?

Clandestine liaisons between single women and married men provide a relatively safe place for the single woman to be vulnerable. She can explore her sexuality, experiment with different ways of interacting, and expose her weaknesses (Richardson, 1986). But the liaison provides a *particularly* safe place for the married man to be vulnerable. It is easier to reveal one's deepest feelings in a relationship that can be readily terminated and safer to discard one's veneer when there is little threat of being trapped or dominated—and easiest yet when displaying one's weaknesses is likely to enchant (Sattel, 1983). Because the double standard is still operative, the risk of betrayal is minimized (Eichler, 1980). The woman will be held accountable and blamed, not the man. It is his marital status that is in fact being protected through the secrecy. The ideology of "protecting" the woman's reputation simply reinforces his safety.

Popular belief holds that the "other woman" has the most potential power because she can destroy the man's whole life by revealing the affair. For potential power to be actual power, however, it has to be recognized and exercised. The women I interviewed did not publicly reveal their affairs or threaten to. The idea did not even occur to them. What a woman wanted was to maintain a high-quality liaison (Richardson, 1985). She had nothing to gain by threatening disclosure and a great deal to lose. Threats would diminish the quality of her relationship, if not end it. Telling the wife required acknowledging the wife's existence, which was not in the single woman's interest (Richardson, 1986: 88–107). If she works with her married lover, she would risk her job and be subject to accusations that she exchanged sexual favors for career advancement. Publicly, she would be labeled a "home wrecker." The fact that she did not recognize her supposed potential power to undermine his marriage testifies to its power over her. "Mutual deterrence" is not their basis for trust; minimization of exposure is. The two are not psychological hostages to each other, but trusted confidantes.

Building a relationship on an assumption of trust increases the trust, if there is no apparent betrayal. One of the consequences of increased trust is increased self-esteen. Being "needed, trusted . . . his one true confidante," the single woman feels ennobled. To be trusted with a secret means you are judged a worthy and moral person. As Simmel has commented, ". . . in the confidence of one [person] . . . in another lies as a high a moral value as in the fact that the trusted person shows himself worthy of it" (1950:348). Listening to his self-revelations and not betraying them, a decision that is "free and meritorious" (Simmel, 1950:348), can give the single woman a sense of moral rectitude and moral superiority that other elements about the relationship do not sustain (for example, "The purity of my feelings for him was so terrific that it made me a good person"; "I still marvel that he considered me worthy enough to know him that well. His wife may have had his name, but I had his soul.").

Because the structural conditions facilitate the free exchange of secrets and an increasing positive regard for the self and the other, women understandably define their experiences as highly intimate ones. One consistent research finding is that feelings of intimacy relate to self-disclosing. Intimacy is perceived as existing when self-disclosures are freely given and are accompanied by positive feelings (for example, Jourard, 1971; Rubin, 1970; Mcallist and Bregman, 1983). What the women are experiencing is the "sort of intimate exchange which we see as a primary component of love" (Rubin, 1974). The idealization of the relationship arises precisely because the man is married, with the constraints of his marital status directly affecting the construction of the nonmarital liaison. Because of his marital status, the intimates perforce become more intimate.

Stage Two: Becoming a We

If the two become trusted confidantes and establish a "special" relationship, the single woman's loving feelings may soon give way to feelings of normlessness and rootlessness, precisely because the relationship is secret. Few, if any, biographical and socialization experiences and few, if any, social supports exist to objectify and validate her relationship. But, as is true of any relationship, the subjectively experienced secret relationship has to appear objectively real in order for it to persist (Berger and Kellner, 1964). In this section, I discuss the processes, including the creation of mutual secrets, through which anomie is overcome and the two become a "We."

Normally, a relationship is objectified through interaction. The married woman has the "constant conversation" with her husband to stabilize her identity, as well as the daily exchanges with friends, relatives, associates, and tradespeople ("Good morning, *Mrs.* ______.") that validate her membership in a socially accepted couple. Since the normal validations are not available to the single woman involved with a married man, the usual means for objectifying the relationship are absent, although the need is not diminished.

Simmel's (1950:358) insight on ritual in secret societies is relevant here. He noted that secret societies devise rituals relatively unfettered by historical and social convention. Highly embroidered rituals can be built up from within the secret society. He proposed that the most typical feature of secret societies, the feature that most distinguishes them from open organizations, is their strong valuation of "rites, formulas, and usages." Through rituals, the members experience the secret society as a "closed unit, a whole, both sociological and subjective" (1950:360).

Structures similar to those described by Simmel arise in clandestine intimate relationships, but, in addition, this research explains how the problem of objectifying the secret relationship is solved. Mutually created rites and mutually created secrets are infused with deep symbolic significance. The rites and objects become the validators. They intensify feelings and prove the relationship exists.

Every woman I interviewed volunteered an example of a rite or an object that confirmed the existence of the relationship. The objects and rites signify to the woman that the relationship exists and has a history and a structure. This identification is referred to as *marking We* (Lester, 1979). Some examples will clarify this process.

Some women mark We intangibly, through the use of private languages, jokes, appellations, phone codes, and celebrations of anniversaries. In describing these, the women frequently emphasize the stability of the rituals. One woman, in a long-distance relationship, commented that she and her married lover wrote each other at the same time each day, "like we were really together." Another talked about the "monthiversaries" they celebrated, and a third emphasized that Tuesday nights were routinely shared with her lover.

In addition to rites and rituals, single women mark We more tangibly, through shared possessions. One woman described in great detail how she and her lover "re-did" her bedroom—choosing colors from paint chips, repainting the walls, sanding the floors, acquiring plants and prints. She summarized, "It's something I wouldn't have done by myself or for myself. We did it for ourselves. It became *our* bedroom." Another woman reported that she began saving mementos, which she placed in a drawer. Her lover began to refer to it as "our drawer." A third said times spent looking at "their photo album" were "very special times when we could remember again." In effect, the bedroom, the drawer, and the photo album are private possessions of both the lovers in which to mark We and preserve a history.

Although probably any relationship that persists can be reconstructed by its participants in terms of their private holdings (Lester, 1979), in these unsanctioned relationships, marking We carries the burden of *proof* that a relationship exists. Moreover, these private possessions remain private. Totally distinguishable from socially validated coupling in which the objects themselves (the ring, the house, the children) become the social basis for the validation, for these illicit couples, the objects are themselves secrets. Because they are not publicly shared, and yet carry so much proof of the existence of the relationship, their symbolic significance intensifies.

For women highly invested in their relationships, the objects can take on a semisacred quality. The reverence suggests a witnessing of holy artifacts, *enshrinement* behavior and attitudes (cf. Cook, 1982). One woman, after a long introduction, brought out "their" scrapbook from its "secret hiding place." Although her manner was talkative before, while the scrapbook rested on her lap, she spoke in short descriptive statements ("This is when we . . .") followed by long silences. As soon as she returned the scrapbook to its place, she resumed her earlier outgoingness. Another woman, after a long preparatory statement, entered her bedroom and positioned herself in front of a bulletin board that held a dried bouquet, a Valentine's Day card, movie ticket stubs, and some postcards. A period of silent viewing followed. Later, she said the board was strategically placed "so I can see it just before I turn off my night-light."

Even for women who were less highly invested in their liaisons or who had negative and angry feelings toward their lovers, the objects that signified that a relationship existed were shared only after a preamble and were handled with great respect. Because the objects are the functional alternatives to *social* confirmation and external validation, they become the manifest and material touchstones in the woman's construction of reality.

The intense meaning of the objects as representations of the relationship is further illustrated by their purposeful *destruction* to signify that the relationship no longer exists. One woman, who experienced an abusive ending to the relationship, said, "I was a wild woman. I ripped and mangled and shredded everything of ours and threw it into the trash!" Another woman, three years after her lover had walked out, said, "I spent New Year's Eve alone, burning our pictures, one-by-one, in the fireplace, chanting, 'Good-bye, good-bye,' over each one." And, a third, after mailing her lover a "Dear John" letter, placed his love letters in a box, sealed it, and "put it outside." To signify the ending of the relationship, the objects are ritually removed, the house "cleansed."

The *ending* of a socially validated relationship is itself socially validated, and the processes for accomplishing it are socially prescribed. The social interaction and "constant conversation" that generated the couple's "we-ness" is replaced by social interaction that acknowledges the couple's demise. Their separation is marked linguistically, socially, and often legally. During the separating process, moreover, each of the partners can talk freely about the break-up and receive social support.

The same autonomy and freedom from social norms that affected the construction of the secret liaison affect its ending. Neither social interaction nor public rituals are available to signify to the self that the relationship no longer exists. Because the relationship is secret, there are few (if any) significant others to talk to about it and even fewer who will provide emotional support. Consequently, the single woman has a paucity of forms through which to "deconstruct" her relationship. The one way she does have is the destruction of the objects that signified its existence. The willful annihilation of the same objects that validated the existence of the relationship signifies its demise.

But before the relationship ends, because these rituals and objects are mutually created secrets, another kind of intimacy is experienced. This is intimacy arising from feeling *attached to* another person, *a part of* a relationship, a whole, both objectively and subjectively. This feeling, like the intimacy arising from exchanging secrets, is one associated with being in love (Rubin, 1974). The single woman, consequently, exists in a social reality of a secretly shared world.

Existing in that world, however, has different consequences for her than for her married lover precisely because she has deferred to his marital status and allowed it to determine the contours of her liaison. The more objectively real and sacrosanct the relationship to her, the more she comes to value the liaison. Consequently, she becomes more committed to preserving it. The more dedicated she is, the more disempowered she becomes. The disempowerment is intensified because of the man's marital status. First, she is denied the social prestige attached to "having" a man and "being in love." Her ability to "attract" a man is not publicly acknowledged. As a result, she becomes more, rather than less, dependent on the married man's attentions. But even more disempowering is how she constructs her life to protect the secret of the relationship's existence. She deepens her sense of intimacy and commitment because she decreases the opportunities for publicly testing the relationship and/or increases her dependence on it.

Because the relationship is a secret one, it is not socially tested. She can cherish her idealization because the relationship is insulated from external judgments and critical appraisals. But, in addition, because she *wants* to see him, she may find herself, "arranging [her] whole life around his, deciding when . . . [she] can go out and when . . . [she] should stay home." To reduce the chances of revealing her secret, she may withdraw from her usual social network and from her family and friends, which makes her even less socially moored and her social identities more fragile. One woman commented, "In a normal relationship you usually don't have to give up who you are. In my relationship, I gave up my family, my identity, my culture, the theater, the arts . . . my therapist." Conversations with friends and family may be truncated as the single woman becomes more matter-of-fact and distant in her intentions, revealing little about her life for fear of revealing all (for example, "I just repressed my life. I didn't talk about anything to anyone."). If she retreats further into social and emotional isolation, her married lover grows more salient. He becomes *de facto* her "whole life." Her withdrawal from others, then, intensifies her dependence on the relationship, her commitment to it, and her love feelings. He is her intimate.

Not all women withdraw so totally from friends and family. However, all the women I interviewed reported episodes such as "lying on the couch on a Sunday afternoon drinking gin, crying, and waiting for him to call"; behavior changes such as "seeing much less of my female friends, so I'd be home if he should call"; routine changes such as "dropping out of the car pool so I could drive the long way past his office"; distancing activities such as "lying to my friends and family about who I was seeing and what I was doing with my time"; and compartmentalizing their liaison, living a disjointed, rather than an integrated, life. Equivalent socioeconomic statuses do not prevent women from relationship disempowerment. Indeed, these illustrations are from women who were socioeconomic equals to their married lovers.

To some degree, women who manage to sustain the relationship sacrifice some independence and autonomy as they construct their lives to accommodate the man's marital status. Their gender contributes to their willingness to (and skill at) accommodating the male, but, it should be reemphasized, it is primarily because of his marital status, not his gender, that she reconstructs her life in the way she does. Unlike these clandestine liaisons, normative male-female relationships are openly constructed, unfettered by a man's commitment to another woman, and have benchmarks that signal the relationship is progressing toward permanency or termination. And they do not require the woman to keep her feelings and significant holdings a secret from others.

The greater the woman's interest in the relationship, the more disempowered she becomes. The less her interest, the more power she retains. The acts required to conceal the relationship create new secrets, limit external testing of the relationship, increase her dependency, and reduce her opportunity for alternative relationships. Understandably, her feelings of intimacy intensify while her power within the relationship diminishes. As a final note, even her power to *end* the relationship diminishes, the more invested in it she becomes. The more dependent the woman on the relationship, the more likely her lover will decide when and how to terminate the relationship, leaving her to emotionally free herself from the liaison, as well as from her feelings of being rejected or abandoned (Richardson, 1979).

Discussion

This paper has gone beyond Simmel by looking at how status and secrecy affect the social construction of secret liaisons between single women and married men. Several salient elements have been identified: how the suspension of the normal rules allows the construction of an alternate reality; how, because the relationship is forbidden, it is not socially tested, thereby contributing to its longevity; how anomie arises and is managed through imbuing rites and objects with intense symbolic significance; how the man's marital status is structurally conducive to idealization of the relationship; and how prioritizing the man's marital status disempowers the woman. These elements may be the same ones that characterize other kinds of forbidden sexual relationships. Although the particulars of any given forbidden relationship may be unique, the contours of them as a *category* may have similar characteristics.

If the status of one of the parties in a secret, sexual liaison is given priority, the relationship will be constructed to protect that person. Subsequently, that person will have greater power in the relationship and greater control over the relationship's construction and denouement. If no status of either party is given priority, the relationship is more likely to be power balanced. A primary example of this is an extramarital relationship between two married people. Because both parties are in equal need of protection and because both parties have the power that accrues from being married, the imbalances are minimized (Atwater, 1982; Lawson, forthcoming).

Marriage, I have argued, confers upon the married greater prestige, greater social-psychological and structural support, and, consequently, greater relationship power than singlehood confers upon the single. Although the effects of marital status are subtle and often masked by more glaring status differences such as gender and socioeconomic status, interactional consequences are real and significant. The status of being married grants an interactional edge to those who are married and elicits an interactional deference to the status from those who are not.

If being married confers as much interactional power as I propose it does, married women involved with single men should enjoy greater power in their liaisons than single women do with married men. Atwater's (1982; 1984) research on "the extramarital connection" of married women supports this claim. Married women enjoy considerable power in their relationships with single men—much more than single women do with married men. The status, married, enhances the gender status, female. The structural limitations of being married work for her, not against her. She has an "oversupply" of men, she is socially moored in a marriage, she can negotiate "emotional equality," she feels in control of the relationship, she is more likely to determine when and how to terminate the relationship than he is, and she has a social structural base to return to when the relationship ends (Atwater, 1984).

This is not to argue, however, that marital status completely overrides gender. We would expect an interplay between gender and marital status. For example, it is unlikely that a single man involved with a married woman would act submissively, put his life on hold, or do the heavy emotional work necessary to sustain the relationship. His gender, male, will have consequences for his experiences in liaison construction that further research would specify.

The research on single women/married men liaisons challenges the implicit assumption that gender is invariably the primary factor in the construction of male-female relationships. The research is consonant with the research agenda of contemporary gender sociology, to discover how gender is shaped in concrete social relationships and to determine its relative effects in different situations (Thorne, Kramarae, and Henley, 1983; Richardson, 1988; West and Zimmerman, 1987). The finding points to an area of analysis that has been overlooked by both gender and family sociologists, namely, "marital privilege" as a determinant and/or mediator of interactional power.

Finally, because we live in a complex, gesellschaft society, it can be argued that the need for secret, forbidden relationships has increased. Secondary relationships, homogenization, and instrumentality reduce the opportunities for individuation and personal trust. Secret relationships provide a harbor from the normative world where an apparently ideal relationship can be constructed and individuation and trust created.

But for whom is the harbor safe? Secret relationships protect the interests of those with the greater status and power—the married man (woman) rather than the single woman (man), the doctor rather than the patient, the adult rather than the child. The more impermeable the boundaries and the greater the status differential, the more likely the interests of the powerful will be met through the construction of secret relationships. Status differences are carried into the forbidden liaison, and rules are generated that protect the person with higher status. In a very profound sense, then, secret, forbidden, sexual relationships are no sociological surprise. They reinforce and perpetuate the interests of the powerful.

Note

1. This is a theoretical argument inductively produced and intended to generate additional empirical research on the topic.

References

Atwater, Lynn. 1982. *The Extramarital Connection: Sex, Intimacy, and Identity.* New York: Irvington.

———. 1984. "Gender and Norms in Extramarital Relationships." Paper presented to the National Council of Family Relations, San Francisco.

Berger, Peter, and Brigette Berger. 1975. *Sociology: A Biographical Approach.* New York: Basic Books.

Berger, Peter, and Helena Kellner. 1964. "Marriage and the Construction of Reality." *Diogenes* 46:1–25.

Blau, Peter M. 1964. *Exchange and Power in Social Life.* New York: Wiley.

Cook, Judith A. 1982. "The Adjustment of Parents Following the Death of a Child from a Terminal Illness." Ph.D. diss., Ohio State University.

Davis, Murray S. 1973. *Intimate Relations.* New York: Free Press.

De Rougemont, Denis. 1956. *Love in the Western World.* Princeton, NJ: Princeton University Press.

Diamond, Timothy. 1983. "Caring Work." *Contemporary Sociology* 13:556–58.

Eichler, Margrit. 1980. *The Double Standard: A Feminist Critique of Feminist Social Science.* New York: St. Martin's.

Gilligan, Carol. 1982. *In a Different Voice: Psychological Theory and Women's Development.* Cambridge, MA.: Harvard University Press.

Glaser, Barney G., and Anselm L. Strauss. 1967. *The Discovery of Grounded Theory: Strategies for Qualitative Research.* Chicago: Aldine.

Hochschild, Arlie Russell. 1983. *The Managed Heart: Commercialization of Human Feeling.* Berkeley: University of California Press.

Jourard, Sidney. 1971. *Self-Disclosure: An Experimental Analysis of the Transparent Self.* New York: Wiley-Interscience.

Karp, David A., and William C. Yoels. 1979. *Symbols, Selves, and Society.* New York: Harper and Row.

Koch, Michael. 1980. "Sexual Abuse in Children." *Adolescence* 15:643–48.

Lawson, Annette. Forthcoming. *Adultery.* New York: Basic Books.

Lester, Marilyn. 1979. "Making Music Together: A Sociological Formulation of Intimate Encounters between Males and Females." Presented at the American Sociological Association Meetings, Boston.

Lorenz, Konrad. 1966. *On Aggression.* New York: Harcourt, Brace and World.

Mcallist, Hunter A., and Norman J. Bregman. 1983. "Self-Disclosure and Liking: An Integration-Theory Approach." *Journal of Personality* 51:202–7.

MacKinnon, Catherine. 1979. *Sexual Harassment of Working Women.* New Haven, CT: Yale University Press.

Reiss, Ira, R. E. Anderson, and G. C. Sponaugle. 1980. "A Multivariate Model of Determinants of Extramarital Permissiveness." *Journal of Marriage and the Family* 42:395–411.

Reskin, Barbara, and Heidi I. Hartmann. 1986. *Women's Work and Men's Work: Sex Segregation on the Job.* Washington, DC: National Academy Press.

Reynolds, Larry T. 1987. *Interactionism: Exposition and Critique.* Dix Hills, NY: General Hall.

Richardson, Laurel [Walum]. 1979. "The 'Other Woman': The End of the Long Affair." *Alternative Lifestyles* 2:397–414.

———. 1985. *The New Other Woman: Contemporary Single Women in Affairs with Married Men.* New York: Free Press.

———. 1986. "Another World." *Psychology Today.* February: pp. 22–27.

———. 1988. *The Dynamics of Sex and Gender: A Sociological Perspective,* 3rd rev. ed. New York: Harper and Row.

Rubin, Zick, 1970. "Measurement of Romantic Love." *Journal of Personality and Social Psychology* 16:265–73.

———. 1974. "Lovers and Other Strangers: The Development of Intimacy in Encounters and Relationships." *American Scientist* 62:182–90.

Russell, Diana E. H. 1986. *The Secret Trauma: Incest in the Lives of Girls and Women.* New York: Basic Books.

Sattell, Jack W. 1983. "Men, Inexpressiveness, and Power." Pp. 242–46 in *Feminist Frontiers,* edited by Laurel Richardson and Verta Taylor. New York: Random House.

Simmel, Georg. [1902–03; 1908; 1917] 1950. *The Sociology of Georg Simmel.* Translated by Kurt H. Wolfe. New York: Free Press.

Stein, Peter J. 1981. "Understanding Single Adulthood." Pp. 9–21 in *Single Life: Unmarried Adults in Social Context,* edited by Peter J. Stein. New York: St. Martin's.

Thorne, Barrie, Cheris Kramarae, and Nancy Henley. 1983. "Language, Gender, and Society: Opening a Second Decade of Research." Pp. 7–24 in *Language, Gender, and Society,* edited by Barrie Thorne, Cheris Kramarae, and Nancy Henley. Rowley, MA: Newbury House.

Waller, Willard. 1938. *The Family: A Dynamic Interpretation.* Hinsdale, IL: Dryden Press.

West, Candace, and Don H. Zimmerman. 1987. "Doing Gender." *Gender and Society* 2:125–51.

10

Intimate Relationships and the Creation of Sexuality

PHILIP BLUMSTEIN
PEPPER SCHWARTZ

The study of human sexuality has been dominated by the presumption that male and female behavior is biologically programmed, and much research has concerned itself with understanding what these programs are and to what extent biological predispositions are modified by social forces. Another prominent assumption posits that each individual has a *true* sexual core self which does not change. Some researchers emphasize that this self emerges over time, through a process of socialization, while others stress that desires are genetic and/or hormonal in origin, but both perspectives share a belief in the immutable core disposition.

The combined force of these two research traditions in the study of human sexuality has almost dismissed from serious scholarly discussion what we believe to be the true nature of human sexuality: that sexuality is situational and changeable, modified by day-to-day circumstances throughout the life course. In our perspective there are few absolute differences between male and female sexuality. What differences we observed are primarily the result of the different social organization of women's and men's lives in various cultural contexts. "Essentialist" theories, that is, theories which assume immutable selves, ignore data which would disturb the assumption. One startling example of the field's willingness to be misled is the unfortunate interpretation of the ground-breaking Kinsey studies and the misuse of the Kinsey heterosexuality/homosexuality scale (Kinsey, Pomeroy, & Martin, 1948; Kinsey, Pomeroy, Martin, & Gebhard, 1953). In this scale, Kinsey and his colleagues categorized individuals not as heterosexual versus homosexual, but on a continuum between exclusively heterosexual and exclusively homosexual. We would like

---

We would like to thank Mary Rogers Gillmore, Judith A. Howard, and Barbara Risman for their helpful comments on an earlier draft of this paper. Blumstein, P., and Schwartz, P., "Intimate Relationships and the Creation of Sexuality," in *Homosexuality/Heterosexuality: Concepts of Sexual Orientation,* D. P. McWhirter, S. A. Sanders, J. M. Reinisch, Eds. (New York: Oxford University Press), to be published in 1989 by Oxford University Press. Reprinted by permission of the Kinsey Institute for Research, Indiana University.

to reexamine the scale, using it to direct research away from essentialist reifications and more in the direction we believe Kinsey himself would have preferred: toward a kinetic model of sexual desire and away from a static and categorical model.

Unfortunately when the Kinsey group constructed the scale of zero to six, they unintentionally endorsed and extended essentialist ways of thinking by establishing a typology allowing for seven kinds of sexual beings instead of only two. After Kinsey there were such people as *Kinsey 4s* instead of simply heterosexuals and homosexuals. While the seven-point scale does enormously more justice to the range and subtlety of human sexuality, in its common usage it does not do justice to Kinsey's own belief in the changeability and plasticity of sexual behavior. Because researchers have inevitably used Kinsey's scale as a shorthand system of sexual identification, they have reified the person as a sexual type. His or her "real" sexuality is discovered and seen as an essence that has been uncovered. It is the final summation of the person's sexual behavior and "psychic reactions."

Such essentialist thinking allows one to ignore concrete behaviors in assigning people to sexual categories. Even the verbal descriptions made by respondents and patients of their *own* behavior and feeling states may be swept aside in an essentialist judgment. As Katz (1975, p. 1371) has written on this general subject, "Persons conceive of essences as inherent qualities which may be manifested, reflected, indicated, or represented by, but do not exist in, conduct. . . . [E]ssences exist independent of observable behavior." Essentialism also allows one to capture the actor with one great biographical sweep, for example, "She is a homosexual," or "He is a bisexual." The Kinsey scale, as it is frequently used to aggregate behavior over a finite length of time or even over a lifetime, encourages the categorization of an actor's biography; for example, "She is a Kinsey 3."

The application of the Kinsey scale is hardly unique in this respect. Essentialism has dominated both lay and professional thinking about sexuality. Sexuality has been perceived as emanating from a core or innate *desire* that directs an individual's sex life. Before Kinsey, this desire had to be either homosexual or heterosexual; after Kinsey this desire could be ambisexual. But in either case, it originated in constitutional factors or in the person's early experience and was a fixed part of the person. This desire has been seen as so powerful that even though behavior might vary over a lifetime, many psychotherapists and sex researchers have continued to believe in the existence of a basic predisposition reflecting the true nature of each individual's sexuality.

We do not deny that there are men and women who come to a therapist with unacted-upon homosexual desires which they believe reflect their true sexual selves. Nor do we deny that most Americans who call themselves heterosexual or homosexual feel strongly that their sexuality is highly channeled. They feel that they have only *categorical desire,* that is, desire for people of only one specific gender.[1] But the commonly held belief in the generality of this pattern has not been challenged to see if it reflects a truly universal experience. And indeed there is evidence to call that belief into question (Blumstein & Schwartz, 1976a; 1976b).

It is our position that it is not primarily categorical desire that determines whether people's sex partners are male or female. Fundamental categorical desire may not even exist. Rather it is culture that creates understandings about how people are sexual and thus determines whether people will be able to have only one sexual focus, to eroticize both sexes, or to experience categorical desire for one sex at one point of their life and categorical desire for the other sex at another point of their life (Herdt, 1981). In our society, because virtually everyone partakes of the dominant essentialist theory of sexuality, large numbers of people experience categorical sexual desire and see it as determining their sexual life. But it is critical not to confuse this particular cultural pattern with scientific confirmation that there is a core sexual orientation within every human being. In our society there are also people whose fundamental sexual desire seems to be produced within the context of a relationship, rather than by an abstract preference for women or men, or whose sense of sexual self never becomes consistently organized. The essentialist understanding of sexuality skirts questions of what experiences and understandings lead to the behaviors that create a sense of self. Essentialism ignores the *process* of the creation of a sense of self.[2]

But it is not only the essentialist nature of the Kinsey scale to which we object. The Kinsey scale, particularly as it is presently used in lax scientific discourse, is limited because it was based on a single cultural model of sexuality. The Kinsey group inadvertently took the dominant model of middle-class male sexuality as a guide for understanding human sexual behavior, when other models, also cultural, but perhaps ultimately more productive, could have been utilized. In the male model, behavior provides the critical data used to categorize core sexual selves. This is because in the modern Western world, men and their observers have used behavior as the indicator of internal psychic processes. This has been particularly true in the analysis of homosexuality because homosexual behavior so violates cultural proscriptions that it has been assumed that such behavior must surely demonstrate an irrepressible core sexual self. Thus, once homosexual acts were discussed scientifically, the use of behavior as an indicator of an individual's true sexuality became more important.[3] Oddly enough, however, homosexual acts tend to be given greater weight than any heterosexual acts which the individual might also perform. In most cases, it is assumed that "psychic reaction" is the crucial factor to resolve any empirical oddities. If psychic arousal is more dramatic in homosexual relations, then a homosexual core self is adduced. How cross-situationally consistent such psychic arousal might be, however, is seldom contemplated.

The cross-cultural record amply suggests that the essentialist model of human sexuality has far from universal fit. Indeed one does not need a cross-cultural perspective; if one looks at the relatively ignored facts of modern Western female sexuality, the essentialist model's inadequacies become clear. As we have observed elsewhere (Blumstein & Schwartz, 1976a; 1977), female sexuality in our culture does not justify an essentialist position. Women are less likely than men to view their sexual acts as a revelation of their "true sexual self," and female sexual choice seems to be based as much on situational constraints as on categorical desire. Desire seems to be aroused frequently by emotional intimacy rather than by abstract erotic taste.

Our sociological vision of sexuality is far different from the essentialist approach of many other sex researchers. Our thesis is simply that desire is created by its cultural context. Sexuality emerges from the circumstances and meanings available to individuals; it is a product of socialization, opportunity, and interpretation. For example, male sexuality in our culture-view is shaped by the scripts boys are offered almost from birth, by the cultural lessons they learn throughout the life course, among them the belief in a sometimes overpowering male sex drive and the belief that men have immutable sexual needs which are manifest over and above individual attempts at repression.

Our approach leads to a different question than the one posed by essentialists. As sociologists we do not wish to proliferate sexual categories, but rather ask, "What circumstances create the possibility for sexual behavior—either homosexual or heterosexual?" This question cannot be approached fruitfully when one is relying on the seven-point Kinsey scale, since concrete behaviors are lost in the data aggregation process used in applying the scale to people's lives.

Within a specific cultural setting there are many factors which facilitate or deter sexual behavior, both homosexual and heterosexual. The two key factors, which we shall concentrate on in this paper, are (1) the *gender roles* culturally available, and (2) the *social organization of opportunities*.

Biological sex is constrained and directed by the roles society offers men and women. Expectations of role performance organize male and female sexuality. Thus in order to understand human sexual behavior and the meaning of that behavior to people, it is crucial to know what members of each sex have learned is appropriate to feel and to do, and what sanctions exist for inadequate or noncompliant role performance.

While there is still much to be understood about the subtle relationship between sexuality and gender, we are substantially more ignorant about the second factor, the social organization of opportunity. By this we mean how society does or does not offer circumstances that permit certain behaviors to occur. These circumstances may be as concrete as a woman being unable to have heterosexual experience because her interactions with men are always chaperoned, or as subtle as her being unable to have sexual relations outside of her marriage because she is a suburban housewife who, in the course of her typical day, never finds herself in the company of men. Even a wife who is propositioned may not have a real opportunity if the cost of giving in to temptation is ostracism from her community, expulsion from her marriage, and a future of being unacceptable to any other loving partner. Similarly, a boy who goes to all-male schools will have different sexual opportunities than one who is never in an all-male adolescent peer group, and a salesman who travels constantly is more likely to have extramarital temptations than a man who never leaves his small hometown.

Opportunity is also shaped in a less objective fashion by the meanings the culture makes available. A wife may not be able to be sexually responsive even if she is alone with a man other than her husband, if she has learned that a healthy woman has little sexual appetite and that what appetite she has can only be aroused in the context of her role as wife and companion to her husband. A man may have difficulty experiencing homosexual desire in himself if he has been taught that such attractions do not exist in typical heterosexually active men.

From these examples it should be clear that we are not describing forces that affect individuals idiosyncratically, but rather we are focusing on the way society organizes social life. This does not mean that everyone acts according to a single cultural mandate. Sometimes social directives are in flux or they are actually in conflict with one another and leave room for individual choice. For example, when women in large numbers were first allowed a college education, there was no deliberate social plan to make them men's equals, nor certainly for them to have sexual appetites resembling men's. The same can be said of the development of safe and effective contraceptive technologies. The latent consequence of men and women having more similar lives, however, has been that attitudes and norms which had functioned well to maintain very different sex lives for women and men were no longer able to sustain their potency and legitimacy.

We would argue that understanding the dynamics of gender roles and social opportunities is a more fruitful approach to the question of why sexual behavior occurs and under what circumstances sexual identities are adopted than is the essentialist paradigm. We do not in this paper perform the larger sociological task of developing a theory of how social opportunities arise in sexual life. Rather we proceed from the idea that social opportunities exist, and examine one type of opportunity structure in depth in order to show the utility of the concept. The source of opportunities we focus on here is intimate relationships, which we see as profoundly important in determining what behaviors will take place.

As an immediate caveat, we must say that in our culture this is truer for women than for men. If Kinsey had used female sexuality as a model, his scale might have been conceptualized not so much in terms of accumulated acts and psychic preoccupations but rather in terms of intensity and frequency of love relationships, some of which might have only incidental, overt erotic components.

Women have been so effectively socialized to link love and attachment, love and sex, that eroticization is more often a consequence of emotional attraction than the trigger for the involvement. In cases where eroticization comes first, it is unlikely to continue without a relationship context; if the attraction is powerful, a relationship may have to be invented in order to sustain and justify continuing the liaison.

Whether this attraction process is the result of women's relatively low position in the social structure (de Beauvoir, 1953), or whether it is a response to cultural themes governing female sexuality (Laws & Schwartz, 1977), or whether women's erotic cues are biologically different from men's (Symons, 1979; van den Berghe, 1979), is a large question; and we are unable to put it to rest in this paper. We can, however, show that in our culture women's sexuality is organized by other than physical cues. For modern Western women, the recognition of love or admiration or the pleasure in companionship or deep friendship most often leads to erotic attraction and response. While women are not incapable of seeking sex for its own sake, this pattern of sexual behavior is relatively rare among them (Blumstein & Schwartz, 1983). Our research indicates that it is overwhelmingly more common for the relationship (or the desire for such a relationship) to establish itself first.

This pattern is less common among men in our culture. While homosexual and heterosexual erotic feelings can develop in an intimate relationship, it is much more common for a man to have sexual attractions (as early as adolescence) to a number of specific persons (some or all of whom may be total strangers), or to a generalized other, or to fantasized persons. If an opportunity exists, and any personal or cultural interdictions can be overcome, he may seek to realize his erotic preferences in one or more concrete sexual contacts. An intimate or committed relationship is not necessary for excitation, and in some cases may even be counterproductive to sexual arousal. Nonetheless most men do form intimate relationships, and this leads us to ask what is the relevance of such relationships for their subsequent sexual behavior and self-identification?

This is a complex question since in some cases the relationship, for example, marriage to a woman, seems to organize the man's sexual behavior and identity, while in other cases, such as the self-defined homosexual man who is married to a woman, it is less central. The husband who has sexual experiences with other men may feel torn, dishonest, and fearful of exposure, but frequently he also feels a need to have a family and an approved social identity (H. Ross, 1971; M. Ross, 1983). He also finds the attraction of conventionality more compelling than the opportunity to have a less compromised homosexual sex life. A different but related example is a man with a previously exclusively homosexual life who decides that heterosexual marriage is important to him and that his homosexuality is too costly. We interviewed such a man, who decided to learn how, in his words, to "be heterosexual" in order to facilitate having children and, as he saw it, stability and respectability. While we cannot say that twenty years after this decision he would experience no residual homosexual desire, we can certainly claim that his attachment to a heterosexual relationship changed his behavior and, we believe, his self-identification.

How it is possible for men such as these to organize their lives in these ways is a question that needs and deserves further research. There is, however, some relevant information in the anthropological and historical records on the interaction of appetites, intimate relationships, and sexual self-identity. It is far from culturally universal to expect intimate relationships to be the major or sole outlet for the expression of sexual feelings or appetites. The modern Western desire for sexual, emotional, and lifestyle coherence is probably a rare accommodation. In the ancient world, for example, a gentleman was expected to marry and father children, regardless of his attraction to males; and even in modern times, there are numerous examples of homosexual behavior occurring in the private lives of married men (Humphreys, 1970; H. Ross, 1971; M. Ross, 1983). This homosexual behavior has not exempted men from performing the male role of their time.

An interesting question is whether the separation of family and sexuality has been possible because of innate sexual flexibility or because men are socialized to be able to separate sexual, loving, and obligation impulses so that they can accomplish sex within whatever format is necessary. Or has this ability led to the existence of dual lives so that the appetite could be fulfilled without threatening home and family? Thus, homosexual behavior could occur without homosexual self-identification, thereby inhibiting the development of an exclusively homosexual lifestyle.

An important question is why is there now such great emphasis on shaping one's life on the basis of one's intimate relationships. Perhaps the same social forces that helped create a bond between love and family and sex for women are starting to apply to men as well. Moreover, recent cultural themes of individual fulfillment and personal growth encourage and shape sexuality by giving people the impression that any disjunction between parts of the self is unhealthy and ultimately an inappropriate way to live. In addition, the ability to identify oneself as a homosexual man or lesbian and be viewed as gay by friends and acquaintances probably diminishes ability to identify with or practice heterosexual desire. The predominance of the essentialist paradigm leads men and women to create a coherent package of behavior, identity, and community, and they are thus more motivated to form same-sex relationships.

While sex role differences are a critical factor in understanding the impact of intimate relationships on sexuality, it is also important to consider the type of relationship. Sexuality is different in marriage as compared to heterosexual cohabitation, and opposite-sex relationships have a different sexual dynamic from same-sex relationships (Blumstein & Schwartz, 1983). An individual's sense of self is in part created by the relationships she or he is in, and most individuals find a transition that might occur, that is, from cohabitation to marriage or from an opposite-sex to a same-sex partner, has an enormous impact on their identity. For example, a man whom we interviewed had married his childhood sweetheart and had what he considered a happy, fulfilling, and monogamous marital sex life until his wife died unexpectedly. This man subsequently, in his words, "became in touch with" early homoerotic feelings and entered into a relationship with a man. He describes himself as having been "obsessed" with his new partner, but also feels that he had been equally taken with his wife. While this man could be labeled as a Kinsey 3, or for that matter as a Kinsey 0 who changed to a Kinsey 6, we argue that it would be more fruitful to look at the circumstances that shaped his sexuality, courtships, marriage, and homosexual relationship. One might also want to know why this man, unlike most men in his society, was sexually galvanized by a tender relationship, rather than by independent erotic desire.

Another example is the case of a woman, unhappily married for twenty-three years, who felt a profound absence of a real "soulmate." She met a woman at her son's college graduation ceremony, and, over a long period of time, the two women gradually fell in love and left their husbands. Not only did the respondent's sense of self change, but so did her sexual habits and desires. Again, instead of trying to determine who the "real person" is, we think it more productive to discover how changing relationships produced some new forms of behavior.

All of this would be theoretically trivial if we were only talking about individual histories. What makes these stories more compelling to a social scientist is that they are reflections of twentieth-century Western opportunities. The manner in which the intimate relationships are conducted is a cultural and historical phenomenon, which, when studied in the aggregate, can show us how sexuality is created.

The organization of opportunity in modern life is formed by the instability of marriage, a high remarriage rate, the ability to survive as an independent unmarried person, and the possibility of meeting eligible sex partners of either sex in institutions that have developed expressly for the purpose of bringing people together. The scenarios described in this paper are uniquely twentieth-century stories and would not have been possible, for example, in nineteenth-century America. There would have been few opportunities for divorce, little ability to live a single or private life, and no conceptualization of the importance of sexual fulfillment or entry into a gay lifestyle. In fact *lifestyle* is a uniquely modern concept. Lifestyle incorporates the notion of sexual choice, and choice has simply not existed for most people in most historical periods. Furthermore, how people behaved within marriage or with a same-sex partner would have been entirely different from the way they would act today. A same-sex relationship in the nineteenth century would probably not be perceived as an appropriate public lifetime commitment.[4]

We are not historians and cannot do justice to the meanings and constructions of everyday sexuality in periods other than our own. We have, however, gathered data in the 1970s and 1980s which show how sexuality is shaped by the available relationship scripts. Our observations are based on two pieces of research: (1) the study of the antecedents of sexual identity and bisexuality, based on a sample of 150 interviews (Blumstein & Schwartz, 1976a; 1976b; 1977); and (2) the study of same-sex and opposite-sex couples, involving questionnaire, interview, and observational data, the overall sample representing approximately 1000 male homosexual couples, 800 lesbian couples, 3600 heterosexual marriages, and 650 heterosexual cohabitation relationships (Blumstein & Schwartz, 1983).

Two areas of couples' sexual lives—sexual frequency and monogamy—are presented to illustrate the contention that intimate relationships shape sexuality.

Sexual Frequency

In all four groups of couples, frequency declines with the duration of the relationship (see Table 1). From this we infer that there is some habituation effect in all kinds of couples that serves to reduce sexual appetite.[5] Within heterosexual couples, this pattern varies by the simple fact of whether or not the pair is legally married. People who live together without marriage are surely different from those who marry, and these differences may in some measure account for the differences in sexual frequency. But they probably do not account entirely for the differences. Rather, we suggest, it is the differences between marital and nonmarital heterosexual relationships themselves that create different opportunities and different motivations for sexual expression.

When we look at the three groups in our study which include women, we notice that those in relationships with men (both married and unmarried) have a greater sexual frequency than those in relationships with other women. We also note that the sexual frequencies in male homosexual relationships come closer to the heterosexual frequencies. The probable reason for these differences in sexual profiles is that men in our culture are allowed and encouraged to desire and demand more sex. They have fewer costs for experiencing or acting on sexual desires (that is, no reduced marketability, no fear of becoming pregnant), and therefore they establish a fairly high sexual frequency in both heterosexual and homosexual relationships. We do not think women in heterosexual relationships have essentially different sexual appetites from women in lesbian relationships, since both groups of women have had similar sexual socialization and have learned similar inhibitions. If the heterosexual women in our study were suddenly put into a same-sex relationship, their sexual frequency would probably resemble lesbians' sexual frequency. The reduction in sexual frequency would occur because the norms of lesbian relationships are different from those of heterosexual relationships and because two women bring different cultural scripts to a sexual relationship than a man and a woman.[6]

Table 1 *Couples Reporting Sex Three Times a Week or More*

Years Living Together	Married Couples	Cohabiting Couples	Male Couples	Female Couples
2 or less	45% (344)	61% (349)	67% (309)	33% (357)
Between 2 and 10	27% (1505)	38% (288)	32% (472)	7% (350)
10 or more	18% (1754)	——	11% (169)	1% (61)

Note: Numbers in parentheses are the number of couples on which the percentages are based. Very few of the cohabitors were together more than ten years.

In our study, men initiated sex more than women in opposite-sex relationships.[7] Men are assigned this role, and women in our society are taught to be receptive rather than aggressive in sexual matters.[8] It makes sense, then, that in lesbian couples, where both partners have experienced female sexual socialization, there would be a mutual reluctance to take the sexual lead. Such inheritance of social conditioning might contribute to lesbians' having an overall lower initiation rate than other couples and hence a lower rate of sexual activity.

Their reluctance to initiate, however, does not simply stem from the internalization of sexual prohibitions directed at women. Additionally, themes in some lesbian subcultures stigmatize sexual aggressiveness as "powerplays" and male-type sexuality, and place a lower premium on genital sexuality, with a corresponding emphasis on other forms of physical intimacy. Moreover, higher standards of relationship satisfaction are demanded in order to legitimate sexual intimacy. Relationship dynamics, rather than essential core sexuality, orient the individual's sexual frequency and sexual pattern.

The internal dynamics of the relationship can affect sexual experience in subtle ways. For example, among all four of the groups of couples in our study, the greater power one partner has, the more likely he or she is to refuse a sexual overture (Blumstein & Schwartz, 1983, pp. 219–221). And among the women in heterosexual couples, the more power they have, the less likely the couple's intercourse is to be restricted to the male prone–female supine position (Blumstein & Schwartz, 1983, pp. 229–230).

On the basis of these findings, and with every indication that there will be greater equality between the sexes in the future, one might hypothesize that the sexual patterns of heterosexual couples will change in response to a more liberated female sexuality. In some couples frequency may increase and in others it may decrease, but in either event these changes will be responses to the structure of the relationship between the partners, not to some inherent capacity of women.

Monogamy

The rules of monogamous conduct provide insight into how male sexuality is affected by intimate relationships. With the exception of the male homosexual couples, the majority of each group of couples feels that the rules of monogamous conduct are a cornerstone of the relationship and should not be broken.[9] Homosexual men, while presently intimidated by the risk of contracting AIDS, nonetheless have a long history of separating sexual desire from intimacy and love, and have evolved a norm of having relationships that allow either occasional or a great deal of sex with persons other than one's partner.

Heterosexual men, both married and cohabiting, have frequently mentioned in our interviews that they would like greater permission for "recreational" sex in their relationships, but the data show that they tend not to pursue it (see Table 2). If these men were in a same-sex relationship, they would have a higher rate of nonmonogamy because the rules of acceptability would be altered.[10] Thus, an element of their sexuality is constructed by their female partner's wishes and by the norms that are shaped by the institution of marriage. Compliance to the norm is, of course, not perfect: many husbands do have extramarital sex, and sex outside their relationship is even more common among male cohabitors. The latter face less stringent guidelines within their relationship and are merely asked to comply with

Table 2 *Respondents Reporting at Least One Nonmonogamous Instance in the Previous Year*

Husbands	11%	(1510)
Wives	9%	(1510)
Male cohabitors	25%	(288)
Female cohabitors	22%	(288)
Homosexual males	79%	(943)
Lesbians	19%	(706)

Note: Numbers in parentheses are the number of respondents on which the percentages are based. Respondents are partners in couples who have lived together between two and ten years.

their partner's wishes rather than with the directives of marital vows. Looking at the difference between married men's and cohabiting men's extrarelationship sex tells us how much the norms of marriage organize sexuality.

This cursory look at sexual expression in intimate relationships is not intended as more than an illustration of the analytic mileage to be gained by conceptualizing sex within the context of social circumstances. Even by looking at relatively crude survey data we can see that sexual behavior is created by relationship expectations and traditions rather than by sexual essences. If we were to look more microscopically within relationships we could see the subtle ways in which intimate interaction affects participants. We could see how friends, neighborhoods, community, law, and other constraints affect sexual conduct. If research on sexuality were to proceed in this direction, if more attention were paid to opportunity structure—of which intimate relationships are but one—we would uncover the social construction of sexuality.

In sum, we look forward to research where situational variables and cultural meanings are seen as the foundation of sexuality. But new research needs to avoid androcentrism so that opportunity structures are not chosen because of their relevance only to men's lives. A useful approach will take into account individual biography without producing a static and individualistic explanation of sexuality. Sexuality is best comprehended by noting and understanding the *processes* which encourage the occurrence of acts and the reason for their discontinuance. We should focus on the act, behaving not as accountants tabulating frequencies, but as behavioral scientists looking at the meaning of the act for the actors. If we continue as we have in the past, focusing on the individual, rather than on the social context that creates his or her behavior, we may end up with interesting biographies but relatively little ability for further prediction or theory construction. We then run the risk of thinking we understand something merely because we have given it a number on a scale.

Notes

1. We would also argue that for most members of contemporary Western society, because of the hegemony of sexual essentialism, once an individual develops a sexual identity, it funnels much of his or her social experience into erotic and nonerotic circumstances which continually reinforce a subjective sense of categorical desire.

2. On the social construction of sexuality, see, among others, Gagnon and Simon (1973), McIntosh (1968), Plummer (1975), and Weinberg (1978; 1983).

3. The Kinsey scale was originally aimed at both behavior and "psychic reactions." The inclusion of the latter construct implicitly acknowledged ways in which purely behavioral tabulations could mislead. However, the conceptual and measurement problems associated with psychic reactions have remained largely unresolved.

4. It is important to note that homosexual behavior leads to the existence of gay male and lesbian couple relationships only under extremely rare historical and cultural circumstances. This means that most homosexuality occurs in very different contexts than much (we do not know how much) heterosexuality. This fact, as obvious as it is, has important implications. Most sensible researchers would be wary of equating heterosexual intercourse between two strangers (for example, a man with a female prostitute) with that in a twenty-five-year marriage. Neither situation reflects an "essence of heterosexuality." Researchers have been less sensitive in the case of homosexual behavior, as though the slogan were "sodomy is sodomy is sodomy. . . ." It is critical to see human sexual behavior as context embedded rather than as a simple expression of the underlying sexuality of the individual.

5. Two other interpretations of these data come immediately to mind. First is the argument that physical aging, which is correlated with relationship duration, is the real causal factor. Multivariate statistical analyses allowed an evaluation of the aging effects net of duration and the duration effects net of aging. Based on these analyses we concluded that physical aging and habituation independently reduce sexual frequency. The other interpretation to consider is that couples with relatively low sexual frequency have greater likelihood of longevity. While we have no direct empirical test of this causal hypothesis, it seems implausible in light of substantial positive correlations between sexual frequency and sexual happiness and substantial negative correlations between sexual happiness and relationship durability.

6. Another way of looking at these data is to imagine a woman living in a heterosexual relationship for ten years followed by a homosexual relationship of the same duration. In the typical case, the total number of sexual acts in the heterosexual relationship would be much greater than the total number of acts within the lesbian relationship. Ought we label such a woman a Kinsey 3 because she was in two ten-year relationships. Or would she be a Kinsey 1 because her sexual activity was more frequent in the heterosexual union? Or would we label her a Kinsey 5 or 6 because of her most recent sexual life, especially if asserted that this relationship was permanent? These data suggest caution in the use of a scale that does not take into account the context and changing meaning of people's emotional and sexual lives.

7. Fifty-one percent of husbands say they initiate sex more than their wives as compared to 16 percent who say the reverse pattern holds true; the remainder say initiation is equal (N = 3612). While the wives are not in perfect agreement with their husbands, they are very close (48 percent and 12 percent, N = 3616). Thirty-nine percent of male cohabitors say they initiate more and 19 percent say their female partner initiates more (N = 646). The female percentages are 39 and 15 percent (N = 648).

8. Sociobiologists have argued that this difference is a reflection of the different reproductive strategies of men and women. Indeed Symons (1979) has applied this argument to the sexual behavior of lesbians. His discussion, however, does not adequately deal with the influence of cultural learning.

9. We asked respondents how important they felt it is that they themselves be monogamous. The percentages saying it is important are husbands, 75 percent (N = 3635); wives, 84 percent (N = 3640); male cohabitors, 62 percent (N = 650); female cohabitors, 70 percent (N = 650); lesbians, 71 percent (N = 1559); and male homosexuals, 36 percent (N = 1924).

10. It should be noted that the percentages in Table 2 are based on data gathered just before the AIDS crisis began to receive widespread attention in the gay community.

References

Blumstein, P., & Schwartz, P. (1976a). Bisexuality in women. *Archives of Sexual Behavior* 5:171–181.

———. (1976b). Bisexuality in men. *Urban Life* 5:339–358.

———. (1977) Bisexuality: Some social psychological issues. *Journal of Social Issues* 33(2):30–45.

———. (1983). *American couples: Money, work, and sex.* New York: William Morrow.

de Beauvoir, S. (1953). *The second sex.* New York: Knopf.

Gagnon, J. H., & Simon, W. (1973). *Sexual conduct: The social sources of human sexuality.* Chicago: Aldine.

Herdt, G. H. (1981). *Guardians of the flutes: Idioms of masculinity.* New York: McGraw-Hill.

Humphreys, L. (1970). *Tearoom trade: Impersonal sex in public places.* Chicago: Aldine.

Katz, J. (1975). Essences as moral identities: Verifiability and responsibility in imputations of deviance and charisma. *American Journal of Sociology,* 80:1369–1390.

Kinsey, A. C.; Pomeroy, W. B.; & Martin, C. E. (1948). *Sexual behavior in the human male.* Philadelphia: W. B. Saunders.

Kinsey, A. C.; Pomeroy, W. B.; Martin, C. E.; & Gebhard, P. H. (1953). *Sexual behavior in the human female.* Philadelphia: W. B. Saunders.

Laws, J. L., & Schwartz, P. (1977). *Sexual scripts: The social construction of female sexuality.* Hinsdale, Ill.: Dryden Press.

McIntosh, M. (1968). The homosexual role. *Social Problems* 16:182–192.

Plummer, K. (1975). *Sexual stigma: An interactionist account.* London: Routledge & Kegan Paul.

Ross, H. L. (1971). Modes and adjustments of married homosexuals. *Social Problems* 18:385–393.

Ross, M. W. (1983). *The married homosexual man.* London: Routledge & Kegan Paul.

Symons, D. (1979). *The evolution of human sexuality.* New York: Oxford University Press.

van den Berghe, P. L. (1979). *Human family systems: An evolutionary view.* New York: Elsevier.

Weinberg, T. S. (1978). On "doing" and "being" gay: Sexual behavior and homosexual male self-identity. *Journal of Homosexuality* 4:143–156.

———. (1983). *Gay men, gay selves: The social construction of homosexual identities.* New York: Irvington.

Part Three

Becoming a Parent: Options and Realities

Part Three focuses on the social context that affects decisions about parenthood or childlessness. Although we cannot possibly cover every possible option, we try to highlight a variety of decisions people may face today. The first essay focuses on the earliest decision, whether or not to carry a pregnancy to term. The next deals with infancy and the differential impact babies have on mothers and fathers in two-parent families. The last two chapters focus on single parents.

Zimmerman's essay on abortion decisions explores when abortion is perceived as a crisis. Although previous work suggests that personality disorders may explain why some women experience abortion as a crisis, Zimmerman's interviews with women terminating a pregnancy suggest instead that the present and anticipated circumstances of a woman's life are the best predictors of whether her abortion experience is traumatic. When a woman has clear future goals, which an unplanned pregnancy would disrupt, and at least some supportive relationship, an abortion is not usually experienced as a crisis. But with no future plans or supportive relationships, abortion becomes a much more difficult event. Zimmerman suggests this personal decision, whether or not to carry a pregnancy to term, is affected quite dramatically by the social circumstances of a woman's life.

LaRossa and LaRossa write about those couples who decide to have a child and how they experience the first year of life. An infant forces parents to be on call continuously, and this reduces personal free time. Indepth interviews conducted by the authors suggest that this leaves mothers and fathers facing a zero-sum game where one "wins" the valued resource of free time only if the other one "loses." The authors find that mothers lose most often. Rather than rely on theories of maternal instinct or the psychologically based need to "mother," LaRossa and LaRossa find that sociological variables—social time, power, commitment, and ideology—do a good job of explaining the disproportionate quantity of child care performed by women.

Finally, both Risman and Fassinger focus on how the experience of parenting shapes behavior. Risman's research on single fathers suggests that despite their lack of training as primary caretakers, these fathers believe they fulfill the role quite capably. Fassinger's interviews with single parents provide considerably more detail to our understanding of single parents. She finds that experience during marriage is a better predictor of the capability to head a household alone than the parent's gender. Those men who believed themselves to be the head of the household while married move smoothly into single parenthood, while those men used to a more egalitarian partner had considerably more trouble adapting to heading a household alone. Women from traditional marriages had more trouble with single parenthood than those who had more egalitarian or even wife-dominated marital histories. Both studies of single parents suggest that experiences during adulthood are crucial for explaining the parenting behaviors of men and women.

All four of these chapters identify different microstructural variables that may affect parents. For example, Zimmerman discusses how close supportive relationships impact the experience of abortion decisions. LaRossa and LaRossa identify ideology and male/female status differentials as variables that promote female responsibility for child care. Risman focuses on how the experience of child rearing and the expectations of others that children need primary caretakers help create male "mothers." Finally, Fassinger finds that previous marital experience can either help or hinder the ability to head a household alone. All these authors support our thesis: many of the aparent sex differences in parenting are a result of social context rather than the internalized femininity of mothers.

11

Experiencing Abortion as a Crisis: The Impact of Social Context

MARY ZIMMERMAN

Abortions in the United States usually occur as very personal and private events, especially when compared to most other medical procedures. Though there are millions of women in U.S. society who have had them, the fact that abortions are so common does not appear to have completely legitimated them. The experience remains one typically enacted with a certain degree of discretion and secrecy. If a woman has an abortion she seldom reveals it to anyone but the most intimate confidantes (Zimmerman, 1977). The relative isolation of abortion situations undoubtedly reflects a reaction to the intense public debate over the morality of abortion and an attempt among abortion recipients to protect themselves from possible negative feedback. But our cultural tendency to view abortion as a private and personal experience is not just a product of its being socially circumscribed to avoid stigma. There also appear to be widely held assumptions about how abortions are experienced emotionally—and why. Women's reactions are typically viewed as highly individualistic, primarily a product of personal attitudes, values, and a unique psychological profile. Thus, a traumatic abortion might be explained in terms of a strong religious upbringing, great love of children, or psychological instability.

Research on abortion experience in the social and behavioral sciences has tended to perpetuate these lay assumptions. Abortion experience has been studied almost exclusively as an individual phenomenon. The focus has been on the abortion recipient, and research questions have dealt with "internal" psychological parameters, especially the possibility of abnormal personality traits. Some studies have also considered demographic characteristics such as race, religion, age, or social class. Rarely, if ever, is abortion studied in the context of interpersonal relationships or as it affects other participants such as the male partner (Shostak & McLouth, 1984). Nor is it examined in terms of possible beneficial or therapeutic effects. The primary object has been to study either the pathology of the women seeking abortions or to study the pathological effects of having abortions (Zimmerman, 1981). In either case, research has been heavily influenced by the notion that there is something wrong with a woman who would seek an abortion, or that there is something illness-producing in the procedure itself. This view was well articulated several decades ago by a physician who characterized abortion as "a sick person and a sick situation" (Galdston, 1958).

The preoccupation with the moral aspects and psychopathology of abortion patients has abated somewhat in recent years. Investigation of the abortion experience solely in psychological terms and the tendency to study it as an individual phenomenon persist and need correction. My purpose is to provide an alternative view, recognizing that however intimate and personal the event, all experience ultimately is socially mediated. I emphasize the saliency of immediate social contexts and relationships for explaining and understanding abortion experiences. Such a perspective need not be limited to abortion. It can also be applied more broadly to enhance our understanding of other types of intimate experiences.

In arguing for the importance of situation or context in explaining actors' behavior and their interpretations of experience, I will draw upon a study of abortion that examined how a group of women experienced each stage of the abortion process, beginning with the discovery of pregnancy and continuing through the abortion decision, the abortion itself, and into the post-abortion period. The study focused on the nature of women's abortion experience in relation to their social roles and networks. Forty women who constituted a representative sample of the abortion recipients in one medium-sized, Midwestern community were contacted at the time they were arranging to have an abortion (a first abortion for all), and were interviewed about their experiences six to eight weeks after the abortion was performed. The interviews were guided by an outline suggested by Lofland (1971) that assured uniformity in the topics covered. Within this general framework, the questions were open-ended and did not limit the content of the women's responses. The interviews began with a discussion of what life was like during the period approximately six months before the abortion. Talk then moved to how she discovered the pregnancy and through a description of each stage in the abortion process up to the time of the interview. The significant others in each woman's social network were identified at the outset. Special attention was placed on discovering how the experience unfolded in the context of these social relationships. Details of the sampling and data collection procedure can be found elsewhere (Zimmerman, 1977).

Experience as "Situated"

The theoretical perspective of symbolic interaction provided a foundation for the interview guide and for subsequent data analysis. According to this perspective, behavior and the meanings established for it *emerge* from interaction between the actor and others (Stone and Farberman, 1981). Attitudes and behavior are "produced" in immediate social situations and circumstances rather than resulting from stable personality traits, attitudes, or predispositions acquired and internalized early in life through socialization or genetic inheritance. From an interactionist view, abortions are "situated." That is, a woman's experience with abortion reflects her social world and how she fits within it. Her abortion experience is the product of her interactions and relationships with significant others, as well as reflecting her social position and how integrated into key social roles she is.

A basic question raised by previous research and by the public debate over abortion is whether or not abortion causes personal trauma or a crisis for the women involved. Accordingly, one of my objectives was to examine whether abortion could be considered a crisis and, if so, under what conditions. This emphasis raised an interesting theoretical problem: How, within a symbolic interactionist perspective, could I handle the concept of "crisis"? Sociologists have no clear theoretical concept of crisis. Instead, they often adopt the common psychological position that a crisis is a personal perception of extreme frustration, difficulty, or inability to cope.

From an interactionist perspective, crisis cannot be viewed individualistically; it must be seen as a product of social interaction. Drawing upon the writing of interactionist theorists such as W. I. Thomas (Volkhart, 1951) and Anselm Strauss (1959), I concluded that sociologically a crisis was an event so divergent from the continuity of an actor's life that in order for the individual to proceed with her (his) daily routine, interaction had to be interrupted until the event (and the actor's identity in relation to it) made sense. A crisis, therefore, could be defined as a nonroutine event temporarily paralyzing the actor, causing a disruption in interaction, and necessitating an interpersonal process of defining the situation. The more severe the crisis, the more extensive the disruption in social roles and relationships. (For a more detailed discussion, see Zimmerman, 1977.)

Patterns in Abortion Experience

My analysis revealed that the women in my sample were nearly evenly divided, based on the degree of disruption abortion caused in their lives. One pattern could be termed relatively "smooth," characterized by a comparatively calm, pragmatic rection to the discovery of pregnancy, relative clarity in making the decision to terminate the pregnancy, unchanged or improved relationships, and no troubled thoughts in the first two months after the abortion. The other pattern was characterized by greater conflict and disruption. This second group of women had a more emotional reaction to pregnancy, experienced greater decision ambivalence, and had troubled thoughts and disjunctures in roles and in relationships following the abortion. The following descriptions of the initial reaction to pregnancy from two women studied more clearly illustrate the two patterns.

> I already knew that I was and I was thinking to myself. I said, "Why waste the seven dollars? I already know I am." [It wasn't a shock then?] No, because I already knew I was and I knew I had to do something about it. . . . (#39)

> I went and got hysterical. I just—deep down I knew that I was but I didn't want to believe it . . . and I just went crazy. I didn't even know what to do, and I started crying and I just felt like everything had fallen out from under me. (#6)

A similar difference in patterns occurred at subsequent stages in the abortion process—for example, in making the decision.

> It was like there weren't any alternatives. That's what I had to do. . . . I never had any second thoughts. . . . If I were out of school or in a different situation, I'm sure there would have been more thought—"Oh, what am I going to do?"—you know, that sort of thing. But I had too many things to do first, and marriage was out of the question. (#22)

> It was the last couple of hours before the deadline that I decided to go ahead . . . one minute I would be saying, "Well, I'll go ahead and have it [the baby]," and then the next minute I would say, "I'm going to have the abortion—that's it. Final" . . . I was real confused. I kept going back and forth. . . . I changed my mind three times a day. . . . (#15).

And also in the post-abortion period:

> I felt great . . . It didn't bother me at all. [My husband] said, "My God, you act like you've never been through it." I felt super. I didn't have any trouble at all. (#5)

> Everything was over with and I felt relieved, but then I felt—wow, I felt so empty. I just wanted to—ugh, I feel like crying thinking about it . . . it still bothers me. (#30)

Once I had identified these two pattens, the next question was to explain why any given woman would come to follow one pattern rather than the other. Here the importance of situation or social context became evident.

Social Context in Shaping Abortion Experience

The women I studied varied greatly in the degree to which they were well integrated into the social world around them. This proved to be the key factor in explaining their abortion experience. The significance of social integration was dramatically illustrated when I encountered a woman who according to the lay assumptions described previously should have had a particularly difficult abortion experience. She and her husband were very active in a fundamentalist religious ministry and were opposed to abortion. But, despite such attitudes and values, this woman experienced a relatively smooth abortion passage. I can explain this seeming contradiction only by the woman's stability in her social roles and concrete plans for the future. Her well-integrated social position and future purpose put the abortion into a meaningful perspective. Another woman who had a smooth experience expressed this phenomenon particularly well.

> It was like there weren't any alternatives. That's what I had to do . . . I never had any second thoughts. . . . If I were out of school or in a different situation I'm sure there would have been more thought . . . [but] I had too many things to do first, and marriage was out of the question. (#22)

When I examined the social integration and abortion experiences of all the women I studied, the explanatory importance of social context and circumstances became clear.

In contrast to the women with smooth experiences, less well-integrated women without a clear sense of social position and future purpose had more difficulty in making sense out of their pregnancy and in deciding on abortion. Those who became pregnant in a context of low social integration were more likely to experience pregnancy as a crisis. Low social integration is a life situation characterized by (1) minimal participation in social groups, clubs, hobbies, or other leisure activities; (2) a lack of close and varied social relationships; (3) a lack of continuity in central role activities; and (4) uncertainty in looking toward the future. Those who were not well integrated were much more likely to experience abortion as a crisis (79 percent) than those who were more integrated (10 percent).

The more integrated women—those who participated more in social groups, hobbies, and so forth, had more and closer relationships with others, continuity and stability in their major roles, and definite future plans and goals—had smoother abortion experiences. In fact, 90 percent of the integrated women had a smooth passage, providing strong validation for Durkheim's classic observation concerning the insulating power of socially cohesive groups (Durkheim, 1951; pp. 210, 214). Furthermore, the impact of the social situation (in this case, social integration) proved to be more powerful in this study than either religion or social class—variables often used in individualistic explanations to indicate distinctive sets of internalized attitudes and values and childhood socialization experiences. Similarly, the women's prior attitudes toward abortion were poor predictors of abortion experience. In fact, only 30 percent of the women reported they had been completely favorable to abortion prior to becoming pregnant and undergoing abortion themselves.

The significance of social context in shaping abortion experience is perhaps most clearly evident when focusing on women's relationships with others. All of the women studied involved at least one other person in their abortion process, and half the women had confided in more than four people before the abortion occurred. The women confided in others because they needed support, especially social support. Although they wanted secrecy in order to avoid criticism, they also sought as much understanding and validation as possible. In so doing, they often compromised their privacy. Women who were less well integrated tended to tell more people about their pregnancy and abortion and to receive hostile and negative reactions. Those less well integrated had less stable relationships, were less able to control who learned of the pregnancy and abortion, and less able to judge who would be supportive. The nonsupportive responses of others contributed greatly to disruption in the abortion experience. The reaction to the woman's situation by those closest to her influenced whether her abortion experience was smooth or troubled much more than did family background, religious attitudes, or beliefs about the morality of abortion.

The impact of others can be seen at each stage of the abortion process. The following comments illustrate how others' reactions affected decision-making clarity:

> The more he kept saying, "Get an abortion," the more I was thinking maybe I should have [the baby] . . . as soon as he quit saying that, I could think a little straighter. . . . (#15)

> I was kind of confused . . . it really didn't start bothering me until these people started talking to me from the church . . . my mom told them I guess and then they came the next day to my house and they were showing me all these things about how I was killing a baby . . . that really got to me . . . I was thinking about calling the guy that was taking me and telling him I wasn't going to go. (#9)

> She wasn't shocked. She said, "Great, if that's what you have to do." You know, she wasn't down on it. I suppose if she had been down on it I would have felt worse about it maybe. If people browbeat you, you do feel worse . . . I felt a little more release that I had spoken out loud about it. It kind of let off some pressure. (#5)

> She called me and I told her and she got rather upset at me . . . it's not really what she said; it's how she was acting. . . . She just was kind of very upset about it. She didn't approve of it. [How did you feel about that? Did it bother you?] Yes, it kind of did. It still does. . . . (#28)

The questions and opposition from others led the women to doubt their abortion decision. As a result, they often reconsidered alternatives previously rejected. Validation of the abortion decision by others helped women put other alternatives aside. Without social validation, many issues involved in the abortion decision remained open to doubt—even into the post-abortion period. All but one (93 percent) of the women who reported confusion in decision making reported receiving negative reactions from others. In contrast, only 38 percent of those who reported decision-making clarity reported receiving any negative reactions. Clearly, the ambivalence of the abortion decision reflected the nature of the woman's relationships—that is, her social context.

Conclusions

This study of women's experience with abortion shows that how abortion is experienced is a result of the situational circumstances in which pregnancy and abortion occur. Abortion can be a crisis but it does not have to be. Whether it is depends greatly on a woman's position—how well integrated she is in social roles and relationships and the way significant others react to her throughout the abortion process. The social context of abortion appears to be more important in shaping daily experience than previously established attitudes, values, or behavior.

This study supports the symbolic interactionist view that human action is constructed in the present and reflects the contingencies of social situations. Although established attitudes, values, and what appear to be relatively enduring personality characteristics may influence the experience, they are subject to and frequently overridden by the situational demands of the present.

References

Durkheim, Emile. *Suicide.* New York: Free Press, 1951.

Galdston, I. "Other Aspects of the Abortion Problem: Psychiatric Aspects," in M. Calderone, ed., *Abortion in the United States.* New York: Hoeber-Harper, 1958.

Lofland, John. *Analyzing Social Settings.* Belmont, Calif.: Wadsworth, 1971.

Shostack, Arthur B., and Gary McLouth. *Men and Abortion: Lessons, Losses and Love.* New York: Praeger, 1984.

Stone, Gregory P., and Harvey A. Farberman, eds., *Social Psychology Through Symbolic Interaction,* Second Edition. New York: John Wiley, 1981.

Strauss, Anselm. *Mirrors and Masks: The Search for Identity.* Glencoe, Ill.: Free Press, 1959.

Volkhart, Edmund, ed., *Social Behavior and Personality: Contributions of W. I. Thomas to Theory and Social Research.* New York: Social Science Research Council, 1951.

Zimmerman, Mary. *Passage Through Abortion: The Personal and Social Reality of Women's Experiences.* New York: Praeger, 1977.

———. "Psychosocial and Emotional Consequences of Elective Abortion," in Paul Sachdev, ed., *Abortion: Readings and Research.* Toronto: Butterworths, 1981.

12

Baby Care: Fathers vs. Mothers

RALPH LAROSSA

MAUREEN MULLIGAN LAROSSA

How do husbands' and wives' everyday lives change when they become parents? By "everyday life" we mean their daily routines—their eating, sleeping, working, and playing routines. Also, how is the everyday life of a new father different from that of a new mother? These are the questions we set out to answer when we began our study of the transition to parenthood.

As studies of the transition to parenthood go, ours is unique in several respects. First, it is a study of parenthood as parents see it. Each interview was essentially open-ended and free-flowing, which is to say that the men and women in the study were encouraged to talk about what was important to them, not what we presumed to be important. Second, it is a participant-informed study. Married in 1970, we had our first child in 1979 which, coincidentally enough, happened to be the point at which we started to analyze the interviews. Thus, we were in the unusual position of experiencing our own transition to parenthood at the same time we were trying to understand the experiences of others. Third, it is a study of change. Each of the twenty couples in the study was interviewed not once but three times, during the third, sixth, and ninth months postpartum. Fourth, it is a study of both first- and second-time parenthood. Whereas most studies of the transition to parenthood focus only on the first birth, we thought it important to view the transition to parenthood as a continuum that, in principle, can extend the length of the childbearing phase. Last but not least, it is a study of social patterns, social processes, and sociohistorical conditions surrounding the transition to parenthood. All too often, researchers look only at whether or not new parents are "coping with" or "adjusting to" the transition to parenthood, while ignoring the transition to parenthood itself. As a result, we know very little about *what actually happens* when peo-

---

This is an abridged and slightly revised and updated version of sections of Chapters 3, 4, and 9 in *Transition to Parenthood: How Infants Change Families* by Ralph LaRossa and Maureen Mulligan LaRossa.

ple become parents; and we know even less about how what happens is linked to larger sociohistorical realities. (For a detailed description of the methodology used in the study, see LaRossa and LaRossa, 1981.)

In our efforts to make sense of the transcripts, we found ourselves increasingly relying on three conceptual frameworks: the conflict framework, the choice and exchange framework, and the symbolic interactionist framework.

The *conflict framework,* of which the major premise is "when confronted with a choice under conditions of real or perceived scarcity, humans will be inclined to choose themselves over others" (Sprey, 1979: 132), proved to be the overarching orientation because of how central the "problem of continuous coverage" is to understanding the transition to parenthood.

A newborn child cannot survive on its own, but is dependent on adults to feed it, protect it from the elements, and teach it to use symbols (most importantly, language) so that it can become a functioning member of society. The helplessness of the human infant places a family that is in the midst of a transition to parenthood within the class of social arrangements that have as their primary function "coverage." For example, a medical hospital in the United States is a "continuous coverage social system"; there is always someone who is on call, ready to respond to the needs of the patients at a moment's notice (Zerubavel, 1979b). The same kind of coverage characterizes new parenthood. Having a baby launches a couple into the responsibilities of continuous coverage for that baby; someone, either the couple themselves or their representative (for example, a babysitter), must always be on call.

The obligation of having to be ready and able to care for their infant son or daughter tends to reduce the father's and mother's free time, the time when they can do what they want to do rather than what someone else (the baby) wants them to do. Indeed, it is the loss of free time accompanying parenthood that surprises and bothers new parents more than anything else (Harriman, 1983; Hobbs, 1965; Hobbs and Wimbish, 1977; LaRossa, 1983). The scarcity of this valued resource creates a conflict of interest between the husband and wife. No matter how much they may try to avoid it, periodically there will arise zero-sum-game-like situations in which one partner's "winning" (being free to pursue his or her own interests) means that the other must "lose" (forgo his or her own interests for the sake of the baby). Conflicts of interest generally result in conflict behavior, tactics, and strategies which theoretically extend from verbal persuasion to the use of force, as both parties in the encounter pursue their own short- and long-term interests, often at the expense of the other.

It is this basic pattern—child dependency resulting in continuous coverage, which means a scarcity of free time, which leads to conflicts of interest and often conflict behavior—that cuts across the experiences of all the couples in our sample; and it is this basic pattern that explains why the conflict framework became the linchpin in our analysis.

Closely tied to the conflict framework is the *choice and exchange framework,* which operates on the assumption that "humans avoid costly behavior and seek rewarding statuses, relationships, interaction, and feeling states to the end that their profits [or outcomes] are maximized" (Nye, 1979: 2). The choice and exchange framework was found to be useful in understanding the organization of men's and women's commitments to activities, like infant care, outside employment, and recreation. The choice and exchange framework also helped us to understand how power relations in families are directly tied to institutionalized sexism and, more specifically, to the dependency of women on men. One reason that the marital power structure in the United States tends to be patriarchal is that women often have to rely on men for economic support.

Not as often associated with the conflict framework but just as important to our argument is the *symbolic interactionist framework.* The basic insight derived from this framework is that "humans live in a symbolic [conventional sign] environment as well as a physical environment," and that "the best way to understand humans is to deal with the mentalistic meanings and values [the symbols] that occur in the minds of the people, because that is the most direct cause of their behavior" (Burr et al., 1979: 46, 49). The inability of infants at birth to use symbols, the different levels of value that fathers and mothers attribute to free time, the definitions of social structures as legitimate or illegitimate, and, finally, the symbolic or ideological aspects of conflict behavior are all crucial to our analysis and, indirectly, to the conflict framework which supports that analysis.

By accentuating the part that sociocultural forces and interactional contexts play during the transition to parenthood, the three frameworks, taken together, form the basis for a sociological—or structural—approach to the transition to parenthood. Up to now, transition-to-parenthood researchers have relied almost exclusively on an individualistic approach, an approach that focuses on biological or psychological explanations for parental behavior. Rossi (1977, 1984), for example, talks about the effect of biologically based gender differences on parenting, while Chodorow (1978) offers a psychoanalytic theory that locates the roots of fathering and mothering in the personality differences between men and women. In contrast, we hypothesize that sociological variables, such as social time, power, commitment, and ideology, do as good a job—if not a better job—of explaining the conduct of fathers and mothers vis-à-vis their children; and we believe that any theory of parenthood that strives to be comprehensive must include sociological as well as biological and psychological factors.

Work and Play, Primary and Secondary Time

The continuous coverage of infants is somewhat unique in that it entails both work and play. Not only is it important to feed, clothe, and carry the baby, it is also important to play with the baby, since it is through play (and especially games) that the child develops a concept of self, which is indispensable to becoming a full-fledged member of society (Mead, 1934).

In his 1965–66 study, Robinson (1977) discovered several things about child work and child play that we think are highly significant. First of all, he found that not only did housewives spend seven times as much time as employed men in child-care activities, and employed women twice as much time, but that while less than a tenth of women's child care was play, half of all men's child care was play (1977: 64–65). When one considers the range of activities that constitute "baby care," it is indeed remarkable that fathers are able to limit their own activities to such a degree. In their study of the content and organization of housework, Berk and Berk (1979) identify approximately sixty discrete tasks that can be categorized as baby care (1979: 265–275). However, only six of these tasks fall under the heading of play. Combining Robinson's and the Berks' surveys thus suggests that fathers are devoting 50 percent of their baby care time to 10 percent of the baby care. We also found that it was not uncommon for new fathers to define short bursts of play with their infants (often immediately upon coming home from work, or after dinner) as efforts which made up for the fact that they were absent all day or which balanced out their inability or unwillingness to take a more active part in the so-called "dirty work" (for example, diaper changing, feeding). The fact that playing is generally "cleaner" than other kinds of baby care and thus more desirable may only partially explain why fathers tend to prefer this form of contact with their children. The other, perhaps more important, factor in the equation is that play requires less *attention* than custodial responsibilities.

Here is what we mean: With the express purpose of measuring different levels of attention, Robinson's research was based on having families keep a log or a diary of their activities over a specified time, usually a twenty-four-hour period. Looking somewhat like a bookkeeper's ledger sheet, a time-diary lists the hours of the day down the left-hand side of the page, and the following seven questions across the top (thus creating seven columns): "What did you do [at this time]? Time began? Time ended? Where? With whom? Doing anything else? Remarks?" (Robinson, 1977: 7). The first question ("What did you do [at this time]?") tapped into the subject's *primary* or main activity. The next-to-last question ("Doing anything else?") recorded the subject's *secondary* activity, which by definition was anything done secondarily and in addition to the primary activity. Robinson found that the comparisons between men and women with respect to primary child care were exactly the same as the comparisons for child care in general; that is, housewives spend seven times as much time in primary child care, and employed women spend twice as much time in primary child care as men (1977: 72). The principal reason for the similar figures can be traced to the correlation between the kind of child-care activity and the amount of attention devoted to that activity. In a footnote, Robinson reports that (1977: 70):

> While over two-thirds of primary activity child care in the 1965–1966 study was "custodial" (feeding, clothing, chauffeuring, etc.) rather than "interactional" (reading, playing, etc.) in nature, the bulk of secondary activity child care consisted of interactional activities.

When we looked at our data in light of Robinson's findings, we came up with another factor that may help explain why fathers devote a greater proportion of their child-care time to play than do mothers. Not only is play cleaner than many other forms of child-care activity, but play also has the advantage of being less demanding in terms of the amount of attention that one must give to that activity. *Fathers, in other words, may choose play over work because play "eats" less into their own free time.*

How does play "consume" less free time? Think of play and work as ideal-typical poles of a hypothetical continuum. Toward the play end of the continuum one would include activities such as piggy-back riding, tickling, and hide-and-seek. Toward the work end of the continuum one would include feeding, diaper changing, putting to sleep, and so forth. In the middle would be those activities that fall between play and work, the borderline cases: reading a story, giving a bath (with toys, of course), going on nature walks. Generally speaking, activities that are toward the play end of the continuum require less parental attention than the other activities. First, these activities are often shorter in duration. A piggyback ride, for example, may last only two or three minutes. Yet at the end of the ride, the parent can legitimately terminate contact with the baby, often with the assistance of the other parent (for example, "Come on now, give Daddy a break, you tired him out"). Second, play activities are typically not as scheduled or as urgently required as work activities. The parent can usually decide when and how long to play ("Not now, later, but only for a few minutes"), whereas activities such as feeding and diaper changing are more on demand; letting one's child go hungry or remain dirty is frowned upon. Third, play activities are less bounded spatially than work activities. Roughhousing can take place anywhere in the house—in front of the television, in the backyard—which means that the parent can more easily integrate personal activities with play. Feeding and diaper changing, on the other hand, are usually done in specific locales, severely restricting the kinds of activities that a parent can perform in addition to child work.

Getting "Down Time"

Primary and secondary are not the only levels of attention. There is logically a third level of activity, *tertiary* activity, which can be defined as time during which there is no social contact whatsoever. Of course, as with primary and secondary activity, tertiary activity must be operationalized in terms of some referent or referents. Thus, for example, a mother at work would be at a tertiary level with respect to her children, while being primarily and secondarily involved with her job. If, on the other hand, her child happens to call her at her office, then during the phone call she would be primarily attending to her child, and secondarily attending to her work.

Rather than think of attention, one may think of social accessibility (Zerubavel, 1979a). In the primary mode one is most accessible to a referent, and in the tertiary mode least accessible to a referent. Hence, primary, secondary, and tertiary time actually represent points on a continuum that extends from being totally attuned or accessible to a referent (total connection) to being totally neglectful or inaccessible to a referent (total separation).

When adults interact with each other, they generally have the freedom to move, within specified parameters and rules, across all three levels. A husband and wife can, for example, be involved in a very intense conversation one moment (primary status), then shift their attention to the television while still maintaining contact with each other (secondary status), and finally move to separate corners of their house to work on their individual hobbies (tertiary status). (Some husbands and wives might define this third move as secondary status because, as far as they are concerned, being in the same house means that they are *with* each other. But let us assume, for the sake of simplicity, that the husband and wife do not define their situation in this way, but believe that any time that they are not in face-to-face contact with each other, they are in a no-contact status.) The advantage of being able to move across all three levels is that husbands and wives can give each other their undivided attention at one moment, and then withdraw completely from each other the next. They can, in other words, coordinate a system of connectedness and separateness such that at one moment they are concentrating on each other, and the next they are essentially removed from each other.

This is very different from what it is like to interact with an infant. If a mother, for example, is alone with an infant at home, she can never move to a tertiary level, but must always be "up" or "ready" to attend to her child's needs. This is indeed one of the biggest surprises for new parents. They soon learn that infants are not only very dependent on them, but that the demands of infants are also nonnegotiable. The simple phrase "I'll be with you in a moment," which works so well in the adult world to delay moving to a primary or secondary level, is useless with someone who does not understand language. ("Infant" is derived from the Latin word *infans* which means incapable of speech.)

We do not mean to suggest that primary contact with one's child is unrewarding, or that some parents do not find pleasure in having an individual who is totally dependent on them. But as the couples in our study suggested over and over again, what can be unrewarding and unpleasant is the *repetitiveness* of that level of contact. No matter how much we love someone or something, satiation (too much of a good thing) reduces the reward value of that person or object (Homans, 1974: 29). Also the *pace* of parent-infant interaction can take its toll. As with assembly-line work (see Blauner, 1964) and air traffic control work, the most alienating and most distressing aspect of baby care is its pace. It is the baby and not the parent who generally controls when shifts from one level to the next will occur. The parents' job is to "keep track" of the child, who, if mobile (crawling or toddling), must be "plotted" in terms of direction, speed, and altitude (height).

It is perhaps worth noting that people who work in situations from which they cannot voluntarily withdraw, from which they cannot take "time-outs" when they want to but must wait to be relieved, have been found to be more prone to "burn-out," the symptoms of which include not only physical and emotional exhaustion, but social exhaustion as well, involving "the loss of concern for the people with whom one is working," taking a "very cynical and dehumanized perception of these people," and treating them accordingly (Maslach and Pines, 1977: 101; also Maslach, 1976). Thus, we suspect that there are parents who develop dehumanized views of their own children as a result of the constant attention they are giving to them, and that the parents who are probably most likely to undergo this experience are those who "cannot do enough for their kids," the supermoms and superdads.

Even when the baby is sleeping, an adult left alone in the house cannot move to a tertiary level. Although the parent will probably not be in the same room as the baby during nap time, the parent is still monitoring the infant, still standing watch. This is not to say that the parent will not feel restored by having an hour or two "off." In reality, however, the "ah" feeling experienced by the parent when he or she carefully closes the door to the nursery after having just rocked the baby to sleep is because now there is time to be primarily involved in his or her own needs while secondarily involved with the baby's needs, rather than vice versa. In short, after a hectic morning of being "up" for the baby—feeding, changing, amusing, watching, consoling, and so forth—the parent can now enjoy a long awaited *semi*-attentiveness.

If there are two adults in the house, the picture can change dramatically. Now each adult can slip into periodic "down times" while the other remains on a secondary level. Sometimes responsibility for the baby is formally arranged, as in those cases where fathers and mothers alternate who gets up in the morning with the baby and who sleeps late. However, more often than not, we suspect, the movement from one level to the next is informal and emergent, a procedure which can sometimes court disaster (He: "I thought *you* were watching the baby!" She: "And I thought *you* were watching the baby!").

If one of the adults refuses to share responsibility for the baby, then the other must always be "up" or "ready." Thus, while one parent watches television, reads a book, works in the den—essentially oblivious to the needs of the baby—the other must be continuously on guard. Again the formal/informal distinction applies. One husband in the sample formally announced to his wife that, as far as he was concerned, she was always on duty—seven days a week, twenty-four hours a day. With other husbands, the results were still the same—the wife always attending to the baby—but the means were more subtle and more informal. Thus, a husband may claim that he, too, is in a secondary status with respect to the baby, but in reality he is technically in second while functionally in third; if the baby starts to cry or moves too close the house plants, he will not feel any compulsion to intervene, but will let his wife take care of it. Even more subtle is the strategy of arranging his activities so that he precludes his having to share in the baby work. The father who decides to pay the bills or perhaps clean the kitchen just when the baby needs to be fed or changed has effectively preserved a tertiary level of contact with his child.

The significance of negotiating protectiveness becomes clear at this point. It is quite common for fathers and mothers to debate over how protective they should be with their babies (for example, "Should we let her cry?"). Although the manifest function of these discussions is to decide what is best for the child, the hidden agenda is often what is best for the husband and wife. Should a father conclude that his wife is too protective ("You are spoiling her"), he can then justify his refusal to respond to the baby's demands. However sincere he may be, the results are still the same—"down time" for the father, often at the expense of his wife. For example, one of the fathers went out virtually every night of the week, despite his wife's protests that he should stay home with her and the baby. One of his responses to her protests was that if she were willing to hire a babysitter, she could join him. Since she refused (she felt that as a working mother it was bad enough that she had to leave her baby during the day; she was not going to leave her at night too), it was, in his opinion, basically *her* fault that the two of them did not spend more time together.

Helping Versus Sharing

The father who refuses, either formally or informally, to do anything is the exception, not the rule. What is the rule—as suggested by our data and other studies—is that fathers will periodically move to a primary or secondary attention level with their infants, thus enabling their wives to get tertiary ("down") time, but that when they do take over, they almost always assume that they are "helping" their wives rather than "sharing" the parental responsibilities.

Mothers are also likely to see fathers as surrogate parents, and, like their husbands, will use words such as "helping" and "babysitting" to denote the father's contribution. It is interesting to note that in the 1701 pages of transcripts, *every* couple would, at least once in their interviews, refer to the husband as "helping" the wife with the baby, whereas not a single couple defined the wife's parental responsibilities in these terms.

There are a variety of ways that a "helping" role can be performed. The first signs that the father will be less involved than the mother in child care can be seen before the baby arrives, during the pregnancy. More often than not, the wife will be the one to think first about and eventually buy several of the how-to books on parenting. If the father does read any of the books, either in whole or in part, it is likely to be as a result of the mother's coaxing. Clearly, from the start, the mother is the one who is "in charge" of the baby. Her purchase of the books reflects what is generally accepted: Babies are "women's work." The fact that she will read the books more thoroughly than her husband directs what is to come: since the father is not as informed about what it means to be a parent, both parents will assume that Mom is the one to orchestrate and implement the child's care. When and if the father does participate, it is presumed to be under the mother's direction.

After the baby is born, performances which reflect and direct the father and mother's separate roles become more sophisticated. Perhaps the most easily recognized is the behavior that ensues the first few times the father holds the baby. Upon being handed his infant son or daughter, he will often say something to the effect that he hopes he does not drop the baby. Then, while he is cradling the baby in his arms, the father will stiffen up, demonstrating both to himself and to everyone in the room (including the baby) that this is not his accustomed role. Often, the coactors in this drama will reinforce the father's definition of the situation by standing very close, as if to be ready to catch the baby should he or she actually fall out of the father's arms. Another typical maneuver is to encourage the father to sit down, preferably in a stuffed chair, so that his arms can be supported. Throughout the scene, the father will ask for and the other performers will readily offer instructions on how to position the arms; where to hold the baby's head, and so forth. Additional touches may include having someone gather everyone in the house so that they can see Daddy holding Junior or, even better, grabbing a camera to capture a "rare" moment for posterity.

In sociological terms, this scene is a perfect example of what Goffman (1961) refers to as *role distance.* The mock or comedic aspects of the performance indicate an attempt by the father to deny "not the role but the virtual self that is implied in the role" (1961: 108). In other words, the father is distancing or disassociating his self from the parental role.

The father's performance stands in stark contrast to the mother's actions when she holds the baby. Even if she does fear that she will drop the baby during those first few days of parenthood, it is considered poor form for her to display that fear. Rather, she is likely to try to appear as if holding the baby is well within her abilities. And the other performers in the room are likely to communicate to the mother that she does indeed look "natural" for the job.

The mother's performance is the flip side of role distance. What she is doing is *embracing* the parental role—disappearing, as it were, "into the virtual self available in the situation," confirming "expressively [her] acceptance of it" (Goffman, 1961: 106).

The role distance/role embracement distinction is actually a continuum, one that may be useful for understanding a puzzling set of findings. Studies indicate that most husbands and wives do not believe that men should do more family work than they are doing now. And among the minority who do feel that men should contribute more, a greater proportion of men than women express an interest in expanding the man's family role (Pleck, 1976). Women, in other words, generally "want" to remain chiefly responsible for the house and for the children.

One explanation—perhaps the most popular—is that women have a psychological investment in their family roles, and become threatened if they cannot count on housework and baby care as their domain. For example, one of the case-study wives was very proud to be a full-time housewife and mother, feeling that these roles constituted her "career" in life. If her husband had decided one day that from then on he would take over a substantial part of the homemaking duties, we have no doubt that this particular woman would have indeed felt threatened.

In terms of what we have been saying, the psychological investment explanation focuses on the role embracement of the mother. Because her self is so closely tied to motherhood, reducing her role performances would undermine her identity. This is probably true for many women, but it does not seem to us to be the whole story. Also operating, we suspect, are the consequences of the father's role distance. To continue our discussion of the variety of ways that helping behavior may manifest itself once the baby comes, consider these role-distancing performances disclosed by the couples: A father "forgets" to change the baby's diaper for the whole time (about six hours) that he is "babysitting" while his wife has gone shopping; he claimed that he was just about to do it. A father just "gives up" trying to feed his infant son and concludes that he is just not "as good at it" as his wife is. A mother reports that her husband did such a terrible job of cleaning their daughter that she finally decided that it was easier for her if she just did it herself. And finally, a mother notes that when her husband did care for the baby he would always ask for her assistance, which meant that she ended up doing most of the work anyway. Thus, another explanation for why mothers do not want more cooperation is that they may not trust their husbands to do a good job or they have learned that their husband's assistance is more trouble than it is worth.

What about the fathers? Although fathers are more inclined to "want" to increase their participation more than mothers "want" them to, the number of fathers who advocate change is still small. Role embracement and role distance can still apply. While the mother embraces parenthood, the father is embracing the traditional male role, which means he sees himself more as the breadwinner than the caretaker. His job, as some of our husbands said, is to "put the food on the table and pay for the kid's college education." Thus, many fathers take exception to the claim that they do not care for or about their children. They point out that although they may not be involved in the day-to-day feeding and cleaning of the baby, they are very much involved in the day-to-day responsibility of providing financial support. Indeed, they argue, because their responsibilities in this realm are so time consuming and energy exhausting, they cannot possibly help their wives more, nor should they be expected to. Even if the wives themselves are employed, many fathers still insist that their jobs are more pressure-laden than their wives' jobs are, and that they still, therefore, should not be expected to help more around the house. (Studies have found that the wife's employment has a negligible impact on the husband's housework and child-care responsibilities [Berk and Berk, 1979; Pleck and Rustad, 1980; Robinson, 1977].) One father in the sample resented the whole idea that men in this society must hold a job, while women can presumably take off when they like to have a baby. The implication was that although men may be "helpers" at home, women are "helpers" in the economic world.

Related, of course, to the father's embracement of the traditional role is the fact that some men have a psychological investment in *not* helping more at home. In their minds, husbands who do too much housework and baby care are not "real men."

The fact that fewer mothers than fathers advocate change is, however, the real puzzle, the solution to which may be linked to the use of the word "help" to denote the father's parental performances. If the wife believes that her husband's contribution to child care is an act of charity, a "gift" from him to her, then each time the husband helps with the baby, he alters the social exchange balance in the marriage. Having done his wife a "favor," both he and she expect that the favor will be returned (quid pro quo). The form of the repayment may not be known. It can, itself, be an act of charity (for example, helping the husband pay the bills), or simply an immediate response to a request (for example, sex even though she is tired). The norm of reciprocity (Gouldner, 1960), nevertheless, dictates that over time role partners will strive for a balanced exchange (Blau, 1964).

Thus, the reason that more mothers than fathers may not be too keen on the idea of having men help more (and significantly, it is in terms of "help" that the surveys are sometimes phrased; see Robinson, 1977, for example) is that mothers may not want to "pay the price." They may not be comfortable with the deferential stance they are expected to take to offset their husband's gratuities (cf. Bell and Newby, 1976).

Of course, the choice may not be theirs to make. The few studies that have examined whether the marital power structure changes after the birth of a child have found that marriages typically become more patriarchal during the transition to parenthood (Cowan et al., 1978; Meyerowitz and Feldman, 1966). Speculation on why this shift occurs has generally centered on the fact that many women quit work when they have their first baby (see Hoffman, 1978, for example). Since power is inversely related to dependency (Emerson, 1962), the increased financial reliance of the wife on the husband is presumed to decrease her power in the relationship, all other things being equal (cf. Blood and Wolfe, 1960). We would hypothesize that the wife's power will typically decrease, regardless of whether there is a change in her employment status. The unrelenting demands of an infant increase the wife's dependency on the husband for "down time." Though she may not like the fact that when she does get relief from her husband it is defined as a gift for which she will be beholden, she is not likely to cut herself off from his aid. Nor is the husband likely to stop contributing care, particularly if he begins to sense that his wife is indeed grateful for his support. Some husbands in our sample, in fact, tried to increase their wives' dependency not by doing more baby work, but by demanding that their wives acknowledge that since they did a lot more than most of their male friends, they should be appreciated more than they are now. In short, we suspect that marriages tend to become more patriarchal after the birth of the first child because of the socially defined character of baby care.

As might be expected, there are always exceptions to the rule. Women can and do increase their power in a relationship by using their children to increase their demands on their husbands (LaRossa, 1977: 45–46). Also, husbands and wives who do not see the husband's contribution as "helping" are less likely to have the power-dependency balance in their marriages dramatically altered.

One final point on helping: One of the few studies to examine how (rather than whether) the marital power structure changes after the first birth found that couples use more "coercive tactics" (power plays, guilt induction, disparagement) with each other when they become parents (Raush et al., 1974). These tactics may very well be related to the power-dependence imbalances that are created by helping behavior during the transition to parenthood. If so, then having a baby could, for some couples, precipitate a cycle of mutual coercion escalating ultimately to the use of physical force. The existence of a relationship between parenthood and marital violence is not unheard of. Gelles (1975) found that a disproportionate number of women are hit by their husbands while they are pregnant. And Straus et al. (1980) recently reported that the most likely conflict to lead to blows between a husband and wife is conflict over children.

The Reification of Infants

After reading the transcripts only once, we realized that the value of parenthood was different for the fathers and mothers in our sample. What we did not immediately realize, but what became more apparent with each successive reading, was the way in which the fathers' and mothers' value differences influenced their interactions with their children. In a nutshell, because of the configuration of the fathers' values, they were more likely to act toward their infants as if they, the infants, were *things* (reifications).

One of the fathers, for example, said that his mind would often wander while he was talking with people. His wife, in particular, would become annoyed when, in the middle of a conversation, she would sense that he had "left." The father said that he was working very hard to break this habit with his wife, but that when he did it with his new son, he did not feel that guilty. Since his son was too young to sense that he was not getting his undivided attention, he could, as he put it, "fink [out]" on his kid. Critical to this father's attitude was his disappointment with very young babies. As far as he was concerned, they could not "interact." When the father made this remark, his wife immediately disagreed, saying that their son, and indeed all infants, could interact, but on a different level. The mother, in other words, seemed more sensitive to the fact that infants may not be able to use symbols, but they can communicate through signs (for example, crying means "I want something"). In general, the mothers in the sample were more sensitive to their infant's abilities than the fathers were.

Another way of describing the different attributions that fathers and mothers gave to their infants is to say that mothers were likely to see their infants as more "interpersonally competent" than fathers saw them. The more interpersonal competence that one imputes to other actors in a relationship, the more satisfied one is with that relationship (Burr et al., 1979). Thus, we would hypothesize that mothers generally enjoy the relationship with their infants more than fathers do.

All of this is not to say that fathers do not want their children, that they do not think they are rewarding. Nor do we mean to suggest that there are not moments when mothers would just as soon hide from their kids, or that mothers do not have other reasons, besides simple enjoyment, for wanting to be mothers. Rather, the point is that the socially determined configuration of values for fathers and mothers is different. To explain what we mean by this, we will apply the often-used intrinsic/extrinsic distinction to parental values.

A *value* "is the position of anything in a preference ordering" (Kuhn, 1974: 107). All social objects, including people, have some value—and often a complex of values—attached to them by others. Essentially, there are two kinds of values—intrinsic and extrinsic. The *intrinsic value* of something or someone is the amount of sheer pleasure or enjoyment that one gets from experiencing that object or person. The *extrinsic value* of something or someone is the amount of social rewards (for example, money, power, prestige, approval, positive self-image, avoidance of stigma or physical pain) associated with having or being with that object or person.

If, for the sake of simplicity, we divide both intrinsic value and extrinsic value into "high" and "low," we arrive at the following ideal types:

A. High Intrinsic Value, High Extrinsic Value
B. High Intrinsic Value, Low Extrinsic Value
C. Low Intrinsic Value, High Extrinsic Value
D. Low Intrinsic Value, Low Extrinsic Value

Configurations "A" and "D" in their most extreme forms would include "love" and "hate," respectively. Thinking in interpersonal terms, an "A" type would be the parent who very much enjoys interacting with his or her child, and who derives prestige and social approval from being a parent. An example of a "D" type would be the parent who has decided not to keep his or her baby because of the lack of both enjoyment and perceived social rewards accompanying the transition to parenthood. Category "B" would, in its extreme form, include fathers and mothers who get a thrill just from being in contact with their kids but who have never seen their children as assets to be displayed or bartered. And finally, category "C" would, in its extreme form, include fathers and mothers who see their children only in utilitarian terms, as commodities in the interpersonal marketplace. Though presented here as dichotomous variables (high/low), intrinsic value and extrinsic value are, in reality, continuous variables (highest . . . midpoint . . . lowest). Hence, whereas it may be difficult to conceive of the four types in their most extreme forms, the chances are that all of us have directly or indirectly known people who more or less conform to one type or another. We may not know, for example, a parent who derives only intrinsic benefits from being a parent, but we can perhaps think of fathers and mothers who just seem to get "a charge" out of being parents, and who seem to be relatively uninterested in the extrinsic payoffs.

The relevance of the typology to understanding the reification of infants is that category "C" is a reified relationship. To see a baby largely in terms of the social rewards which he or she provides is to dehumanize the baby. We recognize that this statement is itself a value judgment, but we believe that "thing-like relationships" is an accurate description of some of the interactions that were described during the interviews. To be more specific, and to return to the central point about father-child relationships, our data suggest that there are many fathers who could be said to, more or less, fall into category "C," many fathers who certainly want and treasure their children, but who do not really enjoy being with their kids. Sure, they will roughhouse with their toddlers on the living-room floor, and will blush when hugged or kissed by their one-year-olds, but when you really get down to it, they just do not have that much fun when they are with their children. If they had their druthers, they would be working at the office or drinking at the local pub—and quite often they are doing precisely that either in fact or in fantasy—but they commit themselves to their kids out of a sense of responsibility.

Relationships which are perceived as primarily obligatory take on a very different character than intrinsically valued relationships. First, obligatory relationships operate at lower levels of attention than intrinsically valued relationships, which is to say that there would be more divided attention, more secondary activity in these relationships. Also, obligatory relationships are generally more routinized, so as to facilitate the addition of other activities (and other people) when enacting the obligatory relationship. Thus, we would hypothesize that Low Intrinsic/High Extrinsic parent-child relationships would be marked by more multiple activities and, because they can be easily routinized, more play activities than High Intrinsic/High Extrinsic parent-child relationships.

The best example of this was provided by the father who complained that his son could not interact and who said that he had developed a series of "tricks" which helped him get through any extended contact with his son. Basically, the tricks were toys and events which kept the baby distracted, and which thus decreased the father's level of attention. The father had also learned what particular sequence of introducing the tricks worked best for distracting the baby the longest. Thus, the father would initiate a routinized series of distractions when his son started to get too demanding.

Reification of children can spiral. Parents who, from the start, assume that their infants are not interpersonally competent may conclude that they do not enjoy being with their children, which can result in a lowering of their attention and routinization of their interaction with their kids. This strategy can prevent the parents from effectively discovering that their children (1) may be more interpersonally competent than they originally thought they were, and (2) are becoming more interpersonally competent with each passing day (because of developmental changes). Not being receptive to these changes may contribute further to the parents' low level of enjoyment when they are with their children, which may mean that they will withdraw even more, and so on. The significance of this hypothetical pattern is that it suggests that child-care differences between couples and between fathers and mothers are not simply a function of internalized value differences being "played out," but are a consequence of *interactional processes* that take place during the transition to parenthood itself.

Aligning Actions and Traditional Divisions of Labor

It is clear from the above analysis that during the transition to parenthood, the probability of misunderstandings, screw-ups, snafus, conflicts of interest, and unplanned consequences is quite high. In a word, things can "get out of line" quite easily. Generally, these misalignments take two forms. *Interpersonal misalignments* are those situations in which there is a misunderstanding or basic conflict of interest between people. *Culture-conduct misalignments* are those situations in which there is a perceived discrepancy between the cultural ideals and expectations of the participants in a social system and their actual or intended conduct; they say one thing and do another (Stokes and Hewitt, 1976).

When people are confronted with either an interpersonal misalignment or a culture-conduct misalignment, they will engage in what are called (reasonably enough) aligning actions (Stokes and Hewitt, 1976). *Aligning actions* are principally verbal activities and include, among other things, *motives* ("answers to questions interrupting acts or programs" [Mills, 1940: 473]), *remedial interchanges* ("corrective readings calculated to show that a possible offender actually had a right relationship to the rules, or if he seemed not to a moment ago, he can be counted on to have such a relationship henceforth" [Goffman, 1971: 108]), and *accounts* ("a statement made by a social actor to explain unanticipated or untoward behavior" [Scott and Lyman, 1968: 46]).

Aligning actions are central to a sociological perspective because they help us to understand a central sociological problem, namely, the existence of continuity and change in social life. Given instances of culture-conduct misalignment (the second of the two forms of misalignment), the major functions of aligning actions are to (1) "maintain culture in the face of conduct that is at variance with it," and (2) "provide a social lubricant that simultaneously permits social change and yet allows conduct to be linked to recognized cultural boundaries" (Stokes and Hewitt, 1976: 848).

With respect to the first function, aligning actions explain how a couple can believe that they have a role-sharing (nontraditional) system when their conduct clearly indicates that they have a role-segregated (traditional) system. The aligning actions in this case define role-segregated conduct as nothing more than a legitimate exception to the rule. Thus, for example, the couple who very much wants to institute an androgynous parental arrangement but who finds it virtually impossible to carry out, given the existing societal constraints, may conduct themselves on a traditional plane but continue to believe that they are "into androgyny" by defining their deviance from their beliefs as "excusable," "justifiable," and so forth. In other words, aligning actions are a form of situational ethics which allows people to hold on to their absolute standards. Of course, aligning actions need not be used conjointly by a couple. A husband may, through aligning actions, continue to genuinely believe that he is sharing the load despite evidence to the contrary. A wife may, through aligning actions, continue to honestly believe that she wants to be with her kids more than anything else in the world despite her efforts to disassociate from them.

The second function of aligning actions—the change function—is perhaps even more important than the continuity function, in that the change function provides a sociological explanation for traditionalization during the transition to parenthood. Several studies have found that traditional marital behavior *increases* during the months following the birth of a first child (Cowan et al., 1978; Entwisle and Doering, 1981; Meyerowitz and Feldman, 1966; Rausch et al., 1974). Explanations for why these changes occur have typically centered on either physiological or personality factors which are supposedly triggered by parenthood (Chodorow, 1978; Rossi, 1977, 1984).

We cannot test the relative validity of the physiological and personality explanations with our data. And this is not the place to embark on a review of studies which have attempted to test these two theories. We can, however, say this: The existing evidence indicates that physiological and personality factors are *not sufficient* to explain traditionalization after birth. As important as these variables may be, no one has yet conclusively demonstrated that physiology or personality, or some combination of the two, is all that is needed to understand why couples shift to a traditional family system during the transition to parenthood.

The inability of physiological and personality theories to explain everything points to the importance of including sociological variables in models of traditionalization. But we must be careful here; in principle, a sociological approach does not mean simply paying homage to societal factors impacting on couples after they become parents. Contending that society "forces" couples into traditional roles is to conceive of a society that is separate from, rather than integrated with, individuals. This approach is nothing more than deterministic reasoning disguised as sociological reasoning. Substituting societal determinism for physiological or personality determinism is *not* in keeping with a sociological perspective.

Thus, for example, when Michael Lamb, a psychologist by training, attempts to explain traditionalization by arguing that "the insistent and undeniable dependency of the baby makes equivocation or ambiguity about role demands more difficult to sustain than in the preparental phase, and our society's expectations regarding nurturant maternal roles are more clearly defined than any other" (Lamb, 1978: 146), he falls short of offering a truly sociological explanation because he leaves open the question of exactly how societal expectations translate into marital behavior. Where Lamb's proposition actually fails is in his implicit assertion that traditional behavior is nothing more than cultural programming. As noted earlier, however, the relationship between culture and conduct is not as smooth as Lamb suggests. Whereas in earlier times traditionalization may indeed have been a puppet-like process, postindustrial society does not provide couples with a "clearly defined" script for how to act when a baby arrives. To the contrary, parental expectations in modern society are extremely complex and highly ambiguous (LeMasters, 1970).

The part of Lamb's statement that, in our opinion, should have been developed more is the beginning, where he says that "the insistent and undeniable dependency of the baby" poses special problems for new parents. Here he is suggesting some social interactional process operating to move the couple toward traditional role behavior. Our data suggest that the dependency of the baby on the parents is indeed an important factor in traditionalization, but that it is not simply a matter of making "equivocation or ambiguity about role demands more difficult to sustain." Rather, it is the dependency of the baby which creates a scarcity of free time, and which places the couple in a more competitive stance toward the other.

Before the transition to parenthood, it is relatively easy for couples (and especially men) to believe that they are nontraditional in the same way that it is easy, during times of economic growth and prosperity, for the middle class to believe that it is not racist. In both situations, valued resources (time in one case, money in the other) are not immediately threatened. However, history has shown that when it becomes apparent that strict adherence to sexual or racial equality can mean personal losses, then the basic axiom of the conflict orientation applies: When resources are scarce, people tend to choose themselves over others. Put simply, under conditions of scarcity, whites become more racist and men become more sexist. But in choosing themselves over others, both the middle-class white and the husband-father are faced with their own culture-conduct misalignments. In all likelihood, their behavior in the economic or temporal "squeeze" is at odds with their stated beliefs before the scarcity. This is where aligning actions come into play. By blaming others (their parents, their bosses, the government, and even the people they are competing with—blacks or women) and/or by justifying their conduct, they try their best to symbolically (but not behaviorally) mend their broken promises. Initially, these aligning actions serve as stopgap measures, helping the people in the system (both the "haves" and the "have-nots") cope with the transition, helping them maintain a consistent and orderly reality to their lives. Over time, the aligning actions help to transform the reality of the system itself.

In order to make our point clear, we should more precisely define what we mean by "traditionalization." Up to now, we have used the term to refer to increases in traditional behavior. This is because the existing studies on the transition to parenthood have employed the term in this way, and because it would not have been meaningful to question their approach until after we had introduced the change function of aligning actions. In truth, limiting traditionalization to behavioral shifts is theoretically vacuous. To know simply that a couple exhibits traditional behavior tells us nothing about whether the husband and wife "have their hearts in it" (role embracement), or whether they are mechanically "going through the motions." In other words, the meaning which the couple imputes to their activity is lost. We are not talking about whether the couple is "bothered" or "gratified" by their behavior. Rather, we are referring to the couple's total way of looking at what they are doing, their world view, their *Weltanschauung*. Although the studies which have focused on the transition to parenthood have equated traditionalization with behavioral change, there are other studies which have attempted to assess the impact of parenthood by comparing couples with and without children, and which indicate that, in addition to changing their behavior, couples may also shift to traditional ways of thinking (Hoffman and Manis, 1978). If both the culture and the conduct of a marriage traditionalize, then *traditionalization is an organizational transformation rather than simply a behavioral change.* This is how we prefer to use the term, and for good reason. Our data suggest that, more often than not, the transition to parenthood initiates a systemic level change in marriage toward a more traditional social organization.

The key to the difference between the continuity and the change function of aligning actions is time. On a short-term basis, aligning actions serve a preservative function, allowing beliefs to persist despite contradictory evidence. But on a long-term basis, aligning actions serve a morphogenic function, allowing beliefs to drift, ever so gradually, in the direction of the misaligned conduct. The presumption being made here is that over extended periods of time "culture follows conduct" (Stokes and Hewitt, 1976: 848). Thus, on a short-term basis, the couple whose conduct after the birth of their child is more traditional than their beliefs can use aligning actions to preserve those beliefs. But on a long-term basis, their willingness to excuse and justify their behavior rather than actually make it conform to their beliefs will result in an adjustment of their beliefs to their conduct. They will, in other words, begin to develop a marital culture that is closer to (but not necessarily in exact correspondence with) their actual conduct. Thus, aligning actions serve as a "social lubricant" for traditionalization in that they allow misalignments to be explained away rather than seriously examined.

The legitimacy of aligning actions is also important. Not all aligning actions are honored—that is, accepted—by the "offended" party as a legitimate explanation for the misalignment. Whether or not an aligning action is deemed legitimate is a function of the social structural and symbolic universe of the people in the interaction. For example, while it is generally considered socially acceptable for a father to say that his career is keeping him from his children, it is not as acceptable for mothers to use this excuse. It is also not as acceptable for mothers to say that they have less patience with their newborns than their husbands do, or that they are not as skilled in feeding, changing, or quieting the baby. If any of these aligning actions were offered by a mother, there is a fairly good chance that they would be disallowed by her husband, her family, her friends, and others. Thus, crucial to the traditionalization process is the availability of aligning actions that legitimate the father's withdrawal from baby care, and the corresponding absence of aligning actions that legitimate the mother's withdrawal from baby care.

The legitimacy of an aligning action is, however, not a given, which is to say that social actors cannot assume that an aligning action will be accepted when it is offered. The critical stage in the "life" of an aligning action is when the aligning action is presented and accepted or not accepted by the other party. Up until this point, the validity of an aligning action for any particular relationship is an open question. Only after the aligning action is presented *and* accepted does it become part of the social reality of the relationship. For example, when a husband says for the first time (perhaps just after he has had difficulty giving the baby breakfast) that he feels that he is inept at feeding his son or daughter, the wife's immediate response to the husband's assertion is critical. If at this point she does not challenge her husband's definition of the situation, or if she takes over responsibility for feeding the baby because of what he has just said, she has effectively endorsed the aligning action, accepting it, at least for the moment, as part of the consensual world. *Thus, the theory proposed here for the traditionalization process is both sociohistorical and interactional. As much as the aligning actions may appear to the husband and wife as realities that are "out there," programming their every move, the fact is that they are part and parcel of the negotiation process itself, intrinsic to the whole idea of social interaction.*

Conclusion

Our objective in this chapter has been to present a sociological view of the transition to parenthood. We believe that the transition to parenthood offers the student of social life a unique opportunity to see in action what Mills (1959) meant by "the sociological imagination." Few family experiences provide so vivid a picture of how biography and history are dialectically related. Few family experiences are so close to the cornerstone of a society.

The picture of parenthood that we have presented may not be as "beautiful" as some people would like. Nonetheless, we think that it will be ultimately beneficial. By laying bare some of the social patterns, social processes, and sociohistorical linkages underlying conflict and sexism during the transition to parenthood, we have at least provided a clue into how we might go about improving the social world of fathers and mothers.

References

Bell, C., and H. Newby (1976) "Husbands and wives: the dynamics of the deferential dialectic." Pp. 152–168 in D. Barker and S. Allen (eds.) *Dependence and Exploitation in Work and Marriage.* London: Longman.

Berk, R. A., and S. F. Berk (1979) *Labor and Leisure at Home.* Beverly Hills, CA: Sage Publications.

Blau, P. M. (1964) *Exchange and Power in Social Life.* New York: John Wiley.

Blauner, R. (1964) *Alienation and Freedom: The Factory Worker and His Industry.* Chicago: University of Chicago Press.

Blood, R. O., Jr., and D. M. Wolfe (1960) *Husbands and Wives: The Dynamics of Married Living.* New York: Free Press.

Burr, W. R., G. K. Leigh, R. D. Day, and J. Constantine (1979) "Symbolic interaction and the family." Pp. 42–111 in W. R. Burr, R. Hill, F. I. Nye, and

I. L. Reiss (eds.) *Contemporary Theories about the Family,* Vol. 2: *General Theories/Theoretical Orientations.* New York: Free Press.

Chodorow, N. (1978) *The Reproduction of Mothering: Psychoanalysis and the Sociology of Gender.* Berkeley: University of California Press.

Cowan, C. P., P. A. Cowan, L. Coie, and J. D. Coie (1978) "Becoming a family: the impact of a first child's birth on the couple's relationship." Pp. 296–324 in W. B. Miller and L. F. Newman (eds.) *The First Child and Family Formation.* Chapel Hill: Carolina Population Center, University of North Carolina.

Emerson, R. M. (1962) "Power-dependence relations." *American Sociological Review* 27 (February): 31–41.

Entwisle, D. R., and S. G. Doering (1981) *The First Birth.* Baltimore, MD: Johns Hopkins University Press.

Gelles, R. J. (1975) "Violence and pregnancy: A note on the extent of the problem and needed services." *Family Coordinator* 24 (January): 81–86.

Goffman, E. (1961) *Encounters: Two Studies in the Sociology of Interaction.* Indianapolis: Bobbs-Merrill.

——— (1971) *Relations in Public.* New York: Harper & Row.

Gouldner, A. W. (1960) "The norm of reciprocity: A preliminary statement." *American Sociological Review* 25 (April): 161–178.

Harriman, L. C. (1983) "Personal and marital changes accompanying parenthood." *Family Relations* 32 (July): 387–394.

Hobbs, D. F., Jr. (1965) "Parenthood as crisis: A third study." *Journal of Marriage and the Family* 27 (August): 367–372.

Hobbs, D. F., Jr., and J. M. Wimbish (1977) "Transition to parenthood by black couples." *Journal of Marriage and the Family* 39 (November): 677–689.

Hoffman, W. (1978) "Effects of the first child on the woman's role." Pp. 340–367 in W. B. Miller and L. F. Newman (eds.) *The First Child and Family Formation.* Chapel Hill: Carolina Population Center, University of North Carolina.

Hoffman, W., and J. D. Manis (1978) "Influences of children on marital interaction and parental satisfactions and dissatisfactions." Pp. 165–214 in R. M. Lerner and G. B. Spanier (eds.) *Child Influences on Marital and Family Interaction: A Life-Span Perspective.* New York: Academic Press.

Homans, G. (1974) *Social Behavior: Its Elementary Forms.* New York: Harcourt Brace Jovanovich.

Kuhn, A. (1974) *The Logic of Social Systems.* San Francisco: Jossey-Bass.

Lamb, M. (1978) "Influences of the child on marital quality and family interaction during the prenatal, perinatal and infancy periods." Pp. 137–164 in R. M. Lerner and G. B. Spanier (eds.) *Child Influences on Marital and Family Interaction: A Life-Span Perspective.* New York: Academic Press.

LaRossa, R. (1977) *Conflict and Power in Marriage: Expecting the First Child.* Beverly Hills, CA: Sage Publications.

——— (1983) "The transition to parenthood and the social reality of time." *Journal of Marriage and the Family* 45 (August): 579–589.

LaRossa, R., and M. Mulligan LaRossa (1981) *Transition to Parenthood: How Infants Change Families.* Beverly Hills, CA: Sage Publications.

LeMasters, E. E. (1970) *Parents in Modern America.* Homewood, IL: Dorsey Press.

Maslach, C. (1976) "Burned-out." *Human Behavior* 59 (September): 16–22.

Maslach, C., and A. Pines (1977) "The burn-out syndrome in the day care setting." *Child Care Quarterly* 6 (Summer): 100–113.

Mead, G. H. (1934) *Mind, Self, and Society from the Standpoint of a Social Behaviorist* (Edited by C. W. Morris). Chicago: University of Chicago Press.

Meyerowitz, J. H., and H. Feldman (1966) 'Transition to parenthood." *Psychiatric Research Report* 20 (February): 78–84.

Mills, C. W. (1940) "Situated actions and vocabularies of motive." *American Sociological Review* 5 (December): 904–913.

——— (1959) *The Sociological Imagination.* London: Oxford University Press.

Nye, F. L. (1979) "Choice, exchange, and the family." Pp. 1–41 in W. R. Burr, R. Hill, F. I. Nye, and I. L. Reiss (eds.) *Contemporary Theories about the Family,* Vol. 2: *General Theories/Theoretical Orientations.* New York: Free Press.

Pleck, J. H. (1976) "Men's new roles in the family: Housework and child care." Working paper. Wellesley, MA: Wellesley College Center for Research on Women.

Pleck, J. H., and M. Rustad (1980) "Husbands' and wives' time in family work and paid work in the 1975–76 study of time use." Working paper. Wellesley, MA: Wellesley College Center for Research on Women.

Raush, H. L., W. A. Barry, R. K. Hertel, and M. A. Swain (1974) *Communication, Conflict, and Marriage.* San Francisco: Jossey-Bass.

Robinson, J. P. (1977) *How Americans Use Time: A Social-Psychological Analysis of Everyday Behavior.* New York: Praeger.

Rossi, A. S. (1977) "A biosocial perspective on parenting." *Daedalus* 106 (Spring): 1–31.

——— (1984) "Gender and parenthood: American Sociological Association, 1983 presidential address." *American Sociological Review* 49 (February): 1–19.

Scott, M. B., and S. M. Lyman (1968) "Accounts." *American Sociological Review* 33 (February): 46–62.

Sprey, J. (1979) "Conflict theory and the study of marriage and the family." Pp. 130–159 in W. R. Burr, R. Hill, F. I. Nye, and I. L. Reiss (eds.) *Contemporary Theories about the Family,* Vol. 2: *General Theories/Theoretical Orientations.* New York: Free Press.

Stokes, R., and J. P. Hewitt (1976) "Aligning actions." *American Sociological Review* 41 (October): 838–849.

Straus, M. A., R. J. Gelles, and S. K. Steinmetz (1980) *Behind Closed Doors: Violence in the American Family.* New York: Doubleday/Anchor.

Zerubavel, E. (1979a) "Private time and public time: The temporal structure of social accessibility and professional commitments." *Social Forces* 58 (September): 38–58.

——— (1979b) *Patterns of Time in Hospital Life: A Sociological Perspective.* Chicago: University of Chicago Press.

13

Can Men "Mother"? Life as a Single Father

BARBARA J. RISMAN

Research on single fathers is vital because more children than ever before are living—at least part of the time—with divorced fathers (Katz, 1979; Orthner, Brown & Ferguson, 1976; Rosenthal & Keshet, 1981). Judges, counselors, teachers, social workers, policy specialists and single parent families themselves all need accurate and verifiable information as to how this emerging family form operates. Single fathers must often fill social roles for which they have not been trained. Do they feel competent to nurture their children, or has their male sex role socialization been so overwhelmingly consistent (e.g., Bandura & Walters, 1963; Chodorow, 1978; Stockard & Johnson, 1980) that by adulthood fathers have neither the inclination nor aptitude to provide primary care for young children?

Individualist and microstructural theorists would give different answers to the question of whether single fathers can be viable primary caretakers for young children. This paper begins with a discussion of these two theoretical perspectives. An assessment of previous literature follows the theoretical discussion. New research which differs from past work in two ways is then presented. The sample used for these analyses is diverse enough to identify what demographic and life-style factors may affect satisfaction with single fatherhood. In addition, the conclusions suggest that microstructuralist theory provides a better explanation than does individualist theory for the experiences of single fathers. The implications of a microstructuralist perspective for

---

A dissertation fellowship from the American Association of University Women supported this research and is gratefully acknowledged. The author would also like to thank Pepper Schwartz, Phillip Blumstein, and Judy Howard for their helpful comments at various stages of this research. In addition, Maxine Atkinson, Mary Gillmore, Wilma Peebles, and Richard Kane provided valuable reviews of this article. Finally, the gender role seminar at the University of Washington provided collective support and criticism for the on-going research of which these analyses are the first product. This is a slightly revised version of an article published in *Family Relations*, Vol. 35, 1986.

professionals who work with single fathers and their children are discussed.

Theory

Most writing about gender differences and parenting (e.g., Chodorow, 1978; Gilligan, 1982; Rossi, 1984; Stockard & Johnson, 1980; Van den Berghe, 1979) is clearly individualist. Authors suggest that by adulthood men and women have developed very different individual personality characteristics. Females have become more nurturant, person oriented and child centered, and males have become more competitive and work oriented. In an articulate and influential statement of this individualistic perspective, Linton (1945) argued that personality develops from habitualized attitudes and as a result of repeated experiences. Intensely held emotions, values and predispositions develop during childhood and coalesce into a person's core identity, which has limited flexibility once formed. Most of the literature on parenting attributes the observed sex differences between mothers and fathers to internalized psychic predispositions: women desire to mother their children while men do not.

Although individualist theorists (e.g. Chodorow, 1978; Gilligan, 1982; Stockard & Johnson, 1980; Van den Berghe, 1979) identify differing social and/or biological determinants for sex differences in parental behavior, they all take for granted the *consequences* of sex role acquisition and focus their debate on *how* sex role acquisition occurs. In particular, individualist theorists often assume that women make better caretakers than do men. They debate whether this is true because women have themselves been mothered by same-sex parents and have therefore developed the desire for intense intimacy or whether the social reinforcement girls receive for doll play and other nurturant behavior is a better explanation for exclusively female mothering.

Although there are as many varieties of structuralism (see review by Mayhew, 1980) as of individualism, all structuralists dispute the assumption that individual motivation, learned through whatever processes, can explain human behavior. When applied to the study of gender (Kanter, 1977; Lorber, 1981; Risman, 1987), microstructuralism rejects the assumption that sex roles are internalized as personality traits. Because behavior is not viewed as immutably fixed by childhood experiences and biological preconditions, the differing parental behaviors of men and women must be explained as adaptive to ongoing interaction, the product of more immediate situational demands.

Individualist and structural theories make very different predictions about the possibility for successful single father households. Individualist theories would predict that single fathers lack both the internal motivation and the expressive skills to provide the intense intimacy necessary for nurturing young children. In contrast, structural theories suggest that human behavior, including family roles, is determined by the social context in which people live. Although mothers are currently expected to shoulder primary responsibility for childrearing, microstructural theory suggests that when that responsibility is shifted to fathers, men will adopt those behaviors which have traditionally been considered mothering.

The present research was designed to test whether individualist or microstructural theories are more accurate predictors of single fathers' lives. Such a theoretical debate is vital to those who work with single parents and their children because social policies, including those which affect single parents, are based on implicit theoretical perspectives. Assumption based on these contrasting theories will lead to very different social policies. For example, an individualist theory suggests that single fathers, and other men interested in primary caretaking, need to be taught to parent. Social workers implicitly using an individualist perspective might suggest the development of special courses or individual counseling for fathers before they be allowed to shoulder primary caretaking responsibility. In contrast, microstructural theory suggests that instead of retraining individuals, social policies designed to aid single parents, men or women, need to focus on restructuring paid work so that it does not create conflict for those persons who also shoulder primary responsibility for young children.

Review of the Literature

Research on single fathers began in the late 1960s in the United States, Canada, England and Australia. The research thus far has been primarily descriptive. Because the methods, samples and therefore results differ dramatically by geographical region, this review focuses mostly on American (i.e., U.S. and Canadian) single fathers.[1] The American studies (Ambert, 1982; Defrain & Eirich, 1981; Gasser & Taylor, 1976; Greenberg, 1979; Hanson, 1979; Mendes, 1979; Orthner et al., 1976; Rosenthal & Keshet, 1981; Santrock & Warshack, 1979) have small samples of predominantly white, middle-class fathers. These men were identified from single parent organizations, by answering media advertisements, or by referrals. Greif's (1985) research on American single fathers is conceptually sophisticated and based on a large sample. But like most other studies, it is based entirely on men who join support groups (e.g., Parents Without Partners), and the data are presented descriptively.

The descriptive findings about American single fathers appear remarkably consistent. Few single fathers (Ambert, 1982; Defrain & Eirich, 1981; Gasser & Taylor, 1976; Greenberg, 1979; Hanson, 1979; Mendes, 1979; Orthner et al., 1976; Rosenthal and Keshet, 1981; Greif, 1985; Santrock & Warshack, 1979) recruit either female kin or paid help to perform the "female" tasks of housekeeping. Homemaking does not appear to be a particular problem for single fathers. Another consistent finding is that although American single fathers do report some problems, such as worry that their daughters lack a female role model, most respondents generally feel satisfied with their perceived competence as single parents and single adults.

With such consistent results, it may appear that the theoretical questions raised here have already been answered: despite their male sex role socialization, today's single fathers believe themselves successful. Unfortunately, there is a major weakness in past research. Most studies have been exploratory, with samples that are small and homogeneous on factors which may affect role performances—income and reason for custody. No previous American study has a large and diverse enough sample to identify respondents in various economic statuses and with a variety of reasons for father custody.

It is important that research on American single fathers includes more diverse samples because the English and Australian studies (e.g., Ferri, 1973; George & Wilding, 1972; Hipgrave, 1982; Katz, 1979; Murch, 1973; O'Brien, 1982), which include more economically deprived families, suggest that financial status is a key factor in men's performance and satisfaction as single fathers. Within one large sample (George & Wilding), those fathers who reported financial problems also felt less competent as parents. An analagous situation exists between samples. Researchers whose samples include many financially deprived families (e.g., Katz, O'Brien) tend to report more serious problems in both father/child relationships and the father's role satisfaction. A single father's economic standing may be an important determinant of his satisfaction with lone parenthood.

One other recent British study provides direction for research on American families. O'Brien (1982) found that the reason for father custody influences the adaptation and success of single fathers. O'Brien categorized single fathers into three groups by the reason for custody: conciliatory negotiators, hostile seekers, and passive acceptors. Conciliatory negotiators had been partners in dual career marriages and gained custory of their children as a result of amicable discussions and joint decisions. Hostile seekers fought for custody, often to punish ex-wives for extra-marital affairs. Finally, passive acceptors had been deserted by their wives.

O'Brien found that conciliatory negotiators were considerably more successful single parents than passive acceptors or hostile seekers. Unfortunately, social class was confounded with reason for custody in this study. When custody was amicably negotiated, both parents were usually professionals, and comfortably middle-class. Hostile seekers had lived in more traditional one paycheck households, while passive acceptors were most often from the lower middle-class and reported severe financial stress. It may be that the reason for father custody is merely one indication of difference in the lifestyle of each social class. If, however, reason for custody and economic status have independent effects on custodial fathers' adjustment, no research thus far can differentiate such effects.

Methodology

The present study was designed so that the sample was large and diverse enough to disentangle the independent effects of economic status from reasons for father custody on father's perceptions of their role in life as single parents. Do all kinds of men, for whatever reason they became single fathers, adopt the behaviors usually considered mothering? Do fathers who face economic insecurity have more problems adopting the role of primary caretaker? In this section, the data collection techniques and resultant sample characteristics are discussed in detail. The dependent variables are then described, followed by a brief presentation of the statistical techniques used in the analysis.

To locate single fathers, advertisements appeared in national single parent magazines and newsletters. In addition, referrals were solicited from social service agencies in Washington state and Boston, Massachusetts. To avoid sampling only respondents who were identifiable via social service agencies or parenting associations, press releases were distributed to Washington state and the national media. These press releases attracted the interest of talk show hosts and radio public service departments across the country. Word of mouth referrals were also thoroughly investigated.

Two hundred eighty-one questionnaires were distributed between 1981 and 1983 and 141 completed surveys returned. This 54 percent response rate considerably underestimates the proportion of eligible single fathers who participated once contacted; questionnaires were often distributed unknowingly to ineligible referrals.[2] A detailed discussion of sampling strategies is available elsewhere (Risman, 1983).

To meet eligibility requirements, at least one child under 14 years of age had to live as a full-time resident in each home. Ninety percent of the respondents reported that their youngest resident child was a pre-teen. This study was designed to measure the relationship between a father and his youngest child. In over three-quarters of these families, at least one child lives with the father all of the time; in the other 23%, the children visit their mother for up to 3 months per year.

Over half (62%, n = 87) of the respondents had little choice in adopting the single parent role,[3] because they had been deserted, widowed, or their wives had refused custody. These men, passive acceptors, had become single fathers through no active effort of their own. The rest were split evenly between having negotiated for custody while still married (n = 26), conciliatory negotiators, and having obtained custody by forceful action against the mother's wish (n = 28), or hostile seekers. The mean length of time these men have been in their current marital status is between 1 and 2 years; over half have been single for over 2 years.

Ninety percent of the single fathers in this study were white. About half these fathers had not graduated from college, one-third were graduates, and the rest had advanced degrees. Over half were employed in professional, managerial, or other white collar jobs, while approximately one-quarter of these fathers work in blue collar jobs. The men in this study were more likely to work in white collar jobs and less likely to work in blue collar jobs than a sample actually representative of the 1981 male labor force (U.S. Census, Statistical Abstract, 1982–1983). Eighty percent of these fathers worked full-time, the rest worked part-time or were currently unemployed. Seventeen percent of these respondents reported an annual income less than $15,000, and almost half (45.5 percent) earn between $15,000 and $29,999 per year. Nearly one-quarter of the sample reported yearly incomes between $30,000 and $50,000, while 14 percent reported incomes above $50,000 annually. Given the mean yearly income of $20,000 to $25,000, these single fathers earned somewhat more money than the average white single father who supported a family in 1980 on approximately $18,731 annually (U.S. Census, 1982).

Reason for father custody and economic status were not related in this study. Although fathers who negotiated custody were more likely than other respondents to work in white collar jobs ($tau\ b = .18$, $p = .02$) they did not earn significantly more money.

Religion did not seem to play a major role in most of these men's lives. Nearly a third reported "no religious preference." Thirty-nine percent were Protestant and almost 20 percent were Catholic. Only 4 percent were Jewish, and the rest reported "other" religions. On a 9 point religiosity scale (1 = not at all; 9 = very religious), the group mean was nearly at 5, indicating less than orthodox religious attitudes.

Previous research has identified three issues as central to the role of single father: (1) the father's experience and skill with the instrumental tasks of homemaking; (2) the nature of the father/child relationship, or the expressive function of parenting; and (3) the father's overall role satisfaction. The present research was designed to address each of these issues systematically. Measures for each dimension were created from items on a 20 page self-administered questionnaire; all measures were based entirely upon the fathers' perception.

The analysis proceeds very simply. Descriptive information on each dimension is presented briefly. Next, the impact of economic status and reason for custody are assessed for each dimension. For a more detailed discussion of methodology see Risman (1986).

Results

The Instrumental Tasks of Childrearing: Fathers as Homemakers

Four out of five single fathers in this study had no outside housekeeping help, either paid or volunteer. Most men did not depend on mother, girlfriend or housekeeper to perform the stereotypically female tasks of cooking or cleaning. Over 80 percent of all fathers reported that they were personally responsible for the varied tasks of housekeeping: grocery shopping, food preparation, house cleaning, and yard work. On the average, fathers ate dinner at home with their children from five to six times per week.

The fathers in this study showed a concern for making their homes child centered. Ninety-two percent of the respondents have children's first aid supplies on hand, and 83 percent have an average of three emergency phone numbers posted for children or sitter's use. When only 8 men in a sample of 141 respondents reported that friends or relatives routinely performed either child care or housework, it is safe to conclude that single fathers manage their households by themselves. They do not find female housekeepers to take responsibility for tasks usually assigned to wives (e.g., Nye, 1976).

Not only do fathers take responsibility for housecleaning and other mundane tasks, but they also report spending considerable time with their children in both household chores and recreational activities. On the average, single fathers and their children do joint household chores at least weekly. They watch TV together weekly, and play sports together more than once a month. These fathers take their children on an educational outing (e.g., museum) or watch spectator sports together monthly. In addition, respondents chauffeur their youngest child to some activity at least once every week.

The custodial fathers in this study are concerned that their children receive adequate health care. Nine out of 10 fathers have a family physician or clinic. Nearly all the children in this study visit a dentist at least once every year (91.4 percent) and half of them visit a dentist twice a year. The vast majority (89.9 percent) of the children do not have any serious health problems.

To measure less obvious aspects of child care, fathers were queried about involvement with their children outside of family activities. Nine out of 10 fathers with children enrolled in schools organized by homerooms knew the homeroom teacher's name. Eighty-eight percent of the respondents could name at least 3 of their youngest child's friends, and only 4.5 percent of these fathers did not know any of their children's friends.

The Expressive Tasks of Childrearing: The Father/Child Relationship

Although the instrumental tasks of homemaking are surely important, the tenor and quality of the father/child relationships are perhaps the most central issue in research on single fathers. Psychoanalytic theorists (e.g., Chodorow, 1978) often suggest that a core attribute of mothering, but not fathering, is the ability and desire to develop intensely intimate relationships with young children. It is essential to ask whether single fathers develop intimate relationships with their young children, or whether children living alone with fathers lack the intense bonds they might have developed with mothers.

In this study, these relationships are measured by the fathers' perceptions of dyadic intimacy between themselves and their youngest child. First, fathers report the extent to which they believe the child discloses his or her feelings. Other measures of dyadic intimacy include frequency of physical affection, questions on closeness, and satisfaction with the relationship.

In general, these men believe their children share almost all of their emotions. Children are more likely to share positive feelings, such as being happy, excited, proud, and smart, than negative feelings such as being worried or lonely.

In addition to reporting a great deal of self-disclosure from child to parent, these fathers report considerable physical contact with their children. When asked how often they were physically affectionate with their children, including cuddling and body wrestling, the mean response was at least once every day. Similarly, when explicitly queried on how often they hugged their youngest child, the mean response was between every day and more than once a day.

Overall, the lone fathers in this study feel very close to ($\overline{X}$ = 8.33 on a 9 point scale), and very affectionate toward ($\overline{X}$ = 7.41), their youngest child. They also generally approve of their children's behavior ($\overline{X}$ = 6.96). Indeed, the fathers are very satisfied ($\overline{X}$ = 7.71) with the relationships they have developed as primary parents.

Fathers' Role Satisfaction

The fathers in this study are generally satisfied with the relationships described above, a satisfaction not a function of their integration into particularly supportive extended kin networks. Although half these men live in the same city as their own parents, they see their relatives either monthly or a few times yearly. Under one-third of these respondents (29 percent) can depend on either relatives or friends as usual babysitters. On the average, relatives care for the children only a few times a year.

Although relatives do not provide routine child care, they do provide emotional support and practical help during a crisis. When a child is ill, 37 percent of all respondents call a relative for emotional support. Another third call a friend or current dating partner, while the rest depend on other sources for support. About one-half of the fathers stay home from work with a sick child, one-quarter report that relatives help care for a sick child during the work week and the rest either pay a sitter or make other arrangements. Single fathers have support networks composed both of kin and friends, but do not depend on others to shoulder routine child-care responsibilities.

Although most respondents do hope to remarry eventually (90 percent), they do not claim to seek a woman to relieve them as primary parent. While a large minority (38 percent) intend to retain primary responsibility, the rest hope to share child care equally. Not one respondent wants a new wife to take the major responsibility for childrearing. Although these men are not searching for a replacement mother, they are concerned with the relationship between a hypothetical spouse and their children. Every respondent feels affection between children and possible wife is at least somewhat important, and almost all (80 percent) felt such affection to be very important or necessary.

The desire to continue intense involvement with their children, even after remarriage, is very strong evidence that these men feel comfortable with the role of primary parent. For example, when asked how often they would rather be childless the mean response is 1.68 on a 9 point scale (1 = never). Despite their statistically deviant lifestyle, these men are glad to be fathers.

The Impact of Social Class

Thus far, this research supports previous findings: single fathers appear to have little trouble fulfilling either the instrumental or expressive functions of single parenthood. Indeed, the respondents in this study report a good deal of satisfaction with their lives. It is now appropriate to turn attention to the impact of financial status on the respondents' perceptions of their lives.

Overall, a father's economic status affects his role as a single parent primarily on instrumental tasks. Not surprisingly, income was positively related to having outside help come into the home (*tau b* = .21, p = .004). This relationship is not, however, strictly linear. Although the respondents are categorized into four income levels, it is those men with incomes over $50,000 annually who are different from the rest. Over half of the most wealthy men (57.6 percent) hire outside help for housekeeping versus 13 percent to 19 percent of men in the three other income categories. These high income single fathers are more likely to hire help for the following tasks: cooking dinner (*tau b* = .15, p = .05); housecleaning (*tau b* = .27, p = .001); and preparing lunches (*tau b* = .17, p = .01). There were no differences by income level in who fixed the families' breakfast, shopped for groceries or children's clothing, performed yard work, or how often the family ate dinner together.

As might be expected, there is also a positive relationship between expensive activities and father's income. For example, there is a positive relationship between the number of yearly visits to a dentist and father's income (*tau b* = .20, p = .002), but 92 percent of all children see a dentist at least once a year. There was also a weak positive relationship between having an established relationship with a family doctor or clinic and economic status (*tau b* = .13, p = .05); 80 percent of fathers who earn under $15,000 annually report such a relationship versus approximately 95 percent of fathers in all other income categories. Father's income is also positively related to the frequency of attendance at spectator sports (r = .22, p = .01) and the frequency of father chauffering a child to an activity (r = .27, p = .001). These findings make intuitive sense, as medical care, children's activities, and spectator sports are expensive. There were no differences by economic status for less expensive activities such as the frequency of family TV viewing, playing sports together, or going on educational outings.

On measures of paternal concern with creating an environment safe for children—the number and types of first aid in the home and whether emergency phone numbers are posted for children or sitters—there are absolutely no differences by economic status. In sum, the wealthiest fathers buy somewhat more housekeeping services and spend more money on recreational activities than do others, but there is no evidence that they are more safety conscious or concerned with their performance on other instrumental tasks.

Fathers' economic status is even less important for the tenor and ambience of parent/child relations—the expressive dimension of parenting. Only one difference related to social class emerged on the expressive dimension: an inverse relationship exists between income and fathers' ratings of disclosure from their children about negative feelings. Children whose fathers earned more money were less likely to reveal when they were sad ($r = -.19, p = .01$), lonely ($r = -.22, p = .01$), or worried ($r = -.20, p = .01$). This cannot be attributed to children in poorer homes having more negative experiences, because when descriptions of children's personalities were analyzed no differences emerged by parental economic status.

The finding that income is inversely related to children's disclosure of negative emotions is surprising, as past research suggests that men who face economic uncertainty have more trouble adjusting to the role of primary parent than do middle-class men. Perhaps this finding can be interpreted by realizing that only *negative* emotions are disclosed more to low income fathers. Past research (e.g., Kerckhoff, 1972) suggests that because middle-class parents have higher expectations for their children's behavior than do poor ones, children may withhold some negative feelings to meet such performance expectations. Therefore, it may be that children of more middle-class, single fathers are withholding feelings to avoid disappointing their fathers.

A cautionary note is necessary. Despite the relationship between income and child's self-disclosure, most fathers in this study report both intimate relationships with their children and satisfaction with those relationships. In fact, there were no differences in role satisfaction based on social class. Although wealthier men were more likely to date frequently ($r = .24, p = .01$), they were no more likely to be seeking a wife. Men with higher incomes are, however, more likely to feel it essential for children and potential spouses to get along ($r = .14, p = .05$).

Despite these slight differences between respondents based on income, the substantive variation between the mean responses in each group is not impressive. Unlike the research conducted in other countries, social class does not seem to be a particularly important determinant of an American man's satisfaction with single fatherhood.

The Impact of Reason for Custody

Although instrumental tasks are not at all related to reason for custody, there seems to be one major difference in the respondents' perceptions of their relationships with children based on why they have custody. Fathers who fought for custody report better relationships with their youngest child than do other respondents. Men who received custody over ex-wives' objections believe their children are more likely to disclose feelings of loneliness ($F = {}_{(2.136)}4.26, p = .02$) than are either fathers who negotiated for custody or passive acceptors. Similarly, although all fathers find childrearing a chore less than half the time, men who fought for custody report feeling that childrearing is a chore less often ($\overline{X} = 3.11$ on a 9 point scale, 9 = always) than do negotiators ($\overline{X} = 4.15$) or passive acceptors ($\overline{X} = 4.13$; $F = {}_{(2.135)}3.25, p = .04$). In addition, although not statistically significant, there is a trend for passive acceptors to more often wish they were childless ($\overline{X} = 1.84$ on a 9 point scale, 9 = always) than do negotiators ($\overline{X} = 1.43$) or hostile seekers ($\overline{X} = 1.43$).

These results are not readily interpreted. It may be that fathers are more likely to want custody of children when they have previously developed intimate relationships. Another explanation, however, is that positive perceptions of the father/child relationship are justifications for the father's decision to pursue custody against the wishes of the mother. Fathers who fought for custody may be particularly likely to ignore negative experiences to avoid cognitive dissonance over their own actions. Whatever the reason for these findings, it is important to remember that the differences based on the reason for custody are not dramatic.

Conclusions: Theoretical and Practical Implications

These results support past research which suggested that, at least in their own perceptions, custodial fathers are competent as primary parents. However, these findings also differ from past research. Economic status seems to be less important as a determinant of life satisfaction among American single fathers than among those in England or Australia. An even more striking difference is that in this research, men who have fought for custody believe they have developed as, if not more, intimate relationships with their children than do other single fathers.

Despite the differences between fathers based on reason for custody and economic status, these findings suggest that men believe they can be competent custodial parents. With this conclusion, based on a large and diverse sample of fathers, it is now possible to assess the usefulness of microstructural and individualist theories for understanding single fatherhood. The ability of men to provide primary care for pre-teenage children challenges currently popular individualist theories which suggest that the personality traits needed to mother are internalized as psychic predispositions, so that by adulthood males have neither the inclination nor skill to care for young children.

This research suggests that childhood experiences and sex role socialization do not create inflexible gender typed behavioral patterns. Instead, as microstructural theory suggests, the situational demands of role requirements influence adult behavior and lead men to mother when they have no wives to depend upon. Perhaps gender differences in our society are based as much on the differential expectations and role requirements males and females face throughout their lives as upon internalized personality characteristics. This study suggests that when males take full responsibility for child care, when they meet expectations usually confined to females, they develop intimate and affectionate relationships with their children. Despite male sex role training, fathers respond to the nontraditional role of single parent with strategies stereotypically considered feminine.

What are the practical implications of this structural perspective on single fathers? The implications for social policy are clear; the traditional assumption that children belong with their mothers after divorce needs to be reexamined. When judges decide what is in a child's best interest, they need not always assume mothers are better primary caretakers than are fathers. Similarly, social workers and counselors employed in Family Court should be aware that females do not necessarily make better mothers. It may be in the arena of child custody men stand to gain—and women stand to lose—by the removal of gender-based societal and judicial inequity.

Notes

1. The early British studies (George & Wilding, 1972; Ferri, 1973; Murch, 1973) were based on much larger samples and commissioned because "motherless" families came to be considered a social problem. Poor fathers were overrepresented in these studies because the sampling technique tended to identify those families who used social service agencies. The respondents in recent British and Australian studies (Hipgrave, 1982; Katz, 1979; O'Brien, 1982) more closely resemble American samples, but still include more economically deprived families.

2. Because social service agencies insisted upon anonymity for the clients they referred and contacted, the percentage of no response due to intelligibility cannot be traced.

3. The overrepresentation of fathers with little choice in adopting the single parent role is a result of sampling techniques designed for a larger study of which these data are but one part. I have no information as to the actual proportion of American single fathers who had no choice, who negotiated or who fought for custody.

References

Ambert, A. (1982) "Differences in children's behavior toward custodial mothers and custodial fathers." *Journal of Marriage and the Family* 44 (1):73–86.

Bandura, A., and R. H. Walters (1963) *Social Learning and Personality Development.* New York: Holt, Rinehart and Winston.

Chodorow, N. (1978) *The Reproduction of Mothering.* Berkeley: University of California Press.

Defrain, J., and R. Eirich (1981) "Coping as single parents: A comparative study of fathers and mothers." *Family Relations* 265–273.

Ferri, E. (1973) "Characteristics of motherless families." *British Journal of Social Work* 3(1):91–100.

Gasser, R. D., and C. H. Taylor (1976) "Role adjustment of single fathers with dependent children." *Family Coordinator* 25(4):397–402.

George, V., and P. Wilding (1972) *Motherless Families.* London: Routledge and Kegan Paul.

Gilligan, C. (1982) *In a Different Voice: Psychological Theory and Women's Development.* Cambridge: Harvard University Press.

Greenberg, J. B. (1979) "Single-parenting and intimacy: A comparison of mothers and fathers." *Alternative Lifestyles* 2(3):308–330.

Greif, G. (1985) *Single Fathers.* Lexington, MA: Lexington Books.

Hanson, S. (1979) "Characteristics of single custodial fathers and the parent-child relationship." Doctoral dissertation, University of Washington. Dissertation Abstracts International, 40 (12), 6438-A.

Hipgrave, T. (1982) "Lone fatherhood: A problematic status. Pp. 171–183 in L. McKee and M. O'Brien (Eds.), *The Father Figure,* London: Tavistock Publications.

Kanter, R. M. (1977) *Men and Women of the Corporation.* New York: Harper Books.

Katz, A. J. (1979) "Lone fathers: Perspectives and implications for family policy." *Family Coordinator* 28(4):521–528.

Kerckhoff, A. C. (1972) *Socialization and Social Class.* Englewood Cliffs, NJ: Prentice-Hall.

Linton, R. (1945) *The Cultural Background of Personality.* New York: D. Appleton-Century.

Lorber, J. (1981) "On the reproduction of mothering: A methodological debate." *Signs* 6:482–486.

Mayhew, B. (1980) "Structuralism versus individuals: Part 1, Shadow boxing in the dark." *Social Forces* 42:91–105.

Mendes, H. A. (1979) "Single-parent families—A typology of lifestyles." *Social Work* 24(3):193–200.

Murch, M. (1973) "Motherless families project: Bristol council of social service report on first year's work." *British Journal of Social Work* 3(3):365–376.

Nye, I. F. (1976) *Role Structure and Analysis of the Family.* Beverly Hills, CA: Sage Publications.

O'Brien, M. (1982) "Becoming a lone father: Differential patterns and experiences." Pp. 184–207 in L. McKee and M. O'Brien (Eds.), *The Father Figure.* London: Tavistock Publications.

Orthner, D. K., T. Brown, & D. Ferguson (1976) "Single-parenthood: An emerging life style." *Family Coordinator* 25(4):429–437.

Risman, B. J. (1983) "Necessity and the invention of mothering: A test of individual versus structural explanations for gender roles." Doctoral dissertation, University of Washington. Dissertation Abstracts International, 44 (11), 3510-A.

Risman, B. J. (1987) "Intimate relationships from a microstructural perspective: Men who mother." *Gender and Society* 1(1):6–32.

Rosenthal, K. and H. F. Keshet (1981) *Fathers without Partners.* Totowa, NJ: Rowman and Littlefield.

Rossi. A. S. (1984) "Gender and parenthood." *American Sociological Review* 49(Feb.):1–19.

Santrock, J. W., and R. A. Warshak (1979) "Father custody and social development in boys and girls." *Journal of Social Issues* 35(4):112–125.

Stockard, J., and M. M. Johnson (1980) *Sex Role Inequality and Sex Role Development.* Englewood Cliffs, NJ: Prentice-Hall.

U.S. Department of Commerce, Bureau of the Census (1982) "Changing family composition and income differentials." *Special Demographic Analyses* CDS-80-7.

U.S. Department of Commerce, Bureau of the Census (1982–1983) *Statistical Abstracts: National Data Book and Guide to Sources.* Washington, DC: U.S. Government Printing Office.

Van den Berghe, P. L. (1979) *Human Family Systems: An Evolutionary View.* New York: Elsevier.

14

The Impact of Gender and Past Marital Experiences on Heading a Household Alone

POLLY A. FASSINGER

Divorce or death of a spouse can turn one's world upside down. The grief and sense of loss can be overwhelming and remain vivid for years. In the context of this emotional turmoil, single parents shape new daily-life patterns and realign their parenting, housework, financial management, and paid work. This paper examines single parents' feelings about one such change: heading a household alone. We know from past research that single parents have numerous responses to becoming sole householders. For example, some single parents feel quite stressed about making decisions without a partner (Kopf, 1976; Orthner et al., 1976) while others are happy to be sole householders because they can live without the constant criticism and tension caused by their ex-mates (Weiss, 1979). In contrast to these reactions of pleasure and displeasure, Greenberg (1979) discovered ambivalent feelings about independence among single parents.

Although the literature tells us single parents do not react uniformly to becoming sole householders, we do not know what causes single parents' different responses. What kind of parent is ambivalent? Which single parents enjoy heading a household alone? I investigated these questions through a grounded theory study of men's and women's reactions to single parenting.

Previous research has examined how gender shapes single parenting. Many believe that gender socialization and a system of gender stratification cause women and men to have different experiences as single parents. For example, Brandwein et al. (1974) speculated that our culture's socialization process left women less prepared to be familial authority figures. Other frequently mentioned gender differences among single parents include their unequal social pressures and social supports (Ambert, 1982; Gasser and Taylor, 1976; Smith, 1980; Spicer and

---

An earlier version of this paper was the recipient of the 1987 Dissertation Paper Award of the American Sociological Association's Section on Sex and Gender. The author thanks Barrie Thorne, Nancy Gilliland, Linda Johnson, Barbara Risman, and Carol Wharton for their helpful comments.

Hampe, 1975) and the greatly disparate economic resources of these men and women (Espenshade, 1979; Schlesinger, 1979; Weiss, 1984; Weitzman, 1985).

Because of these findings, I originally anticipated that parents' gender would be the strongest indicator of pleasure or displeasure with single parenting. However, I discovered a variety of reactions to single parenting *among* mothers and *among* fathers and unexpectedly found similar responses to single parenting within groups of men and women. I concluded that gender alone is not a reliable determinant of men's and women's reactions to single parenting.

I argue instead that single parents' gender and previous marital experiences intersect to shape parents' responses to heading a household alone. A person's previous marital experiences (what I call "marital history type") together with their gender influences whether or not she or he sees single parenting as liberating, confining, enjoyable, or distressing. I discovered that parents with similar marital histories have common reactions to single parenting; past marital experiences offer a baseline from which parents judge current responsibilities. Gender is important because it corresponds with different sets of experiences and duties within each marital history type. The following pages outline specifically how gender and marital history type together influence single mothers' and single fathers' feelings about heading a household alone.

Study Background

Evidence for this paper comes from a grounded theory study of single parents' reactions to their changed responsibilities (Fassinger, 1987). Through notices in school newsletters, day care centers, programs such as Parents Without Partners, and referrals, I contacted divorced single parents[1] who resided with their children. All interviewees were residents of a Midwestern city whose population was approximately 120,000 in 1980. The city is predominantly white (97 percent); all respondents are white.

Of the twenty single mothers and fourteen single fathers with whom I spoke, the mothers were slightly younger than the fathers ($\overline{X} = 34$ for women, $\overline{X} = 39$ for men) and had been single parents for a somewhat longer time. These fathers, who had slightly larger families, were more economically advantaged than the women (men's median 1984 salary = \$22,000, women's = \$16,800). All parents had at least a high school education and many had attended trade school or business school. A high percentage of these women were professionals; many were nurses or teachers. Fathers were mostly in professional or administrative positions.

Interviews were semistructured; questions focused on changes in the parents' daily lives since becoming single parents. I transcribed all interviews and analyzed the information using a version of the constant comparative method (Glaser and Strauss, 1967) and a strategy suggested by Charmaz (1983) of line-by-line coding of the data. Comparisons revealed that some single parents were overwhelmed by decision-making changes, some were proud of their new duties, and some seemed rather nonchalant.

I continually searched for underlying patterns in parents' reactions to sole householding. I looked for similarities based on parents' reasons for becoming single parents (for example, desertion, own choice), tenure at single parenting, income, age, marital status, education, number of children, gender of children, and reason for custody.[2] Although numerous studies asserted that these factors are related to significant variations among single parents (Gasser and Taylor, 1976; Greif, 1985; Hetherington et al., 1976; Rosenfeld and Rosenstein, 1973; Schorr and Moen, 1979), when compared by these traits, I found no consistent themes in parents' responses to being sole householders.[3]

Moving beyond suggestions offered in the literature, I examined differences in single parents' responses based on factors the parents implied were significant, such as tenure as a married parent, beliefs about why the marriage ended, previous personal investment in the marriage, and work commitment. I discovered that the kind of marriage the parent previously had, or their "marital history type," played a prominent role in single parents' reactions to becoming sole householders.

I then delineated the single parents' marital history types. Since my questions often led parents to describe division of labor and decision-making structure in their past marriages, I focused on these two dimensions. I determined that single parents described four basic marital history types, which differed according to spouses' participation in decision making, parenting, housework, and income-earning. These types include what I call segregated marriages, modified-segregated marriages, integrated marriages, and primarily wife-shaped marriages.[4]

Marital History Types

I created this typology and allocated single parents into these categories solely on the basis of one spouse's (the single parent's) perception of his/her marriage. Although this technique is not the most valid way to describe marital behavior (Safilios-Rothschild, 1969), my focus is on single parents' *perceptions* of their experiences. I rely on the parents' own constructions, because they utilize these images to assess their past and present interactions. I argue that single parents' perceptions of their marriages serve as reference points for their reactions to single parenting.

The following marital history types are ideal types. None of the four completely represents the single parents' past marriages. I relied most on a couple's decision-making pattern to delineate among marital history types. For example, segregated marriages always had male-controlled decision-making. Although decision-making was the main distinguishing factor, involvement in parenting, housework, and paid work were secondary, discriminating traits.

Segregated marriages are what many sociologists would call traditional marriages. These marriages are "segregated" because husbands and wives have separate, nonoverlapping spheres of control. Men head these households and have responsibility for income-earning and major decision-making. Women in these marriages are usually full-time homemakers; parenting and housework are their responsibility. Eight of the twenty women and two of the fourteen men in my sample came from segregated marriages (see Table 1).

Modified-segregated marriages have slightly less male-dominated decision-making and family finances. Wives from modified-segregated marriages act as junior partners. Mothers, often part-time employees, are responsible for the housework. Yet, these husbands are likely to aid periodically with parenting. Seven women and seven men with whom I spoke came from modified-segregated marriages.

Integrated marriages come closest to what some sociologists refer to as egalitarian marriages. However, these men and women do not necessarily uphold an egalitarian ideology. Parenting may be primarily the responsibility of the mothers, yet fathers do much child care. Housework is shared equally or is done more often by the wife. Decision-making and care of family finances are shared responsibilities. Spouses with

Table 1 *Marital History Type of Single Parents by Parent's Gender*

	Gender of Single Parent	
Marital History Type	Female	Male
Segregated Marriages	8	2
Modified-Segregated Marriages	7	7
Integrated Marriages	0	5
Primarily Wife-Shaped Marriages	5	0
TOTAL	20	14

integrated marriages are usually employed full-time. Although no women in my sample reported this marital type, five single fathers came from integrated marriages.

Wives have a very active, if not dominant, role in *primarily wife-shaped marriages*. These mothers are often the decision-makers and frequently handle finances. Nonetheless, wives do not dominate these families; husbands seem to have significant influence and veto power. Parenting and housework are usually the mothers' domains, but she receives some aid from her spouse. These fathers and mothers are usually full-time workers. Five women and none of the men in my sample came from primarily wife-shaped marriages.

No fathers suggested they had a primarily wife-shaped marriage, and no mothers felt they had an integrated marriage; this pattern may stem from husbands' and wives' perceptual differences. Men and women might tend to overestimate their own input into family affairs and underestimate their spouses' involvement. Thus, although men and women may think they were active family members, their ex-spouses' perceptions could differ. Or men may not admit they had primarily wife-shaped marriages because this implies they lacked power. Finally, perhaps few men from primarily wife-shaped marriages become single fathers; they may have difficulty gaining custody due to their wives' strong family control.

In the following pages, I describe single parents' reactions to becoming sole householders in light of these four marital history types, and I contrast single mothers' and single fathers' experiences. A gender difference exists, I would suggest, because of men's and women's separate positions within their past marriages. For example, although I spoke with both fathers and mothers from segregated marriages, the prior experiences of these men and women were quite dissimilar. Accordingly, their current reactions to daily responsibilities were dramatically different.[5]

Reactions to Sole Householding

During our discussions, single parents distinguished between two major components of householding: being responsible for household tasks (such as paying bills and earning an income) and making decisions about minor and major household plans. Parents spoke of their responsibility for household tasks as incorporating a diffuse, holistic sense of responsibility for family and home. They discussed decision-making by referring to the array of minor and major daily decisions they faced.[6] Parents' reactions to both elements of heading a household are outlined below. I first describe the parents' marital history type to help the reader clearly differentiate among single parents' past experiences and to illustrate, in part, how I was able to classify parents. I then describe the parents' reactions to becoming sole householders. The discussion begins with women's feelings.[7]

The Women

The eight *mothers from segregated marriages* experienced the most drastic changes in their sense of family and household responsibility. These women had very traditional marital experiences, including gender-segregated division of labor and male-controlled family authority systems.

In some cases, mothers described segregated marriages as places with little room for a woman's voice. That was Marge's experience.[8] Her husband was oppressive and domineering. She explained:

> I guess before it was almost like he had a lid on me. One of my girlfriends said to me, "When you first moved there, I thought you'd ask him how many times a day you could breathe when he was at work and you'd make darn sure that you didn't take that extra breath until he came home." . . . It was like being in a corner with

nowhere to turn. I had nothing to say about nothing. He made the decisions to do everything and I was supposed to accept what he says, do what he said, and like it 'cause that was the way it was. I mean nobody was gonna change it.

Mothers from segregated marriages had three distinct reactions to their changed household task responsibilities. First, these women were the most likely of the mothers to feel doubtful about whether they could handle being a sole householder. Such doubt sometimes manifested itself as an early, powerful fear of single parenting. Judy's husband traveled extensively and rarely was home. Even so, the thought of being a sole householder was almost paralyzing to her.

> I got scared. I realize now that I was more afraid of being alone with the kids than I was of losing him, per se. That was my big fear. Then I begged him to stay.
>
> Q: What were you afraid of?
>
> Being alone with the kids, being 100 percent responsible for the household. Even if all he did was send in the paycheck and show up every once in a while, there was another person there that I could at least expect to do things. It wasn't like I had to do it all myself. I was really afraid of being alone, afraid of my competence. Really afraid.

Second, women from segregated marriages (especially mothers with preschoolers) felt most overwhelmed by heading a household. As Maggie noted:

> It's all the roles a single parent has. Like duties, with a married couple there are certain roles a male plays. He takes the car for the oil change, the income tax, the bills, etc. They are often the money managers. The woman does the household duties. There are certain tasks delegated to one or the other. But knowing that I must do it all. . . . I don't know, it's not frustrating, 'cause that leads to anxiety. I think it can be overwhelming. That's a better word. 'Cause you don't always know what to do first.

Judy also felt inundated by tasks.

> For me to go out and start a career at a minimum-an-hour job and at the age the kids were then, where they needed more day care, more physical care and things, and the housework . . . everything just seemed so overwhelming to me. I just didn't see how I could do it all. And I sat around and watched my house get dirtier and dirtier and me more and more overwhelmed by it.

In fact, many women from segregated marriages felt that sole householding was the most frustrating aspect of their lives. When I asked about her sources of frustration, Maggie said:

> Probably it's knowing that you are totally responsible. In keeping up the house to getting groceries, balancing the checkbook, everything. If I screwed up my life, knowing that what I do is going to affect my child. It's not really getting a break. . . . It's a constant concern, a pressure to know there is really no one else to turn to.

Ann described how this responsibility crept into even minor, everyday activities.

> The frustrating thing is that I am responsible for everything. That, not just her but everything, financial, everything I have to do. I was remembering once when my parents came up. [We drove somewhere] and I sat in the back seat and I thought, my God this is weird 'cause I am not driving. You know? I couldn't remember the last time that happened. And I remembered the first time my daughter could close the door herself and lock the seat belt herself. I thought, "This is great! I don't have to do that."

Third, in spite of their fears and frustrations, mothers from segregated marriages did derive some pleasure and esteem from being householders. Although doubtful as they began single parenting, over time a number of mothers were pleasantly surprised by their capabilities. For example, Nancy observed:

> The real satisfying part is the feeling of incredible accomplishment and, look at what I did by myself. At first it was just overwhelming and I thought I would never do it. . . . But basically I have been responsible for all that I have been able to do. It's [a] real source of pride in my life.

Maggie communicated her pleasure in mellow tones.

> I feel like I have been successful. It is satisfying. It's a feeling of accomplishment.
>
> Q: What have you accomplished?
>
> Raising a family on my own. Financially, we are quite secure. . . . I feel like I have given my kids a lot.

Also, being totally responsible for household decisions felt like an enormous task to mothers from segregated marriages. They had neither expected nor wanted to be family leaders. Maggie communicated these mothers' sense of bewilderment.

> I was a dependent wife. . . . My first thought was, how am I gonna survive? Not financially, but who is gonna make my decisions? They were almost made. I kinda knew what day to day would be. But when he was gone, I wondered, "Now, how is this gonna work? Where is my decision-maker?" I wasn't prepared for it.

In sum, mothers from segregated marriages felt quite overwhelmed by their household and decision-making responsibilities. Of the mothers, these women were the most distressed about sole householding.

The seven *women from modified-segregated marriages* felt more strained about sole decision-making than they did about gaining responsibility for household tasks. Most of these women previously had been involved in many household decisions and responsibilities while also working part-time. However, they did not think of themselves as their families' main decision-makers when they were married. Like Jo, they felt their husbands were in charge.

> I thought of him as the head of the family. I thought that he was the one who should probably have the final say . . . should have control of the situation.

Mothers from modified-segregated marriages usually saw themselves as junior partners in decision-making and householding when they were married. For some, like Betsy, sole decision-making was a completely new experience.

> You have to remember that I went from my mother's house into marriage and I never really had to make any major decisions on my own. There was never anything another person didn't have some input on.

Initially, mothers from segregated marriages felt bewildered by sole householding. However, mothers from modified-segregated marriages were qualitatively different. They had been active in decision-making. At the onset of single parenting, their frustrations focused on their lost decision-making support. They wanted a helper and missed their spouses' assistance. Some decisions now seemed more perplexing and difficult to tackle. Paula recounted:

> We were organized before and decision were planned ahead. We knew what was going to happen. Before, he went out and scouted about where we should move, looked into things, and found the best deals. Now I think, how am I going to do all this if I move? Find a house? Get a job? Before, there were two to do it.

These mothers struggled with self-doubt and uncertainty about decisions early on. They second-guessed their opinions and longed to hash over decisions with someone. Paula explained these feelings well during a discussion about her children.

> I have made all the decisions [about them]. And it's always . . . I haven't talked it out fully? Did I miss something? Did I make the right decision? Did I not think of something? It's much easier to have someone there to talk it out with. Maybe somebody to say, "Yeah, you said this, too." And blame them a little bit. I don't know. But it's a responsibility I am still not secure in.

Pam and her husband had been separated for four months when we spoke. At that time she debated about some large issues, such as custody privileges. Yet, even everyday decisions seemed troublesome. When I asked about difficult things she dealt with, she did not hesitate to say:

> Making decisions. I am finding decisions difficult to make. . . . I plan to go slow. I know that I am going to have to make these decisions and no one else is going to make them. That's the most difficult thing.

This was not a chronic response of these single mothers, however. Over time, many women from modified-segregated marriages slowly discarded their uncertainty and developed security and confidence in their decision-making and householding. Although mothers from segregated marriages also moved in this direction, they developed security and confidence more slowly and tentatively.

As evidence of increased decision-making comfort, mothers from modified-segregated marriages cited their numerous achievements. For example, some were proud to have managed a family for years. Others felt good about their families' improved financial situation. Although mothers from segregated marriages also communicated pride in sole householding, mothers from modified-segregated marriages spoke less tentatively. Margaret was quite animated when she explained:

> I never thought I would ever feel this way. I didn't feel this way before he left. I feel very secure with who I am. My abilities and what I can do. I don't need to grab hold of somebody to save me. I love rock and roll music, and [do you know] the song "I need a hero?" I don't need a hero. I am capable of just trudging through life all by myself. And I don't have to grab hold of somebody to save me and to be a parent to the children.

Jo clearly contrasted her past and present sources of confidence:

> I think I am probably more confident, in achieving things for myself. I think when I was married my confidence lay in what could be provided for me and now I feel confident that I can get it for myself. That I can go out and get it for myself. Before I felt like maybe things came to me because I was married to such and such a person. . . . I feel like I could probably handle situations better than I could before and I think maybe because I am the only one who can handle them now I have to. Where before somebody else probably stepped in and handled something for me.

In *primarily wife-shaped marriages,* wives were a dominant, if not controlling, force in family decisions. Grace explained:

> When it came to the decisions in the household, I tended to make most of them. Peter would be part of the process but I would be the director most of the time. And I am strong willed and if I really wanted something, I would really want it.

These women often felt like household heads when they were married. When I asked Carol if she had felt this way, she replied:

> Yes, in a lot of respects. And I don't know where that started. I don't know if it was me being . . . I mean I never felt that I was a dominant person. I never felt like I was headstrong. A lot of time I would sit back and wait for something. For him to do what I felt had to be done or should be done. And it would never

> get done. And it wasn't until I would get there and do it that it would get done.

Consequently, unlike the women from modified-segregated marriages, these women did not seem troubled or feel disrupted by a lost decision-making partner. Nor was their early single parenting marked by doubts or second-guessed decisions that typified women from modified-segregated marriages. At most, mothers from primarily wife-shaped marriages became more thoughtful about choices. For example, Arlie felt more introspective.

> Being single, I have had to look at a lot of different things and decide what is best. And look from both sides of the issue. Maybe if I thought it was right and Joel thought it was wrong there'd be a balance in there. And now I have to contemplate every decision I make as to whether it's the right decision. I have always been one of those that had always wanted to just [go] full steam ahead on a project or something. Or if I wanted to do something, I want to do it right now. No matter what it would be. And now I have to stop and look at the outcome.

The five mothers from primarily wife-shaped marriages contrasted strikingly with women from segregated marriages. Women from primarily wife-shaped marriages did not seem overwhelmed by responsibilities, unlike women with more traditional marital histories. On the contrary, mothers from primarily wife-shaped marriages enjoyed sole householding. Some, like Carol, even regarded it as their greatest satisfaction.

> The most satisfying thing? . . . I think it's kinda a reaction to the marriage I was in. That's, I'm the boss. I am the decision-maker. I was the decision-maker anyway, and now I don't have to convince somebody else that I think this is the way it should be done. . . . Things are just easier. Now when I see something that has to be done, it can be done and it's done the way I feel it should be. And that's a good feeling.

During their marriages, decision-making had become conflict-ridden for some mothers from primarily wife-shaped marriages. They often had felt caught in a bind. Although ultimately the family decision-makers, these mothers tried to involve their spouses in decisions. This was a very draining exercise; the husbands usually were reluctant participants. And these men frequently criticized or derogated their wives' actions and decisions. Because of this, after her separation, Carol felt like a ball and chain had been lifted from her.

> I think I felt a real stifling living with this person. So many times when I would suggest something it was laughed at or, "We can't do that." Well instead there should have been, there wasn't the moral support to go ahead and do it. I let him do that to me. I let him stifle me. . . . Now that that's not there, I don't have to worry about it. And if I want to do something, I do it. If I want to.

I am not saying that mothers from primarily wife-shaped marriages never tired of decision-making. Having no break from decision-making often was exhausting. However, mothers from primarily wife-shaped marriages did not think that sole decision-making was a major obstacle or hardship. Unlike mothers from segregated marriages, these women were not surprised to be capable householders; they rarely cited this as an accomplishment. If anything, mothers from primarily wife-shaped marriages felt that single parenting had a positive impact on their already relatively high self-confidence.

In sum, mothers from segregated marriages never expected to be sole householders. They doubted they could manage, often felt overwhelmed by their duties, and were very frustrated with sole householding. Mothers from modified-segregated marriages felt less pressure and frustration. Still, they longed for a decision-making partner and often second-guessed their decisions, particularly early on in single parenting. Mothers from primarily wife-shaped marriages had been decision-makers and family leaders when they were married. They did not feel taxed by sole householding, nor did they yearn for a partner. Women from primarily wife-shaped marriages whose spouses were passive or had often disagreed with them were the most satisfied with their new responsibilities.

The Men

As discussed above, women from segregated marriages often felt engulfed by the demands of householding. However, one could say that responsibility for a household was not an issue for *men from segregated marriages;* their lives changed little with respect to heading a household. The two men from segregated marriages saw themselves as their families' leaders when they were married and felt ultimately responsible for the well-being of their households. If they now felt some greater pressures, their concerns were specific and concentrated on housework and/or parenting. Neither father mentioned changes in a larger, more diffuse sense of household responsibility, unlike the women from segregated marriages.

Men from segregated marriages were quite confident in their decision-making, especially with regard to householding, financial management, and parenting. Carl even seemed to feel adversely about any advice or decision-making support. He explained that,

> I always [think] back to my old man. He won't give advice. It made me a better man. But it seems like I just do that naturally. I ask myself and I say, "What do I do?" I'll figure it out.

Fathers from segregated marriages did not believe that heading a single parent household was significantly different from their previous responsibilities. For example, when Carl described how single parenting influenced his life, he remarked:

> It's a natural thing. Everybody says, "You have responsibility." But I don't feel it. It comes natural. A lot of people tell me that.

The seven *men from modified-segregated marriages* had rather traditional marital backgrounds, too. These fathers thought of themselves as heads of their previous families and believed they had dominated family decision-making. Like fathers from segregated marriages, most men from modified-segregated marriages seemed generally confident and comfortable with their household responsibilities and decision-making. For example, Vince remarked:

> Oh, I have no trouble making decisions. I mean that's just a part of my character to be able to make decisions. Sometimes maybe a little too impulsively, but I don't have trouble making decisions.

However, unlike fathers from segregated marriages, these men did not feel they carried the total burden of decision-making and money management when they were married. They believed they were senior partners, and thought of their wives as assistants. For example, Gene was describing his marital responsibilities when he said:

> I felt like the stress was more on me than it was on both of us. I felt like the partner with the overwhelming responsibilities.

Gene's depiction of his wife as a partner highlights an important difference between the experiences of men from segregated marriages and men from modified-segregated marriages. Hints of wives' contributions crept into men's descriptions of decision-making in modified-segregated marriages. Gene's experience was perhaps a bit unusual; he thought that his wife should have been more involved as a helper or partner.

> I made most of the decisions with very little support or feedback from my spouse 'cause she was real passive and I didn't like that. I suppose she wanted somebody to make decisions for her. . . . I kept pushing her to be more responsible and make more decisions or joint decisions. And if she wouldn't immediately, I would go ahead and do it.

Vince also was a bit of an exception among fathers from modified-segregated marriages. He gave his wife a lot of decision-making control in order to avoid conflict. Yet, it was clear from

Vince's description that he retained as much power as he desired.

> In the marriage, the path of least resistance was to let her make the decisions. Because we had a power struggle relationship, where she felt inadequate, down in relation to me. Not as much status in terms of job, career, income. And she was always struggling for control, control, control. . . . I would play an active role in decisions I thought were important but in general I didn't play much of a role at all in day-by-day things.

Because they saw themselves as decision-makers and household leaders when they were married, many fathers from modified-segregated marriages felt little change in their household responsibilities after they became single parents. If these fathers felt more accountable for an area of their lives, they focused on parenting or some other isolated duty, as did fathers from segregated marriages.

Although becoming a sole decision-maker was often very demanding for women from modified-segregated marriages, these fathers hardly noted a change. Particularly in the early years of single parenting, mothers from modified-segregated marriages missed their spouses' decision-making support and guidance. At this time, mothers from modified-segregated marriages were often full of self-doubt and uncertainty. In contrast, the few men from modified-segregated marriages who spoke of lost decision-making help seemed relatively untroubled. They hesitantly "guessed" the past aid had been helpful or said they "kinda" missed having support.[9] For example, Sid seemed ambivalent about sole decision-making. Early in our discussion Sid said he enjoyed independent decision-making; later he seemed nostalgic about having occasional help. He admitted:

> Earlier I said it's nice to be able to make your own decisions, but I guess in some ways I kinda miss that [partnership] too. Share and talk and discuss. There wasn't a lot of that but. . . .

Steve had no problems with sole decision-making. However, he said that being a married parent made decision-making easier, because a helper enabled one to think clearly. When asked if decision-making was different as a single parent, he replied:

> Oh, I guess in discussing it. I think I could sort things out easier, just discussing it. So I guess from that standpoint, yes, it's different.

Without a decision-making helper, Rod took decisions a bit more seriously. Even so, he showed no doubt or stress about this responsibility, unlike many mothers from modified-segregated marriages.

> It occurred to me that when you have two adults in the house, maybe for the same reason that people feel that collective responsibility is easier to shoulder, when you make a decision, it's always easier if you feel like it was talked out and worked out in a group. I guess I do sometimes. You don't have that feeling when you are a single parent. Because all of your decisions are going to seem more arbitrary than if you had two people there to discuss it. I guess that makes me take them a little more seriously. To think about them a little more and to realize that what I decide on is going to be the way it is.

In sum, fathers from modified-segregated marriages reported few transformations in decision-making. Yet, these fathers were more likely than fathers from segregated marriages to notice any lost aid, be more thoughtful about decision-making, and/or feel a bit of strain from this task.

Fathers from modified-segregated marriages also appreciated their added control over decision-making as single parents. While married, some fathers from modified-segregated marriages felt restricted by their wives' opinions, as did Rod who believed that,

> Since becoming a single parent, I think that I do have more control over, I realize that what is going to happen is more my choice. . . . Where we are going to live I will choose. If we

> buy a house I am going to choose. I will be able to sit down and look at my checkbook and my income and decide whether we are going to buy a house or not without anything extraneous interfering.

Vince made similar comments.

> In a sense I feel more control of my life overall than I did when I was married. And that's nice. I have more control over the tension I live with. . . . I have more control over how to schedule my life. . . . Marriage, depending on the circumstance I think, has to involve a lot of negotiations and common agreement about how to spend time, how much is jointly and not, and at least at the moment it's nice to be free of that.

Although these fathers liked having more decision-making power, their enjoyment or relief was minimal in contrast with mothers from primarily wife-shaped marriages. And unlike mothers from modified-segregated marriages, fathers from modified-segregated marriages did not derive greater confidence and esteem from sole decision-making.

Of the fathers, the five *men from integrated marriages* had the strongest feelings about their new household responsibilities. Integrated marriages were the most egalitarian. These fathers, for example, did not believe they had headed their households when they were married; most called their past marriages a partnership. For example, Roger described his marital decision-making by saying,

> The way I think it was like a kinda mutual thing. If I would suggest, then she would suggest and we discussed it and it went.

Even if one spouse tended to dominate decision-making, these men generally regarded themselves and their wives as active contributors to household plans. Larry believed that,

> When we were married it was pretty much equal. We really had few arguments. We just got along. . . . And we did most of the joint decision-making, I think we just kinda blended. I may have done a little more, my say did mean more, but how much more I couldn't say. We had give and take there. It surprises me to think about it, to see how balanced we were.

Although men from integrated marriages commented mostly on parenting and keeping up a home, a number felt an increased, diffuse sense of total responsibility. For example, I asked Roger what was most difficult about being a single parent. He looked puzzled; then he said:

> I don't think you can just pick one of them out for me, I can't. I can't pick one of them out, it's all together. It's all together anyway. You have to raise the kids and the household has to be kept clean and keep the kids healthy and feed them decent food to keep them happy. And it's all rolled into one.

Irv felt more overall responsibility as a single parent because he could not share pressures and duties. At one point he admitted:

> I guess one way to look at it is, there is nobody else to blame for what goes wrong except me. Whereas before I guess there was always a scapegoat. You could always blame your partner for whatever.

Only fathers from integrated marriages were skeptical about managing a household alone when they first became single parents. This might seem odd since of the fathers, men from integrated marriages had been the most involved with daily household activities. Yet, fathers from integrated marriages had been accustomed to a partnership with another adult.

Uncertainty about managing alone was most severe among fathers from integrated marriages whose wives had left them unexpectedly. For example, early on, Larry was filled with anxiety. He described his then-frequent self-inquisitions.

> It's very devastating at first. How in the world am I gonna do it? Can I? Am I gonna be able to? And I was rock bottom at the time.

Men from integrated marriages reacted to decision-making responsibilities very differently than other fathers. In fact, their feelings often seemed similar to those of women from modified-segregated marriages perhaps because both groups felt they had had valuable decision-making partners. Fathers from integrated marriages openly missed their decision-making partners. They regretted being unable to "check things out" with someone. For example, when talking about adjustments in his life, Roger said:

> I guess the biggest change would be making all the decisions on my own. Like, not the major decisions, but the everyday things. 'Cause usually like, I don't know it's kinda hard to give an example. Just everything. 'Cause like now this time of [the] school year I have to find my youngest one a sitter. He is gonna go to kindergarten. I have to find a sitter for him and usually we had, we decided on where he was gonna be and she usually was the one that usually did all the arrangements on that. . . . We were kinda, we kinda made decisions together.

Fathers from integrated marriages felt encumbered by numerous decisions, as did mothers from segregated and modified-segregated marriages. Irv felt that sole decision-making was his greatest source of stress.

> Everything is just, is your decision. What happens to the house is *your* [his emphasis] decision. What happens to the kids is your decision. What happens to the color of the drapes is your decision. What happens if the house is clean is your decision. There is no sometime relief. . . . It's, it's a lot harder, a lot more pressure.

Martin agreed that he, too, was troubled about relying solely on his opinions and choices. When asked about his greatest frustrations, he replied:

> It gets back to decisions. It's always there. You, at least I do, always have some self-doubt about decisions. It would be so nice to have someone to bounce them off of, to test them out, give them a feel. . . . I think the worst part of that is being wholly responsible for the decisions and nobody really to try out those decisions on. To test them out and talk about them. To decide, to have someone else decide or have someone else help out and decide major things with you. That's really one of the tougher things. That really wears you down after a while. It's always on you. You are always the one that has to make this choice.

Of the fathers, men from integrated marriages were most hesitant and doubtful about decisions, as was Larry.

> The question always comes up in your mind, as to am I doing the right thing? Is my judgment good enough? In the marriage we could always discuss things. Now otherwise, as a single parent you can't really discuss it with the kids. Some things you can, some things you can't.

Two final reactions to decision-making and householding by fathers from integrated marriages seem almost contradictory in comparison with the ideas mentioned above. However, these comments must be placed in appropriate context. First, even though many fathers from integrated marriages felt burdened, frustrated, and uncertain about sole decision-making, doubts gradually declined and over time they gained esteem and satisfaction from decision-making (as did mothers from modified-segregated marriages). Martin displayed some of this self-admiration. After a year of single parenting, he said:

> I have been able to make decisions more quickly now out of necessity. And that's made me feel good about myself . . . I am proud of getting on day to day. I am proud of that. People come up to me and say, "I don't know how you are doing it." And I say I don't either, frankly. It's just a hell of a labor. A lot of effort to run a career with all that's attendant outside, and a family.

When Larry spoke of the pleasures of single parenting, he had been alone for over five years.

> I have been able to realize that I can do it myself. That I don't need the other person to interact with. The kids know that Dad can do it. Being able to totally, I suppose, be my own boss. I can come and go as I please, within reason. [And] I suppose it's just having them for six years. Having custody and just knowing that we are a family, even if there is one spouse missing. That we can do things together, the kids and I, other than the kids and us. And just knowing that, that you can still be a family, without half the family.

Second, while fathers from integrated marriages missed another adult's support and cooperation, they enjoyed having more control over their lives, more so than other fathers. Karl realized that as a single parent,

> One had only oneself to consult with. There wasn't any more negotiating about what was going to happen. When I made a decision, that was it. We are going on vacation. That's it. My daughter will go to this school. That's my decision. It's time for a checkup. I want to buy a fancy leather chair. I would just do all those things without, you know, it's real nice to have that kind of freedom. Just sort of charting one's own course without baggage. To do what one wants. What one would like.

Pleasure with independence and increased control was strongest among fathers from integrated marriages who had been single parenting for years. Of course, in relation to other men, fathers from integrated marriages were less independent when married. Thus, they had the greatest potential to gain control over their lives as single parents.

In sum, men from segregated marriages were confident about decision-making and secure as their families' leaders. When they were married, men from modified-segregated marriages felt responsible for household tasks but not for sole decision-making. Even so, these fathers only slightly missed their wives' decision-making help. Being a sole decision-maker caused these men to become perhaps more thoughtful about choices. Men from integrated marriages had the strongest feelings about their new responsibilities. Early on these fathers were most likely to express uncertainty about sole householding. Many keenly missed their decision-making partner and wanted to thrash out ideas with someone. As a result, fathers from integrated marriages sometimes felt taxed, frustrated, or overburdened by decisions; they felt hesitant and doubtful at times, especially early on in single parenting. Still, of the fathers, men from integrated marriages were most pleased with having more control over their lives and were proud of their families' survival and their success as sole householders.

Discussion

In many ways these findings lend further credence to microstructural perspectives on behavior. As Risman (1987) explains, most research on gender utilizes an individualistic model, which assumes that gender socialization and resultant personality development bring about stable, gendered behavior in men and women (Chodorow, 1978; Weitzman, 1979). However, Risman's evidence illustrates that social structural factors promote behavior we normally attribute to gender. For example, Risman found that some of single fathers' parenting behaviors (for example, with respect to intimacy) are more akin to mothers' parenting than married fathers' actions. She argued that this similarity occurred because single fathers have more in common experientially with mothers (since they are primary caretakers of children) than with married men who are not primary parents. Thus, Risman concluded that men's and women's behavior often may differ because they are embedded in different social situations and networks.

My findings also may be interpreted from a microstructural perspective. Microstructuralists assume that structural elements of parents' lives (in this case, their past decision-making patterns and division of labor while married) create the circumstances within which single parents forge their behaviors. If one's structural position is similar (as when both women from modified-segregated marriages and men from integrated marriages state they were decision-making partners), then one's responses are likely to be similar (as when women from modified-segregated marriages and men from integrated marriages both mentioned that they missed having decision-making support). In my study, parents' gender alone is not a reliable predictor of parents' responses to single parenting. However, gender is relevant because it leads the parents into one of two possible structural locations within each marital history type, and these locations correspond with common reactions to single parenting.

This study illustrates that gender and marital history type intersect and shape adults' lives in many ways. As a result, we have a more complex portrait of single mothers and single fathers. Many past researchers assumed women and men have discrete, nonoverlapping realities. For example, Bernard (1972) asserted there were two marriages ("his" and "hers") in every marriage. Bernard's thesis ignored heterogeneity among men and among women and implicitly promoted an individualist paradigm. By investigating how gender and marital history type overlap, we can see why some mothers and fathers react similarly to single parenting. Because families have numerous structures (that is, patterns of labor and decision-making), men and women have a variety of experiences and reactions to families. Therefore, one's gender is not a clear key to one's reality. However, marital history type provides a context in which gender is enacted in families.

Aside from the theoretical implications of my findings, this report has practical value as well. For example, it can encourage those who develop programs and policies for single parents to appreciate single parents' diverse situational constraints, material conditions, and social networks. Microstructuralists believe we can redesign social settings to promote social change. Instead of assuming that men's or women's behavior is rather inflexible due to their gendered personalities (as would the individualist perspective), programs informed by microstructuralism would anticipate that fathers' and mothers' actions will change as their social situations and interactions alter. For example, I discovered that women from segregated marriages often were very stressed about single parenting. In the future, we could protect women from these severely negative reactions by instructing them about the hazards of segregated marriages. Overall, the applied implications of my project are clear: programs expecting single fathers or single mothers to be rather homogeneous will fall far short of their goals.

Notes

1. One respondent has been a single parent twice—once due to divorce and once due to her spouse's death.

2. Although many have asserted that reason for custody has significant effects on fathers' reactions to single parenting (Gasser and Taylor, 1976; Mendes, 1976; O'Brien, 1982), Risman (1986) found that reason for custody had few effects on fathers' satisfaction with single parenting. In my sample, 28.5 percent of the fathers gained custody because the mother left home and did not want to live with the children, 28.5 percent negotiated the arrangement with their ex-wives, and 43 percent fought for custody. A number of the parents in my sample had joint legal custody; however, every parent lived with his/her children at least six months of the year.

3. One exception to this pattern is years of single parenting. I later discovered that this variable had a significant effect on single parents' reactions, but mainly within the context of the parents' marital history type.

4. These marital types differ somewhat from the typology developed by Scanzoni (1980) and extended by Atkinson and Boles (1984). Scanzoni primarily delineates marital types by the wife's paid work pattern. In contrast, my typology is based on a couple's decision-making, division of labor at home, and labor force participation. The Scanzoni head-complement and senior-junior partner types do correspond roughly to what I call segregated and modified-segregated marriages, respectively. However, Scanzoni's third type of "equal

partners" represents marriages in which wives work full-time and see their income-earning responsibilities as equivalent to their spouses. In contrast, in "integrated marriages" spouses do not necessarily see themselves as co-breadwinners, yet wives usually work full-time, and spouses believe that decision-making and household responsibilities are shared generally. In addition, I have a fourth category, "primarily wife-shaped marriages," which does not correspond to the types developed by Scanzoni or Atkinson and Boles. Atkinson and Boles' notion of the "wife as senior partner" perhaps comes closest to "primarily wife-shaped marriages." Families see the occupations of senior-partner wives as more important than the husbands' jobs. In primarily wife-shaped marriages, however, wives do most of the decision-making, yet they are rarely the families' main income-earner.

5. One might assume, accordingly, that reactions of men and women from integrated marriages would be less divergent than those of women and men from segregated marriages. However, I cannot verify this because I did not speak with any women from integrated marriages.

6. I analyze elsewhere the impact of marital history type and gender on parents' comments about particular, isolated responsibilities and decisions related to financial management, housework, paid work, and parenting (see Fassinger, 1987).

7. Parents' reactions to their current responsibilities were not used to classify their marital history type. Instead, parents' descriptions of division of labor and decision-making patterns in their past marriages were examined first. Once the four basic marital history types were delineated, I compared and contrasted parents' feelings about their new duties.

8. Names and occupations used to describe these single parents are fictitious. In developing substitute occupations, I did not change the general nature of the parents' work (for example, professional occupations were replaced with other professional occupations).

9. Perhaps fathers from modified-segregated marriages missed their spouses' decision-making aid more than they admitted. They might have been reluctant to express these feelings for fear of seeming too dependent. Although fathers from modified-segregated marriages may have been motivated by such impression management, fathers from integrated marriages were not; they easily expressed their sorrow over lost decision-making help.

References

Ambert, A. 1982. "Differences in children's behavior toward custodial mothers and custodial fathers." *Journal of Marriage and the Family* 44 (February): 73–86.

Atkinson, M., and J. Boles. 1984. "WASP (wives as senior partners)." *Journal of Marriage and the Family* 46 (November): 861–870.

Bernard, J. 1972. *The Future of Marriage.* New York: Bantam Books.

Brandwein, R., C. Brown, and E. Fox. 1974. "Women and children last: The social situation of divorced mothers and their families." *Journal of Marriage and the Family* 36 (August): 498–514.

Charmaz, K. 1983. "The grounded theory method: An explication and interpretation." Pp. 109–126 in R. Emerson (Ed.), *Contemporary Field Research.* Boston: Little, Brown.

Chodorow, N. 1978. *The Reproduction of Mothering.* Berkeley: University of California Press.

Espenshade, T. 1979. "The economic consequence of divorce." *Journal of Marriage and the Family* 41 (August): 153–163.

Fassinger, P. 1987. Transitions in the Lives of Single Parents: Heading a Household and Parenting Alone. Unpublished Ph.D. dissertation, East Lansing: Michigan State University.

Gasser, R., and C. Taylor. 1976. "Role adjustment of single parent fathers with dependent children." *The Family Coordinator* 25 (October): 397–401.

Glaser, B., and A. Strauss. 1967. *The Discovery of Grounded Theory.* Chicago: Aldine Press.

Greenberg, J. 1979. "Single-parenting and intimacy: A comparison of mothers and fathers." *Alternative Lifestyles* 2 (August): 308–330.

Greif, G. 1985. *Single Fathers.* Lexington, Mass.: Lexington Books.

Hetherington, E., M. Cox, and R. Cox. 1976. "Divorced fathers." *The Family Coordinator* 25 (October): 417–428.

Kopf, K. 1976. "Meeting the social and emotional needs of the single parent." Pp. 37–38 in S. Burden, *The Single Parent: Proceedings of the Changing Family Conference V.* Iowa City: University of Iowa Press.

Mendes, H. 1976. "Single fatherhood." *Social Work* 21 (July): 308–312.

O'Brien, M. 1982. "Becoming a lone father: Differential patterns and experiences." Pp. 184–195 in L.

McKee and M. O'Brien (Eds.), *The Father Figure.* London: Tavistock.

Orthner, D., T. Brown, and D. Ferguson. 1976. "Single-parent fatherhood: An emerging family life style." *The Family Coordinator* 25 (October): 429–437.

Risman, B. 1986. "Can men "mother"? Life as a single father." *Family Relations* 35 (January): 95–102.

———. 1987. "Intimate relationships from a microstructural perspective: Men who mother." *Gender and Society* 1 (March): 6–32.

Rosenfeld, J., and E. Rosenstein 1973. "Towards a conceptual framework for the study of parent-absent families." *Journal of Marriage and the Family* 35 (February): 131–135.

Safilios-Rothschild, C. 1969. "Family sociology or wives' family sociology?" *Journal of Marriage and the Family* 31 (May): 290–301.

Scanzoni, J. 1980. "Contemporary marriage types." *Journal of Family Issues* 1 (March): 125–140.

Schlesinger, B. 1979. "One-parent families: Knowns and unknowns." *Social Science* 54 (Autumn): 25–28.

Schorr, A., and P. Moen. 1979. "The single parent and public policy." *Social Policy* 19 (March–April): 15–21.

Smith, M. 1980. "The social consequences of single parenthood: A longitudinal perspective." *Family Relations* 29 (January): 75–81.

Spicer, J., and G. Hampe. 1975. "Kinship interaction after divorce." *Journal of Marriage and the Family* 37 (February): 113–119.

Weiss, R. 1979. *Going It Alone: The Family Life and Social Situation of the Single Parent.* New York: Basic Books.

———. 1984. "The impact of marital dissolution on income and consumption in single-parent households." *Journal of Marriage and the Family* 46 (February): 115–127.

Weitzman, L. 1979. *Sex Role Socialization.* Palo Alto, Calif.: Mayfield.

———. 1985. *The Divorce Revolution.* New York: Free Press.

Part Four

The Interconnections Between Work and Family

The chapters in Part Four show very clearly that we cannot study intimate relationships in the family as if they were isolated from the world of paid work. Each article identifies different ways by which the economic sector affects intimacy. Gerson's article on employed women also suggests that choices about the family eventually affect the world of work.

Spade's chapter sets the stage for this final section by introducing what she calls a "sex-integrated" approach to the connections between work and family. Most past research has been sex-segregated, studying the effect of paid work on men and women quite differently. For men, work has been seen not as a choice or a variable but as a given. For women, however, paid work has been viewed as immediately problematic for the family. The focus of most studies of women's employment has been on understanding to what extent the wife's job causes disruption in the family. Spade proposes a sex-integrated model that focuses on how the conditions of *both* parents' employment shapes behavior at home.

The next three chapters by Hertz, Gerson, and Cohen implicitly use such a sex-integrated model. Hertz interviewed dual-career corporate couples and found, not surprisingly, that their marriages were relatively egalitarian. What makes Hertz's findings so intriguing is that these couples did not consciously choose to pioneer the dual-career lifestyle, nor were most of them feminist when they married. Instead, Hertz finds that despite their intentions to fulfill traditional domestic roles, these corporate women found themselves with career opportunities they did not expect, and eventually with lifestyles they could not afford without their paycheck. Marital equality was a consequence of hectic lives. Employment opportunities and career constraints led to changes in their marital relationships.

Gerson and Cohen use a sex-integrated approach, but each author focuses exclusively on one sex. Gerson explains how employed women in contemporary society are faced with structural dilemmas if they try to combine paid work with childbearing and child rearing. We have no national maternity leave policy, too few day care facilities, and even less national commitment to assuring quality care for preschool children. Yet, Gerson identifies particular social network variables that do lead some job-committed women toward motherhood. These variables include (1) stable relationships with men who strongly desire children, (2) perceived costs of childlessness, and (3) reasonable alternatives for lowering the time and energy of parenthood, particularly with involvement from men anxious to be fathers.

Cohen studied husbands and fathers. In-depth interviews reveal that many fathers feel constrained from more active involvement with their children because of their jobs. Almost all the men in Cohen's study believed that their responsibilities as fathers were primarily nurturing and caretaking. Breadwinning was not considered the most important family responsibility. Cohen's research raises serious questions about previous theories that have assumed men to be primarily work-oriented. The men in Cohen's study defined themselves at least as much by their family roles as by their success at work.

Finally, Staples argues that whatever ideologies about the family exist, we are all constrained to live within the limits of our economic situation. Staples shows that although black Americans hold quite traditional family values, they live in unconventional family settings. Why? Because in our society the very definition of a husband is a man who can *at least* earn an income; therefore the high rates of unemployment among young black males make them less marketable as spouses. Staples suggests that until our economic system reduces racial inequities, many black women will not have the option to marry because there are too few eligible black men. Perhaps if Cohen's thesis that men are important to families over and above their breadwinning capacity was more widely disseminated, both men and women might realize that males can be valuable family members even without paychecks.

These chapters support our general thesis because each one identifies different sociological variables that affect the relationship between paid work and intimate relationships within the family. Spade discusses how the actual conditions of work may affect an individual's behavior at home. Hertz discusses how the time and energy necessary for career mobility creates a new type of marriage when two careerists live in one family. Gerson identifies how the social context of employed women's lives pushes them either toward motherhood or childlessness. Cohen suggests that work constraints preclude greater male involvement in child rearing even when fathers desire more active family roles. Finally, Staples shows us that the economic system in which we live sets the parameters for our choices: the high level of unemployment among black men makes the possibility of stable nuclear families for the majority of black women and children unlikely. Clearly, some of the most important microstructural factors that shape our intimate relationships can be traced to the economic circumstances of our lives.

15

Bringing Home the Bacon: A Sex-Integrated Approach to the Impact of Work on the Family

JOAN Z. SPADE

It is time for a change in the way we approach the question of the impact of work on dual-worker families. The conceptual perspectives underlying such research are often outdated because they are sex-segregated in orientation. Currently men's and women's employment are treated differently, as are their roles in the family, much of which derives from the individualist paradigm elaborated in the introduction. Instead, the alternative theoretical model proposed here focuses on how actual conditions of work experiences (for example, closeness of supervision or complexity of the job) of men and women similarly influence orientations toward their families and activities in the home. Because this model includes women as well as men and uses the same conceptual definition of work and family for both sexes, I refer to it as the sex-integrated model.

A sex-integrated model adds to our understanding of the impact of work on the family because occupational conditions of both spouses affect interaction in the home. Previous studies overlook this issue because they are based on outdated definitions of male and female roles in society. Academically and culturally, work has been defined as a male activity and family as a female activity. Given the current changes in the labor force, this perceptual segregation of work and family by sex is no longer a practical model for research, particularly analyses of dual-worker families (Miller & Garrison, 1982; Berheide & Chow, 1983; Dussert, 1985).

Over the past twenty to thirty years participation of women in the labor force has increased significantly, precipitating changes in the structure of work and the structure of the family. Women's orientation toward work has changed, they are delaying marriage and child rearing for educational and occupational pursuits (Regan & Roland, 1985), and they are more likely to stay in or reenter the labor force after the birth of children. An effect of the tendency toward increased edu-

The author would like to thank Michael Farrell, Carla Howery, Sue Jansen, Melvin Kohn, and Beth Vanfossen for their careful review of this article.

cation and uninterrupted work careers for women today is that women are more likely to be committed to their jobs (Regan & Roland, 1985; also see Spenner & Atkinson, 1985; Bielby & Bielby, 1984) and to increase their status in the work force (Consumer Research Center, 1984).

Consequently, a large proportion of the women in intact families are in the labor force (64 percent of the women with school-age children and 50 percent of the women with preschool children [U.S. Department of Labor, 1984]). This increase in women working outside the home has an impact on the interpersonal relationships in their families. Dual-worker families must meet the same needs and demands confronting all families, but the person-hours available to accomplish such tasks are reduced considerably. Families can adjust to these extra pressures in various ways, but individual responses of both husband and wife are critical as they accommodate to the increased demands on their time and emotions.

The sex-integrated model addresses the question of how variations in the work responsibilities of men and women influence their attitudes toward, and behaviors in, their families. Research supports the assumption that the conditions of work shape orientations and behaviors outside of work. The sex-integrated model extends such findings by examining the influence of occupational conditions on individuals' orientations to family issues. Today, more than ever, men and women are spending a considerable number of hours at various work activities. It is, therefore, important to analyze the influence of microstructural conditions of the work of wives as well as husbands on processes in the home (for example, decision making, division of labor, and marital satisfaction).

The Sex-Segregated Model of Work and the Family: An Outdated Approach

A traditional sex-role perspective prevails in the literature and research that analyze work and family relationships. In their review, Feldberg and Glenn (1979) organize research on work into "sex-segregated models"—the work model for men and the gender model for women. Long-Laws refers to this as the "myth of mom and pop—men work; women do not" (1976:34). Such sex-segregation is also evident in the sociology of the family as illustrated by the use of two different chapters on work in a review of family literature: one on "men's work" and the other on "wife/mother employment" (Burr et al., 1979). The result of the conceptual segregation of men's and women's work and family roles is a scarcity of research examining both husbands' and wives' jobs in dual-worker families.

These orientations reflect traditional, middle-class assumptions regarding roles necessary to fulfill the needs of the family system, which are formalized in functionalist theory. Although this perspective is not overtly acknowledged in the research, its influence is far from dead. The man's work is taken as a given; it is expected and normal (Parsons, 1954) and viewed as a predominant experience in men's lives, despite contradictory evidence (Pleck, 1983). The impact of men's jobs on their families is generally ignored with the exception of research on the effects of atypical work schedules and demanding careers on family life, or studies of the influence of fathers' social class on sons' occupational choices and social mobility. These analyses deemphasize the part men play in interpersonal relationships within the family.

When a woman works, however, the impact of her job on the family is viewed as problematic for the family. The impact of the wife's job occurs when the pattern of role relationships in the home is disrupted by the woman working outside the home (Parsons et al., 1953). Women's jobs are perceived as secondary or extra, with actual job activities ignored. The concern is only that the woman is employed, ignoring that she may be either a physician or a factory worker. Studies of the impact of women's work, therefore, emphasize the influence of women's work on others: their husbands, the children, and society. Examples of family processes assumed to be influenced by the outside employment of women are marital satisfaction (Burke & Weir, 1976; Benin & Neinstedt, 1985); power (Blood & Wolfe, 1960; Hood, 1983); husbands' participation in family labor, or performance of "feminine" tasks (Condran & Bode, 1982; Coverman, 1984; Maret & Finlay, 1984); the mental health of husbands' and wives' (Kessler & McRae, 1982; Ross et al., 1983; Fendrich, 1984); children's participation in household chores (Propper, 1972); and children's attitudes (Acock et al., 1982). The focus of the majority of these studies is to understand the perceived disruption resulting from women moving out of their homes and into the labor force. Although these are important issues for the family, in most of these studies the role of the husband in the home is ignored, as are the conditions of work of both husband and wife.

These sex-segregated definitions of work are reflected in the methods used to describe men's and women's jobs. Women's jobs are usually measured by the number of hours worked, often coded as part-time, full-time, or not working. Men's jobs, however, are defined by assessing the conditions of work. Measures of men's work range from simple white-collar/blue-collar dichotomies to sophisticated factor analyses of different occupational characteristics. Using these two different methods to measure husbands' and wives' work creates a situation in which it is impossible to compare the impact of work on men and women.

The Sex-Integrated Model of Work and the Family

Using the sex-integrated model, the character and processes of family life reflect the occupational conditions of both husband and wife. The model rests upon two basic assumptions. The first is that occupational conditions shape the values, orientations, and behavior of wives as well as husbands. The second assumption is that values, orientations, and behaviors that are shaped by occupational conditions influence men's and women's behavior in their roles as husbands, wives, and parents. Thus, the sex-integrated perspective suggests that microstructural variables outside the family sphere influence behaviors and conditions within the family.

The sex-integrated model combines assumptions from the exchange and social learning theories. Using exchange theory, the activities and skills learned on the job (for example, supervisory or decision-making techniques) can be viewed as a resource that husbands and wives use to influence family bargaining (Hood, 1983; LaRossa, 1977). Underlying social learning theory is the argument that behavior that is rewarded in one context will be repeated and generalized in other situations. Since work is continuous and rewarded (with weekly paychecks and an occasional promotion), it is likely that the behavior and attitudes resulting from job activities influence behavior in other settings including family orientations and behavior.

While the sex-segregated model focuses heavily upon culturally defined sex roles in structuring the nature of the work activity for men and women, the sex-integrated model concentrates on the consequences of work activities for behavior off the job. The sex-integrated model contrasts with the sex-segregated model in key ways. First, the sex-integrated model is not concerned with the causes of employment, while the sex-segregated perspective rests on the assumptions that work is an economic necessity for men and an extra activity for women. Second, the consequences of the work activity are viewed very differently in these two models. The impact of work on the family is viewed as shaping the values and orientations that men and women bring to their families in the sex-integrated model, not in fulfilling or disrupting their family roles. Consequently, the questions asked by each perspective differ greatly. The sex-integrated model asks, "How does the type of work we do shape our orientations and behaviors in the home?" while the sex-segregated model asks, "How does the social structural position of men influence their families?" and "How do families adjust to the mothers' absence from their homes *if* they work?"

The sex-integrated model should be viewed as only one of many possible perspectives for viewing the impact of microstructural work conditions on families. The relationship between work and family is a complex one, and many variables influence this interaction, including the possibility of family structure on work conditions (Coverman, 1984). However, conditions at work are less negotiable than conditions within the family, and negotiations with bosses and more powerful employers are less likely to occur than adaptations within the family sphere. Therefore, it is important that we explore how work, as a factor in microstructural experiences, influences conditions and gender relationships in the home.

Research Supporting the Sex-Integrated Model: Impact of Work on the Individual

A fundamental premise of the sex-integrated model is that the social situation can influence an individual's orientation and behavior, because the work situation carries over to impact family relationships. A variety of social psychological analyses find that individuals' formation of personal beliefs, preferences, and orientations toward others and themselves is related to group experiences (Breer & Locke, 1965) and the influence of significant others (Morse and Gerkin, 1970). Wilensky (1960) provides two models that explain the impact of work on off-work activities: the compensatory and spillover models, the latter of which is favored (Rice et al., 1980). The spillover model predicts that "objective structural conditions of work" influence behaviors off the job (Meissner, 1971; Rice et al., 1980).

Research conducted by Kohn and colleagues, assessing the influence of occupational self-direction on various measures of values, intellectual functioning, and social orientation, provides further support for the spillover of work into values and orientation unrelated to the job. Occupational self-direction is defined as the ability to exercise "initiative, thought and independent judgment at work" (Kohn, 1977: 139–140), and includes measures of job complexity, closeness of supervision, and routinization of work. Higher levels of occupational self-direction are associated with a self-directed orientation (Kohn & Schooler, 1983a; 1983b); lower levels of alienation (Kohn, 1983); more flexible psychological functioning (Kohn & Schooler, 1983c; Miller et al., 1983; Slomczynski et al., 1981); and selection of leisure activities that require higher levels of intellectual involvement (Miller & Kohn, 1983). Furthermore, Kohn and his colleagues find that it is occupational conditions, not sex of the individual, which influence self-conceptions and social orientation (Miller et al., 1983; Schoenbach, 1985).

Impact of Work on the Family

The second premise of the sex-integrated model is that occupational conditions may also influence the person's participation in his or her family. If the nature of the work activity influences the relationship of individuals to others and their perceived competence in other settings, then it is likely that these perceptions will impact family situations. For example, people whose microstructural networks at work require that they deal with highly complex issues are likely to perceive themselves as capable of handling complex problems in other settings, whereas people who are highly supervised are not likely to see themselves as having the wherewithal to change the course of events either on or off the job.

An excerpt from Piotrkowski's (1979) study of thirteen working-class and lower-middle-class families is valuable in illuminating the impact of work on the family. These comments of a male computer operator are an excellent illustration of how routine work spills into the home.

> I think a boring job, a job that doesn't take too much mentally from a person and doesn't take too much physically from a person, affects his home life also. I think he tends to become lazy.

> I do, personally. . . . Once I started getting into the job being boring, less mentally aware—I feel like I'm walking in a daze all the time. I mean, it's just something personal about me, but I just feel like I'm walking in a daze all the time.

Another example, from Rubin's interview with a mother of four who has been married thirteen years, illustrates the influence of work patterns on the home. Both the woman and her house were unkempt and disordered. The woman apologizes to Rubin, noting, "It's just that I'm so disorganized that I never finish anything I start" (Rubin, 1975: 181). This woman then goes on to describe the positive carryover from her former job in a bank office.

> You know, it's funny, but I'm very organized when I work. I guess you wouldn't believe it, would you, but my desk was as neat as a pin. There was never a paper out of place. I even used to be more organized around the house when I was working. (182)

For the male computer operator in Piotrkowski's study and the female bank worker in Rubin's study, the microstructural conditions of their work had an impact on their families' functioning and process.

Although other studies have focused on how men's and women's work affect various aspects of family life, much of this research is sex-segregated, examining either men's *or* women's work, but not both simultaneously. Some studies, however, have begun to examine the relationship between occupational conditions and family life and, as the two examples illustrate, evidence supports the impact of both men's and women's occupational conditions on family processes. The following sections review these studies as they relate to the impact of work on children and on husband-wife interaction.

Impact of Work on Children

Research indicates that men's and women's occupational conditions influence their parental values and the transmission of occupational values to their children. Kohn and his colleagues included an aspect of family relationships, parental values, in their analysis of the influence of occupational conditions on men's orientation. They found, as others had found before, that working-class parents tend to value conformity for their children and middle-class parents tend to value self-direction. However, they expanded upon previous research by including actual occupational conditions in their studies. They find that occupational self-direction has a consistent and significant impact on men's parental values. Controlling for social class, men with higher levels of occupational self-direction value self-direction for their children; whereas men with little opportunity to exercise self-direction at work value conformity for their children (Pearlin & Kohn, 1966; Kohn, 1969; Slomczynski et al., 1981). In another analysis (Kohn et al., 1986) using samples from the United States and Poland, they find that husbands' and wives' occupational self-direction are related to values for their children and to their children's values in Poland and the United States.

Other researchers support the findings of Kohn and his colleagues. In an analysis of 186 couples, I found that occupational self-direction is related to the values men and women hold for their children (Spade, 1984a). In addition, there is some evidence that occupational self-direction of one spouse may influence the other spouse's values for their children. Acock and his colleagues (1982) also found that women's occupational statuses are related to their children's values. Women in lower-status jobs are more likely to have children who are traditional in their religious and sexual beliefs, militaristic, and committed to the work ethic than women who work in high-status jobs. However, for lower-class women, Ferree (1980) finds that working outside the home, in and of itself, influences the values of the women and is related to an increased support of feminism.

Mortimer's (1976) analysis of social mobility suggests that men's occupational conditions spill over to influence sons' occupational values. Although research on social mobility has found little movement in social class from fathers to sons, Mortimer reexamines the issue, including fathers' occupational conditions. In her analysis, the relationship between fathers' and sons' occupational values is better predicted by fathers' occupational conditions than by differences in social class indicators. Mortimer's findings add support to the assumptions of the sex-integrated model since occupational conditions of the fathers predict whether or not vocational values are transmitted to their sons.

Impact of Work on Husband-Wife Interaction

The research on the impact of work on husband-wife interaction is even more sex-segregated. The majority of these studies examine only the impact of wives' work on the family and tend to use broad measures of work (for example, employed/not employed, occupational status, work commitment).

In my own research on reciprocity or equality in spousal relationships (Spade, 1984b), I find that higher occupational self-direction of both husbands and wives is related to perceptions of greater reciprocity in the relationship for themselves as well as their spouses. Furthermore, wives' occupational self-direction remains statistically significant in predicting their own *and* their husbands' perceptions of reciprocity in regressions that control for educational backgrounds, occupational self-directions, and hours worked for both spouses as well as number of years married and number of children.

Seccombe (1986), however, finds that occupational self-direction of neither spouse predicts division of household labor in the home. Other research (Condran and Bode, 1982), my own included, finds that husbands and wives tend to have different perceptions of how much work in the home is done by each spouse. Since Seccombe does not examine the differential perceptions of household labor by sex, the correlation between work and family may be weakened in her study.

Research on occupational status indirectly measures women's occupational conditions and is related to the question of whether their work influences their families. Higher occupational status tends to be associated with a variety of job tasks, independent assignments, and the need for initiative—relationships very similar to Kohn's occupational self-direction. Keith and colleagues (1981) find that husbands of wives with higher occupational status were more likely to participate in household tasks and score higher on life satisfaction.

Work commitment also correlates with women's job status (Safilios-Rothschild, 1970; Sobel, 1963) and, thus, work commitment also indirectly measures occupational self-direction. In her analyses of the relationship between work commitment and husband-wife relationships, Safilios-Rothschild (1970) finds that women with high commitment are more likely to have husbands who give in more often, are more "permissive," and share decision making with their wives. Hoffman (1963) also examines work commitment, finding that women who are committed to their work are less punitive and more affectionate toward their children.

Conclusion

The arguments in this paper point to several interesting new frontiers in the study of the impact of work on the family as well as the "traps" of the sex-segregated approach. We must go beyond the categorization of women's work as either employed or not employed to learn about the impact of women's work on the family. We must also look at the impact of men's as well as women's work on the family. Finally, we need to look at the impact of their jobs together as they influence the family. Men and women do not operate in a vacuum, either outside or inside the home. We need to consider both jobs simultaneously in our analyses.

Consequently, continued research and exploration of theoretical premises are called for. Current studies have failed to answer the questions that follow from a society in which over one-half of the mothers of school-age children are employed. Obviously, we can no longer assume that workers are male and that females are primarily concerned with familial activities. To adequately assess the impact of work upon the family we must develop conceptual models that analyze the work role of women as well as men.

The sex-integrated model presented here is an attempt to meet these needs. The sex-integrated approach differs from previous conceptual models in arguing that the occupational conditions of both men and women influence their values, orientations, and behaviors in the family. As stated earlier, the sex-integrated model rests upon two basic assumptions: that occupational conditions shape the values, orientations, and behavior of both men and women; and that the values, orientations, and behaviors that are shaped by job conditions influence men's and women's behavior in their roles as parents and husbands and wives. Consequently, the impact of the microstructural conditions of work on the family in the sex-integrated model is that of shaping the values and orientations that men and women bring to their families.

The value of the sex-integrated model is that it goes beyond traditional, individualist assumptions about the roles of men and women in our society to look for those characteristics of the microstructure surrounding work that influence the person and the family. The excitement of the sex-integrated model lies in the discovery of the multitude of previously unrecognized interactions between work and the family.

If we are to understand the impact of work on the family, we need to examine the microstructural conditions of work, which affect both spouses, those conditions of work that influence the person and their interactions with others. These microstructural conditions change as the structure of the work world changes and as the individual's place in the work structure changes. Therefore, we need to examine how changing occupational relationships affect attitudes and orientations. And we need to consider work histories of men and women as we study families. In addition, we need to clarify the microstructural conditions of the home, looking at behaviors and interactions free from gender biases, and seek out better ways to study interactions surrounding the division of labor and marital interaction.

Work is part of the macrostructure that determines microstructural conditions affecting men's and women's lives and those of their families. The sex-integrated model and other gender-free models will help free us from the paradigms that narrow our focus on individuals' adaptive strategies without recognizing the power of structure in shaping our lives.

References

Acock, Alan C.; Barker, Deborah; and Bengston, Vern L. 1982. "Mother's Employment and Parent-Youth Similarity." *Journal of Marriage and the Family* 11: 441–455.

Benin, Mary Holland, and Nienstedt, Barbara Cable. 1985. "Happiness in Single- and Dual-Earner Families: The Effects of Marital Happiness, Job Satisfaction, and Life Cycle." *Journal of Marriage and the Family* 47: 975–984.

Berheide, Catherine White, and Chow, Esther Nagan-Long. 1983. "The Interdependence of Family and Work." Paper presented at the American Sociological Association meeting, Detroit, Michigan.

Bielby, Denise Del Vento, and Bielby, William T. 1984. "Work Commitment, Sex-Role Attitudes, and Women's Employment." *American Sociological Review* 49: 234–247.

Blood, Robert O., Jr., and Wolfe, Donald M. 1960. *Husbands and Wives: The Dynamics of Married Living.* New York: Free Press.

Breer, Paul E., and Locke, Edwin A. 1965. *Task Experience as a Source of Attitudes.* Homewood, Ill.: Dorsey Press.

Burke, Ronald J., and Weir, Tamara. 1976. "Relationship of Wives' Employment Status to Husband, Wife and Pair Satisfaction and Performance." *Journal of Marriage and the Family* 38: 279–287.

Burr, Wesley; Hill, Reuben; Nye, F. Ivan; and Reiss, Ira L., Eds. 1979. *Contemporary Theories About the Family.* Volume 1. New York: Free Press.

Condran, John G., and Bode, Jerry G. 1982. "Rashomon, Working Wives, and Family Division of Labor:

Middletown, 1980." *Journal of Marriage and the Family* 44: 421–426.

Consumer Research Center. 1984. "The Working Woman: A Progress Report." New York: The Conference Board.

Coverman, Shelly. 1985. "Explaining Husbands' Participation in Domestic Labor." *Sociological Quarterly* 26(1): 81–97.

———. 1984. "Gender, Domestic Labor Time, and Wage Inequality." *American Sociological Review* 48(5): 623–655.

Dussert, Claudine. 1985. "Impact of Women's Employment on Themselves and on Their Children." Paper presented for a round-table discussion at the American Sociological Association meeting, Washington, D.C.

Feldberg, Roslyn L., and Glenn, Evelyn Nakano. 1979. "Male and Female: Job Versus Gender Models in the Sociology of Work." *Social Problems* 26: 524–538.

Fendrich, Michael. 1984. "Wives' Employment and Husbands' Distress: A Meta-analysis and a Replication." *Journal of Marriage and the Family* 46: 871–879.

Ferree, Myra Marx. 1980. "Working-Class Feminism: A Consideration of the Consequences of Employment." *Sociological Quarterly* 21: 173–184.

Hoffman, Lois Wladis. 1963. "Parental Power Relations and the Division of Household Tasks." Nye, F. Ivan, and Hoffman, Lois Wladis, Eds. *The Employed Mother in America.* Chicago: Rand McNally.

Hood, Jane C. 1983. *Becoming a Two-Job Family.* New York: Praeger.

Keith, Pat M.; Goudy, Willis J.; and Powers, Edward A. 1981. "Employment Characteristics and Psychological Well-being of Men in Two-Job Families." *Psychological Reports* 49: 975–978.

Kessler, Ronald C., and McRae, James A., Jr. 1982. "The Effect of Wives' Employment on the Mental Health of Married Men and Women." *American Sociological Review* 47: 216–227.

Kohn, Melvin L. 1983. "Occupational Structure and Alienation." Kohn, Melvin L., and Schooler, Carmi, Eds. *Work and Personality: An Inquiry into the Impact of Social Stratification.* Norwood, N.J.: Ablex.

———. 1977. *Class and Conformity: A Study in Values.* Second Edition. Chicago: University of Chicago Press.

Kohn, Melvin L., and Schooler, Carmi. 1983a. "Job Conditions and Personality: A Longitudinal Assessment of Their Reciprocal Effects." *Work and Personality: An Inquiry into the Impact of Social Stratification.* Norwood, N.J.: Ablex.

———. 1983b. "Occupational Experience and Psychological Functioning: An Assessment of Reciprocal Effects." Kohn, Melvin L., and Schooler, Carmi, Eds. *Work and Personality: An Inquiry into the Impact of Social Stratification.* Norwood, N.J.: Ablex.

———. 1983c. "The Reciprocal Effects of the Substantive Complexity of Work and Intellectual Flexibility: A Longitudinal Assessment." Kohn, Melvin L., and Schooler, Carmi, Eds. *Work and Personality: An Inquiry into the Impact of Social Stratification.* Norwood, N.J.: Ablex.

Kohn, Melvin L.; Slomczynski, Kazimierz M.; and Schoenbach, Carrie. 1986. "Social Stratification and the Transmission of Values in the Family: A Cross-national Assessment." *Sociological Forum.* 1: 73–102.

LaRossa, Ralph. 1977. *Conflict and Power in Marriage: Expecting the First Child.* Beverly Hills, Calif.: Sage.

Long-Laws, Judith. 1976. "A Feminist View of Marital Adjustment." Gurman, Alan S., and Rice, David G., Eds. *Couples in Conflict: New Directions in Marital Therapy.* New York: Jason Aronson.

Maret, Elizabeth, and Finlay, Barbara. 1984. "The Distribution of Household Labor Among Women in Dual-Earner Families." *Journal of Marriage and the Family* 46: 357–364.

Meissner, Martin. 1971. "The Long Arm of the Job: A Study of Work and Leisure." *Industrial Relations* 10: 239–260.

Miller, Joanne; Schooler, Carmi; Kohn, Melvin L.; and Miller, Karen A. 1983. "Women and Work: The Psychological Effects of Occupational Conditions." Kohn, Melvin L., and Schooler, Carmi, Eds. *Work and Personality: An Inquiry into the Impact of Social Stratification.* Norwood, N.J.: Ablex.

Miller, Joanne, and Garrison, Howard H. 1982. "Sex Roles: The Division of Labor at Home and in the Workplace." Turner, Ralph, and Short, James, Jr., Eds. *Annual Review of Sociology.* Palo Alto, Calif.: Annual Reviews, pp. 237–262.

Miller, Karen A., and Kohn, Melvin L., 1983. "The Reciprocal Effects of Job Conditions and the Intellectuality of Leisure-Time Activities." Kohn, Melvin L., and Schooler, Carmi, Eds. *Work and Personality: An Inquiry into the Impact of Social Stratification.* Norwood, N.J.: Ablex.

Morse, Stanley, and Gergen, Kenneth J. 1970. "Social Comparison, Self-Consistency, and the Concept of Self." *Journal of Personality and Social Psychology* 16: 148–156.

Mortimer, Jeylan T. 1976. "Social Class, Work and the Family: Some Implications of the Father's Occupation for Familial Relationships and Sons' Career Decisions." *Journal of Marriage and the Family* 38: 241–256.

Parsons, Talcott. 1954. "Age and Sex in the Social Structure of the United States." *Essays in Sociological Theory.* New York: Free Press.

Parsons, Talcott; Bales, Robert F.; and Shils, Edward A. 1953. *Working Papers in the Theory of Action.* Glencoe, Ill.: Free Press.

Piotrkowski, Chaya S. 1979. *Work and the Family System: A Naturalistic Study of Working-Class and Lower-Middle-Class Families.* New York: Free Press.

Pearlin, Leonard I., and Kohn, Melvin L. 1966. "Social Class, Occupation, and Parental Values: A Cross-National Study." *American Sociological Review* 31: 466–479.

Pleck, Joseph H. 1983. "Husbands' Paid Work and Family Roles: Current Research Issues." Lopata, Helena Z., and Pleck, Joseph H., Eds. *Research in the Interweave of Social Roles: Families and Jobs.* Volume 3. Greenwich, Conn.: JAI Press.

Propper, Alice Marcella. 1972. "The Relationship of Material Employment to Adolescent Roles, Activities and Parental Relationships." *Journal of Marriage and the Family* 34: 417–421.

Regan, Mary C., and Roland, Helen E. 1985. "Rearranging Family and Career Priorities: Professional Women and Men of the Eighties." *Journal of Marriage and the Family* 47: 985–992.

Rice, Robert W.; Near, Janet P.; and Hunt, Raymond G. 1980a. "The Job-Satisfaction/Life Satisfaction Relationship: A Review of Empirical Research." *Basic and Applied Social Psychology* 1: 37–64.

———. 1980b. "The Relationship Between Work and Nonwork Domains: A Review of Empirical Research." *Academy of Management Review* 5: 415–429.

Ross, Catherine E.; Mirowsky, John; and Huber, Joan. 1983. "Dividing Work, Sharing Work, and In Between: Marriage Patterns and Depression." *American Sociological Review* 48: 809–823.

Rubin, Lillian Breslow. 1976. *Worlds of Pain: Life in the Working-Class Family.* New York: Basic Books.

Safilios-Rothschild, Constantina. 1970. "The Influence of the Wife's Degree of Work Commitment upon Some Aspects of Family Organization and Dynamics." *Journal of Marriage and the Family* 32: 681–691.

Schoenbach, Carrie. 1985. "Effects of Husband's and Wife's Social Status on Psychological Functioning." *Journal of Marriage and the Family* 47: 597–608.

Seccombe, Karen. 1986. "The Effects of Occupational Conditions upon the Division of Household Labor: An Application of Kohn's Theory." *Journal of Marriage and the Family* 48: 839–848.

Slomczynski, Kazimierz M.; Miller, Joanne; and Kohn, Melvin L. 1981. "Stratification, Work, and Values." *American Sociological Review* 46: 720–744.

Sobel, Marion G. 1963. "Commitment to Work." Nye, F. Ivan, and Hoffman, Lois Waldis, Eds. *The Employed Mother in America.* Chicago: Rand McNally.

Spade, Joan Z. 1984a. "Occupational Structure and Men's and Women's Parental Values." Paper presented at the Second International Interdisciplinary Congress on Women, Groningen, The Netherlands.

———. 1984b. "Work and Changing Relationships in the Home." Paper presented at the Annual Meeting of the Society for the Study of Social Problems, San Antonio, Texas.

Spenner, Kenneth I., and Atkinson, Maxine P. 1985. "Work Commitment, Sex-Role Attitudes and Women's Work: New Evidence and a Proposed Resolution." Paper presented at the ISA Research Committee on Stratification and Mobility, Harvard University, Cambridge, Mass.

U.S. Department of Labor. 1984. *Families at Work: The Jobs and the Pay.* Washington, D.C.: U.S. Government Printing Office.

Wilensky, Harold L. 1960. "Work, Careers, and Social Integration." *International Social Science Journal* 12: 543–560.

16

Dual-Career Corporate Couples: Shaping Marriages Through Work

ROSANNA HERTZ

The dual-career marriage challenges a number of principles of traditional marriage. Employment and its rewards still shape a couple's life chances; but instead of a single career or job-defining marital roles, there are two careers qualifying each spouse as a "breadwinner." Many dual-career couples live better than their more traditional counterparts, but ambiguity and confusion surround the marriage of two careers. No one partner in the household can claim authority based on "bringing home the bacon." Questions as to whose career and time commitments should take precedence are befuddled by similar (and competing) employer demands. Arriving at a division of labor for household tasks is complicated by both spouses' daytime absence from the home. Traditional corporate careers require the husband (as employee) and the wife (as his aide) to join forces in what Papanek (1975) referred to as the "two-person career." Dual-career marriages have, in this sense, two husbands and no wife.

Ambiguity and confusion about social roles are common among people experiencing social change. New expectations about behavior are only dimly perceived as new practices emerge. Marital roles are no exception. In this regard marital roles are not viewed as "fixed" in early childhood socialization or biological conditioning. Instead, as the microstructural approach suggests (Risman, 1987), behavior of husbands and wives is adaptive to ongoing interaction. But simply resocializing individuals to believe that a gender division of labor does not produce marital equality is not enough; instead, as Lorber (1986) argues, social change depends on reorganizing the social world. What makes the experience of the couples in the study important is that their efforts to define a new set of roles did not precede the marriage but, rather, occurred only after the

---

Revised from an article in *Families and Work* edited by Naomi Gerstel and Harriet Engle Gross by permission of Temple University Press. For a lengthier discussion of dual-career couples and methods used in this study, see Rosanna Hertz, *More Equal Than Others: Women and Men in Dual-Career Marriages.*

practical implications of change began to emerge. For example, wives' careers demanded long hours in the office making them unable to be at home cooking dinner. Husbands learned to cook not because of a broader ideology but out of necessity. Not unlike a picture slowly brought into focus, the practical implications of change in their situations took time to appear as something comprehensible: marriage as a relationship apart from, yet dependent on, their individual careers.

The dual-career marriage consolidates three careers; his, hers, and theirs. The marriage, the "third career," bears remarkable similarities to the career one makes in work, especially in a new industry. That is, everyone knows what the title "manager" is, but few have a clear sense when they embark on a career just where they will end up—though, of course, everyone has plans. Career marriages are similar; but in addition to wanting to be a "husband" or "wife," each has to comprehend and work at that role as it emerges over time.

Without many models to use as benchmarks, couples tend to measure themselves against the traditional husband and wife roles, a model that provides insufficient and often contradictory advice. The third career (marriage) is "made," not imitated or created automatically, and therefore it involves confusion and uncertainty. Thus, their unease in dealing with an ambiguous situation leads to frustration in trying to make a new reality fit an old model. Far from being the avant-garde of a social movement with an articulate vision of something they wanted to create, they are struck by their lack of ideological prescriptions about equality of marital roles. Instead, they simply practice it. Though rough edges remain to be smoothed, marital roles have been shaped in the direction of the objectives espoused by many feminist theorists, but largely without prior indoctrination of either spouse in the ideology of equality. That is, microstructural conditions (their opportunities and rewards) are far more important in explaining changes in those couples' behavior than ideology. His and her careers are microstructural causes that helped create the "third career," the marriage. In this article, I will discuss the process through which dual-career couples "make" their third career.

The Sample

Data were collected in semistructured, in-depth interviews with twenty-one dual-career couples. Participants in this study were selected from a pool of couples identified by informants in corporations located in the Chicago metropolitan area. I located couples in which husbands and wives were similarly situated professionally and organizationally. This close "matching" to one another in terms of earnings and employer-work requirements was necessary in order to assess how the absence of clear inequalities in income or career status would effect relations between husbands and wives and their accommodations in the household division of labor, financial arrangements, child care, and career strategies. Prior studies tended not to distinguish between jobs and careers. As a result they focused on husbands and wives whose work locations and opportunities were not equally valued or rewarded. Thus, it is unclear if employment opportunities or gender beliefs shape these marriages. By matching husbands and wives as closely as possible, this study illuminates how social relations are negotiated.

Each husband and wife was individually interviewed about his or her attitudes regarding work and family. The median age for males was thirty-six and for females thirty-four. The median number of years married was nine; 65 percent of the couples had children. Because they were corporate dual-career couples, they were quite affluent: the median joint income was $90,250 in 1981–82. Wives' median income was $40,200; husbands' median income was $47,500. Seventy-one percent live in the city. (For a lengthier discussion of dual-career couples and methods used in this study, see Hertz, 1986.)

Career Beginnings: His Career

The men in this study grew up in the 1940s and early 1950s. For them working was expected, not a matter of choice. Their lives reflect the prototypical middle-class male career pattern: college, graduate training, and then a series of jobs. Their lives followed a neat, orderly sequence as they moved directly from one stage to the next. Fifty-two percent of the men went directly from college to graduate school. Another 24 percent of the men went to the military after college graduation before proceeding to graduate school. Many men prepared for careers by their choice of undergraduate majors. Unlike women, whose undergraduate majors are a bit more evenly distributed, almost two-thirds of the men majored in social science (specifically economics), and only one-quarter majored in the humanities (specifically history).

Forty-three percent of the men married when they graduated from college. In the majority of these cases, wives supported husbands while the latter earned advanced degrees. However, 48 percent of the men married after completing graduate education when their wives typically were just completing graduate education. In the former group, husbands and wives went through graduate school in turn-taking fashion, and in the latter group it was the husbands who supported their wives through advanced training. At the time of these interviews, thirteen men held corporate positions as managers or vice-presidents, eight men were either corporate lawyers or doctors, and three men were self-employed.

The early part of the men's careers did not involve a change in attitude about their role as breadwinners. Change took place more subtly as a result of their wives' entry into the labor market. Whereas the academic market has a limited number of universities in any geographical area, forcing academic couples to commute more often (Gerstel and Gross, 1984), in the 1980s employment opportunities in the Chicago area for these corporate couples are much more abundant. Therefore, these corporate husbands and wives could afford to limit their geographical mobility and choose between positions in the immediate area and in the process maintain a dual-career *locally*-based marriage. The issue of how men's careers developed in tandem with their wives' and how that altered the social roles of husband and wife will be discussed.

Career Beginnings: Her Career

Caught in the middle—between an old dream and a new reality—best captures the story of the lives of these women. The last issue to emerge out of the turbulent sixties was the question of women's rights. Most of these women graduated from college before 1972, the year in which the Senate passed the Equal Rights Amendment; few really had plans or thoughts of careers. Rather, they dreamt of traditional roles as wives and mothers. Work was a waystation to fulfilling that dream.

These women were neither visionaries nor activists in the women's movement, nor enthusiastic adherents to its ideology even when it became visible. It is possible that the reason these women were unaffected by changing women's roles can be attributed to a self-selection of early corporate women from pools of women not involved in the antiwar or student movements. This study asked questions only about present and past participation in the women's movement and beliefs about feminism. It is also possible that single women in the higher echelons of the corporate world might respond differently than these married women. As these women reconstructed their pasts from the vantage points of the 1980s, their feelings about how little the women's movement did to help them integrate their personal and professional lives appears to explain their present sentiments. Their views on feminism and the women's movement echo Hewlett's (1986) remarks about the lack of support the movement gave women who wanted families in addition to careers. Feminism in the 1980s was typically viewed as antifamily and antimale. Little had been done to guarantee these women maternity leaves and adequate child care. They saw themselves as "isolates." That is, each woman was alone in her respective corporation fighting for the ability to have (not even to integrate) a family with her career. The women with children were quick to tell me how they had paved the way for other managerial women to be granted maternity leaves.

> When I found out I was pregnant, I then told my boss, and he was shattered, even though he knew that I was trying to get pregnant. You know, a "You're doing this to me" kind of reaction. "How am I going to tell the other guys on the block that I've got a pregnant manager?" He started out by informing me that I had the same amount of maternity leave policy as the secretaries, which is essentially that you don't get paid. You are promised a job of equivalent status if you return within approximately six months. I told him that was all very nice, and I told him I would call him.
>
> Now I was the first woman manager on corporate staff *at all.* And I was the first nonsecretarial person to get pregnant. This corporation had no experience and the maternity policy was written at that time. . . .

There were exceptions, of course; a few women worried about how their present decisions to have children would effect other women who were in lower corporate positions. But even for this minority, feminism was not perceived as moving beyond achievements in female employment. The following quote expresses the dilemmas of having children and the "situational factors" (Lorber, 1981; Gerson, 1985; Hertz, 1986) of corporate climbing that discourage women from having children.

> I think feminism has a lot to do with my concern about having a child, and that's one of the things that I had wrestled with. I am thought of as likely to be the first woman in our firm who would be elected principal, and there isn't one now. . . . If I even have a child, then I've confirmed all sorts of stereotypes—"Oh my God, there's another one who just went out and had a kid after we've put all these years into her. How are we ever to have any women as principals if they all leave?"—and I may damage the opportunity for women who come behind me.

Instead of ideology fueling career decisions in the 1970s, these women were the beneficiaries of labor market openings. They were in the right place at the right time. For many this meant that early job experiences after college provided them with sufficient training to move into managerial positions. For others employment backgrounds allowed them to join the first large group of women to enter advanced-degree programs and obtain credentials that were later translated into corporate careers.

Although both groups of women drifted into the work force, at some point something changed that placed them in career tracks instead of more peripheral occupations. At the time these interviews were conducted, these wives, as well as their husbands, occupied a fairly varied array of management or managerial-level corporate positions. For example, five women were vice-presidents, two were directors, nine were managers, three were professionals, and two were consultants. Each foresees a reasonable probability of promotion. None sees herself locked into the position that she presently occupies. However, some do foresee corporate moves (within Chicago) as critical for their career advancement. Their dreams of career success today match those of their husbands and their male colleagues.

How is it that these women came to acquire and invest in corporate careers at variance with traditional expectations? To answer this question, it is necessary to analyze the process through which they made career investments. The decision to work was eased by the fact that most of these women had acquired college degrees in disciplines that qualified them for salaried positions in corporate settings. Despite the apparent applicability of many of these degrees to a white-collar job market, the majority of these women did not consciously decide to major in fields that would qualify them for salaried positions. Most thought that their degrees and college experience would transfer into employment, but they had no initial goals for business careers of the sort for which they saw men being trained. One woman, typical of this group, describes her thoughts about her "career start."

> So I was somewhat directionless and unfocused at that point. Chicago seemed as good a place to be as any, and my boyfriend was here. In 1966 it was relatively easy for women with math and philosophy degrees to get good-paying jobs in data processing. The whole career start was accidental.

Moreover, fully two-thirds did not begin to pursue careers until some time after they were married. In order to avoid confusion over the process of career investment, I will analyze these two groups separately, drawing them together later to discuss general issues.

The women who married before beginning careers married either before they finished college or shortly after receiving their college degrees. They married under the middle-class "rules" of the old dream, thinking that once their grooms had completed their graduate studies, they would assume their place beside them as homemakers and wives. As one woman explained:

> At that point I really didn't have any long-term career goals. My goals had stopped when I graduated from college and I hadn't really thought through what I intended to do after that. . . . Here I was with the thought that I was going to obviously get married and have children at a young age and do all those nice things that my mother did.

The initial employment histories of these women are simply not based on long-term career goals for themselves; instead, they are directly linked to their husbands' future career prospects.

> We both had degrees in journalism but I followed him—his career. Every six months they would send him someplace else. His first job was in Georgia, and I worked as a news editor for the *Dublin Herald*. . . . Six months later he got transferred to Chicago, and I followed him here and I got a job as a secretary at a TV studio, and six months later he got transferred to Philadelphia . . . and I worked as an assistant director for an advertising agency. . . . He was pursuing his career, and I was picking up whatever I could.

So although the majority of these women were not thinking in terms of careers or career goals, they were gaining job experience and skills as they followed their husbands' leads.

Until this point they are pursuing one career—his. How is it that these women came to have careers of their own? Even though they expressed satisfaction with their work and feelings of self-confidence about their early employment histories, it is unclear that labor force participation by itself explains a shift in thinking about careers. Similarly, even though these women recall their traditional aspirations prior to marriage, marriage itself allowed their career goals to take hold. Both employment opportunities and husbands' encouragement appear critical. However, it is difficult to assess the relative contributions of employment opportunities and the marital relationship, especially since these data were gathered in the context of reconstructing personal histories.

Once these women began to consider themselves in a career path, they sought to acquire the additional training or certification necessary to enhance their chances of promotion. Fully 71 percent of the women earned a postgraduate degree in a career-related field. The percentage of women who earned postgraduate degrees is the same for those married before and after they began their careers.

For the one-third of the women who married in their mid-to-late twenties, employment was an assumed part of their marital relationship. Although their lives did not include following a husband from one position to the next, career beginnings for half this group were incremental as well. Regardless of which route they took to their careers, women's career decisions became intertwined with their husbands'.

Changing Gender Roles: The Choice to Work Outside the Home

Although employment prior to marriage or at the beginning of marriage, to help husbands financially, has always been part of the traditional female role, all the women talked about having chosen to seek a job beyond these early years. There are two dimensions to this choice: a gender-role decision and an economic decision. One woman compared male and female expectations about employment:

> I made a choice to work and I like it. And I do it because I like it. I mean I wasn't socialized to think I'm a bad person if I didn't work, when most men never really had that choice. They've always known they were going to work. They were going to support a family, and they never were able to make a choice. But I did. It's very important to me, or I wouldn't have made the choice.

Although this may sound like a personal and idiosyncratic choice, it is in fact a gender-role decision. Implicit in the choice to work outside the home is not only a comparison of women's and men's roles but a confrontation between traditional values for women and their new desires. The choice to work outside the home constitutes a decision *not* to pursue a traditional role as homemaker. This decision has been eased by the fact that few encountered direct opposition in their choice—for example, from a husband who insisted on his wife's occupying a traditional role.

Employment was conceived of as something they should do because "we had to have more money." Almost from the very beginning of their marriage, her earnings constituted a significant contribution to their shared lifestyle. They did not just live on his salary, banking hers. Instead, they lived on both incomes, and their lifestyles expanded accordingly—including their rent or mortgage, their bills, the places they chose to go, and so on. They became dependent upon their dual earnings. Put differently, their joint earnings determine their standard of living, and at the same time, their standard of living determines how much money they need to earn. Both husbands and wives made comments like: "We could live on one salary. We could adjust. But we couldn't live today the way we live on two salaries."

These women cannot choose to opt out of the labor force and give up their "choice to work outside the home." Without planning to do so, they have accrued financial obligations and debts. Women, then, come to experience the same kind of career pressure as men.

At the time when many of these women took their jobs, no real decisions had to be made about *future* investments in careers. These women assumed that, in the early stages of a career, the opportunity costs were relatively low: since little investment had been made, little cost would be incurred if they left the workplace. Questions concerning her career only became salient when children became an issue. Decisions thus appeared much less significant at an earlier time. In fact, earlier behavior came to be recognized as decisions made only as time passed and career investments grew to the point where couples faced fairly significant costs if she forsook her career.

Making the Marriage

> It's two separate lives in some ways. It's like a dual carriageway, and we are both going down those carriageways at more or less the same speed, I would say. While those carriageways don't cross one another, if something happens on one of them, something necessarily happens on the other one.

Because both husbands and wives have careers, the marriage can no longer respond entirely to the demands of only one spouse (or spouse's career). Marriage can no longer serve to define a division of labor between breadwinner and homemaker and, with that division of labor, a relative priority or valuation of the different activities. If two careers are to be nourished, they must also be constrained by a set of rules for how competing career demands are to be balanced and how the homemaking or reproductive activities of the marriage are to be organized. Among the couples I interviewed, the predominant mechanism for negotiating individual careers is based upon marriage as a third career. For these couples, marriage represents *both* the social contract entered into by a man and a woman for purposes of gaining intimacy, love, and children, and all the other intangibles of such a union *and* the conjoining of two careers.

This conception of a shared career infuses marriage with a different meaning than the traditional pattern. Couples do not always articulate a clear statement about the equity of careers and the equality of spouses. Yet the practice of balancing the demands of two careers produces an outcome in which, if both careers are to survive, some vision of mutual benefit must be invoked on a daily basis. This criterion serves to distribute or accomplish reproductive/homemaking tasks (broadly and narrowly conceived) and is referred to as a guide when either spouse confronts a situation that challenges or potentially affects the other spouse's career. Marital equity is not taken for granted; it is worked at. As one typical husband put it:

> I certainly don't think this is a gloriously equal marriage marching off into the sunset. I think we struggle for equality all the time. And we remind each other when we are not getting it.

Put differently, it is not an ideology of marital equality that determines careers; instead, it is because of the two careers that equality becomes an issue. Indeed, couples rarely spoke directly about equality. They spoke instead of trying to strike a balance between careers and family commitments by keeping each other in check so that neither spouse could tip the scale in favor of his or her own career. Although symmetry may produce feelings of equity, attempts to maintain symmetry provide a constance source of conflict within dual-career marriages. One husband explains how individual career involvement is a catalyst for assessing family involvements.

> There is this constant pressure of trying to balance things, constantly reassessing how much time we spend in family and careers. [Could you give me an example?] Sure. Every day. Every week. Trying to figure out how much time to spend—whether you should be with the kids, or with Ann, or working. . . . You make definite tradeoffs. You *both* make a tradeoff. It's also hard because we both frequently talk about it. How much of a tradeoff each one of us should be making—whether we are both making the same amount or whether the other one feels that one of us is spending too much time on the job.

Although couples do not keep ledgers, most have instituted rules over job choices and moves. One couple decided to establish a rule to prevent recurrent disagreements surrounding job moves. The wife explained how this a priori rule reflected their sense of marital equity:

> What we have tried to do is set the ground rules before we are faced with a specific decision. [Why?] To give it some neutrality. . . . Whoever did not have the offer made the basic decision to move. If he had an offer, I had first crack at rejecting the city. It's really a veto power.

Other couples had different mechanisms for achieving parity, including rules about lateral moves as well as promotions.

Although it is difficult to directly assess equality in the household division of labor and in marital roles, these couples exhibit a greater degree of symmetry than has been reported by research on traditional families. Whether these couples are more egalitarian than those studied in previous research—which suggested that dual career marriages do not always lead to equality—is difficult to discern (Holmstrom, 1973; Poloma and Garland, 1971; and Pleck, 1977). The findings from prior research and this study are not strictly comparable, and definitions of equality remain to be tightened.

The marriage thus comes to operate as a constraint on the unbridled pursuit of one career to the possible disadvantage of the other. But it also operates as a buffer, cushioning the negative impact of failures or reversals in one or the other career. The unpredictability of careers and responses to them demands such an arrangement, and paradoxically, it forges an emphasis on equity and symmetry for each career. Were it not that marriage is so elevated in importance that it can constrain as well as buffer, then one might refer to the relationship merely as a convenience. But the marital tie operates as a legitimate constraint on careers, and it stimulates a review of the gender roles associated with marriage. Again, as is the case with marital roles, it is the practice of combining two careers, not the articulation of a nonsexist ideology, that shapes decisions and informs change.

A Step out of Traditional Gender Roles

First-hand knowledge about the organization of family life comes from what we observed our parents doing. Even if couples had friends in dual-career marriages, they were more likely to compare themselves with their parents, not with friends. Like the husband quoted below, the majority of men and women in this study came from families that had clearly defined roles and expectations for husbands and wives.

> I was a product of a family where the mother didn't work ever and whose job, in her mind, and her responsibility, in that marriage, was the maintenance of the household, the parenting function, cooking meals, and keeping things organized. So that when my dad got home he didn't have to put up with anything. . . . Joan [his wife] says, "I'm not going to scurry around here at ten to six and clean up the house so it looks neat and clean when you get home, so you think that's the way it's been all day. You can help clean it up." But that was not the way my mother was. I guess I wouldn't have as honest a view of the world, life, and I wouldn't enjoy it as much if someone with a broom was dusting a path in front of me as I walked.

Gender roles continue to play a part in determining the form of marital relations, and it takes a constant struggle not to fall back on the old ways of marriage—the old rules and roles—that these individuals witnessed as children in their parents' homes.

Yet things have changed for these couples. Again, there was no ideological underpinning to their marriages that caused the roles of husband and wife to be dramatically altered. The break with their traditional upbringing is simple to explain: as women's careers became as demanding as their husbands' there was no time for a wife to be a "wife." The initial change, then, was in the wife's role. Thus, as wives and husbands became "duplicates" of one another (at least as workers outside the home), her "new" role altered his. The invisible work of the home is now in plain view, and although couples do hire household labor (and wives were responsible for supervising help) (Hunt and Hunt, 1977; Hertz, 1986), many chores remain to be done around the home. One husband explains how this change came about for him and his wife:

> We don't consciously say that we're going to share, but it just turns out with both people working you can't have one do everything. If one of us were relying on the other to fix meals, we'd both starve.

Her career alters not only the meaning of "wife" but, in the process, his role as husband. This role expansion is fundamentally different for men and women: she has moved outward, discovering the world of making a living; he has moved inward, discovering the intricacies of running a home. Time, tolerance, and enjoyment determine who performs which tasks. As one husband explained:

> There were no initial arrangements. It was just an agreement that both of us would share in the housework. There is nothing like "You do the laundry and I'll do the pots and pans." There is just an understanding that we were both working and that we both have responsibilities to other things.

Work impacts family life because of time constraints and demands put on each individual. In turn, the couple (both individuals with such constraints) is forced to figure out an organization for running the household that takes into account the work constraints, and that, in the process, accomplishes the equivalent of a frontal assault on the gender-based allocation of duties. This is another way of saying that what is experienced as a breakdown of traditional gender roles in the family need not necessarily be the product of a conscious strategy of confronting gender inequality. Often the role changing is discussed as "new interests" or "hobbies" such as men's interest in cooking when, in fact, the "interest" was generated because those men's wives were not around to cook meals and the men were getting tired of having frozen foods. Similarly, a number of women expressed a real lack of interest in cooking and indicated their relief in not being forced to perform—precisely because their jobs did not leave them the time or their work provided sufficient income to purchase those services directly.

However, lingering ambivalences are connected with giving up clearly defined husband-wife patterns. These stem from the couple's failure to fulfill what are conceived of as traditional gender roles.

Couples sometimes do fall back on traditional roles. One man uses the derogatory term, "squaw work," to explain his own awareness of the inequality built into a traditional division of labor but nonetheless remains an intermittent feature of their marriage:

> You have to realize I was in the 4-H Club with the cows and my wife was in the 4-H Club with home economics. That tells a lot about where we started. But we have migrated away from all that. . . . Even today my wife is not embarrassed by doing the squaw work. She kind of likes to do the housework. It gives us an old-fashioned feeling to our marriage every once in a while and that is a nice touch.

Women in this study also worry about emasculating their husbands by asking them to do more around the house, even when they employ full-time housekeepers. As a result, they retain some aspect of household work as their exclusive turf. One woman reserves one chore for herself, despite her husband's insistence.

> I don't like the way he looks doing the laundry. Well, to me it's something that women do. It represents a nurturing activity to me—something very feminine. Maybe it's my way of showing him I still have that.

This was typical: remnants of a traditional division of labor were defended by the wives as much as, or more than, the husbands.

It is in the emotional arena that men feel most slighted. The attention wives once showered on their husbands is reduced because they no longer have the time or energy, or perhaps even the need to do so. Further, although men are involved in the domestic arena, their feelings are not necessarily aligned with their actions. As one man put it:

> You know, I don't consider myself the ultimate liberated man. In terms of the pendulum swing, I'm pretty far in that direction [left]. But, you know, when she's had to work on Saturdays or Sundays to finish a big project, I take care of the kids, and I'm not overly thrilled about it. But I do it.

Career Development and Choice

Even if the steps out of traditional gender roles are somewhat tentative and cause some discomfort, the conjoining of two careers does open some real possibilities for change in careers. In most cases, the development of careers is alternating in character. His career comes first and makes possible hers or investments leading to hers. Her career makes possible shifts in his career. Perhaps more important than the alternation of investments is that the large and stable portion of family income coming from the wife's career makes possible career shifts for him. Because the dual-career marriage frees men from sole economic responsibility, the men can be less obsessed by work, less aggressive, and even less motivated because the weight of this responsibility is shared. One man explains how this has made a difference in his life:

> I'm not a workaholic. I'm pretty comfortable at what I'm doing. I probably could make more money if I was interested in working a lot harder, but I would have to sacrifice a lot of things for that—like time with my family, personal time, a lot of things. I'm just not willing to do that, and in part I don't have to do that because my wife works.

A woman describes the freedom she feels her career gives her husband:

> The woman who works and makes as much as the man gives the man flexibility and freedom in his job. He doesn't have to worry incessantly: "What if something happens—what if I die or what if I get fired or what if I hate this career and I'd rather refinish furniture and start my own business?" He has more flexibility because of the economic freedom.

Men did not just fantasize about a career change: several enacted one. For others a career shift was in the talking stages. In all cases the wives encouraged such moves. In this regard, the career marriage paves the way for career choice. One man, after having a disagreement with the president of his company, made good on his intention to "strike out on his own" in the consulting field. He explains how this was possible.

> We [he and his partner] went into business with virtually no clients. The fact that Susan was working and making a good income was significant. The decision would have been different if that had not been the case. We couldn't have afforded it. She and I talked about my leaving the company, and she agreed with me.

But the business was not on a solid footing, and this started to affect their marriage.

> It's good we started to make money when we did. It took a bit longer than we expected. We'd both reached a point where, if we hadn't started being more successful within a year, I probably would have gone back into the job market. If I hadn't, she would have been pretty unhappy about it. She was feeling the pressure of carrying the financial responsibility and feeling the sacrifice that we were making collectively was beginning to add up.

Shared economic responsibility is these couples' goal, and it is only for brief periods that either spouse is willing to assume full economic responsibility.

In short, the career marriage offers husbands freedom to explore career alternatives and career shifts much like the choice reserved for middle-class women in a more traditional pattern. Women in this study have not yet done the same, but that may be because their careers are newer (in terms of their thinking of their employment as a career and in terms of the number of years they have actually spent in their chosen fields). His career change may eventually make possible alternatives in her career trajectory.

Communication and Support

Despite moments of doubt, ambivalence, and conflict, dual-career couples often develop a communication style that they believe is quite different from that which characterizes traditional marriages. Husbands and wives with careers spend the bulk of their time engaged in similar activities, which, while often drawing on different kinds of expertise, share a rhythm and a structure; this situation is far different from the chasm that separates paid employment and housework. Thus, these spouses understand each other's lives and experience a high degree of empathy: "She has a sense of what I'm doing 'cause she's out there doing the same damn thing every day."

One woman explains how a shared understanding makes her relationship with her husband different from that of traditional husbands and wives:

> Another aspect of my traveling and his traveling is that each of us understands what travel is to the other and it's not sitting at home thinking that it's glamorous or exciting and that I'm being left out, as a lot of wives who are very resentful of their husband's traveling. We don't give each other hassles about traveling.

Most couples talk about the day's events over dinner or in bed, whether there is one earner or two. But what is striking in these cases is the similarity of the talk. She talks finance and he talks marketing. It is the content of her end of the conversation that has changed.

Although they can support one another through similar organizational experiences, they are not conduits linking one firm to the next. The majority talk about personal problems, office politics, and unusual events. Unless couples are in the same field, they do not talk about the details of their jobs because of the specialized knowledge needed to understand the finer points. Even when they are in the same field, they do not necessarily talk about the specifics of the work, especially when issues are confidential. The similarity of their employers' organizational structure, however, provides a basis for shared understanding and communication.

> We talk a lot about common problems in respect to interrelating to the other associates. Her study teams are like my study teams. Her problems of having a junior associate who doesn't seem to be able to get his or her game together is the same as my problems, and we are a resource to each other in saying, "Have you tried this or that?"

These couples, then, have the quintessential modern marriage—theirs is truly a companion marriage. Yet there is also the potential for competition for status between spouses. Sometimes spouses pointed out that their talk leads to disagreement about who knows best and who is really the expert. Couples try to resolve this problem by carving out distinct areas of expertise. One man explains how this operates in his marriage:

> Our work coincidentally overlaps an awful lot. . . . But we each have a reasonable working knowledge of where the other person is stronger. There's some recognition that I know more about certain things and she knows more about other things. . . . Sometimes we interrupt each other when we're talking about things, but if it is my area that I know more about, she backs off, and vice versa.

The carving out of distinct areas of professional turf allows each partner to avoid getting too close to the world the other occupies outside the home. It is one way in which the marriage buffers the careers and keeps husbands and wives from developing the petty jealousies and conflicts characteristic of co-workers in the same office.

Conclusion

At the outset, I suggested that the dual-career couple represented a situation with two husbands and no wife. However, the epigram ignores synchronous movements in other directions, including that of limiting the career aspirations and goals of husbands and wives and opening new avenues of expression for each. This combination of new limits and new openings marks a fundamental departure from traditional marital arrangements for those couples who are willing to undertake the challenge of negotiation. And the negotiation terrain included not just two parties or areas of interest—his and hers—but a third: theirs. Their career, the marriage, is a set of shifting boundaries that defines mutual interests in careers *and* a relationship that, more than the traditional marriage, poses a potential counterweight to the influence of employment.

The third career forces a clearer set of limits on the demands of the other two, offering the possibility that marriage and family could exert some influence on what employers can ask of their employees. But because dual-career marriages are few and far between and careerists tend to be located in organizations that are capable of resisting collective demands from managerial workers, the influence of marriage on work organizations tends to be reduced to selective incidents of individual resistance or, more commonly, individual opportunities forgone in order to sustain the balance between his career and hers. This fact makes even more important the definition of a set of principles that can guide the pursuit of two careers and permit an acceptable union between them and family. In this sense, norms of equity and reciprocity must be much more open to discussion and debate. Since neither husband nor wife can claim sole authority on the basis of breadwinning, rules of conduct and a division of labor must be created to service the equally compelling demands of two careers. However, as corporations restructure their employment opportunities to allow some women to become full participants with career mobility, her career emerges alongside his career. This social change in employment opportunities fosters greater symmetry between individual husbands and wives. His and her career are microstructural causes that help create their marriage. But, as I have attempted to show, concerns with equity between husbands and wives rarely precede the construction of dual-career marriages. Rather, those concerns commonly *follow* investments in two careers.

References

Gerson, Kathleen. 1985. *Hard Choices: How Women Decide about Work, Career and Motherhood.* Berkeley: University of California Press.

Gerstel, Naomi, and Harriet Gross. 1984. *Commuter Marriages: A Study of Work and Family.* New York: Guilford Press.

Hertz, Rosanna. 1986. *More Equal than Others: Women and Men in Dual-Career Marriages.* Berkeley: University of California Press.

Hewlett, Sylvia. 1986. *A Lesser Life: The Myth of Women's Liberation in America.* New York: William Morrow.

Holmstrom, Lynda Lytle. 1973. *The Two-Career Family.* Cambridge, Mass.: Schenkman.

Hunt, Janet G., and Larry L. Hunt. 1977. "Dilemmas and Contradictions of Status: The Case of the Dual-Career Family." *Social Problems* 24: 407–416.

Lorber, Judith. 1981. "On the Reproduction of Mothering: A Methodological Debate." *Signs* 6: 482–486.

Lorber, Judith. 1986. "Dismantling Noah's Ark." *Sex Roles* 14: 567–580.

Papanek, Hanna. 1975. "Men, Women, and Work: Reflections on the Two-Person Career." *American Journal of Sociology* 78: 852–872.

Poloma, Margaret M., and T. Neal Garland. 1971. "The Married Professional Woman: A Study in the Tolerance of Domestication." *Journal of Marriage and the Family* 33(August): 531–540.

Pleck, Joseph H. 1977. "The Work-Family Role System." *Social Problems* 24: 417–427.

Risman, Barbara. 1987. "Men Who Mother." *Gender and Society* 1: 6–32.

17

Reluctant Mothers: Employed Women in the '80s

KATHLEEN GERSON

Far-reaching changes are taking place in the work and family patterns of American women. Even seasoned observers, armed with statistics, are suggesting that changes in women's behavior amount to no less than a "subtle revolution" (Smith, 1979). As women's workplace participation has reached a historic high, the birthrate has also dropped below the replacement rate to a historic low. If current trends continue, the generation now in its prime childbearing years will not bear enough offspring to reproduce itself. It is no coincidence that the rise in the number of women workers occurred alongside a sharp decline in women's fertility. Women's employment and family decisions have always been closely connected, and recent changes simply underscore the interactive, indeed inseparable, quality of this relationship.

This article explores the relationship between women's work and family decisions by taking a close look at the women most responsible for recent changes in female employment and childbearing patterns. It examines the lives of a strategic group of women now in their prime childbearing years, all members of a generation in which large numbers have departed from the well-worn paths of their forebears. As the generation whose own life choices are most responsible for dramatic demographic shifts, this group is especially well positioned to illuminate the causes, consequences, and meaning of the subtle revolution now under way. (For a description of the methods and sample employed in this study, see Gerson, 1985, Appendices B and C.)

Alternative Adult Pathways: Social Forces and Life Plans

Although women form a diverse group, this analysis focuses on the choices, plans, and strategies adopted by one rapidly growing

This article is a revision of Chapter 7 in *Hard Choices,* University of California Press, 1985.

subgroup, nondomestic women attempting to combine parenthood with full-time work outside the home. It contrasts these work-committed mothers (and future mothers) with domestic and permanently childless women. In the face of structural barriers and ambiguities, these "reluctant mothers" challenged both the assumptions and the social arrangements that make career and motherhood incompatible. As they struggled to resolve the contradictions between strong work and family commitments, they developed coping strategies that undermined the foundations of gender inequality at home and at work and that redefined inherited assumptions about what is possible for women in the modern world.

Unlike domestically oriented women, these women were committed workers who viewed children as potentially costly to their work careers. Unlike permanently childless women, however, they decided over time that childlessness held greater costs than motherhood. Faced with cross-pressures to have a child *and* a career, these women thus neither wholeheartedly embraced motherhood nor rejected it completely. Rather, they approached parenthood reluctantly, aware of the problems it posed, yet fearful that a different course would hold even greater dangers. I analyze here the process by which this group of work-committed women became, or planned to become, "reluctant mothers" and the roles of men, material and social resources, and ideological change in structuring this process.

Examining the forces that have shaped these women's decisions clarifies the more general process by which women choose between work and family commitments as their work aspirations interact with their desires to bear and rear children. The experiences of these women also show how work and family decisions emerge from the broader social context in which they occur.

There are four general patterns that a woman's life course can assume, whether she was born into the working or the middle class. These four patterns are based on two especially important dimensions around which distinct groups of women form. First, women differ in their early expectations about the goals they plan to pursue as adults. Exposed to a diverse, complex set of experiences as children, women, like men, develop a variety of conscious and unconscious aspirations long before they are able to test these wishes as adults. For some, these early images take the shape of well-formed plans in which the future appears as certain as the past. For others, these goals are more amorphous, assuming the form of vague hopes that may or may not be realized.

However misty or clear, these early desires form the baseline for adult life. Some plan to build their lives around the traditional feminine commitments to home, husband, and children; these women expect their own lives to resemble the domestic model that has been so prevalent in the recent past. Others view marriage and motherhood with trepidation and aspire to the less traditionally feminine pursuits of work advancement. Because their numbers have been few in the past, members of this latter group may be less convinced that their life choices are guaranteed than are those who start with domestic aspirations. Their lack of certainty, however, in no way diminishes the power of their feelings. The aspirations that women take into adulthood may thus center around domestic or nondomestic goals.

Once established, these early orientations are subjected to the real constraints and opportunities encountered in adulthood, the second dimension that distinguishes groups of women from each other. The social circumstances adults confront can support or undermine their original goals. Initial goals can prove viable, leading them down a life path wholly consistent with early expectations, or these early plans can ultimately turn out to be uninviting or even impossible, encouraging or perhaps requiring individual change. Unexpected events can lead adults to reevaluate their past assumptions and reorient themselves toward the future. Thus, pathways through adulthood may either follow or diverge from the beginning baseline.

People differ in the extent to which they are exposed to change-inducing experiences. They consequently vary in the degree to which change characterizes their developmental path. When the pace of historical change is slow, most people are insulated from events that might shake up their views of the world or their proper place in it. Under these circumstances, most people tend to assume that their lives are preordained and rooted in the natural order of things. Even during periods of accelerated social change, many are able to move stably through life without veering significantly from an expected path.

Periods of rapid change increase the likelihood of exposure to triggering events that promote and sometimes force individual change. At these times, people who might otherwise assume that the order of their lives is a given find that they must undergo personal change in order to adapt to changing social circumstances. These people experience turning points when they abandon old assumptions and confront new possibilities.

Women can be distinguished by their initial orientation toward work and family (determined primarily by early childhood experiences) and the subsequent experience of stability or change in adulthood. Some of those who began adulthood wanting to become mothers and homemakers stayed on the domestic path; others veered away from the private sphere and into the workplace. Among those who entered adulthood ambivalent toward motherhood and aspiring for workplace accomplishments, some remained on this nondomestic path, and others moved toward domesticity over time. Those whose initial life plans did not change enjoyed supportive circumstances that sheltered them from challenges to their goals or from enticements to new directions. In contrast, unexpected obstacles or opportunities faced those who did change as they moved through the early stages of adulthood. Figure 1 illustrates these alternative pathways.

Whether respondents developed a new orientation or sustained an old one, structural cross-pressures made it difficult for them to implement and sustain their decisions and preferences. Women who chose to place family and children before other life commitments confronted the dilemmas of how to overcome the isolation that homemaking can impose and how to defend their choices against the growing social devaluation of domestic pursuits. In contrast, women who established committed ties to the workplace faced dilemmas about whether and how to integrate children into their lives. Although each group faced a different set of obstacles and central concerns, both confronted dilemmas that lacked established, institutionalized solutions. Both faced

Figure 1 *Alternative Adult Pathways*

Baselines		Present Work-Family Orientation
(childhood goals and expectations)		(present situation combined with future plans)
Domestic (expected to marry, bear children and either be a homemaker or work intermittently in a traditionally female occupation)	→ / ↗	*Domestic* (is or expects soon to be a homemaker or mother with loose, if any, ties to work)
Nondomestic (oriented toward full-time work or career, not oriented toward bearing and rearing children, or both)	↘ / →	*Nondomestic* (oriented either toward full-time work or career with no plans for children or toward full-time work or career in combination with one or two children)

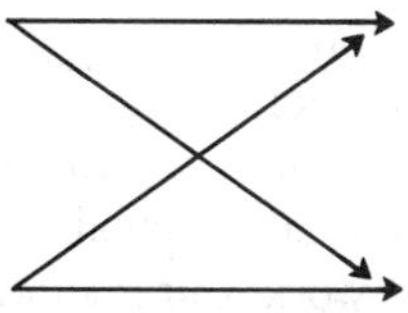

different forms of "structural ambiguity" in which they were forced to choose between mutually exclusive but equally problematic alternatives.

The structural ambiguity faced by the women studied here took different forms and provoked different reactions, depending on the particular orientation a woman developed. Whatever her orientation, however, structural ambiguity produced more than psychological ambivalence. It necessitated strategies of adjustment—strategies that tended either to reproduce traditional patterns of gender relations or to act as a force for change. As respondents reacted to the particular form of structural ambiguity they faced, they either created new social arrangements or reproduced old ones. Because they all faced historically unprecedented conditions, however, none could avoid the active struggle either to invent new responses or to preserve old ones.

Figure 1 shows how each group developed two possible responses to the dilemmas posed by the structural ambiguity of their respective situations. Among those with domestic orientations, some had the resources and the desire to make full-time homemaking a career. Others, more frustrated at home or without the financial resources to stay home full-time, were either currently in, or planning to join, the paid labor force part-time. Among those with nondomestic orientations, some concluded that they would never have children; others were either preparing to, or currently attempting to, combine full-time employment and parenthood.

Whether they opted for childlessness or attempted to combine work and motherhood, women committed to nondomestic paths made choices that promote social change far beyond the scope of their private lives. In particular, those who planned to combine motherhood with career pushed for structural and ideological changes in the workplace and at home that would ease their parenting responsibilities and reduce the work penalties that motherhood threatened to entail. They thus joined their childless counterparts in forging new, if fragile and only dimly perceived, pathways for adult women. As long as the social forces that led these women away from domesticity persist, this group will also persist in its efforts to remove the obstacles that continue to block nontraditional paths.

The Childbearing Decision Among Work-Committed Women

The committed worker's approach to childbearing was one of deep ambivalence, which is well illustrated by this thirty-year-old woman's struggle to develop enthusiasm for childbearing amid fears that motherhood would upset the delicate balance of her professional and personal life.

Q: Over the next five to ten years, do you plan to work, raise a family, or do both?

A: I think I plan to combine working with raising a family. And the reason I say I *think* is that, if I want to have a family, I'm sure I'll want to combine working with a family. I'm having a little trouble wanting a family. I'm not quite sure where that's coming from.

Q: Where do you think it's coming from?

A: I'm not sure that I like children. It's more than that. I'm stretched so many ways now, in terms of demands on my time. And I feel that a baby, if I commit myself to a baby, I can't let it go for a week like I can the garden. I'm a little afraid of that extra commitment. That's just going to be a little more than I can take. I'm not sure yet what has to give where. I'm afraid of having kids, and yet that's hard because I know I'm going to hate myself when I'm sixty if I don't have any kids. It's a real up-in-the-air situation in terms of what I really want to do.

In contrast to those whose ambivalence about children led them toward childlessness, however, reluctant mothers planned to add, or had already added, children to their lives. These women confronted different constraints and brought different resources to bear on the decision to have a child than did their childless counterparts. They were more likely to find themselves in relationships that would be seriously jeopardized by childlessness. They were also in a better position to minimize the negative impact children threatened to have on their lives. This group thus faced cross-pressures that lowered the perceived costs of childbearing and raised the costs of childlessness above a tolerable level. Childlessness became harder to choose and less attractive, leading these women to add children to their already established commitments at the workplace.

These features of their situation also made reluctant mothers less inclined to discount and more inclined to focus on the potentially dire long-term consequences of childlessness. They thus developed coping strategies to reduce the perceived costs of motherhood and discounted instead the costs of combining work and family. In contrast to their childless counterparts, they came to believe that they could integrate mothering into their lives without significant sacrifice to themselves, their work, or their children. This upwardly mobile office manager concluded, for example, that bearing a child would pose no major obstacle to achieving her rapidly rising work aspirations.

Q: Why do you plan to have children and work at the same time?

A: I don't want to have to give up anything to have children. I don't want to have to change my life-style at all. I look at it as an addition to my life. I'm not planning on changing anything.

Several factors led these women to decide that they could successfully combine work and motherhood without "giving up anything." First, men played a critical role in shaping these women's responses to the motherhood dilemma. The pressures exerted on reluctant mothers by their male partners pushed them toward motherhood rather than away from it. Second, given the social and emotional pressures they faced, reluctant mothers were less able than childless women to discount the costs of childlessness. They were also better positioned to develop contextual supports for combining work and motherhood.

Men's Parenting Motivations

The women who chose childlessness lacked a committed relationship or, paradoxically, had a valued relationship that children threatened to undermine. Reluctant mothers generally faced the contrasting situation: forgoing children threatened to undermine a relationship more than did having them.

Reluctant mothers typically had partners who, directly or indirectly, encouraged and pressured them to bear children. In contrast to the stereotype of the manipulative and overanxious wife coaxing her reluctant husband into parenthood, these respondents found themselves being pushed toward childbearing by husbands impatient to become fathers. This computer programmer explained:

Q: So you're feeling a lot of pressure at this point to have a child?

A: Mostly it's from my husband. Not because he's deliberately doing it, but because I know he wants to make babies, and he has been very serious about talking about it. When are we going to do it, this and that, until finally I said, "Please back off because I'm not ready for this yet."

Q: Do you think it would affect your marriage if you decided to never have children?

A: Yes, because if I decide I won't have children, my husband has to decide if he wants to keep me. . . . Because he wants a family, and I think that's really important to him. I would prefer not to do that, having a baby just because the husband wants it, simply to please him. If I'm to go through being pregnant, I prefer to be deliriously happy about it.

The male desire to have children and the prospect of losing a spouse or partner if she opposed this desire were often decisive in opting for motherhood.

Pressure from a spouse also operated in more subtle ways. Just as an uninterested partner pushed some women away from motherhood, mild forms of support pushed others toward it.

Male support became especially powerful when it led a woman to equate a committed relationship with children. In this context, children implied costs and problems, but they also expressed the value of the relationship itself. Thus, at twenty-seven, this lawyer viewed child rearing not as a form of individual fulfillment, but rather as a biological and emotional extension of her commitment to a man.

Q: What would you say are your main motivations for having a child?

A: I see it closely as an identification with my husband. He wants them. He's *very* family-oriented. It's never been discussed, but it would bother him if he didn't think he was going to have them. But if I found I was biologically unable to have them, I don't think I would adopt. Having kids will really be a hassle and complicate life. It's going to be very inconvenient, and I think a strong reason I want children is to have a child with my husband rather than to have children per se.

Finally, even though reluctant mothers did not define children as the fulfillment of their identity or nurturing needs, they often viewed them as a way of fulfilling their spouses' needs. Depriving their partners of children meant depriving themselves of the pleasure of giving something important to the person they valued most.

Just as an uninterested or openly hostile spouse dampened the desire for children among permanently childless women, so an encouraging or assertive one led reluctant mothers to overcome or at least act against their ambivalence toward childbearing. These accounts suggest, furthermore, that theories that picture men as universally uninterested in children and uniformly underdeveloped in their nurturing needs, capacities, and desires oversimplify men's orientations toward parenting and women's experiences with men. These male partners' parenting motivations went beyond the desire to reproduce offspring merely to prove manhood or to perpetuate the family name and genetic structure. At least in the eyes of their female partners, these men possessed a genuine desire and ability to nurture children. (Recent research by Pruett, 1983, on a sample of primary caretaking fathers supports this conclusion.) Were these parents or would-be parents not of the male gender, one might be tempted to label their motives as a need or desire to "mother." Similarly, reluctant mothers' reasons for wanting babies resemble those commonly attributed to men for wanting to father children.

As the strength and legitimacy of the nondomestic path for women have grown, men have faced added pressure to acknowledge their parenting motives and to push for children in their marriages. Because men do not typically view their options as a choice *between* work and family, they are less likely to focus on the negative consequences children might exact from their work careers than are their nondomestic female partners.

If we credit these reluctant mothers' perceptions, we must conclude that both men and women vary significantly in their desires to bear children and in their reasons for doing so. We must also conclude that men's and women's parenting motivations are related and interactive. Reluctant mothers appear to have responded as much to their partners' desires to procreate and nurture as to their own. Despite their own ambivalence, reluctant mothers were propelled slowly and haltingly toward motherhood by their partners. These accounts challenge the tenacious view held by social theorists, psychoanalysts, and ordinary people alike that women uniformly become mothers primarily to fulfill strongly felt needs to nurture, and men typically seek parenthood grudgingly.

Perceived Consequences of Childlessness

Because these respondents experienced strong contextual pressuress favoring motherhood, they were less able to insulate themselves from their fears of what childlessness implied in the long run. They therefore tended to focus on the negative consequences of childlessness rather than discounting them.

As pressures mounted, reluctant mothers were increasingly haunted by the costs of permanent childlessness: social disapproval, consignment to a lonely and desolate old age, and the loss of a major life experience with intrinsic value beyond its social measure. The fear of these costs had powerful psychological ramifications for work-committed women facing pressures to parent. An upwardly mobile worker with an eager spouse worried:

Q: How do you think you'd feel if you never had children?

A: Guilty, guilty. I really think that my approach toward having children at this point in my life is more based on what is expected of me than what I expect of myself. I think the only reason I'm considering having children right now is because it's heresy not to consider having children. The strongest thing will be the guilt and putting up with the disapproval. I don't think there's ever an end to the push. You get the pressure all your life from one place to another. It's just incredible.

Although childlessness had been the path of least resistance in early adulthood, fears of the negative consequences of never having children took on greater significance as respondents entered their thirties. At thirty, this same respondent conceded:

Q: But the negative consequences of *not* having a child also bothers you?

A: That's right. I'm going to hate myself when I'm sixty. I won't have any grandchildren, nobody to take care of me in my old age, all that kind of stuff.

Thus, although children were not welcomed in the present, the long-term consequences of childlessness grew increasingly more ominous for these reluctant mothers. They gradually came to see parenthood as their best chance for establishing intimate, enduring interpersonal bonds. Some even concluded that rejecting motherhood would foreclose the possibility of meaningful human relationships altogether. A lawyer, for example, viewed children as her only protection against an otherwise impersonal world.

Q: What are your main reasons for wanting children?

A: I think it would be really sad to be forty or fifty years old and not have a family. I think families are extremely important. Our society is getting so splintered as it is that I think it's really nice to have this close group of people, besides just your spouse.

Despite parenthood's drawbacks, reluctant mothers began to switch their focus from its costs to its intrinsic benefits. These included not only the continuation of the family unit but also the experience of creating a human being and adding balance, fullness, and renewed purpose to a life skewed too heavily in favor of work. Although strongly committed to work, this accountant came to view child rearing as the ultimate challenge.

A: When you go into life and everything, you're living day to day. You can have one job or another job, you can do something, but whatever you do is not an influence as much as raising a family. So I think it's really important. It's the most challenging thing that anybody can do.

Reluctant mothers responded to social and personal cross-pressures by focusing on the costs of childlessness rather than discounting them. Torn between fears of the disruption that children would cause and offsetting desires to please their spouses and affirm their interpersonal commitments through children, these women mustered a variety of reasons, some positive and some negative, to bolster their halting commitment to motherhood.

Coping Strategies

Consciously and unconsciously, reluctant mothers developed coping strategies designed to lower the costs of children and ease the way toward childbearing. Some strategies rebounded on male partners who exerted pressures in favor of parenthood. Because their partners desired children, reluctant mothers could bring more leverage than their childless counterparts to the process of negotiation with their partners about how to rear their shared offspring. Spouses and male partners thus found themselves pulled more fully into the parenting process and pushed to redefine their beliefs about proper child-rearing practices and the actual sexual division of labor within the home. These women reacted to the dilemma they faced, using whatever material and ideological leverage they could muster to control and limit the costs of motherhood.

Since reluctant mothers rejected childlessness and were unable or unwilling to loosen their work commitments, only one viable response remained: lower the costs of children. This group developed three strategies to accomplish this task. They decided to limit the number of children they bore; they struggled to bring their male partners into the parenting process; and they redefined their traditional notions about how to rear children. Each of these strategies represented some form of change—in how they organized their lives, in how they dealt with the people around them, or in how they theorized about mothering.

In their search for a way to combine committed work with motherhood, reluctant mothers typically changed their beliefs about the nature of proper child rearing and early childhood development. These ideas were more malleable than the relatively intransigent and slowly responding structures of work and marriage. Bereft of viable structural alternatives, ideological change became the path of least resistance. Caught between pressures to procreate and to achieve at work, reluctant mothers surrendered traditional beliefs that their own mothers had lived by and passed on to them.

A: I'm the opposite extreme of where I came from . . . where I felt you had to be home full-time in order to raise a child in terms of what the *child* needs. I don't think that's true anymore. Before, I felt a mother, to be a good mother, should be home with her children. Not only is it not necessary, but it might not even be best. Besides, those are the terms on which I'm willing to have a family.

The emerging beliefs of this group of women contrasted sharply with the views and behavioral patterns of their mothers, currently domestic women, and women committed to childlessness. They also represented a break from reluctant mothers' own earlier views. To ease the integration of work and family, reluctant mothers rejected traditional views and challenged the widely espoused notion that working mothers have a deleterious impact on their offspring. This process offered an escape from an otherwise irresolvable double bind, but it also required a difficult break from past assumptions and parental messages. A respondent with high work aspirations explained:

Q: What brought about the change in your attitude that work and child rearing couldn't be combined?

A: I just don't think it's true. I don't think it was true for [my mother]. I believe that I can manage to combine anything I want to, and I can do it well. I feel like a lot of the messages I got growing up were that, in fact, you couldn't combine career and family, that if I were to marry and have a family, that would be the end of my life. And I think I adopted them without understanding that, and I acted on them. Now that I have begun to separate from my parents' views, and particularly my mother's, I don't think that those are valid for me.

For some, ideological change occurred after their children were born. Faced with the experience of domesticity, they realized that, regardless of the dangers they had been told their return to work would entail, staying home was not acceptable. They thus developed new notions of good mothering that better fit their needs. Ambivalent emotions that included both guilt and a certain fragile confidence that their children would not be harmed emerged side by side. A biologist and mother of three returned to work after the birth of her first child despite her concerns and doubts.

A: I'd never held a baby in my life, and just the idea of this individual being in my charge was overwhelming. And then I found out there's nothing to it. I went back to work with guilt feelings that I should be home, but I could see that [my children] were great.

Q: Why did you decide at that point that it was okay to work?

A: At that point, I wasn't sure if the children were fine. I was still having tremendous guilt feelings, and I did for the next couple of years. But staying home was not for me. I loved my children dearly, and I felt I was a very good mother. I loved my husband dearly. But I wasn't going to sacrifice my life for these individuals. I wanted something for myself, too.

Fear, guilt, and doubt were especially common among those who lacked the moral and financial support of a male partner. This clerk and single mother, for example, considered desperate measures when divorce left her perched on an economic and emotional precipice.

Q: Did you ever worry that Laurie would suffer from your working?

A: I did. She was about two when I first separated. She started getting hyper attacks. It really scared me. I thought, "Oh, what have I done?" I was going through a very depressed, worried period, and I wrote my brother and asked if maybe I should give her up for adoption, giving her to a family, because maybe I'm not giving her enough. He said, "No. Your daughter, you keep." I think I would have regretted it. My ideal isn't the way it happened, but I don't regret the way it happened, either. I guess I'd never be happy being a housewife because, to me, there's no way to measure the value of it.

Given their lack of other acceptable alternatives, guilt and doubt, however deeply experienced, did not thwart reluctant mothers' determination to combine work and child rearing. Instead, they emphasized the benefits working mothers offer their children. They turned the traditional ideology on its head and began to develop a new philosophy of mothering that hinged upon the conviction that, at least in some instances, full-time mothering can actually harm children. Inherited beliefs and prevailing theories notwithstanding, reluctant mothers concluded that their own children would be better off because they would be mothered less.

Reluctant mothers came to believe, first, that an unhappy mother would produce an unhappy child. If full-time mothering produced disastrous consequences for the mother, it would produce disastrous consequences for the child as well. This divorced bank officer concluded that a hired, but happy, caretaker was preferable to a miserable full-time mother.

Q: Has working interfered with your ability to raise a family?

A: No, because if Janet and I had stayed home together, we would have driven each other nuts. I would not have been as good a mother as I am now. Thank God there are all these lovely people who are willing to watch my child when I'm gone and give her certain things that I'm not ready or able to give.

Work-committed mothers also argued that they would bring energies, ideas, experiences, and resources to child rearing that full-time mothers could not offer. An accountant reasoned:

A: Also, I think that, if I'm challenged and alert, it's something I could probably communicate to my children.

Reluctant mothers thus believed that their absence could and would be offset by benefits they were uniquely positioned to provide.

Third, reluctant mothers focused on money. If full-time homemaking would impose financial strains on the household, they reasoned, then a child would suffer more from economic deprivation if its mother stayed home than it would from maternal deprivation if its mother worked. The fact that a working mother could provide money in place of time also justified the choice to work. This lawyer offered the same rationale for working full-time that men have historically relied on to justify their absence during the day.

A: I plan to have children, probably two; and my idea is to take off work, maybe four months, and then go back. I might want to work part-time, but that's just not feasible; so I don't even think about it. I think about going back to work full-time. And you also have to have enough money to make it comfortable, because if you've got economic strains [the child will suffer].

Fourth, reluctant mothers argued that by working they would protect their offspring from the dangers of "overmothering." They directly challenged the belief that children need constant care and attention from one primary caretaker, preferably their biological mother. Instead, they argued that children can be overindulged and overprotected by an ever-present, overzealous mother lacking other major commitments. Reluctant mothers came to believe that their children would actually have a better chance for healthy development precisely because their mothers would be occupied elsewhere.

A: I'm not sure I'm right in saying there's *no* bad in all that comes from being gone all the time during the day. But I had the opportunity to see both families where the parents are at home and the parents aren't at home. To tell you the truth, the kids are better off if they don't have Mommy home all the time, keeping them babies. And I think in a way, too, it might help them to learn responsibility and self-reliance and things like that.

Finally, reluctant mothers questioned the widely accepted assumption that mothers who do not work shower their children with attention and affection. They argued instead that housework and other activities so preoccupy most full-time homemakers that they are no more likely to attend to their children's needs than are working mothers.

Q: So you don't think the children will suffer if you work?

A: No, I don't think so. You figure that a mother who is home all the time, even though she might be around, is still preoccupied with something else. She spends a lot of her time doing housework or whatever; so I don't see the difference. When a family gets together at night, their main concentration right then is on each other; so I think it's something that *would* work out.

This argument may not be as farfetched as it superficially appears. Bane (1976: 15–17) reports that television has become a major babysitter for most children, including preschoolers, and that the difference in the amounts of time working and homemaking mothers spend exclusively with their children is "surprisingly small." The average preschooler, for example, watches television about one-third of his or her waking hours, regardless of who is caring for the child. Reluctant mothers concluded that the quality rather than the quantity of time spent with offspring was the decisive criterion for defining good mothering and responsible child rearing. In their view, working did not seriously compromise the overall texture of the relationship between parents and children. They argued instead that working actually improved the quality of familial bonds. This rather simple substitution—of quality for quantity of time a mother spends with her child—opened up the otherwise inaccessible option of combining motherhood with committed work.

Q: You said that when you were younger, you saw working and raising children as incompatible. Why don't you feel that way any more?

A: Because it's the quality of time that you spend with them, I think. That's where I was a little bit confused. I thought you had to spend all your time with them and be a mother and housewife or just full-time working, but you can do both.

Ideological change required not only a leap of faith into uncharted territory, but a considerable amount of discounting as well. Confronted with a traditional set of beliefs (however ill-supported by evidence) that argues that mothers of young children who indulge their "selfish" desires to work run the risk of producing damaged offspring, reluctant mothers had to struggle to minimize such a possibility in their own minds. Because they were experimenting but would not know the results for some time, they found themselves waiting and hoping that all would turn out well. But they also braced themselves for unanticipated contingencies. Reluctant mothers chose to travel an uncertain path, the outcome of which they knew they could not foresee.

Q: Will working interfere with your ability to raise a family?
A: I'll try very hard not to let it. But clearly it will be different for my kid than it was for me having a mother at home all the time. Whether that's going to be a positive thing or a negative thing, only time will tell.

Reluctant mothers also discounted the costs children threatened to exact from workplace accomplishment. Although the fear of work costs remained, they struggled to minimize such threats as well.

Q: Do you think having children will affect your progress at work?
A: I think that is in the back of my mind. . . . Probably the reason why I've never actively gone out to have a kid is that concern. But again, I keep pushing that concern aside and saying that it's not going to affect [anything], which may be foolish.

Whatever their qualms, the process of ideological change lowered the perceived costs of children to a level that made the choice for motherhood possible. In the midst of uncertainty, reluctant mothers developed a strong commitment to creating new ways of integrating work and family life. For this group, there was no other acceptable choice. They concluded, unlike their domestic and childless counterparts, that responsible mothering and committed work are not incompatible. As this aspiring worker declared:

Q: What are the main reasons you plan to work and raise a child at the same time?
A: Because I don't think just raising kids would be fulfilling for me. If I had to give work up, I don't think I would have children. But I don't see why I would have to give it up. I don't think they're incompatible.

Psychoanalytic theory notwithstanding, beliefs about what constitutes correct child rearing and good mothering are as much ideological constructs as established scientific "fact." There are, of course, some demonstrably wrong ways to rear a child, such as extreme abuse, deprivation, or neglect; but that leaves much room for variety in terms of who cares for the young, how much time is focused upon them exclusively, and how many caretakers are actively involved. Caretaking by the biological mother is neither the only safe option nor a guarantee of a "successful" outcome. It is thus difficult to resist the conclusion that persistent beliefs about the harmful effects of working mothers serve more to control women's behavior than to protect their children. These beliefs can be considered ideologies in the truest sense of the word: important control mechanisms that prevent some women from acting in their own behalf and that induce guilt in those who do.

The argument that modern theories of child rearing are ideologies that serve, to some extent, as mechanisms of social control is supported by the historical record. Full-time mothering is a relatively rare and historically recent social construction, as are the beliefs that support and justify this particular family form. Before the industrial revolution, children were afforded neither maternal indulgence nor constant adult attention, and they were not deemed to need them (Ariès, 1962; Ryan, 1981; and Shorter, 1975). Because these children appear to have developed into healthy, functioning adults, these examples call into question the scientific basis for concluding that all children require a specific and universal form of mothering for proper development.

Despite the power of ideological prohibition, however, reluctant mothers were compelled to change the terms of the discourse about motherhood. They rejected the received wisdom of their childhood and many of their peers and substituted a set of beliefs that better fit their own needs and circumstances.

Ideological change, then, helped reluctant mothers cope with the motherhood dilemma. The pressure to challenge traditional beliefs and values, however, would not have been present if larger historical forces had not created a dilemma in the first place. Pressure from changing social structures gave impetus to change in ideas. Structures created the need and impetus for change, but ideological responses helped shape the specific contours that change assumed. Once confronted by these structural dilemmas, reluctant mothers had little recourse but to alter their beliefs to better fit their circumstances. This psychological reformulation subsequently affected behavior, easing the way toward motherhood while simultaneously justifying a continued attachment to work.

Social Consequences of Nondomestic Mothers

We have seen how nondomestic women facing historically unprecedented circumstances developed new responses to the structural dilemmas arising from their emerging commitment to a life beyond domesticity. Whether they opted for childlessness or moved reluctantly toward motherhood, they constitute the cutting edge of social change. They did not just respond passively to the constraints that confronted them; rather, they took actions that shaped the contours of change as well as the conditions of their individual lives. Whether these women were childless or struggling to combine motherhood with committed work, their choices represent the emergence of new alternatives that, if successfully implemented, inevitably necessitate new social arrangements. Their actions and those of others like them have already promoted changes in family organization, workplace dynamics, and accepted beliefs about good mothering.

Because work arrangements were the most resistant to change, the most concerted efforts focused on changing domestic organization, decisions, and beliefs to better fit the demands of work. If nondomestic women's rising demands and dilemmas are to be met, however, work as well as family organization will have to change—for men as well as for women. As increasing numbers of women find that they cannot or will not turn back to domesticity, the impact of nontraditional choices will mount at home and at work. In some form, it will reverberate throughout the structures of marriage, child rearing, and the workplace, going far beyond occasional isolated changes in women's "roles."

The path of least resistance led all nondomestic women toward relatively less mothering. They reduced their fertility and the proportion of time spent with offspring. Nondomestic women also subjected men to increasing pressure to parent more, to participate more fully in domestic activities, and to make way for them at the workplace.

As the proportion of women committed to work has climbed, their aspirations have risen and their determination to reject domesticity has solidified. The momentum of these forces has fueled resistance, rebellion, and demands for change. This buildup of forces for social change must eventually find some avenue of expression. If childlessness remains the unpopular choice it has historically been, then new arrangements for rearing children, new beliefs about their care, and new conceptions of men's and women's capacities and behavioral alternatives will become the most viable route to change.

Structural Forces and Women's Lives

How, then, do social arrangements structure women's choices? First, women are especially subject to the dilemma of "packaged" choices. Not only are they reared with conflicting expectations, but they also confront ambiguous structures that often require them to choose among a number of desired goals. It is particularly difficult for women to build strong bases in both the domestic and the public spheres, and decisions in one sphere limit the range of options in the other. Trade-offs are thus built into the structure of choice: whether a woman opts for work, motherhood, or some combination of the two, she must accept the costs of what is forgone as well as the benefits of what is chosen ("opportunity costs," in the language of economics). In this sense, women face a set of dichotomous choices in which work and family commitments are posed as competing, alternative commitments. Their work and family decisions are inextricably linked; choices in one sphere depend on the opportunities, incentives, and constraints posed in the other.

The responses of the women in this study to the contradictory, ambiguous, and packaged alternatives they faced developed out of, and depended on how, they negotiated four especially important factors in their social environment. Taken together, these factors defined the range of options available, determined which among them appeared most (or least) desirable, and ultimately shaped the respondents' definitions of their situations and varied life choices.

First, the building of, or failure to build, a stable relationship with a male partner, together with this partner's orientations toward bearing and rearing children, had a powerful impact on women's work and family choices. A stable, permanent marriage promoted female domesticity in a number of ways. It fostered a belief in marriage as a safe, secure place that permits and rewards economic dependency; over time, it tended to narrow a woman's occupational options, as wives' work decisions were subordinated to those of their spouses; and it ultimately offered an attractive alternative to unsatisfying workplace experiences. Similarly, a stable marriage promoted a context in which childbearing came to be seen as a natural outgrowth of the relationship itself. Stable marriage thus not only made female domesticity possible for a number of the respondents, but it also fostered an environment in which bearing children and withdrawing from the workplace to rear them seemed natural, inevitable, and desirable. Indeed, strong pressure or encouragement from a mate was enough to lead some working women to become reluctant mothers, despite their own ambivalence and the potential danger to their work careers.

In contrast, when men were not a stable part of these women's lives, when having children threatened the relationship even when it was stable, or when men rejected participatory fatherhood, women found convincing reasons to choose work over family.

The experience of blocked versus expanding workplace opportunity had a similarly powerful impact on the respondents' choices. Stable marriage tended to pull some women into the home, but constricted work opportunities tended to push them out of the workplace. Blocked work mobility dampened expectations for future work accomplishment, imposed few costs for workplace withdrawal, and enhanced the pull of domestic commitments. In this context, some women tended to opt out of the workplace to embrace domesticity and motherhood as the preferred alternative.

If blocked mobility tended to enhance the pull of marriage, motherhood, and domesticity, then expanding workplace opportunity, unexpected promotions, and the promise of a career ladder reinforced the choice in favor of work even when it had initially been considered temporary. Upward job mobility competed directly with women's domestic pursuits. Rewarding work did more than provide economic independence outside of marriage, although this alone expanded these women's alternatives. It also provided another source of personal identity and social reward.

The experience of workplace advancement increased the immediate social, economic, and emotional rewards of working; it fostered a belief in future rewards at work; and it raised the costs of leaving work, even for a short time, to have a child. Upward mobility at the workplace nourished work aspirations and raised the perceived costs of motherhood. Expanding occupational opportunities drew some women into the workplace; eroding domestic supports pushed others out of the home.

Third, when the spouse of a stably married woman was able to provide an income that was perceived as adequate, women were not pushed out of the home or away from domesticity. Male economic support both permitted these respondents to withdraw from work to rear children and sheltered them from exposure to unexpected work opportunities that might have initiated a process of change.

In contrast, women who experienced economic squeezes in the household were likely to be pulled into the workplace, despite their earlier plans or preferences. When this occurred, it often triggered a chain reaction of events that ultimately altered work and family decisions. The perceived need for a second income not only forced some women into the world of work; it also delayed childbearing decisions, limited the number of children a family could afford and the time a mother could devote to their care, and provided a period for unanticipated work opportunities to initiate a reassessment of family as well as work aspirations. Perceived economic squeezes thus led some stably married women to pursue nondomestic pathways and to reconsider their commitments to motherhood as well as to work.

Finally, the perceived rewards and costs of a domestic life-style shaped these women's work and family decisions. Some women found mothering and homemaking the fulfilling experience they had hoped it would be. Others were surprised to find that, contrary to their earlier expectations, the life of homemaking or full-time motherhood was decidedly disappointing. As growing numbers of their neighbors, friends, and peers left the home for work, these women found the increasing isolation and devaluation of full-time mothering and housekeeping too costly to bear. This decline in the social supports for motherhood, together with the rise in supports for alternative choices such as working and childlessness, led many to reject the domestic patterns more typical of earlier generations.

Some or all of these four factors precipitated critical turning points for most of these respondents. At such times, unanticipated events, which ultimately reshaped the course of their lives, intervened. For the individual experiencing them, these events seemed random and their effects idiosyncratic and personal. From a broader perspective, however, this apparent randomness takes on an orderly form. No matter how fortuitous a divorce or new job opportunity may have seemed to the woman confronted with change, these events are rooted in shifts taking place in the structure of American work and family institutions.

The process of individual change was thus closely linked to the social environment in which individual development took place. As the pace of social change has quickened, the probability has increased that women will be exposed to unanticipated events that promote, and even require, change in their lives. Periods of accelerated social change make individual change not only possible but probable. In such periods, stability becomes as uncertain and difficult to accomplish as change; neither is assured, and both call for explanation.

Despite the forces promoting nondomestic responses, supports and incentives for domestic patterns remain. Because they were exposed to a more traditional set of constraints and opportunities, some women responded to the dilemmas they faced by reproducing domestic patterns. Even among those who veered away from initial goals, the direction of change was not uniform. Although underlying social forces have pushed ever more women into the workplace, obstacles to change have led others to follow a more domestic path. Some women developed high workplace aspirations, aiming for jobs they had once considered out of reach and turning away from domestic orientations, while others reduced their career aspirations and turned instead to traditional feminine pursuits. In negotiating transitions through adulthood, the women in this study veered in different directions, developed divergent orientations, and stressed different abilities even when they started with similar goals, desires, and orientations.

In short, the fact of social change did not determine a uniform outcome in individual lives. These women faced dilemmas, not clear-cut choices. They had to make decisions amid contradictory circumstances, and the process was full of ambiguity and conflict. It involved development and negotiation in which women struggled with and against their employers and male partners to define and control their situations.

These women responded to their dilemmas in genuinely creative ways. Their choices, their struggle to create viable life paths, often led to extensive personal growth. In many respects, these women have been sailing in uncharted waters. Taken together, their efforts are changing the social order as well as their own lives. Their individually creative responses have combined to create new social forms—forms springing from changes in social structure but defined and implemented by individuals. Because these women's biographies have intersected with social structures in transition, they have created history. They have been not just passive receivers of change, but also its authors.

These findings about the process by which women negotiate the choice between work and family have a number of important implications for understanding women as a social group. They highlight the inadequacies of theories that posit either that early childhood experiences are the major determinant of women's adult choices or that women's behavior can be fully understood as the result of universal patterns of male domination. Instead, the extent, type, and permanence of change in women's social position must be located in the changing social order and in the process by which different groups of women make different choices in response to variable circumstances.

References

Ariès, Philippe. 1962. *Centuries of Childhood: A Social History of Family Life.* New York: Knopf.

Bane, Mary Jo. 1976. *Here to Stay: American Families in the Twentieth Century.* New York: Basic Books.

Gerson, Kathleen. 1985. *Hard Choices: How Women Decide about Work, Career, and Motherhood.* Berkeley and Los Angeles: University of California Press.

Pruett, Kyle D. 1983. "Infants of Primary Nurturing Fathers." *Psychoanalytic Study of the Child* 38:257–77.

Ryan, Mary P. 1981. *The Cradle of Middle Class: The Family in Oneida County, New York, 1790–1865.* New York: Cambridge University Press.

Shorter, Edward. 1975. *The Making of the Modern Family.* New York: Basic Books.

Smith, Ralph E. 1979. "The Movement of Women into the Labor Force." In Ralph E. Smith (ed.), *The Subtle Revolution: Women at Work.* Washington, D.C.: Urban Institute.

18

Becoming and Being Husbands and Fathers: Work and Family Conflict for Men

THEODORE F. COHEN

Introduction

Many core assumptions are often made about men's and women's lives. From the biological facts that women conceive and bear children and the sociological observation that they have been the primary nurturers of children stem many of our preconceptions about women's nature, actions, and capabilities (Wortis, 1974). Trapped within concepts like the "maternal instinct," women have had to struggle to prove that they are more than just agents of reproduction. They have been relatively successful. These are, by now, fairly familiar critiques of much traditional sociological work on women (Oakley, 1974).

For men, the core assumption has traditionally been that "men work." Work activity has often been explicitly portrayed (Bernard, 1983; Liebow, 1967; Parsons, 1942; Zelditch, 1974) or implicitly accepted (Goetting, 1982; Rubin, 1979) as men's chief activity, their "master role," the very essence of what makes them men.

> It is of fundamental significance to the sex role structure of the adult age levels that the normal man has a "job" which is fundamental to his social status . . . [I]t is perhaps not too much to say that only in exceptional cases can an adult male be genuinely self respecting and enjoy a respected status in the eyes of others if he does not "earn a living" (Parsons, 1942: 607).

David and Brannon's (1976) notion of the "Big Wheel" suggests that men's *success at work* is used as a badge of their masculinity; the more successful a male is in his job, the more masculine he appears to himself and others. Additionally, work has been portrayed as the activity to which men attach the most importance. They are seen as deeply psychologically involved in their work roles (Pleck, 1983) or as displaying considerable

---

An earlier version of this paper was published in the *Journal of Family Issues,* March 1987.

"role attachment" (Goffman, 1966) to their paid work.

Other, far-reaching presumptions follow the emphasis on men's work. Work comes to be seen as men's principal *family* role; they are "breadwinners" or "providers," with the fruits of their work portrayed as their major contributions to their families. If a man fails entirely (Liebow, 1967) or falls short (Rubin, 1976) in fulfilling his "Good Provider Role" (Bernard, 1983), then he fails or falls short as a man, husband, and father. On the other hand, men supposedly succeed in their family roles by what they do outside *and away from* their families. The resulting male absence from home and family for the bulk of their waking hours has been accepted as an appropriate allocation of men's time and energy.

Finally, since work is so frequently described as men's central role, regardless of their marital or parental status, the transitions into or out of these roles appear deceptively simple for men to navigate. As illustrated in Figure 1, since work remains as a constant centerpiece across their life cycles, men's experiences becoming husbands and fathers seem reducible to increasing the number of others dependent (in part or full) upon their work activity.

Men are not often described as adding very many other activities or radically altering their social identities with marriage or fatherhood. Consider the following example of this depiction of men's family experiences:

> Since the role of adult male in our society dictates a primary identity with occupational status, thereby deemphasizing conjugal identity, men are likely to experience a relatively mild identity shift as they pass from the status of single person to that of mate. . . . The social status, and therefore personal identity, of a man is relatively independent of his marital status . . . (Goetting, 1982:213).

In the following passage Rubin compares the role experiences of American men and women:

> For women, family is at the core of their lives; for men it is at the periphery. For a man, marriage is what he "does" in addition to what he "is." . . . First he's a "doctor, lawyer, merchant, chief." *Then some small part of him becomes a husband and father as well* [emphasis added]. Work, not family, is a man's most important social task (Rubin, 1979:109).

Both of these quotes illustrate the extent to which the "men work" presumption is embedded in sociological analyses of men's lives and family life. This presumption is incomplete to inaccurate. Of course, men have worked to support their families. However, men may have performed additional activities or possessed attachments that were less visible to social scientists. As informants men were absent from most of the sociological investigations of marriage and family life (Blood and Wolfe, 1960; Miller and Swanson, 1958) due in part to their long physical absences from home and family (and thus researcher) during the day. Still, there is more than methodological oversight at work here. Family research is guided by prevailing perspectives. As Pleck (1979) points out, until the feminist critique emerged, family studies were guided by a traditional perspective that made functional the traditional division of labor. In the functionalist framework that dominated family sociology for so

Figure 1 *Traditional Approach to Men's Roles*

Status:	Boy ⟶	Man ⟶	Husband ⟶	Father
Role:	Nonwork ⟶ (Play or school)	Work ⟶	Work ⟶	Work

long, work was not only what men were described as doing but was also what they *ought* to be doing in order to achieve the most efficient familial division of labor (Parsons, 1942; Zelditch, 1974). Thus, the possibility that men may have done or felt more within their families never became dominating research concerns.

This approach has been overgeneralized to "men" as opposed to "some men." Despite the findings of nearly a decade's worth of research (Lewis and Salt, 1986; Pleck, 1983; Pleck and Lang, 1978) indicating that *at least some men* are more psychologically involved in their family roles than work roles, the traditional presumption continues to influence social scientific analyses of men and families.

Even if most men's *chief* activity as men, husbands, and fathers has been to work, the traditional analysis of men's family lives is still open to some important criticism. First, the sources of men's behavior are debatable. The most frequent explanation for men's allocation of their time, energy, and priorities has been male gender socialization. More specifically, men are believed to be work-centered as a consequence of the kind of socialization they have received (David and Brannon, 1976). This socialization has explicitly prepared men to see work as their ultimate life pursuit and, less directly, tied them to this role by hampering the development of more nurturant and expressive personality traits that are inappropriate for their occupational roles. As a result of this kind of gender training, men supposedly come to see certain roles and activities as more appropriate and attractive to them and other (especially familial) pursuits as inappropriate and undesired. Thus, men's concentration of energies is depicted as the product of a socialization that leads them to choose to immerse themselves in work activities and to deemphasize their family activities.

This kind of explanation ignores the role played by microstructural factors in shaping role behavior. In order to enact a role at least two factors must be present: choice *and opportunity.* For example, entering marriage and parenthood are not enough to cause one to act in any given way. These events merely confront people with certain situational demands and constraints. Individuals may respond to these differently, depending largely on their conceptualizations of what is appropriate role behavior and on the availability of opportunities to behave in the desired manner. "Choice," then, is related to "role attachment" (Goffman, 1966) in that the degree to which men choose to enact a role depends largely upon the degree of role attachment they possess. "Opportunity," on the other hand, is dependent largely on the commitments they have made and the consequences of those commitments (Becker, 1970; Goffman, 1966). Too much of the literature on men and families overlooks the importance of their opportunities, thus implying that what (little) men do in the family reflects their choices and preferences. Microstructural theory reminds us that people's actions are circumscribed by the social organization of experiences available to particular types of actor (Risman, 1987).

In the present analysis, both the *opportunities* men have and the *role conceptualization* they choose to enact are being hypothesized as continuous variables that range in value between extreme points. In other words, men may have anywhere from very narrow and traditional notions of what husbands and fathers are supposed to do, to very broad conceptualizations of appropriate behavior. Likewise, they may be locked into occupational and social situations that restrict their opportunities to perform marital and parental roles, or, at the opposite extreme, they may have *no* constraints on their opportunities for familial involvements.

If we treat opportunity and role conceptualization as if they were dichotomous, the relationship between them can be schematically presented (see Figure 2). This typology illustrates four possible combinations of men's notions of appropriate family roles and their opportunities for enacting these levels of role behavior. Cells A and D represent instances wherein behavior reflects matched levels of opportunity and role conceptualization. The type of

Figure 2 *Relationship Between Role Conceptualization and Opportunity*

		Conceptualization of Roles	
		Broad	Narrow
Opportunity	High	A	C
	Low	B	D

man represented by Cell A can involve himself fully in what he defines in a broad sense as an appropriate and extensive involvement by husbands and fathers. Cell D represents men who are blocked from high levels of familial participation, but expect little involvement in their family roles. Thus, they don't miss these opportunities. Instead, they may define their roles as largely breadwinning and seek no opportunities for greater levels of involvement in other dimensions of family life.

Cells B and C are more complex cases. They represent cases where discrepancies exist between what men wish to do and what their opportunities allow them to do. Cell B contains men who would prefer to be more actively involved with their wives and/or children than they currently are, *given the opportunity.* At present, they lack such opportunities. Finally, Cell C represents an equally complicated case of men who have opportunities to increase their family involvements available to them and, yet, *choose* not to. Neither of these types are particularly well explained by more traditional individualist frameworks that depict socialization as the major determinant of the choices people make and, thus, the behaviors they display. I will return to and expand upon this typology in a later section, relating it to findings obtained in this research.

A second, related criticism stems from the failure of most studies to examine nonbehavioral dimensions of men's roles. This results in an inability to identify real though unobservable changes in men as indicators of the impact of marriage and fatherhood and a tendency to equate whatever men do most frequently with what's most important or meaningful to them. As others have noted (McKee and O'Brien, 1982; Pleck, 1983), this has resulted in potentially inaccurate and misleading depictions of men and families. In the pages that follow, I will highlight and examine from a microstructural perspective discontinuities between men's accounts of their role attachments and performances. In other words, men's failure to actualize in behavior what they report feeling will be explained in terms of their opportunities and the social expectations for their behavior.

Study Design

The data reported in the following pages are findings from an exploratory study of men's familial roles and role transitions. The central objectives were (1) to detail how a sample of men defined and enacted their marital and parental roles, (2) to document the kinds of effects getting married and becoming fathers had on informants, and (3) to empirically challenge the adequacy of the "men work" version of the male role.

The data were obtained through intensive, semistructured interviews with a nonprobability sample of thirty Boston area men, nearly equally divided between recently married, childless men (14) and married men with young children (16). Given my dual concerns with "becoming and being" husbands and fathers, I deliberately restricted the sample to men in the early years of marriage or fatherhood. Such men could comment on their activities as husbands or fathers, yet were still new enough to these statuses to recall their lives outside marriage or before fatherhood. For similar reasons, the sample was restricted to men in intact first marriages and to fathers with one (or few) child(ren). They were thought to be the best candidates for detailing the nature and impact of the transition in question. The fourteen married, childless men were married an average of 1.9 years, while the subsample of fathers were married an average of 4.6 years. The sixteen new fathers had first become fathers

2.1 years before being interviewed. Ninety percent of the sample, including all of the childless men, were in their first marriages; thirteen of the sixteen fathers were first-time fathers. Two fathers had two children, and one man had four. More than two-thirds of the men had wives who were employed outside the home. Of the nine wives who were not employed, eight were new mothers.

The sample was a purposive, nonprobability sample drawn from three different sources. Twelve of the thirty men were located through community agencies and institutions in a mostly working-class Boston suburb. Eight more informants were obtained by "snowball sampling" the initial participants. The remaining men were referred to me by my network of colleagues, friends, and neighbors.

The sample intentionally included men from a variety of socioeconomic and ethnic backgrounds. Socioeconomically, the informants ranged from a high-school-educated janitor to a Ph.D. physicist. Half (13 of 26) of the employed informants worked in traditional blue-collar or low-level, white-collar occupations. Three men were full-time graduate students and one other was a full-time househusband. The sample appears less equally representative of different classes when looking at years of education: eighteen of the thirty men had four years of college (9 men) or more (9 men). It is unclear whether education or occupation would have a greater effect on men's role transitions and definitions. Clearly, occupations may act as either resources or obstacles to what men can do by influencing their availability to their families as well as their abilities to provide what is needed or desired. Education, on the other hand, helps shape role expectations and definitions. Given these complexities and the exploratory nature of the research no simple class comparison will be made. Instead, I will suggest ways in which aspects of men's socioeconomic position *might* account for the attitudes and behaviors men reported.

Informants' ethnic backgrounds included Italian, Irish, Portuguese, and French Canadian. In its racial and religious composition the sample was less diverse. There was only one nonwhite and one Jewish informant. Again, given the exploratory nature of the study, the emphasis on both "becoming" and "being" husbands *and* fathers and the relatively small nonprobability sample, it was not possible to incorporate all potentially important factors into the sample or the analysis. Having decided to explore differences between social classes, I could not include in a sample of thirty men racial and religious variations as well. Race, ethnicity, and religion may be important factors in shaping men's role definitions, transitions, and performances and future studies ought to seek out their effects on men's family lives. Given all of the aforementioned limitations of the sample, none of the findings presented are offered as generalizations to the population of husbands and fathers, but as potential areas for further investigation and validation.

Data Collection and Analysis

Each informant was interviewed once, by the author, about his life before marriage, his premarital expectations of marriage and reasons for marrying, behaviors as a husband (including housework, sex, decision making, and conflict management), changes wrought by marriage, and satisfaction with marriage. The new fathers were asked these same questions and comparable ones about fatherhood (for example, why they had children, what they expected fatherhood would be like, what they did as fathers, how fatherhood changed their lives). Special attention was devoted to the effects of fatherhood on men and their marriages and on similarities and differences in the two role transitions and the responsibilities of both roles. Men were also asked a series of questions about work, designed to qualitatively measure men's attachment to their work and its connections to the family.

Interviews proceeded from a schedule of more than 100 questions, drawn partly from prior research (Rubin, 1976; Oakley, 1980) but mostly original to this study. Each interview did not consist of an identical set or sequence of items since new ideas and themes were pursued as they emerged. A concerted effort was made to keep the interviews flexible and somewhat informal in tone. It was especially necessary to employ such a strategy with male informants. For them, discussions about the most private and intimate dimensions of their lives are infrequent to absent given men's lack of available opportunities for, and the potential impropriety of, such self-disclosure. Ninety percent of the interviews were conducted in informants' homes; of the remainder, two were done at the informants' workplace and one was conducted at my home. The average interview lasted slightly under two hours, though they ranged from just over one to three and one-half hours long.

All interviews were tape recorded and later transcribed. Once gathered, the data were analyzed thematically. As with interview questions, occasionally the existing literature on families, women, or men was used as sources of analytical themes. In other instances, themes emerged directly from the interview material through the use of the "constant comparative method of qualitative analysis" (Glaser and Strauss, 1967). Dominant patterns in men's accounts were used to build analytical categories. As alternatives or variations on these themes appeared, modifications were made and new analytical categories were developed. What follows are the major findings and a discussion of their implications for reconceptualizing men's lives.

Findings and Discussion

Becoming Husbands and Fathers

In becoming husbands and fathers, informants took on responsibilities and constructed roles that, once in place, restructured their social lives. In both transitions, men had to respond to new situational features, demanding more of them than merely that they "work." Thus their experiences *becoming* husbands and fathers did not consist of simple, linear additions of breadwinning responsibilities, but rather a wholesale "remaking" of their lives.

Although men's entrances into marriage and parenthood required them to restructure their intrapersonal and interpersonal lives and their role activities, the transitions were very different. Becoming a husband is a process that unfolded gradually, sometimes commencing long before the official entrance into marriage. Much of its impact was thus absorbed prior to legally and formally being a husband. By restricting analyses to a comparison of the lives men led just prior to their legal marriages with their lives afterward, the full impact of marriage is largely missed. It appears, then, as if their lives were altered little by becoming husbands. If, however, we broaden the examination and include the impact of coupling and exclusivity on men, we are in a better position to understand "becoming a husband."

Because of the opportunity during exclusive coupling to alter much of their social and psychological environments to fit the requirements of the new relationship, men could "become husbands" before marrying. "Being a husband" means acting in a manner that is consistent with the particular expectations of one's wife as much as the more generalized societal expectations of men's marital roles. Since the specific other who defines his status as a husband is the same person that makes him a partner in the pre-marital relationship that eventuates in marriage, men had the opportunity to assimilate and test many of the behaviors that would be expected of them as husbands. Men had the opportunity to undergo more than *anticipatory socialization*; they could actually enter the role prior to being formally assigned the status of husband, behave in ways that allowed them to partially experience what being married was like, and thus do more than simply prepare themselves for a future role.

Fatherhood offered men no such opportunity. As Rossi (1983) has observed, the transition to parenthood is sudden, irrevocable, and comes on the heels of little or no prior training. Unlike the process of becoming a husband, the "other" who is the key object for his becoming and being a father was not present in men's lives until after informants were formally fathers. Thus, men were unable to feel like fathers beforehand or to identify with a father role until after the actual birth of their children. Although men had expectations, images, and fantasies about their soon-to-be-born children, this "imaginary fatherhood" left them unprepared for the postnatal alterations in their lives. They had to adjust to their new social relationships (with their children) and new roles (as fathers) at the same time that they were experiencing new day-to-day environmental conditions and the effects of these conditions on their marital and social lives, and acquiring a new sense of who they were and what their lives now entailed.

The following two comments illustrate how some men contrasted the transitions to marriage and parenthood and how the gradual nature of the marital transition understates its real though deceptive impact.

> With marriage we took our time to figure out what we wanted to do and how. . . . We kept living the way we had and whatever adjustments we made to each other we made as we realized they had to be made. With kids it's completely different; you have to change spectacularly, immediately, once that kid is there. You can't take your time, you gotta learn that immediately. (36-year-old househusband)

> As much reading as we did [about parenthood], we just weren't prepared for what it was really like. . . . With marriage, we had pretty much drifted into being married without realizing it. Actually getting married was just formally recognizing something that had happened. (31-year-old retail manager)

In both marriage and fatherhood men had to remake nearly every dimension of their lives, but in fatherhood they had to do so immediately after birth. The suddenness of these alterations may account for the perceptions expressed above. The process of "becoming a husband" may, in fact, have changed men's lives from some premarital point in almost as complete a manner as parenthood changed husbands' lives. Since these changes can be drifted into and adjustments made gradually, even those whose lives were most directly changed failed to perceive the extent of the changes. Although the consequences were similar due to the difference in process, men may have understated the impact of marriage and exaggerated the consequences of fatherhood.

Parenthetically, the interviews also suggested that men's experiences becoming parents were different from women's experiences in some important respects. For example, there was less in men's prior socialization that prepared them to be fathers and, during pregnancy, no real and direct father-child connection that compares to the connection between mother and child. Thus, as expected, informants were less prepared for parenthood than women. However, this led to an interesting outcome after their children were born. Whereas women have been reported to experience disappointment over the lack of fit between their romantic expectations and the reality they faced as mothers (Oakley, 1979; 1980), for men the reactions were more mixed. Men, too, were forced to confront a harsher, more demanding reality than they'd imagined, but they were equally surprised by greater than expected involvements in fathering. For example, consider this comment from a 25-year-old food service worker.

> I change my son, feed him, bathe him. . . . I don't know, I think I'm getting a lot more out of the relationship than most other fathers have. . . . My perception was that at five years old the father took over—take him to the ball game, camping, do this or that with him—but before that [I thought] it was all mother. [I thought fathers might] take the baby, hold him, look at him and then, "Here you go, back to mother." But I am glad it's like this; I'm getting a lot more out of him, watching him grow. I'm understanding a little more about why mothers feel about their children as strongly as they do.

Although the preceding comments compared the transitions to marriage and fatherhood, a more important point must be stressed. Both transitions resulted in more significant changes in men's lives than has been assumed under traditional conceptualizations. More than "some small part of . . . [a man]" (Rubin, 1979: 109) was affected by becoming a husband and father. Men may have appeared to be less affected than they were because they continued to perform the same *public* activity—work—and did not typically seek outlets to express any difficulty they were experiencing with the transitions to marriage or fatherhood. Since they continued in the same activities and, because of their emotional reserve, appeared psychologically unaffected, men's lives might look unchanged. However, this narrow understanding of men's roles as husbands and fathers fails when men's role attachments are held up to more careful scrutiny.

Some of the most important changes initiated by becoming a husband and/or a father are unobservable when looking at how men might be experiencing these role transitions. One such change is an alteration in how one perceives oneself, leading to a reduced emphasis on self-interests. A 33-year-old engineer described becoming a husband as having initiated a change in how he thought about life:

> We were two very independent people. . . . Before [marriage] it was putting myself first; being married means putting my wife first.

A 42-year-old teacher added the following, similar, comment:

> Making any plans—what to do with one's job—it's part of a *joint* procedure. It's not like your life is not your own, but it *is* something shared. *As this corporate entity* [emphasis added], a lot of the decisions that you would make on your own you now make in collaboration with another person.

Becoming a father was described in the following terms by a 33-year-old administrator:

> You have a child, you look in the mirror and you're not the same guy you thought you were. . . . It's really just . . . something creeps into your life and then all of a sudden it dominates your life . . . changes your relationship to everybody and everything . . . and you question every value you ever had. . . . And you say to yourself, "This is a miracle."

Others expanded upon this. Nearly 80 percent of the sample responded affirmatively when asked whether they felt changed by marriage while *all* of the fathers reported feeling changed by fatherhood, citing changed routines, altered self-concepts, restructured priorities, and greater commitments to work. Both marriage and fatherhood were also described as making men feel more constrained or "less free." Finally, it should be noted that marriage and, especially, fatherhood led some informants to new emotional responses (Greenberg, 1986; Richman, 1982). They found themselves feeling more and expressing their feelings more easily, as evidenced by the following comments about the impact of marriage and fatherhood.

> [Being married] means really sharing your life with another person [including] your thoughts and your hopes, your fears and frustrations. That's one of the biggest "perqs" of the whole thing . . . after you get married it becomes fashionable to let your feelings out. (30-year-old production manager)
>
> I think [fatherhood's] calmed me down a lot more. [Now] when I see a sad movie on TV I might get a lot closer to watering up than I ever would have. . . . It's almost like I've been completed in a way. (25-year-old food handler)

Being Husbands and Fathers

Both marriage and parenthood are multidimensional. For my informants, this entailed doing more as husbands and fathers than just working. Economic responsibilities represented only *one* of a number of dimensions of men's family lives, thus challenging the traditional depiction of men in families. These other dimensions include the emotional, psychic, community, legal, and economic "stations of marriage" (Bohannan, 1970; Goetting, 1982), as well as a variety of intrapersonal, interpersonal, and role performance (for example, housework and childcare) dimensions. Men's sense of themselves, their hierarchy of priorities, their relationships with others, and their performance of various tasks were all affected by their statuses as husbands and fathers in ways that go beyond most sketches of men in families. This is especially true of men's understanding and performance of expressive friendship roles in marriage and nurturant roles in fatherhood. These components of men's marital and parental roles, not breadwinning, were stressed by the majority of informants as the central elements of their familial roles.

In defining what it means to be a husband, nearly all informants answered in ways that highlighted the friendship, companionship, and intimacy expected of husbands.

> To me it's so simplistic. It's something that was always there. . . . It's having the best friend you can have. She's my best friend. It's very important to me and I'll always be her best friend; her feelings will always come before me. It's having a good friend like that . . . (25-year-old warehouseman)

This was also identified by nearly 90 percent of those who answered as the "best thing" about being married. Only 37 percent of informants (11) even explicitly included breadwinning in their answers to what it means to be a husband. Even when specifically asked about a husband's major *responsibilities,* only half of those who answered identified "breadwinning." Likewise, only five of sixteen fathers included "providing" among what they saw as a father's "main responsibilities" toward his children. More common were references to fathers' nurturant activities; their roles as teachers, role models, companions, or as emotional supports for their children.

It is findings like these that most call for rethinking the nature and depth of men's family roles since they cast men in more affective and nurturant poses (see also Greenberg, 1986; McKee and O'Brien, 1982), which are often overlooked. There are, however, two points to add here lest these findings be misunderstood.

First, a comparison with women's experiences is, again, in order. Although the husbands and fathers in my sample departed some from traditional formulations of men's lives, they did not match the family roles and involvements of their wives who, from men's own accounts, continued to bear the brunt of "family work." For example, although all but five men reported doing at least some housework, only four men described relatively equal divisions of housework, with a fifth informant claiming responsibility for all the household chores. Thus, unlike more optimistic portrayals of men's involvement in housework (Beer, 1983), 83 percent of the sample (25 men) fit a pattern wherein wives bore responsibility for all or for the bulk of household chores. Childcare was less skewed toward wives though they more typically engaged in "primary" and "secondary childcare," and were less likely than their husbands to obtain "downtime" (LaRossa and LaRossa, 1981). Furthermore, housework and childcare continued to be contested dimensions of family living.

Additional differences between informants and their wives were revealed in men's accounts of decision making, sex, and intimacy. It was not a case of the "husband's marriage" and the "wife's marriage" (Bernard, 1972) becoming one and the same marriage, but rather one wherein the "husband's marriage" failed to resemble what has been written about men. The same may be said about fatherhood. Although women probably continue to find their lives more affected by marriage and parenthood than men do, informants appeared to be more affected by these events than men have been thought to be.

Furthermore, all of the husbands and fathers in my sample did not display the same levels of involvements in their families or enact their husband and father roles in the same way. Understanding the differences and their causes will be important steps in identifying how men's lives may be miscast by more traditional and individualistic thinking about family and gender.

Accounting for Men's Familial Role Performances

Returning to the relationship between opportunity and choice, we can begin to examine how informants' family role enactments were shaped. The traditional approach to men's roles as work-oriented suggests that whether they have opportunities for greater participation in their families (Cell C) or not (Cell D), men would neither miss nor seek out opportunities for greater levels of involvement due to their socialization into a work-centered male role. In its extreme, this implies that most men will *choose* not to so involve themselves in their families. Within my sample such men were rare, comprising less than 20 percent of the sample.

Based on my interviews, I would characterize the majority of informants as men whose opportunities for participation in their familial roles fell short of their preferred levels of involvement (Cell B). These were men who were disturbed by the seemingly unreasonable demands made upon them by their jobs and the intrusion of their jobs into their family lives. In their present situations they might *appear* not to miss or desire greater levels of familial involvement; their words suggest otherwise. It is this group of men who are the least accurately understood under the traditional "men work" presumption.

When faced with a discrepancy between what people say and do, sociologists are often advised to suspect what people report and turn instead to what they do. In this research, informants repeatedly expressed strong attachments to their roles as husbands and fathers that were not always matched by a comparable level of behavioral involvement. For example, nearly 90 percent of the sample defined their marital and/or parental roles as their most important social roles (see also Lewis and Salt, 1986; Pleck, 1983; Pleck and Lang, 1978). Work, on the other hand, was mentioned by only one informant as his most important role, ranked last among the roles mentioned by 19 percent of the sample, and went entirely unmentioned by more than half of the informants. Certainly this is the reverse of what we see when we examine men's lives. It is important, therefore, to look past the actual behaviors men reported and seek to understand why men didn't report even greater levels of role performance in their family roles, given what they claimed to feel. There are at least two microstructural sources for the incongruity between men's words and deeds.

I have suggested here that the demands of the occupational system were met at the expense of the family. There were accounts suggestive of both structural and emotional interface between informants' work and family lives (Piotrkowski, 1979). With little flexibility, men's jobs demanded that they be away from home for anywhere from forty to more than sixty hours a week. An extreme example of structural dominance of work over family can be heard in the following comment from a 31-year-old retail manager:

> Work eats into our time. Before, [my wife] worked part-time evenings and I worked part-time days so we had much more time to spend with our daughter and weekends to spend all three of us together. Now, we have *at most* one day off a week together. . . . I have fantasies about being able to have a livable income off of [business out of home] and spend all day with my daughter. If I could do that I would like to.

A 26-year-old banker echoed the frustration expressed above:

> We don't see each other enough. . . . I'm tied up [in class] two nights a week, all night. I don't come home for dinner, I come home a quarter past ten, eat dinner, sit down for about ten minutes to read the paper and then go to

> bed. There's no time for conversation; whatever we talk about, we talk about during dinner. . . . All of a sudden, the week is gone and we've spent all of an hour and a half together. That's lousy. . . I make money, big deal! Obviously, it's important . . . but is it worth getting an ulcer? Is it worth not seeing my wife?

Although most situations were not this severe, nearly half of the sample acknowledged feeling that the job "took too much time away," "made too many demands" on their time, or kept them away too much. The demands of the job also often intruded into the emotional climate of the home. Despite their wishes to the contrary, many men were unable to keep their feelings about their jobs divorced from their attitudes and behaviors at home. This should not be seen as a reflection of the relative priority accorded to work and family but rather a normal, though culturally unpopular, process. Whether positive or negative, feelings about work carry over into home and family life (Piotrkowski, 1979:31). Among my informants it was the negative feelings that were carried over. In the home these work-initiated feelings took a variety of forms, including emotional withdrawal, "pouting," "ranting and raving" or "getting real crazy," and an inability to relax even at night. One informant described laying awake in a "cold fear" at night, while another admitted, on occasion, "dreaming about it." A typical description of the intrusion of work into the family is the following account by a 28-year-old tool and die maker:

> Sometimes it happens; it just comes out—"Grrr"—and then I say to myself, "Geez, I wasn't supposed to do this and still I am doing this anyway." . . . If I am a little bitchy I'll tell her, "I'm in a bad mood, cope with me. If I yell at you don't take it personally."

Using physical absence from the home and inability to emotionally sever work from family as indicators of men's relative role attachments and chosen levels of involvement in work and family ignores the sociological significance of the structure of work in our society. As long as the occupational system operates on a "male model," assuming economic support by "Husband-Economic-Providers" (Gronseth, 1972) and homes tended to by wives/mothers, jobs can demand a level of investment in work that ignores the familial needs of workers. Thus, men's actions in the family will likely fall short of the levels of attachment revealed in my interviews. Men may appear to make that choice, based on their allocations of time and energy, because of their required participation in an occupational system that operates "as if" the family did not exist (Kanter, 1977).

In addition, men's notions of appropriate familial role behaviors are produced and then reinforced or challenged by a culture that is still less than wholehearted in embracing the idea of family-oriented men. Thus, subtle, yet powerful, pressures from peers, kin or co-workers could restrain men from developing deeper levels of involvement or restrict them from fully expressing the role attachments they currently possess (Lein, 1979). This normative or cultural constraint may even limit men's social-psychological involvement in their families in a similar way that structural constraints restrict men's opportunities.

This situation is still more complex. Neither opportunities nor choices are static. Over time, previously nonexistent opportunities may emerge or, as was the case with a few informants, existing opportunities for higher levels of involvement may disappear or diminish. Thus, one cannot predict what kinds of husbands and fathers these men will be from either reports of their present behaviors or their desires or expectations for the future.

Furthermore, opportunities may be pushed upon them independent of choice, such as when wives expect and then demand greater levels of involvement in housework or childcare than men are giving. Interestingly, such external pressure led some informants to the development of hitherto unanticipated attachments.

Finally, we must recognize that opportunities

are themselves the products of choices. Men's actions can create opportunities for greater involvement and participation in their family roles. The most extreme case of this kind, a 36-year-old househusband, simply decided that he preferred full-time familial involvement to paid labor. A less extreme example was a 29-year-old physicist who, knowing the occupational risks involved, had "drawn the line," choosing to maximize his family involvement despite the institutional demands made upon him.

People are not passive victims of structural arrangements. "We make choices as best we can to attain the values we hold dear" (Fischer, 1982:4). Still, we are not entirely free to enact whatever types of role behaviors we choose. The options available to us are greatly influenced by the social and cultural contexts, the "circumstances" within which we live (Fischer, 1982; Risman, 1987). With certain exceptions (Bernard, 1983; Gronseth, 1972; Pleck, 1983), most analyses of men and of families have proceeded on the individualist assumption that men's roles were solely reflections of their choices as produced by their socialization into masculinity.

The Influence of Social Class

Using the model sketched above, one can assess the impact of social class on the family lives informants revealed. The middle-class men who were most visibly distressed by the excessive and inflexible demands made upon them by their work illustrate how, by structuring men's work situations, social class indirectly affects their family lives. Although professional men, in particular, are often portrayed as obsessed with work and relatively unaffected by family roles and relationships, such a picture inadequately applies to my informants' accounts. Instead, informants appeared to possess family role attachments that at least matched those that they had toward their jobs, even if their allocation of time and energy suggested the contrary. Middle-class informants found themselves in relatively successful occupational positions making it difficult for them to leave such positions, or risk losing them, without great sacrifice and material loss. The occupational and familial structures differ greatly, though, in the degree to which they can be molded or bent to fit personal wants or needs (Margolis, 1979). Having made commitments to their jobs that could not be abandoned without considerable risk, most men continued to fit their family lives around their jobs. Their continued, though disgruntled, performance of such work roles indicates not their relative role attachments but that their opportunities for greater involvement in the family were constrained by their role commitments to an inflexible occupational structure.

Working-class informants presented a different pattern. They experienced fewer competing attachments between occupational and familial roles because of the nature of their work. They held jobs that offered them little gratification and even less to enhance their self-images. Despite their rather strong familial role attachments, some of the negative carry over of work into family affected the quality of their family role performances. Although they neither retreated (Liebow, 1967) nor emotionally withdrew (Rubin, 1976) from the family, neither were they invulnerable to the effects of their jobs on their home lives. Furthermore, like many middle-class informants, they faced problems stemming from the inflexible demands of the job. Their options for finding other, more gratifying work were constrained by their financial positions, the skills that they had to offer, and the structure of occupational opportunities.

Although middle- and working-class men had to confront the intrusion of work into the family, there were differences in degree and kind. Middle-class men faced more structural competition and more of a conflict between work and family role attachments. Working-class men experienced a less extreme structural competition between work and family and little conflict of competing role attachments due to the absence of strong occupational role attachments.

Other differences between working- and middle-class men no doubt exist. However, no simple class comparison can be made here between the role performances of working- and middle-class husbands and fathers. In fact, in many instances, men were more similar across class lines than they were different. This supports the possibility that certain kinds of class distinctions in family life may be blurring (Caplow et al., 1983). For example, the similarity between working- and middle-class informants' accounts of the importance of marital intimacy and communication is strikingly different from earlier analyses of class and family life (Rubin, 1976). Similarly, working- and middle-class men did not significantly differ in their attitudes toward their wives' working, their performance of housework, or their emphasis on nurturant aspects of fathering. Although the difference between classes may be shrinking, more systematic research and analysis are needed before current class distinctions can be reliably delineated.

Men's Familial Involvements: Past, Present, and Future

Earlier I suggested that we cannot predict from their reports of their current familial involvements what kinds of husbands and fathers informants will be in the future. As later life stages confront men with new situational demands (that is, more children, greater occupational demands, less time, new experiences with children as they grow), men's familial involvements are likely to be affected.

This raises another question. To what extent can we accurately compare men's behaviors as husbands and fathers to what they recall of their own fathers? Consistently, men described their own fathers as having been uninvolved in their upbringing (or less involved than desired) due to what was perceived as an excessive commitment to work. Yet we must remember that informants' recollections of the fathering they received are memories from late childhood and/or adolescence. It is at least possible that their fathers may have been more like my informants as fathers of infants and toddlers than informants are capable of recalling. As their own children age, the demands on informants will shift from mostly physical and custodial care to emotional attention and support. These are qualitatively different. We cannot predict whether those men who are most adept at caring for very young children will be equally competent or comfortable with older children, or even desire to be. Furthermore, the opportunities for them to be emotionally involved and supportive may become restricted, leaving them at a less than desired level of involvement. If so, they could be remembered by their sons and daughters in similar ways to the ways they recalled their own fathers.

Summary and Conclusion

The weight of the evidence obtained in this research suggests that men's lives may contain greater attachments to, and be more profoundly affected by, marriage and fatherhood than is usually assumed. In fact, once men entered into their marital and parental roles their lives were "remade"; new responsibilities were incorporated into their lives, old activities took on different meanings, self-concepts and priorities were recast. Much of this cannot be observed from the behaviors men display, but were nonetheless very real consequences of becoming husbands and fathers. It appears as if certain roles, unlike hats to be put on and discarded when appropriate, have the potential for "remaking" the actors performing them.

Although all of the husbands and fathers in the sample did not respond in the same way to these life altering role transitions, neither were their experiences reflections of traditional conceptualizations of men's lives. This suggests a second kind of remaking. If becoming husbands and fathers remade men's lives, their experiences dictate that we remake our assumptions and recognize that, for at least some, the old notions of men's lives do not apply (Lewis, 1986). These are inadequate bases for understanding all men. Moving away from them may require looking beyond what men do, to what they say and feel, and reconsidering reasons they don't do more.

Additionally, we should ask ourselves what sorts of measures might enable more men to actualize in behavior the deeply felt family commitments described by my sample. For example, changes in the structure and culture of the workplace that allowed men and women to realize both occupational and familial aspirations would make more likely an increased level of men's real involvement in families (Bohen and Viveros-Long, 1984; Kanter, 1977; Piotrkowski, 1979). Like the few men in my sample whose work schedules left them free to be home during morning and/or afternoon hours, at least some men would find their family involvements expanded and enriched by these opportunities. Likewise, eliminating or reducing the wage gap between women and men would make it more economically feasible for more men to choose, like my househusband informant, to take on a full-time family role. Such alternative work opportunities must be at least partly accompanied by value changes within and outside the workplace that illustrate to men that acceptance of these benefits will not jeopardize their occupational futures or cast aspersions on their masculinity.

Finally, social scientists can move away from theories and models of men and families that explicitly or implicitly presume that all men are work-centered. By implying that all (or most) men are attached to their work roles and not their familial roles, we contribute to the idea that men somehow "ought to be" that way. I am not suggesting that we begin, instead, to portray men as basically family-centered. Neither approach adequately recognizes the importance of microstructural factors in shaping behavior. To continue to use the traditional "men work" presumption as characteristic of all men, however, is to deny the existence of the sentiments, values, and behaviors mounting from this and other recent research.

References

Becker, Howard. 1970. *Sociological Work: Method and Substance*. Chicago: Aldine.

Beer, William. 1983. *Househusbands: Men and Housework in American Families*. South Hadley, Mass.: J. F. Bergin.

Bernard, Jessie. 1972. *The Future of Marriage*. New York: Bantam Books.

———. 1983. "The Good Provider Role: Its Rise and Fall." Pp. 125–144 in Arlene Skolnick and Jerome Skolnick (eds.), *Family in Transition* (4th ed.). Boston: Little, Brown.

Blood, Robert, and Donald Wolfe. 1960. *Husbands and Wives*. New York: Free Press.

Bohannan, Paul. 1970. "The Six Stations of Divorce." Pp. 33–62 in Paul Bohannan (ed.), *Divorce and After*. New York: Doubleday.

Bohen, Halcyone, and Anamaria Viveros-Long. 1984. "Balancing Jobs and Family Life." Pp. 320–329 in Patricia Voydanoff (ed.), *Work and Family: Changing Roles of Men and Women*. Palo Alto, Calif.: Mayfield.

Caplow, T., H. Bahr, B. Chadwick, R. Hill, and M. H. Williamson. 1983. *Middletown Families*. New York: Bantam Books.

David, Deborah, and Robert Brannon. 1976. *The Forty-Nine Percent Majority: The Male Sex Role*. Reading, Mass.: Addison-Wesley.

Fischer, Claude. 1982. *To Dwell Among Friends: Personal Networks in Town and City*. Chicago: University of Chicago Press.

Glaser, Barney, and Anselm Strauss. 1967. *The Discovery of Grounded Theory*. New York: Aldine.

Goetting, Ann. 1982. "The Six Stations of Remarriage: Developmental Tasks of Remarriage After Divorce." *Family Relations* 31 (April): 213–222.

Goffman, Erving. 1966. *Encounters: Two Studies in the Sociology of Interaction*. Indianapolis: Bobbs-Merrill.

Greenberg, Martin. 1986. *The Birth of a Father*. New York: Continuum.

Gronseth, Eric. 1972. "The Breadwinner Trap." Pp. 175–191 in Louise Kapp Howe (ed.), *The Future of the Family*. New York: Simon and Schuster.

Kanter, Rosabeth Moss. 1977. *Work and Family in the United States: A Critical Review and Agenda for Research and Policy.* New York: Russell Sage Foundation.

LaRossa, Ralph, and Maureen LaRossa. 1981. *Transition to Parenthood: How Infants Change Families.* Beverly Hills: Sage.

Lein, Laura. 1979. "Male Participation in Home Life: Impact of Social Supports and Breadwinner Responsibility on the Allocation of Tasks." *Family Coordinator* 28 (October):529–534.

Lewis, Robert. 1986. "Introduction: What Men Get out of Marriage and Parenthood." Pp. 11–25 in Robert Lewis and Robert Salt (eds.), *Men in Families.* Beverly Hills: Sage.

Lewis, Robert, and Robert Salt (eds.). 1986. *Men in Families.* Beverly Hills: Sage.

Liebow, Eliot. 1967. *Tally's Corner.* Boston: Little, Brown.

Lopata, Helena Znaniecki. 1971. *Occupation Housewife.* New York: Oxford University Press.

Margolis, Diane Rothbard. 1979. *The Managers: Corporate Life in America.* New York: William Morrow.

McKee, Lorna, and Margaret O'Brien. 1982. *The Father Figure.* London: Tavistock.

Miller, Daniel, and Guy Swanson. 1958. *The Changing American Parent.* New York: John Wiley.

Oakley, Ann. 1974. *The Sociology of Housework.* New York: Pantheon.

———. 1979. *Becoming a Mother.* New York: Schocken.

———. 1980. *Women Confined: Towards a Sociology of Childbirth.* New York: Schocken.

Parsons, Talcott. 1942. "Age and Sex in the Social Structure." *American Sociological Review* 7 (October):604–616.

Piotrkowski, Chaya. 1979. *Work and the Family System.* New York: Macmillan.

Pleck, Joseph. 1979. "Men's Family Work: Three Perspectives and Some New Data." *Family Coordinator* 28 (October):473–480.

———. 1983. "Husbands' Paid Work and Family Roles: Current Research Issues." Pp. 251–333 in Helen Lopata and Joseph Pleck (eds.), *Research into the Interweave of Social Roles: Families and Jobs* (Vol. 3). Greenwich, Conn.: JAI Press.

Pleck, Joseph, and L. Lang. 1978. "Men's Family Role: Its Nature and Consequences" (working paper). Wellesley, Mass.: Wellesley College Center for Research on Women.

Richman, Joel. 1982. "Men's Experiences of Pregnancy and Childbirth." Pp. 89–103 in Lorna McKee and Margaret O'Brien (eds.), *The Father Figure.* London: Tavistock.

Risman, Barbara. 1987. "Intimate Relationships from a Microstructural Perspective: Men Who Mother. *Gender and Society* 1 (March):6–32.

Rossi, Alice. 1983. "Transition to Parenthood." Pp. 418–428 in Arlene Skolnick and Jerome Skolnick (eds.), *Family in Transition* (4th ed.). Boston: Little, Brown.

Rubin, Lillian. 1976. *Worlds of Pain: Life in the Working Class Family.* New York: Basic Books.

———. 1979. *Women of a Certain Age: The Midlife Search for Self.* New York: Harper and Row.

Wortis, Rochelle. 1974. "The Acceptance of the Concept of the Maternal Role by Behavioral Scientists: Its Effects on Women." Pp. 360–376 in Arlene Skolnick and Jerome Skolnick (eds.), *Intimacy, Family and Society.* Boston: Little, Brown.

Zelditch, Morris. 1974. "Role Differentiation in the Nuclear Family." Pp. 256–258 in Rose Coser (ed.), *The Family: Its Structures and Functions* (2nd ed.). New York: St. Martin's.

19

Changes in Black Family Structure: The Conflict Between Family Ideology and Structural Conditions

ROBERT STAPLES

Historically, family theorists have argued that family structure and achievement interact with one another (Goode, 1963; Parsons and Bales, 1955). While that may have some validity for certain ethnic groups in America, none of those groups share the history and current social conditions of the black population in the United States. The peculiar history of black Americans, combined with structural conditions inimical to family formation and maintenance, have precipitated a crisis in the black family.

The basic theoretical perspective that informs the present analysis of black family life is that of exchange theory. This theory focuses on the reinforcement patterns, the history of rewards and costs, that lead people to do what they do. Essentially it argues that people will continue to do what they have found rewarding in the past. The basic premise here is that certain kinds of family structures exist when there is an exchange of rewards; on the other hand, family arrangements that are costly to one or both parties are much less likely to continue (Blau, 1964; Homans, 1961).

We assume, first, that being married is important to the majority of blacks, especially women. The fact that a near majority of black Americans are not married and living in traditional nuclear family units is not a result of any devaluation of marriage qua institution but rather a function of limited choices to find individuals in a restricted and small pool of potential partners who can successfully fulfill the normatively prescribed familial roles. While many blacks fail to marry, the history of black marriages shows only a minority surviving a lifetime with the same people. Exchange theory suggests that a person will not remain in a relationship where the services

---

The author is grateful to Paul Rosenblatt for his comments on an earlier draft of this paper. This article is slightly revised from when it appeared in the *Journal of Marriage and the Family,* November 1985. Copyrighted 1985 by the National Council on Family Relations, 1910 West County Road B, Suite 147, St. Paul, MN 55113. Reprinted by permission of the publisher and author.

provided seem relatively meager compared with what the person knows about other relationships. It appears, then, that blacks do not marry because the perceived outcome, derived from knowledge of past rewards and costs, is one where alternative sources of goal mediation are preferred risks (Thibaut and Kelley, 1959). This cost-benefit analysis is mediated by structural conditions among the black male population that give rise to dissonance between black family ideology and actual family arrangements.

Black Family Ideology

The popular image of blacks as a group pressing for change in the area of race relations and economic opportunities often is translated into the image of a radical group in the forefront of social change. Other than being opposed to unfair discrimination against any group and favoring liberal social and economic policies, blacks often hold very traditional, even conservative, attitudes on other social issues—attitudes that place them in the mainstream of American mores and folkways. Some years ago Robert Hill (1972) noted that blacks have a strong work, achievement, and religious orientation. In particular, they believe strongly in the institution of the family. Gary and his associates (1983) found that the greatest source of life satisfaction among their black subjects was family life.

Their unconventional family arrangements and lifestyles easily can mislead outsiders to assume that blacks are strongly in accord with newly emerging alternative family lifestyles. While they are tolerant of people—especially blacks—who live in other than nuclear families, the family ideology of most blacks is in the direction of traditional family forms. Several studies, for instance, show that black women wish to marry and maintain traditional roles in the conjugal relationship (Broderick, 1965; Kulesky and Obordo, 1972). One indication of the black value of marriage is the fact that in the past more black women entered into a marital union than their white counterparts. In 1973, among black women 65 years and over, only 3.5% had never married, compared with 6.9% of white women (U.S. Bureau of the Census, 1978).

Among the most traditional of values is that of motherhood and childrearing. Except for college-educated black women, almost all black women bear children unless infertile. The role of mother is regarded as more important than any other role, including that of wife (Bell, 1971). While respectful of a woman's right to control her body, blacks tend to have a more negative attitude towards abortion. The Zelnik and Kantner (1974) study revealed that 35% of white teenagers terminated their first pregnancy by abortion compared with only 4% of black teenagers. However, some of this racial variation may reflect differential access to abortion rather than differential inclination. The black mother's childrearing techniques are also more traditional. She is more likely than the white mother to use physical, rather than verbal, punishment to enforce child discipline. Threatening the child with withdrawal of the mother's love, used by some white mothers, is uncommon among black women, which is one reason that the black mother-child bond remains strong throughout adult life (Nolle, 1972; Scanzoni, 1971).

Although there has been a noticeable increase in feminist ideology among women in the past 20 years, black women are greatly underrepresented in the women's liberation movement. Many black women continue to perceive racism—not sexism—as the biggest obstacle to their career and family goals. They are relatively uninvolved in such prominent feminist issues as pornography, sexual harassment, abortion, comparable pay, rape, etc. Moreover, they are more traditional in their definition of the roles that men and women should play in society and the family (Hershey, 1978). While their attitudes remain very traditional, the family lifestyles and arrangements of blacks are definitely unconventional. After examining the contemporary forms of black families, I explain it as a conflict between family ideology and structural conditions.

Changes in Black Family Structure

Probably the most significant change in the black family during the past 30 years has been the proliferation of female-headed households. When the Moynihan Report (1965) was first issued in 1965, more than three-fourths of all black families with children were headed by a husband and wife. In 1982 barely one-half of all such families included parents of both sexes. Those households headed by black women had a median income of $7,458 in comparison with the median income of $20,586 for black married couples and $26,443 for white married couples (U.S. Bureau of the Census, 1983).

One of the most visible reasons for the dramatic increase in households headed by women has been a corresponding increase in out-of-wedlock births as a proportion of all births to black women. Approximately 52% of all children born to black women in 1982 were conceived out-of-wedlock. This high percentage of out-of-wedlock births is attributed largely to teenage pregnancies. Among women who turned 20 during the second half of the 1970s, 41% of blacks but only 19% of whites had already given birth. Within that same group of young black women, about 75% of all births were out-of-wedlock, compared with only 25% of births to young white women (U.S. Bureau of the Census, 1984). Although black women were twice as likely to have had nonmarital sexual intercourse as whites by the age of 19, their rate of sexual activity was remaining constant, while such activity was rapidly increasing among white teenagers (Zelnik and Kanter, 1977).

Not only has the number and proportion of black female-headed households grown rapidly, but the majority of adult black women are not married and living with spouses. In 1982 approximately 56% of all black women over the age of 14 were separated, divorced, widowed, or never married. Under the age of 30, the majority of them fall into the never-married category; past age 30 most of them are listed as divorced or separated, with a small percentage counted among the widowed. The high divorce rate creates a number of female-headed households among black women over age 30. While one out of two white marriages will end in divorce, two out of three black marriages will eventually dissolve; moreover, black women who divorce are less likely than their white counterparts to remarry. Currently, one in four adult black women are divorced (U.S. Bureau of the Census, 1983).

Some 20 years since the publication of the Moynihan Report (1965), the figures he cited as evidence that the black family was deteriorating have doubled, almost tripled in some areas. How is it that a group that regards family life as its most important source of satisfaction finds a majority of its women unmarried? Why does a group with more traditional sexual values than its white peers have a majority of its children born out-of-wedlock? Finally, we must ask how a group that places such importance on the traditional nuclear family finds a near majority of its members living in single-parent households. While a number of reasons have been cited by theorists, I suggest that the dominant force can be found in structural conditions of the black population.

Family Ideology vs. Structural Conditions

The basis of a stable family rests on the willingness, and ability, of men and women to marry, bear and rear children, and fulfill socially prescribed familial roles. In the case of women, those roles have been defined traditionally as the carrying out of domestic functions such as cooking and cleaning; giving birth to children and socializing them; providing sexual gratification, companionship, and emotional support to their husbands. There is abundant evidence that black women are willing and able to fulfill those roles (Staples, 1973). Conversely, the roles of men in the family are more narrowly confined to economic provider and family leader, but there are indications that a majority of black American males cannot implement those roles. When it comes to a choice between remaining single or getting married, individuals often do a cost-benefit analysis. Marriage is frequently a quid pro quo arrangement. The desire to enter and maintain a conjugal relationship is contingent on their perception of the benefits that can be acquired and, conversely, of the anticipated costs (Blau, 1964).

When selecting a mate, black women must consider the nature of the pool from which they will draw. In 98% of marriages with a black female bride, the groom will be a black male. Hence, her pool consists of unmarried black males with a variety of attributes. The most distinguishing characteristics of that pool is the shortage of men relative to the number of women during the marriageable years. According to the U.S. Bureau of the Census (1983), there are almost 1,500,000 more black women than men over the age of 14. By the Census Bureau's own account, the undercount of black males means that about 925,000 black males exist that were not added to the black population total. It should be noted that the uncounted black male is likely to be transient and unemployed (Joe and Yu, 1984). Since there is an excess number of black males at birth, the subsequent shortage of black males over the age of 14 must be attributed to their higher infant mortality rate and the considerably greater mortality rate of young black males through such causes as homicide, accidents, suicide, drug overdose, and war casualty (Staples, 1982; Stewart and Scott, 1978).

The major problem for black women, however, is not the quantity in the available supply of potential mates, but the quality. Whereas black women may select a mate on the basis of a number of attributes, a minimum prerequisite is that he be gainfully and regularly employed. According to a study by Joe and Yu (1984), almost a majority of working-age black males fail to meet those minimum prerequisites. After an analysis of the economic and census data, they concluded that 46% of the 8.8 million black men of working age were not in the labor force. Based on 1982 statistics, they found that 1.2 million black men were unemployed, 1.8 million had dropped out of the labor force, 186,000 were in prison, and 925,000 were classified as "missing" because the Census Bureau said it could not locate them.

Furthermore, their study overstates the number of "desirable" and available black males in the marriage pool. Even with the census undercount, there are still a half million more black women over the age of 14 than black men. Also, we must subtract from the marriage pool black men with certain characteristics by which they substantially outnumber black women. Among those characteristics would be blacks serving in the Armed Forces. Approximately 90% of them will be male. The U.S. Bureau of the Census (1983) reports that there were 415,000 blacks under arms in 1982, representing 20% of all United States military personnel. It can be stated reliably that a large number of those black males had poor prospects for employment in the civilian labor force (Stewart and Scott, 1978). While the salaries and other benefits of military personnel have improved in recent years and a number of black soldiers are currently married, the military does take out of circulation a number of marriage-age black males by stationing them in foreign posts and isolated military stations. Furthermore, once their period of enlistment ends, black veterans experience a higher rate of unemployment, even in relation to black civilian males with no military service (Stewart and Scott, 1978). Hence, military service only postpones the entry of black males into the ranks of the unemployed, one reason black males have a higher rate of reenlistment than their white counterparts.

Included in the factors that reduce the number of desirable black males in the marriage pool is the high rate of underemployed black males. The U.S. Civil Rights Commission (1982) reported that black men are undereducated for their jobs and have greater difficulty translating education into suitable occupations. Even college-educated black males have an unemployment rate four times greater than their white peers. Among black males employed in the labor force, one out of three will suffer from unemployment in a given year (Staples, 1982). However, these facts serve to explain why black marriages dissolve, not why they never take place. In Hampton's (1980) study, the respondents who reported the highest number of employment problems had a marital disruption rate three times higher than the overall rate for the sample.

Another group of black males regarded as undesirable or unavailable are those confined to mental institutions or who are otherwise mentally unstable. While their exact number is unknown, black males are more likely to be committed to mental institutions than are black women, and the strictures of racism are such that blacks are more likely to suffer from mental distress. In 1970, 240 nonwhites per 100,000 population were confined to mental institutions, compared with 162 whites per 100,000 population. Blacks also used community mental health centers at a rate almost twice their proportion in the general population. The rate of drug and alcohol abuse is much greater among the black population—especially males—based on their overrepresentation among patients receiving treatment services (U.S. Dept. of Health, Education and Welfare, 1979:163–183). It is estimated that as many as one-third of the young black males in the inner city have serious drug problems (Staples, 1982). Many of the mentally unstable, drug and alcohol abusers will have been included in the figures on black males who have dropped out of the labor force or are incarcerated in prison. The magnitude of the problem simply reinforces the fact that black women are seriously disadvantaged in choosing from the eligible and desirable males in the marriage pool.

A large category of black males who fit into the desirable group must also be considered not available. By all reliable estimates, the black male homosexual population is considerably larger than the black female homosexual population (Bell and Weinberg, 1978). Based on the often-quoted Kinsey estimate (Kinsey et al., 1948) that 10% of the adult male population is homosexual, that would mean about 800,000 black men are not available to heterosexual black women. Of course, many of these gay males do marry, for a variety of reasons, and serve well in the roles of husband and father; but, due to the increasing public tolerance of overt male homosexuality, it is reasonable to expect that fewer gay males will choose to enter into heterosexual marriages in the future. Finally, it should be noted that black men marry outside their race at a rate twice as great as that of black women (Heer, 1974; Staples, 1982).

Although the shortage and desirability of black males in the marriage pool largely affects the non-college-educated black woman's marriage chances, the college-educated black female is not spared the problem if she desires to marry within her race and socioeconomic level. In 1980 there were 133,000 more black women enrolled in college than black men—about 57% of all black college students. Moreover, black male students have a much higher attrition rate than their female peers. In the University of California system, for instance, only 12 of every 100 black male students graduate within four years. Thus, in 1981, 36,200 of 60,700 bachelor's degrees awarded to blacks went to women (60%); and between the years 1976 and 1981, black women receiving bachelor's degrees increased by 9%, and comparable black males declined by 9%. These same trends existed for graduate degrees during the years 1976–1981: black women declined by 12% and black men by 21% in the receipt of the master's degree; in the receipt of the first professional degree, black women increase by 71% while black men declined by 21%; and at the doctoral level, black men declined by 10%, while black women increased at a rate of 29% (National Center for Education Statistics, 1983).

College-educated black women do have the option of marrying men with less education and making a viable choice. In the past as many as 50% of college-educated black women married men of a lower socioeconomic level (Noble, 1956), but increasingly there is resistance among these women to marrying down. Almost one-third of college-educated black women remain unmarried past the age of 30 (Bayer, 1972; Staples, 1981). Of course, they face a similar shortage in the marriage pool of male high school graduates and must compete with lesser educated black women for these same men. Also, such middle-level men tend to marry early and have the most stable marriages in the black community (Glick and Mills, 1974). The marriage patterns of college-educated black males tend to put college-educated black women at a disadvantage. Many of these men marry women of a lower educational level, and the interracial marriage rate is highest in this group of black men (Heer, 1974; Staples, 1981).

Structural Conditions and the Changing Black Family

There is no great mystery as to what has happened to the black family in the past 20 years: it is an acceleration of trends set in motion during the 1960s. A highly sexualized culture—via media, clothing and example—has conveyed to American youth the notion that nonmarital sexual relations are not only acceptable but required for individual fulfillment. Women are reaching puberty earlier and emotional maturity later. Furthermore, the consequences of teenage sexual behavior are counteracted somewhat by easier access to effective contraceptives and abortion; and the number of pregnant teenagers has not really increased—only the proportion of births to that group of women as a result of the rapid decline in births to older married women.

While the nonmarital sexual activity rate of black and white teenage women is converging, the black female is more likely to be engaged in unprotected intercourse and less likely to marry or have an abortion if she becomes pregnant. According to Zelnik and Kantner (1974) only 8.5% of their black sample (15–19 years) entered into marriage as an outcome of premarital pregnancy, compared with 50.8% of comparable white women. In addition, 35.5% of white women had their premarital pregnancies terminated by abortion, in contrast to 4.9% of similar black women.

While it is reasonable to question the wisdom of young black women attaining motherhood at such an early age, their decision to bear the children and raise them alone reflects their traditional values and limited options in life. Among black males their age, the official unemployment rate is 52%, and as many as 75% of young black men remain outside the work force (Malabre, 1980). While employment may be easier for black women to obtain, it often will be in dead-end jobs that pay only half the wages earned by white males. Rather than remain childless and husbandless, these women choose to have the children and raise them alone. A good explanation of these life choices is given by Hortense Canady, president of Delta Sigma Theta sorority (1984:40): "having a child is probably the best thing that's ever going to happen to them in their whole lifetime and the only thing they can contribute—this is not true in most other countries in the world. But if you belong to a class or a group of people who have no educational opportunities stretching out before them, no other goals, that's probably the single, best thing that's ever going to happen to you in your life."

Having limited educational and career options to set against bearing a child is not the only reason for the increase in female-headed households. A welfare system that often requires men to be absent from the home is part of the problem; and black women realize that the meager welfare payments are more reliable than a class of men who may never know gainful employment in their entire lives. In general, unemployed men do not make good husbands and fathers. Since employment and income are the measure of a man's masculinity in this society, men who have neither do not tend to feel good about themselves or act very positively toward their wives and children. In the Hampton (1980) study, for example, husbands who were not satisfied with themselves had a fairly high level of marital disruption.

However, the major reason for the increase in black female-headed households is the lack of "desirable" men with whom to form monogamous marriages. According to Joe and Yu (1984), between 1976 and 1983 the number of black families headed by women rose by 700,000, and the ranks of black men out of the labor force or unemployed increased by the same number. The same trend has existed for the past 25 years: almost 75% of black men were working in 1960, and black families headed by women accounted for 21% of all black families in the same year; but by 1982 only 54% of all black men were in the labor force, and 42% of all black families were headed by women (Joe and Yu, 1984).

Having a child out-of-wedlock and failing to marry accounts for 41% of all black households headed by women. Another 51% are divorced or separated from their spouses (U.S. Bureau of the Census, 1983). These marriage disruptions are generally susceptible to the same structural conditions that plague never-married black women. Unemployment and underemployment, the public assistance complex, the educational system, and the health care system all produce economic and psychological alienation in the black male. As Hampton (1980) found, the pressures that push many black males out of other social institutions within society also work to push them out of marital relationships. For every 1,000 black married persons with spouses present, the number of divorces increased from 92 in 1971 to 233 in 1981; the comparable increase for whites was from 48 to 100. Black separations increased from 172 to 225 per 1,000 married persons in the same period; white separations rose from 21 to 29 (U.S. Bureau of the Census, 1983).

A number of social characteristics place blacks at risk for divorce. They have a higher rate of urbanization, greater independence of women, earlier age at marriage, earlier fertility, a higher education and income levels for the wife and lower income status for the husband (Cherlin, 1981). Most black marriages involve a wife who is more highly educated than her husband (Spanier and Glick, 1980). In one out of five black marriages, the wife earns a higher income than her husband (U.S. Bureau of the Census, 1983). This incongruity between the socially assigned roles of the male as the primary provider and the wife as a subordinate member of the marital dyad may undermine the husband's self-esteem, frustrate the wife, and create marital dissatisfaction for both partners. In Hampton's (1980) study, the highest percentage of disrupted marriages (27.4%) was observed among wives with incomes accounting for 40% or more of the family's income. His explanation is that, when women have other means of support in the form of welfare or their own earnings, they may be less constrained to remain in a personally unsatisfying relationship. Alternatively, the wife may be satisfied with the husband's role; but her high income may threaten the husband's authority and status, undermining his self-concept so that *he* becomes unhappy.

These problems of the black family are only variations of the general problems of American families. The direction of change in the family structure is basically the same for all racial groups in the United States and for the same reasons. Guttentag and Secord (1983) demonstrated that unbalanced sex ratios have certain predictable consequences for relationships between men and women. They give rise to higher rates of singlehood, divorce, out-of-wedlock births, and female-headed households in different historical epochs and across different societies. According to Ehrenreich (1983) the breakdown of the family began in the 1950s when men began a flight from commitment to the husband and father role. In the case of the black family, it stems from the institutional decimation of black males.

Summary and Discussion

The past 30 years have culminated in the gradual disintegration of the black nuclear family. Changes in the black family structure are in tune with the changes in American families. A number of social forces account for the increase in singlehood, out-of-wedlock births, divorces, and single-parent households. As women have become economically and psychologically independent of men, they have chosen to remain single or leave marriages they regarded as not satisfying their needs. Simultaneously, the growing independence of women and the sexual revolution of the 1960s and 1970s have allowed many men to flee from the responsibility attendant with the husband and father roles (Ehrenreich, 1983).

While these sociocultural forces impact on the marriage and family patterns of many Americans, they are more pronounced among blacks due to one critical etiological agent: the institutional decimation of black males. As an Urban League report concluded, "The attrition of Black males . . . from conception through adulthood finally results in an insufficient number of men who are willing and able to provide support for women and children in a family setting" (Williams, 1984). Thus, many black women are denied a real choice between monogamous marriage or singlehood. Most do choose to bear and raise children since that is deemed better than being single, childless, and locked into dead-end, low-paying jobs. While many would prefer a monogamous marriage, that is no longer possible for the majority of black women. The same forces that drive many black men out of social institutions also propel them out of the family.

Those forces have their genesis in the educational system. Black women are more educated than black men at all levels except the doctorate. This, again, is in the overall direction of change in American society. White males have also been losing ground to white women in educational achievements. The reasons for the ascendency of women in the school system are unclear. Some speculate that because teachers are disproportionately female, the behaviors tolerated and most encouraged are those that are more natural for girls (Hale, 1983). The higher educational level of black women endows them with educational credentials and skills that make them more competitive in the job market. The changing nature of the economy has placed women at an advantage. While industrial jobs have been declining, the service and high technology sector of the economy have been expanding. Black women are more highly concentrated in the expanding sector of the economy while black men are overrepresented in shrinking industrial jobs.

One consequence of the aforementioned factors has been the attrition of black men in the labor force. Almost 46% of the black men of working age were not in the labor force. As a rule, unemployed males are not good marriage prospects. The percentage of black women heading families alone in 1982 (42%) corresponds closely to the percentage of black males not in the labor force. Along with the number of black males not gainfully employed is the imbalance in the sex ratio, especially in the marriageable age ranges (18–35 years). Guttentag and Secord (1983) have shown that unbalanced sex ratios have certain predictable consequences for relationships between men and women. They give rise to higher rates of singlehood, divorce, out-of-wedlock births, and female-headed households in different historical epochs and across different societies. Another analysis by Jackson (1971) revealed that among blacks the proportion of female-headed households increases as the supply of males decreases. On the other hand, the proportion of female-headed households decreases when the supply of black males increases.

The crisis of the black family is, in reality, the crisis of the black male and his inability to carry out the normative responsibilities of husband and father in the nuclear family. The family's disintegration is only a symptom of the larger problem, that problem being the institutional decimation of black males. And we should be clear that the institutional decimation of black males represents the legacy of institutional racism. The implications of this problem extend beyond the family. A majority of black children live in one-parent households today, and the median income available to those families is less than $7500 per year. While many children rise out of poor families to become successful adults, the odds are against them. Large numbers of them, especially the males, will follow their biological fathers to prison, the ranks of the unemployed, and an early grave. Only by resolving the problems of the black male can we restore the black family to its rightful place in American society. The future of the race may be at stake.

References

Bayer, A. 1972. "College impact on marriage." *Journal of Marriage and the Family* 34 (November): 600–610.

Bell, A., and Weinberg, M. 1978. *Homosexualities.* New York: Simon and Schuster.

Bell, R. 1971. "The related importance of mother and wife roles among black lower class women." Pp. 248–255 in R. Staples (Ed.), *The Black Family: Essays and Studies* (2nd ed.). Belmont, CA: Wadsworth.

Blau, P. 1964. *Exchange and Power in Social Life.* New York: John Wiley.

Broderick, C. 1965. "Social heterosexual development among urban Negroes and whites." *Journal of Marriage and the Family* 27 (May): 200–203.

Canady, H. 1984. Quoted in "Words of the week." *Jet Magazine* (March 19): 40.

Cherlin, H. 1981. *Marriage, Divorce, Remarriage.* Cambridge, MA: Harvard University Press.

Ehrenreich, B. 1983. *The Hearts of Men: American Dreams and the Flight from Commitment.* Garden City, NY: Doubleday.

Gary, L., Beatty, L., Berry, G., and Price, M. 1983. *Stable Black Families. Final Report.* Institute for Urban Affairs and Research. Washington, DC: Howard University Press.

Glick, P., and Mills, K. 1974. *Black Families: Marriage Patterns and Living Arrangements.* Atlanta: Atlanta University Press, 9.

Goode, W. 1963. *World Revolution and Changing Family Patterns.* Glencoe, IL: Free Press.

Guttentag, M., and Secord, P. 1983. *Too Many Women: The Sex Ratio Question.* Beverly Hills, CA: Sage.

Hale, J. 1983. *Black Children.* Provo, UT: Brigham Young University Press.

Hampton, R. 1980. "Institutional decimation, marital exchange and disruption in black families." *Western Journal of Black Studies* 4 (Summer): 132–139.

Heer, D. 1974. "The prevalence of black-white marriages in the United States, 1960 and 1970." *Journal of Marriage and the Family* 35 (February): 246–258.

Hershey, M. 1978. "Racial differences in sex role identities and sex stereotyping: Evidence against a common assumption." *Social Science Quarterly* 58 (March): 583–596.

Hill, R. 1972. *The Strengths of Black Families.* New York: Emerson Hall.

Homans, G. 1961. *Social Behavior: Its Elementary Forms.* New York: Harcourt, Brace and World.

Jackson, J. 1971. "But where are the men?" *Black Scholar* 4 (December): 34–41.

Joe, T., and Yu, P. 1984. *The "Flip-Side" of Black Families Headed by Women: The Economic Status of Black Men.* Washington, DC: Center for the Study of Social Policy.

Kinsey, A., Pomeroy, W., and Martin, C. 1948. *Sexual Behavior in the Human Male.* Philadelphia: W. B. Saunders.

Kulesky, W., and Obordo, A. 1972. "A racial comparison of teenage girls projections for marriage and procreation." *Journal of Marriage and the Family* 34 (February): 75–84.

Malabre, A., Jr. 1980. "Recession hits blacks harder than whites." *Wall Street Journal* (August 21): 1.

Moynihan, D. P. 1965. *The Negro Family: The Case for National Action.* Washington, DC: U.S. Government Printing Office.

National Center for Education Statistics. 1983. *Participation of Black Students in Higher Education: A Statistical Profile from 1970–71 to 1980–81.* Washington, DC: U.S. Department of Education.

Noble, J. 1956. *The Negro Woman College Graduate.* New York: Columbia University Press.

Nolle, D. 1972. "Changes in black sons and daughters: A panel analysis of black adolescents' orientation toward their parents." *Journal of Marriage and the Family* 34 (August): 443–447.

Parson, R., and Bales, R. 1955. *Family, Socialization and Interaction Process.* Glencoe, IL: Free Press.

Scanzoni, J. 1971. *The Black Family in Modern Society.* Boston: Allyn and Bacon.

Spanier, G., and Glick, P. 1980. "Mate selection differentials between blacks and whites in the United States." *Social Forces* 58 (March): 707–725.

Staples, R. 1973. *The Black Woman in America: Sex, Marriage and the Family.* Chicago: Nelson-Hall.

———. 1981. *The World of Black Singles: Changing Patterns of Male-Female Relations.* Westport, CT: Greenwood Press.

———. 1982. *Black Masculinity: The Black Male's*

Role in American Society. San Francisco: Black Scholar Press.

Stewart, J., and Scott, J. 1978. "The institutional decimation of black males." *Western Journal of Black Studies* 2 (Summer): 82–92.

Thibaut, J. W., and Kelley, H. W. 1959. *The Social Psychology of Groups.* New York: John Wiley.

U.S. Bureau of the Census. 1978. *Current Population Reports.* March 1977, Series P-20, No. 314. Washington, DC: Government Printing Office.

———. 1983. *America's Black Population, 1970 to 1982: A Statistical View, July 1983,* Series P10/POP83. Washington, DC: Government Printing Office.

———. 1984. *Fertility of American Women: June 1983,* Series P-20, No. 386. Washington, DC: Government Printing Office.

U.S. Civil Rights Commission. 1982. *Unemployment and Underemployment Among Blacks, Hispanics and Women* (November). Washington DC: Government Printing Office.

U.S. Dept. of Health, Education and Welfare. 1979. *Health Status of Minorities and Low-Income Groups.* Washington, DC: Government Printing Office.

Williams, J. 1984. "Black males' problems linked to family crises." *Washington Post* (August 1): A-6.

Zelnik, M., and Kantner, J. F. 1974. "The resolution of teenage first pregnancies." *Family Planning Perspectives* (Spring): 74–80.

———. 1977. "Sexual and contraceptive experience of young unmarried women in the United States, 1976 and 1971." *Family Planning Perspectives* 9 (May/June): 55–59.

Conclusion

Throughout this book we have shown how gender is continually constructed and adapted during everyday interaction. We have learned how lovers, friends, and family affect one another, and we have seen how these relationships are embedded in a hierarchical gender system.

Three articles in this volume particularly help illustrate how sexual inequality organizes interpersonal relationships. Cheal's research shows how bridal showers utilize female solidarity to buttress the negative consequences of economic dependency. The van club described by DiIorio gives insight into why women acquiesce to subordination. The "lady vanners" are willing to accept male domination because they need a partner to survive economically in the future. Similarly, LaRossa and LaRossa show how women in dual-worker families continue to lose more of their freedom to child care than do their husbands, because they have less power to win time off.

Other articles, however, make us acutely aware that men's lives and relationships are also limited by a patriarchal gender system. The most obvious example is what happens to men who, because of racial inequities in our economic system, cannot fulfill the traditional male breadwinner role. As Staples shows, such men are deprived not only of a job but also of family relationships. From a different point of view, Swain's research illustrates ways in which the gender system limits male friendship. Although men may achieve intimacy with friends, they must do so covertly in order to escape ridicule and other negative sanctions.

While both men and women are constrained by traditional gender systems, it is to be expected that women, being most subordinated, are more actively desirous of change. It has been primarily female activists who have sought to create a society where gender does not set societal expectations, opportunities, or placements in social systems. The phrase "the personal is political" indicates the feminist movement's understanding that even personal relationships are constructed within, and can support, political or hierarchical systems. Women have much to gain from the nongendered world envisioned by Lorber. But men also have much to gain. Although some men react defensively to contemporary feminism by reasserting traditional male privileges, others have begun to reevaluate their beliefs about masculinity and conclude that a nongendered world offers them benefits as well. This "new man" is attracted to being free to parent, express intimacy, and escape sole financial responsibility for his family.

Contemporary intimate relationships have been profoundly affected by feminism, and we hope this continues to be the case. But we need to remember that collective action is only one source of social change. When necessity forces homemakers to reluctantly enter the labor force they may reassess male dominance and renegotiate marital roles. Similarly men who share child rearing with an employed wife may become so devoted to their children that they demand sole or joint custody after divorce, thus creating new kinds of families.

What does the future hold for men and women in intimate relationships? Surely the increasing necessity for two paychecks to support one family will further erode male dominance in marriage. And as female labor force participation continues to increase, we believe men's domestic labor and parental responsibilities will increase within two-parent families and among those who are divorced. But economics is not the only factor we need to consider. Changes in relationships may also occur because AIDS may eventually alter courtship norms in a conservative direction in the heterosexual world as it has already done in homosexual communities. Ironically, the sexual double standard among heterosexuals may finally cease not because men want women to have the same sexual options as themselves, but because men have adopted the "safer" behaviors that were previously the province of women. What will these new sexual standards mean for today's adolescents? For gay men who have radically altered their lifestyles? The only sure answer is that developing norms will result from forces outside the individuals (for example, the risk of disease) and the negotiation of behavior between intimates.

The articles in this book have shown some of the ways that gendered behaviors in intimate relationships are changing and identified those behaviors most resistant to change. Our aim has been to illustrate how intimate relations are structured by their social context and how male/female hierarchy shapes the expression of love, loyalty, sex, and friendship. Understanding the constraints of this gender system is, we hope, the first step in helping to create a world where intimate relationships are based on individual desire and negotiation rather than on socially decreed and enforced gender roles.